TRANSFORMATIVE CURRICULUM LEADERSHIP

THIRD EDITION

James G. Henderson
Kent State University

Rosemary Gornik
*South Euclid–Lyndhurst City Schools
and Perry Public Schools*

PEARSON

Merrill
Prentice Hall

Upper Saddle River, New Jersey
Columbus, Ohio

Library of Congress Cataloging in Publication Data

Henderson, James George.
  Transformative curriculum leadership / James G. Henderson, Rosemary Gornik.
— 3rd ed.
      p. cm.
  Includes bibliographical references and index.
  ISBN 0-13-113896-0
  1. Education—United States—Curricula. 2. Curriculum planning—United
States. 3. Educational leadership—United States. I. Gornik, Rosemary. II. Title.
  LB1570.H45 2007
  375'.000973—dc22   2006018269

Vice President and Executive Publisher: Jeffery W. Johnston
Executive Editor: Debra A. Stollenwerk
Senior Editorial Assistant: Mary Morrill
Assistant Development Editor: Daniel J. Richcreek
Production Editor: Kris Roach
Production Coordination: Thistle Hill
Design Coordinator: Diane C. Lorenzo
Cover Designer: Candace Rowley
Cover image: Corbis
Production Manager: Susan Hannahs
Director of Marketing: David Gesell
Senior Marketing Manager: Darcy Betts Prybella
Marketing Coordinator: Brian Mounts

This book was set in R Life Roman by Laserwords Pvt. Ltd. It was printed and bound by R.R.
Donnelley & Sons Company. The cover was printed by R.R. Donnelley & Sons Company.

Pearson Education Ltd.   Pearson Education Australia Pty. Limited
Pearson Education Singapore Pte. Ltd.   Pearson Education North Asia Ltd.
Pearson Education Canada, Ltd.   Pearson Educación de Mexico, S.A. de C.V.
Pearson Education—Japan   Pearson Education Malaysia Pte. Ltd.

10 9 8 7 6 5 4 3 2 1
ISBN: 0-13-113896-0

PREFACE

NEW TO THIS EDITION

The changes we have made for this edition of *Transformative Curriculum Leadership* are based on our goal of making the book more accessible, practical, integrated, and realistic while clarifying the paradigmatic features of transformative curriculum leadership. We use the paradigm concept as it was originally articulated by Thomas Kuhn in his groundbreaking and highly influential book *The Structure of Scientific Revolutions,* published in 1962. For Kuhn, a paradigm serves as a problem-solving exemplar for a disciplinary community in the sciences. It identifies a particular discipline's central problem, and it provides a way to study, and perhaps even solve, the problem.

We have written this third edition to function as an exemplar for disciplined curriculum problem solving. For purposes of clarity, the book is organized into three sections; however, in the context of the day-to-day work of transformative curriculum leadership, all of the book's topics are deeply embedded in one another.

Although much of the technical training of teachers can be handled in brief workshops, this is not the case for the elevated curriculum judgment we are advancing in this book. For this reason, we have added a new section titled "Sustaining the Curriculum Wisdom Problem Solving." We focus on two key topics in this section: building local learning communities in chapter 8 and engaging the broader public sphere in chapter 9.

FOUR KEY FEATURES OF CURRICULUM WISDOM PROBLEM SOLVING

Our paradigm, which we call *curriculum wisdom problem solving,* possesses four key features. Although these features appear in the second edition, they have been clarified and more carefully organized in this third edition. As we worked closely with educational practitioners over the past 6 years, we noticed the integral relationship between teaching for 3S understanding—referring to the integration of Subject matter understanding with democratic Self and Social understanding—and undertaking a personal journey of understanding. In effect, we recognized that teaching for 3S understanding requires the cultivation of deep *self-understanding.* Given this vital relationship between personal and professional awareness, we decided to highlight Rosie Gornik's journey of understanding in this edition. Readers will come to know her well as they study this book. Her many autobiographical narratives and vignettes have been written to inspire self-insight, and we hope her stories invite readers to create their own narratives of self-examination and self-discovery as democratic educators committed to constructivist best practices.

Curriculum wisdom problem solving possesses three additional key features. Because the problem of teaching for 3S understanding is quite complex, it requires a sophisticated *reflective inquiry.* In effect, it requires the incorporation of a multi-faceted democratic curriculum inquiry into problem-solving reflection. Although the integration of disciplined inquiry and reflection is widely accepted and understood in the medical field, this is not the case in the education field. We have worked hard over the past 6 years to further explore and refine the reflective inquiry map that we first presented in the second edition, and readers can be assured that our guidance in chapter 3 on how to practice reflective inquiry has been carefully field-tested in a variety of educational settings. Chapters 2 and 3 are placed in the book's first section, titled "Two Fundamental Challenges," to acknowledge the paradigmatic relationship between the *method* of reflective inquiry and the *problem* of teaching for 3S understanding.

Section II, "Four Interrelated Decision-Making Processes," highlights the third key feature of curriculum wisdom problem solving. Educators who are inspired to exercise this type of professional judgment must deliberate over a wide range of interconnected curriculum matters. They must think about the relationship between program designing, instructional planning, teaching, evaluating, and organizational life. In effect, their decision making must be *ecological.*

Although most educators have little experience with such systemic deliberations due in part to the current dominance of narrow technical teacher training and the standardized management of education, we have been pleasantly surprised at how quickly motivated teachers and administrators can learn to deliberate in this ecological way. The key is the motivation, and we have written this book with such motivated educators in mind. We recognize that these professionals are this text's audience. They are the educators who will initiate transformative curriculum leadership. Curriculum wisdom problem solving cannot be forced; it is an *invitational* paradigm that must be advanced one person at a time by dedicated educators who appreciate the many benefits of teaching for 3S understanding.

Curriculum wisdom problem solving is a subtle art that must be gradually cultivated with the support of others. In effect, the curriculum wisdom paradigm advances a very high standard for professional judgment. A commitment to refining the art of curriculum deliberation is the fourth key feature of curriculum wisdom problem solving, and the cultivation of this art requires a sustained effort over time. We envision a future in which an increasing number of educators see themselves as practicing a form of professional artistry that is vital to their society's democratic well-being.

PRACTICING TRANSFORMATIVE CURRICULUM LEADERSHIP

The final organization of this book was field-tested in a five-week graduate course at Kent State University during the summer of 2005. Eighteen teacher leaders from a variety of public and private schools in northeast Ohio took this course, called "Curriculum Leadership." It was remarkable how quickly the class organized itself into a dynamic learning community. Although there was some initial dissonance over the fundamental challenges of chapters 2 and 3, this dissipated during the first week as the 18 teacher leaders realized that not only were they capable of practicing curriculum wisdom problem solving, but also that creating contextually relevant transformative curriculum leadership plans was personally rewarding and professionally compelling. Their overall enthusiasm and determination is exemplified in the following excerpt from Christine

Fishman's leadership plan. Christine is an experienced teacher, working to become an elementary school principal. She writes:

This coming school year, I have been placed in a new grade level at my school. I will be teaching third grade, and I am anticipating a learning curve which will require more time but which affords me great opportunity to gain new perspective. Given the finite amount of time in a day . . . , I struggle in the selection of reasonable goals, knowing it might be best to choose only modest ones. In designing, planning, and teaching the curriculum, I believe one of the structures which will make a powerful impact upon my relationship with students and upon student learning would be to implement at least one study which uses a project approach. This mostly constructivist method promotes deep, disciplined understanding of subject matter but is easily infused with opportunities for democratic self and social learning. Students use their own background experiences and questions to fuel the study, conducting fieldwork in small groups and making many decisions about what they'll study and how they'll gather, share, and use the knowledge they've gained. The culmination of the project usually involves some public display of the artifacts of learning, and I've found that this display invites comments by parents and other staff members. These small scraps of conversation and a few photos on our classroom website can actually form an inroad for others to reconsider their understandings about learning, teaching, and the purpose of school. This "back door" to organizational development is often the most welcoming entrance for time-stressed teachers and administrators. . . . As the year unfolds, I expect to find many opportunities across all subject matter disciplines to teach this way. Although I can't precisely fix the details of planning, I know that my heightened awareness of the wisdom paradigm will cause me to find them revealed in daily interactions where I didn't notice them before.

This excerpt from Christine's leadership plan illustrates how dedicated educators can work in quietly personal ways to cultivate curriculum wisdom problem solving. In a few short sentences, Christine clearly articulates her commitment to building a local learning community and to engaging the broader public sphere.

How many educators are willing to exercise such curriculum leadership? No one can precisely say, but until we try, we will never know. As we refined this third edition, we were encouraged by the enthusiastic response to the contents of this book. As a result, we feel that there may be a significant number of educators who are willing to work as transformative curriculum leaders, despite the dominance of standardized management policies in education.

This book is a testament to the spirit of democratic freedom that resides within the hearts and minds of many dedicated, courageous educators, and this spirit is beautifully captured in Christine Fishman's vision of her future as a transformative curriculum leader:

I have high hopes for my future role in education. They've been shaped not only by the experiences I've had over my career, but by the influence of great thinkers such as John Dewey. I have also set high expectations due to the encouragement of my family, colleagues, and friends. I want to create that place where goodness can flourish, where performance is expanded, and where freedom and fairness abounds. I want to avoid the meager harvest of micromanagement, with its aseptic garden in which there is no growth lest I plant it. I am concerned that the people I care for, I also care with. My goals for this utopian paradise must be tempered, however, with a cognizance of the political realities of the current environment. I have heard conflicting advice, such as "Change nothing your first year as a principal" and "Come on strong, or they'll walk all over you." And through it all, I am trying to be brave. Am I intimidated? You bet. But my call will not be ignored, and there is nowhere for me to go but forward.

ACKNOWLEDGMENTS

Since the publication of the second edition in 2000, we have worked with hundreds of educational practitioners in northeast Ohio and throughout the United States who are deeply committed to teaching for a *Subject* matter understanding that is integrated with a democratic *Self* and *Social* understanding. These highly dedicated teachers and administrators have helped us explicate the paradigmatic problem of *teaching for 3S understanding.* They have assisted our efforts in both articulating this organizing problem for curriculum work and exploring its problem-solving nuances. This third edition could not have been written without their valuable input. We thank them and applaud their deep sense of professionalism. Wherever these educators work, they add to the quality of life in their communities.

We wish to acknowledge the helpful insights of several individuals. Richard Hawthorne was the coauthor of the first and second editions of this book. Dick's many insights into the work of transformative curriculum leadership are carried forward in this edition. We organized an informal peer review team to review the final manuscript. Their feedback was quite helpful, and we wish to thank these individuals. They are Barbara Brandt, Elizabeth Brooks, Laurel Chehayl, Diane Craig, Kent den Heyer, Christine Fishman, Kathleen Kesson, Daniel Marksz, and Kerry Peterson. Our special thanks to Amanda Hosey Dugan, senior project editor at Thistle Hill Publishing Services, for her excellent work throughout the production process.

We also want to thank the reviewers of this edition for their insightful comments. They are: Donna Breault, Georgia State University; India Broyles, University of Southern Maine; Francine Hultgren, University of Maryland; Valerie J. Janesick, University of South Florida; Thomas E. Kelly, John Carroll University; Marcella L. Kysilka, University of Central Florida; Dan Marshall, Pennsylvania State University; Cynthia J. Reed, Auburn University; Jennifer Snow-Gerono, Boise State University; and Olusegun A. Sogunro, Central Connecticut State University.

Finally, we want the readers of this book to understand that the theory underlying the practice of transformative curriculum leadership is a particular synthesis of 90 years of curriculum theorizing, particularly in North America. We present this synthesis in chapter 9 for those readers who may be interested in this book's theoretical underpinnings. Here in the preface, we want to acknowledge these curriculum scholars. Without their disciplined studies into the nature of curriculum work, this book could not have been written.

Contributing Authors

Theoretical Discussions

Chapter 3   Michelle Thomas
Chapter 8   Michelle Thomas

Case Narratives

Chapter 9   Kent den Heyer
Chapter 9   Kathleen Kesson

BRIEF CONTENTS

CONTENTS

CHAPTER 1

INTRODUCING TRANSFORMATIVE CURRICULUM LEADERSHIP

We have argued that any model of curriculum planning is rooted in a cluster of visions—a vision of humanity, of the universe, of human potential, and of our relationship to the cosmos. . . . What is of the most extraordinary import, of course, is which particular vision we decide to choose, for the choosing of a vision allows us to become that vision.

(Macdonald and Purpel, 1987, p. 192)

This book advances a specific professional goal, which we hope you will find inspiring and compelling. We offer advice on practicing a particular type of curriculum judgment. Because practicing this judgment is a professional leadership challenge involving deep-seated changes, we describe this work as *transformative curriculum leadership.* This chapter introduces this form of educational leadership and explains its importance, and we will set the stage for our introduction and explanation through a historical comparison and through three contrasting teacher leadership vignettes.

A HISTORICAL COMPARISON

Franklin Bobbitt, who was a professor of educational administration at the University of Chicago, is considered one of the founders of the American curriculum field. In 1918, he published *The Curriculum,* which was the first general curriculum text in North American education. Bobbitt (2004/1918) describes his book as "an introductory textbook in the theory of the curriculum" (p. 10). He advances an understanding of life that serves as his frame of reference for theorizing curriculum. He writes:

> Human life, however varied, consists in the performance of specific activities. Education that prepares for life is one that prepares definitely and adequately for these specific activities. . . . These will be the objectives of the curriculum. They will be numerous, definite, and particularized. (p. 11)

A few years later, Bobbitt published *How to Make a Curriculum* (1924). He compared the making of a curriculum to the planning of a journey; he envisioned this journey as a path containing about 700 standardized objectives.

We also envision curriculum as a journey, but our understanding of this journey is quite different from Bobbitt's influential publications. Bobbitt framed the organizing problem for curriculum as a trip through numerous, precise achievements. *We think this is a very limited way to proceed with an educational journey.* Consider why we make such a challenging assertion. Educators can work hard to ensure that their students achieve what Bobbitt called "behavioral objectives" and what are now called "standardized test performances." Assuming that most of the students do achieve the uniform and systematized goals, due to the educators' efforts as well as the active support of parents and other curriculum stakeholders, can we now say that these students have completed their educational journey? With reference to current educational standardization, consider these questions. Just because students may test well, do they understand the subject matter? Perhaps more importantly, do they understand *why* they studied the required subject matter? Can they apply what they have learned? Can they use what they have learned to engage in collaborative learning, critical thinking, creative problem solving, and other important information-age skills and dispositions? Do they see the relevance in what they are learning? Do they experience continuity in their curricular journey? Is the overall trajectory of their educational path beginning to make sense to them, or are they just mindlessly negotiating adult-imposed objectives? Are they becoming enthusiastic lifelong learners? Do they have a sense of the bigger picture of education? Are they cultivating an understanding of what constitutes a good life? Are they acquiring a feel for the moral purposes of their growth?

We think such questions should serve as the frame of reference for curriculum decision making, and we think it is unfortunate that the way Bobbitt framed the organizing problem of the curriculum field has been so influential for so long. It is time to make a fundamental change in orientation. It is time for a new frame of reference, which we will characterize as a paradigm shift, and one goal of this introductory chapter is to explain our curriculum book's organizing problem. Compare Bobbitt's above interpretation of curriculum-as-journey to ours:

> In a freedom-loving society, a quality human life is realized through a holistic, disciplined, and personalized journey of understanding. Education facilitates this journey through disciplinary subject matter understanding embedded in democratic self and social understanding. Students are provided with active meaning making experiences that cultivate a personal responsibility for lifelong learning, a generosity for diverse others, and a commitment to fair play and social justice.

As you read the introductory chapter in this book, you will notice that two key characteristics of curriculum work are associated with the way we frame the organizing problem of the field. First, educators who choose to facilitate their students' personalized journeys of understanding cannot do so without undertaking a similar journey of understanding. Teaching for holistic understanding requires a journey of self-understanding as an advocate for democratic education. Curriculum work is experienced as a public intellectual process. In order to capture the spirit of this process, one of the leading scholars in the field today transposes the Latin noun *curriculum*, which means the course to be run, into its Latin infinitive form, *currere*, which means to run the course. You will be introduced to William Pinar's curriculum-as-currere notion later in this introductory chapter, and you will learn that chapters 2–8 in this book make use of this currere frame of reference.

Second, our interpretation of curriculum work requires the practice of a sophisticated deliberative judgment. Many years after Bobbitt's influential publications, another University of Chicago professor argued that because curriculum is positioned at the intersection of theory and practice, curriculum workers must engage in case-by-case deliberations that are informed by a theoretical eclectic artistry and that culminate in a practical artistry. This professor's name was Joseph Schwab, and he first published his argument in 1969 in an article "The Practical: A Language for Curriculum." As you read this introductory chapter, you will notice how Schwab's curriculum argument has influenced the creation of this book. The practice of a sophisticated or "elevated" judgment, informed by an eclectic and practical artistry, is a central focus of the text.

The curriculum judgment we are advancing can be explained by returning to the way Bobbitt framed the organizing problem of the field. Imagine a team of educators deciding on the best educational course of action for the students under their care. Based on careful deliberations, they decide that a particular group of students (though not all the students) needs a highly structured curriculum emphasizing specific standardized achievements, and they teach this group of students in this way. Because their decision is informed by case-by-case deliberations and not on a one-size-fits-all orientation, they pragmatically see this course of action as only a means to a larger purpose. In fact, with reference to this larger purpose, they worry about their decision. If they teach only for standardized achievements, will they be unnecessarily limiting this group of students' educational opportunities? Will the students be acquiring a deep understanding of subject matter? If the students are focused only on standardized learning performances, what will they be learning about themselves, about their fellow students, and about how to live a good, productive life?

Because such curriculum questions worry these educators, they commit themselves to a particular type of professional development. They commit themselves to improving their curriculum judgments through a disciplined *understanding* of teaching for subject matter *understanding* in a society with democratic ideals. They appreciate the reciprocal nature of this understanding challenge. They know that their individual journeys of understanding are closely tied to their students' individual journeys of understanding.

THREE TEACHER LEADER VIGNETTES

Consider the following three vignettes. They will also help set the stage for our explanation of why this book was written.

Vignette 1

Robert has just left the professional development seminar he facilitated with a smile. He had carefully planned this Saturday morning class, and he feels deeply satisfied for several reasons. As he drives home, he reflects back on why he feels so good. He was not paid to teach this seminar, nor were his "students" paid to attend, and so he feels a deep sense of professional pride that 15 of his school district colleagues volunteered some of their precious weekend time to work with him. Blood, sweat, and tears went into the creation of this seminar, which focused on introducing and practicing teacher behaviors that have been demonstrated to improve student achievement on the state's mathematics proficiency tests. Because students take these tests at different points in their schooling, the seminar included primary, middle school, and high school teachers.

As Robert thought about these teachers' interactions, the phrase "the left hand doesn't know what the right hand is doing" came to mind. He works in a highly rated school district that is quite large. Because the district employs over 400 educators, it wasn't surprising that many of the seminar participants had not met one another. It was fun helping them recognize that they are on the same team—that everyone is pulling for the same goal, which is to improve students' standardized test scores. Celebrating that sense of common purpose was deeply satisfying, particularly because all the seminar teachers immediately recognized the need to work more closely with one another. As the seminar proceeded, a wonderful sense of team spirit had emerged. He almost felt like the head coach on an inspired and winning football team!

Robert was especially gratified by two comments that kept surfacing in a number of ways throughout the morning. Everyone appreciated the clarity of the seminar he had designed. He was precise in his articulation of the goals of the class, and he didn't waddle in ambiguities and long-winded discussions. Time was not wasted on the "fog of education." He worked with mathematical precision as he introduced specific instructional activities that have been proven to result in higher student test scores. He smiled as he thought about his performance. He had worked hard over many years to become an accomplished high school mathematics teacher, and now this disciplined preparation had paid off. He had become a professional leader who could effectively assist his colleagues in making curriculum judgments that were attuned to the state's educational mandates. He knew how to efficiently help his fellow teachers become accountable and to, therefore, contribute to the school district's proud tradition of achieving high test scores.

Robert also felt good about all of the positive feedback on the instructional strategies that he introduced. It seemed everyone felt that his or her specific teaching repertoire had improved. Everyone now possessed a wider array of strategies for day-to-day curriculum work. He experienced a craftsmanship pride in what had been accomplished, and for a moment he thought about the teachers in the school district who were critical of the state's accountability mandates. Did they not understand that these mandates challenged, or even forced, teachers to improve their instruction? Had these critics lost sight of the overall purpose of education? He thought about the phrase "no child left behind," and he was proud of the fact he was working as a curriculum leader who would make sure all the students in his school district would acquire the basic competencies of reading, writing, and arithmetic. Yes, he was proud of what he had accomplished on that Saturday morning, and it was only the beginning of a long professional journey.

Vignette 2

Diane has just left her principal's office with a smile.[1] She had just negotiated a measure of freedom to teach language arts, mathematics, and social studies in accordance with her best professional judgment. As a fourth-grade urban teacher, Diane felt lucky to be working with an elementary school principal who had an understanding of what is required to teach for students' subject matter understanding. Diane thought that it

---

[1] Thanks to Debra DeBenedictis for her assistance in the creation of this vignette.

certainly helped that Jane, her principal, was once a highly creative third-grade teacher, but Diane hoped that Jane would not get in trouble with the school district's superintendent, who had been a successful high school football coach and was a real rah-rah, team-player, data-driven kind of guy. Diane was concerned for Jane because Jane had just given her permission to play by her own rules. She did not want to abuse this freedom and hurt Jane's administrative career. On the other hand, she certainly deserved this opportunity, because she was a highly respected teacher with 20 years' experience, and she had clearly demonstrated that her students were learning their subject matter.

Diane thought back on how she had convinced Jane that her fourth-grade students didn't need the "drill/skill" curriculum and extra tutoring that the district was providing, at great expense, to teachers in targeted grade levels. Her fourth graders' scores on the state achievement tests carried enormous political consequences because these scores were part of the district's annual report card, which was sent to the state administrators and published in the local newspapers. Diane felt like she was working in a high-stakes pressure cooker, but she had made her peace with this uncomfortable reality because she loved working with 9- and 10-year-olds. She was raised by parents with a deep love of learning, and the first teacher she encountered who shared this passion for education was her fourth-grade teacher. When Diane decided to become an educator, it was partially due to the professional inspiration of this special teacher.

Diane had prepared for her meeting with Jane by crafting an argument with three main points. She began by reminding Jane that her students' class-composed letter to the editor, which had recently been published in the local newspaper with a great deal of fanfare, emerged out of the "mock legislature" activities that were part of an integrated language arts and social studies unit. This learning approach encouraged active meaning making, creative writing, and a deep understanding of social issues, and these desired educational results were clearly exhibited in the students' letter to the editor. The students were not just functioning as glib game show contestants, who would memorize material that would be forgotten in about two months. Fortunately, Jane understood this because she did not equate standardized test performances with authentic performances of understanding. As Diane was making this argument, she assured Jane that her lessons would continue to be informed by the state's language arts and social studies standards. She was not rejecting these standards, just the superficial standardization that was interfering with her teaching creativity. Diane felt fortunate that she was a respected teacher who was known to be dedicated to her students' constructivist learning. Without this professional reputation, Jane may not have bought this part of her argument.

Diane was also clearly able to demonstrate to Jane the specific ways in which the drill/skill curriculum and tutoring—though implemented in the spirit of equity underlying the No Child Left Behind Act—would actually be inequitable for some of her students. These particular students were fragile learners and easily frightened. To ask them to acquire mathematics and language arts skills without a sense of meaningful context and with the help of tutors who did not know them well would actually inhibit their learning. They needed to work out of a strong sense of personal ownership. They needed to work with books and stories that they have chosen and to study facts and skills that have been set in familiar settings by a teacher who knows them. They needed the caring support of adults who understood their particular sensibilities, and they did not respond well to decontextualized curriculum activities and pull-out tutoring.

Diane felt that her third point served as the icing on the cake and was perhaps the part of her argument that Jane found most compelling. Though her urban school district was under an enormous amount of pressure to improve students' test scores, there was also a strong push to "professionalize" the faculty. Diane had two master's degrees, one in curriculum and instruction and one in reading, and was constantly sharing articles and introducing books to her teaching peers. Her principal and other school district administrators knew this. Though they might wince when she publicly complained that teachers were being treated like sheep, they applauded her professional leadership and her commitment to urban education. Diane argued that her freedom from the shackles of the drill/skill curriculum and tutoring would serve as an incentive to other teachers. They would know that if they could demonstrate that they could teach for subject matter understanding, they would be provided with the same discretionary latitude for their curriculum judgments. As she walked down the hallway to her classroom, Diane felt a deep sense of pride. She had become a poster child for her school district's commitment to continuing professional development, and she welcomed the challenge.

Vignette 3

Liz and Harry have just left a friend's house and are driving to a coffeehouse for a late Saturday night dessert.[2] Their friend had rented a video, *Radio,* which the three of them watched over dinner. Liz and Harry were so deeply inspired by the movie that they wanted to talk to each other alone before calling it a night. The movie was based on the true story of a teacher who is also the football coach and athletic director at a public high school in South Carolina. This teacher decides that his football coaching "curriculum" will include the services of an adult African American male with a disability. The coach, who has repeatedly seen the man pushing a shopping cart through town, decides to invite "Radio," who has this nickname because of his passionate interest in radios, to work as an assistant to the football and basketball teams. The drama of the movie revolves around the coach's curriculum decision.

Liz and Harry felt deeply affirmed by the dramatization of this true story. They talk excitedly about the depiction of a public school educator, who does not work as a stereotypic football coach obsessed with winning. The coach, possessing a deep love for the game of football, had always been able to engender a deep understanding of his "discipline," but he now reaches deep within himself to attain a new level of professionalism. With, ironically, Radio serving as his "teacher," the coach grows in his ability to inspire a deep sense of humanity and justice; ultimately, the coach's curriculum decision results in enormous benefits for the school's students, teachers, and administrators, as well as for the entire community. Liz and Harry see themselves as

----

[2] Thanks to Elizabeth Brooks for her assistance in the creation of this vignette.

educators committed to this type of growth, and they feel that their professional identity has been confirmed by this uplifting and well-acted story. Like the coach in the movie, their curriculum judgments are attuned to teaching for subject matter understanding while cultivating an inspired self and social awareness.

As Liz and Harry talk about the movie, they reflect back on a recent curriculum decision. They are both seventh-grade social studies teachers, working on separate teams in a fairly large public, suburban middle school. Each team includes a mathematics, language arts, social studies, and science teacher. They have recently worked with their teammates on the creation of an initial design for an interdisciplinary unit on urban issues that will focus on poverty among urban youth. The goal of the unit is to facilitate a deep understanding of the No Child Left Behind (NCLB) Act. The unit will be successful if students demonstrate awareness that the public sentiment of "no child left behind" is more than political rhetoric; it is an important principle of democratic living. The unit will incorporate math, language arts, and science concepts and skills into active learning activities. The unit's lessons include a field trip to a welfare/workfare agency and a simulation facilitated by two social workers. The students will exhibit their understanding through the creation of nonfictional or fictional case narratives, which will be organized into a readers' theater performance to take place at an upcoming school–community event.

As the curriculum leaders for this interdisciplinary unit, Liz and Harry have encountered two main obstacles. Two of their teammates are concerned that the unit would be too "political" for the community, and the principal and the school district's curriculum director expressed similar reservations. Liz and Harry argued that the critical examination of current government policies is an important part of students' social studies education. Though they are making headway with this argument, they soon realized that this is not the main concern. The central obstacle was the NCLB Act itself. Several of the teachers, as well as the principal and the curriculum director, were quite concerned that the unit's learning activities would not improve students' test scores. Though the curriculum might have intrinsic educational merit, there may not be sufficient payoff. Too much time might be wasted on activities and ventures that would not contribute to the district's bottom line!

While lamenting the ironies of their situation, Liz and Harry suddenly had an idea that might have its own payoff. For several years they have been part of a study group committed to inquiring into the relationship between democracy and education. This group meets twice a year and was started by a social studies education professor at a local university. They discuss a preselected book at each meeting and engage in other inquiry learning activities, and the district has given them continuing education credit for their participation. They decide to call the professor to request a showing of *Radio*. They would like everyone in the study group to watch the movie and then brainstorm with them on how best they can negotiate the enactment of their urban unit. There certainly must be ways to advance their curriculum ideas, and the study group contains smart people who can assist their deliberations. The movie has recharged them; as they dig into their dessert, they look forward to the upcoming leadership challenges. With a renewed sense of determination, they realize they have embarked on a vitally important professional journey.

THE BOOK'S PURPOSE

This book's professional goal can be explained with the help of these three vignettes. This text has been designed to inspire the sustained practice of curriculum judgments that are attuned to student performances of subject matter understanding that are embedded in democratic self and social understanding. We will call this professional goal *curriculum judgment for 3S understanding,* in which the term *3S understanding* refers to the integration of *Subject* matter understanding with democratic *Self* and *Social* understanding.

3S understanding is a complicated curriculum and teaching goal. It is not easy to understand 3S understanding! The first vignette is a moment in the professional life of a teacher leader who practices curriculum judgments attuned to students' standardized test performances. Because this focus represents the dominant decision-making orientation in education today, it is readily understood by curriculum stakeholders, defined as those who participate in and/or have a stake in curriculum decision making, such as teachers, administrators, students, parents, community leaders, and local and state politicians.

THE STANDARDIZED MANAGEMENT PARADIGM

The dominant decision-making orientation could be characterized as the standardized management paradigm. It is an appealing paradigm because of its simplicity of purpose and its straightforward approach to accountability. Administrators manage teachers through the creation and maintenance of an accountability system geared to students' learning achievement as measured by carefully selected standardized tests. Anyone who follows professional sports can appreciate the logic of these systems. Coaches must demonstrate steady progress in the business of winning, or they are fired. Consequently, coaches and their athletes feel continuous pressure to improve. When this logic is applied to education, it has the same effect: Teachers and administrators feel continuous pressure to improve their practices. Because a high percentage of educational systems tenure their teachers, it may be the administrators who get fired; or, perhaps, no one gets fired, but the school loses students and/or gets shut down.

One problem with this dominant paradigm is its lack of subtlety. It is based on a one size-fits-all logic (Cuban, 2003). As pointed out in the first vignette, accountability systems may indeed pressure some teachers to improve their instruction, but what are the long-term consequences of this "improvement"? Because standardized test performances cannot be equated with performances of subject matter understanding, how shall we interpret the quality of the education of those students who score well on a test? Do they really understand the subject matter? Have they cultivated a disciplined mind? Are they acquiring a love of learning? Have they learned to appreciate the importance of education?

There are at least two other problems with the standardized management paradigm. It lacks flexibility and does not encourage moral responsibility, points that were brought out in the second vignette. Curriculum judgments, like legal and medical judgments, must be made on a case-by-case basis. *Particular* students in a *particular* classroom in a *particular* school year may benefit from *particular* practices aligned to *particular* standardized tests, but this does not hold for *all* students at *all* times for *all* educational goals. Deciding on the best educational course of action for a group of students, which is the focus of curriculum judgments, must be handled in a deliberative manner. It requires eclectic and imaginative problem solving (Eisner, 1994; Schwab, 1978). Therefore, when schools are considering the merits of a particular educational program, a number of questions can be raised. Who is benefiting from the educational program, and how are they benefiting? Are there students who are being left behind, poorly treated, or even ignored? What is the educational program's impact on student motivation, retention, and graduation? What is the impact on the educators who are required to work in accountability systems? How does the program affect human relations—between teachers and their students, between teachers and parents, between teachers and teachers, and between teachers and administrators?

Raising these critical curriculum questions does not mean that the standardized management paradigm is all bad. It simply points out that this paradigm is limited; it is not all good. It does provide some assurance that students are acquiring basic knowledge and skills, but at a cost. As the authors of this book, we think educators can make better curriculum judgments. They can make decisions that are attuned to performances of 3S understanding, which, of course, is the focus of the third vignette. Educators who elevate their curriculum judgments in this way might decide to teach for a particular type of standardized test performance but only because they had decided that this type of learning achievement would be appropriate for particular circumstances *as a means* to realize broader educational purposes.

THE CONSTRUCTIVIST BEST PRACTICE PARADIGM

Educators cannot practice curriculum judgments attuned to performances of 3S understanding without developing their individual capacities to teach for subject matter understanding. We stress this point because educators can become so preoccupied with democratic self and/or social learning that they lose sight of their subject matter teaching responsibilities (Dewey, 1938/1963). We will not make that mistake in this book. We will be advocating for a balanced, holistic education that integrates subject matter, self, and social learning. Consequently, we applaud the standards that have been created by all the professional teaching associations in the field of education. Collectively, these standards fall within the parameters of the constructivist best practice paradigm (Zemelman, Daniels, & Hyde, 1993). This chapter's second vignette features a moment in the professional life of a teacher leader who is deeply committed to this basic orientation.

The focus of constructivist teaching is on facilitating the construction of meaning; hence, the use of the "constructivist" term (Brooks & Brooks, 1993; Henderson, 1996). Students are treated as disciplined, active meaning makers. Though they may be asked to engage in some drill and memorization, the ultimate goal of the instruction is to facilitate student understanding. Constructivist teachers are heartened when their students say, "Now, I get it!" Because there is no one precise way to "get it" and because student understanding cannot be seen but only inferred, teachers must rely on public and idiosyncratic demonstrations of meaning. This introduces a certain ambiguity into the constructivist best practice paradigm that some curriculum stakeholders find objectionable. Much like the high school teacher in the first vignette, they want more precision in education.

THOMAS KUHN'S PARADIGM CONCEPT

We are using Thomas Kuhn's *paradigm* concept to convey such fundamental differences in problem-solving orientation. His notion of paradigms achieved widespread academic visibility with his publication of *The Structure of Scientific Revolutions* in 1962. Kuhn argues that scientific disciplines are characterized by "puzzle-solving" informed by a dominant "exemplar." The exemplar has two functions: It posits the organizing problem for a particular disciplinary field (it constructs the puzzle), and it presents a way to study and, perhaps, solve the problem (it constructs a methodology). Kuhn's thesis is that scientific disciplines advance in a constructivist, "paradigm shifting" way that can be unpredictable, tension-filled, and highly politicized. Brown (1988) nicely summarizes Kuhn's thesis:

> Only in crisis does the scientific community abandon its normal, puzzle-solving rules. Some members . . . inaugurate a deliberate scrutiny of fundamental assumptions. . . . An innovator may come forward with a revolutionary new paradigm. . . . The crisis moves to resolution as certain community members switch loyalties to the new paradigm. Once adhering to the new paradigm, these community members are in a "new world," incommensurable with the old one. At first slowly, they eventually attend to increasingly divergent problems, apply novel methods, and think in new terms. (p. 19)

In accordance with Kuhn's historical analysis, when professionals advance a paradigm, they are making two interrelated moves. They are framing and justifying the organizing problem of their field, and they are stating how this problem should be studied and, they hope, resolved. In effect, paradigm advocates are saying, "Our work should be organized in this way so as to address this problem."

The application of Kuhn's paradigm concept to curriculum work is complicated. As Brown (1988) notes, Kuhn was a historian of scientific communities, and there are serious problems applying his critical analysis to educational contexts. While advocates of the dominant standardized management paradigm promote education as an applied science, this is not the case for advocates of the constructivist best practice paradigm—or for advocates of the third vignette's paradigm, which we will shortly introduce. Due to the subtleties and idiosyncrasies of human meaning making, constructivist educators generally argue that education is more art than science. For example, Eisner (2004) writes:

> Artistry as a concept provides a vision of human possibility. . . . Too much of what we do is mired in tradition and stale habit; too much is formulaic and prescriptive. There is a paucity of genuine invention in education and the concept of artistry might help alleviate the constraints that over-formalized and highly technologized processes sometimes impose. . . . It provides a new platform for envisioning and

assessing education. It invites what I have called *productive idiosyncrasy.* There is no pressing need to turn children out of school in a common mold even if it makes comparisons among them easier. (pp. 15–16)

Because educational artistry is a central feature of the constructivist best practice paradigm, as well as the third paradigm, paradigmatic tensions in education can be compared to debates about artistic styles. Such debates are not easily settled, and Brown (1988) quotes Kuhn (1977) on this point:

> When traditions do change, the accompanying controversies are usually resolved far more rapidly in science than in art. In the latter . . . controversy over innovation is not usually settled until some new school arises to draw the fire of irate critics; even, then, I presume, the end of controversy often means only the acceptance of the new tradition not the end of the old. (p. 27)

The three vignettes reflect this complication; because standardized management is the dominant paradigm in curriculum work, advocates of the other two paradigms may, indeed, find themselves involved in very personal and highly complex debates and negotiations that have no final resolution.

THE CURRICULUM WISDOM PARADIGM

Though teaching for subject matter understanding is a necessary feature of the curriculum judgment we encourage, it does not go far enough. We want educators to take one further step; we want them to integrate the subject matter learning into democratic self and social learning. *We think the organizing problem of education should be the facilitation of a particular 3S understanding.* Though complicated in its details, the rationale for this paradigm is easy to explain. Consider the exemplars of subject matter understanding. These are experts in a particular field of disciplinary or interdisciplinary study who practice their expertise in many settings, including universities, hospitals, and businesses. With reference to their particular subject matter, they are "smart" people, but smart people are not necessarily "good" people. We think educators should be encouraging their students to be both smart and good, and our reference for goodness are the democratic values of society. These values hold a society together and allow for the realization of the best in each person; therefore, these are the values that should be emphasized in education—particularly public education.

This curricular focus on 3S understanding can be characterized as the *curriculum wisdom paradigm.* Wisdom is defined in the *Oxford English Dictionary* as "the capacity of judging rightly in matters relating to life and conduct; soundness of judgment in the choice of means and ends; sometimes, less strictly, sound sense, especially in practical affairs." Though wisdom is an elusive and ambiguous concept (Robinson, 1990), it refers to practical judgments directed toward subtle matters of goodness. It denotes curriculum decision making that is focused on the cultivation of enduring values that stand the test of time.

In the world of education, we seldom talk about wisdom. Of course, we talk about knowledge. Knowledge is at the center of the educational project. Increasingly politicians and policy makers are using instrumental language when they talk about what teachers and educational leaders should know: They want educational decisions to be "data driven" and for teachers and educational leaders to use research-based information. The image here is one of gathering bite-sized facts, especially "scientifically proven" facts, and bringing them to bear on curriculum decisions. This orientation is, of course, expressed in the first vignette. Often missing from this picture are the more qualitative dimensions of educational judgments: values, aesthetics, justice, and meaning, to name just a few. Thinking in these more expansive terms would require that we ask different kinds of questions, aside from the instrumental *what works:* Does this educational decision benefit all people equally, especially those who have been marginalized in the past? What kind of "good life" does this policy envision? Does this curriculum plan add to the beauty, the richness, and the harmony of a community's life? Will this decision foster generosity, compassion, and benevolence? What will be the effect of this decision seven generations from now? What does our community really care about? What is worth doing? How can we create a better world?

Asking deeper and more meaningful educational questions and facilitating public discussions around these questions is a challenging task. If curriculum workers in societies with democratic ideals are to succeed at this task, they will have to develop their own democratic wisdom tradition. This is important, because all curriculum decisions are, at their heart, moral decisions. They touch the core of what it means to be human, to live in community with others, to find meaning and purpose, and to create a more just and peaceful world. To meet these moral challenges, we will need to become morally wise, which will be neither easy nor unproblematic. Moral wisdom is not something that you "get" and then "have." It is not a thing, but a process; not singular, but plural; not static, but dynamic; not a technique, but an inquiring way of living.

The two social studies teachers in the third vignette possess a love of curriculum wisdom; the film *Radio* affirms their professional identity. They are passionate about teaching for a subject matter understanding that is embedded in democratic self and social understanding. Because their curriculum judgments are attuned to performances of students' 3S understanding, these two teachers serve as professional exemplars for this book.

THE PARADIGMATIC GOAL OF THE TEXT

The book's goal can now be explained with reference to Kuhn's paradigm concept. We will be offering curriculum leadership advice that falls within the curriculum wisdom paradigm, which is a problem-solving orientation that builds on and deepens the constructivist best practice paradigm. Because accountability systems prevail in education today and are generally backed by the force of law, educators who want to teach for 3S understanding will need to negotiate with advocates of the standardized management paradigm. In day-to-day practice, the three paradigms are deeply embedded in one another; they are not separate, distinctive orientations.

Table 1.1 EDUCATIONAL PARADIGMS		
Educational Paradigm	**Organizing Problem**	**Problem-Solving Cycle**
Standardized management	Student performances on standardized tests	Goal-setting, decision-making, and reflecting activities aligned to high-stakes standardized tests
Constructivist best practice	Student performances of subject matter understanding	Goal-setting, decision-making, and reflecting activities that facilitate students' subject matter meaning making
Curriculum wisdom	Student performances of subject matter understanding embedded in democratic self and social understanding	Goal-setting, decision-making, and reflecting activities that facilitate students' subject matter meaning making in a context of active democratic learning

Table 1.1 has been created to help you envision the three paradigms. Keep in mind, however, that it is an oversimplification of a complicated professional and political reality. The "Organizing Problem" heading refers to how learning problems are framed and, consequently, how they shape the curriculum problem solving, while the "Problem-Solving Cycle" heading refers to how educators move through recurring sequences of setting goals, deciding how to act, experiencing the consequences of specific actions, reflecting on these consequences, and revisiting and, if necessary, resetting goals. We will explore Table 1.1 in more detail in chapters 2 and 3.

LOOKING AHEAD: AN OVERVIEW OF THE REMAINING CHAPTERS OF THE BOOK

The general organizing problem of facilitating students' 3S understanding can be broken down into two fundamental challenges that must be integrated into four decision-making processes. The term *curriculum* may denote specific *products* in your mind, including school district frameworks, scope and sequence charts, course syllabi, and textbooks. However, this is a limited understanding of curriculum. Curriculum products are, we hope, the results of informed problem-solving *processes*. This book works at this process level. Our goal is not to hand you a fish but to teach you how to fish—as an imaginative, creative problem solver!

We will introduce two fundamental challenges of transformative curriculum leadership in chapters 2 and 3. In chapter 2, "Reconceptualizing Subject Standards," we will explore the challenge of rethinking educational standards from a curriculum wisdom orientation. In chapter 3, "Cultivating Reflective Inquiry," we will explore the importance of integrating reflective practice and democratic curriculum inquiry when teaching for 3S understanding.

We will introduce four key decision-making processes associated with transformative curriculum leadership in section II of the book, and these four processes will be presented in separate chapters. In chapter 4, "Designing and Planning for 3S Education," we will discuss the designing and planning decisions that underlie teaching for 3S understanding. In chapter 5, "Teaching for 3S Understanding," we will discuss the ongoing teaching decisions that emerge in the day-to-day 3S educational work. In chapter 6, "Evaluating 3S Education," we will discuss the comprehensive evaluative decisions that are an integral feature of 3S education. In chapter 7, "Organizing for 3S Education," we will discuss organizational decisions that provide supportive structures for 3S education. How should teachers' workdays and work years be organized so that their 3S educational efforts are encouraged and sustained?

The integration of the two fundamental challenges into the four decision-making processes constitutes a very high professional standard. To sustain such high-level problem solving, educators must consider the value of establishing local professional and stakeholder learning communities. This challenge will be addressed in chapter 8, "Building Local Learning Communities." This problem solving could also be sustained through leadership projects in the larger public arena. This topic will be explored in chapter 9, "Engaging the Broader Public Sphere." In this concluding chapter you will learn that this text is based on a particular disciplined interpretation of curriculum-based teaching. If this interpretation could be used to network educators, to influence the public imagination, and to create effective policy instruments, wisdom-oriented educators would gain invaluable sources of support.

Figure 1.1 provides a snapshot of the organization of this book. You will notice that we have placed the chapter 2 challenge of reconceptualizing subject standards in the image's central circle. Paradigmatically speaking, chapter 2 serves as the text's organizing problem. It provides the focus for curriculum problem solving, and it is a constant reminder that transformative curriculum leadership is a particular kind of standards-based reform. Notice how the chapter 3 challenge of cultivating reflective inquiry is also in the image's central circle. This placement recognizes the vital importance of integrating reflective practice and democratic curriculum inquiry in 3S education. Also, the four decision-making processes are situated on the rays of the four-point star that extends from the circle. We want you to understand that unless the two fundamental challenges are integrated into the four decision-making processes, the curriculum judgments will not be properly disciplined. This four-point star also depicts the entire problem-solving gestalt as a "moral compass" for democratic education and as a form of professional artistry. Furthermore, note how the decision making processes are placed in an interconnected and recursive circular pattern. Though we discuss the processes in separate chapters for clarity of presentation, we want you to understand that in actual practice it is not possible to precisely demarcate where one decision-making process ends and another begins. Finally, note that the topic of sustaining the wisdom problem solving is positioned below the star. We want you to understand that the activities of building local learning communities and engaging the broader public sphere support the star.

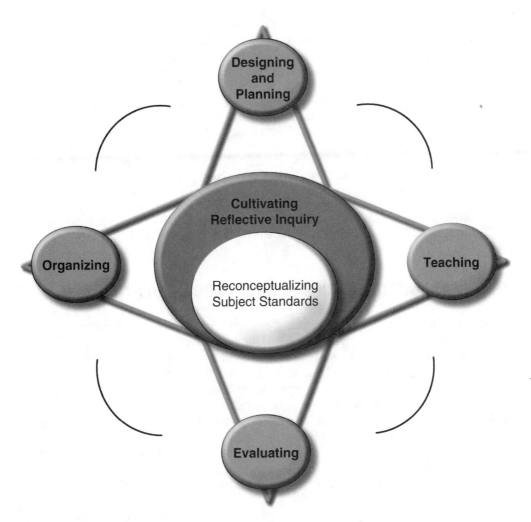

Figure 1.1   **Sustaining the Curriculum Wisdom Problem Solving**

We present this image in a pragmatic spirit. We have gained a certain amount of experience with the curriculum wisdom paradigm, and we have noticed that if educators are to make headway with this professional orientation, they must tackle certain challenges and decision-making processes. We have organized this book around these topics. However, our advice is general in nature. As you undertake the leadership challenges associated with the curriculum wisdom paradigm in your work setting, you may encounter other challenges and processes. If this occurs, we hope we have provided you with sufficient guidance to practice curriculum judgments informed by a love of democratic wisdom. This is, in a nutshell, our pragmatic intention.

Figure 1.1 will appear at the beginning of each chapter, and the topic under discussion will be highlighted. The repetition of Figure 1.1 makes an important point. We want you to understand that all the topics in this book are interrelated. Transformative curriculum leadership is a broad-based and systemic reform effort, described by Eisner (1994):

> The reform of education not only requires deeper and more comprehensive analysis of schools; it must also attend to the dimensions of schooling that must be collectively addressed to make educational reform educationally real. This attention must go well beyond changes in individual aspects of educational practice. . . . Applied to schools, it means that the school as a whole must be addressed: . . . the intentions that give direction to the enterprise, the structure that supports it, the curriculum that provides its content, the teaching with which that content is mediated, and the evaluation system that enables us to monitor and improve its operation. . . . To approach the reform of schools ecologically or, as others put it, systemically, requires, at the very least, attention to intentions—what aims really matter in the educational enterprise as a whole? (pp. 10–11)

TRANSFORMATIVE CURRICULUM LEADERSHIP DEFINED

As we mentioned at the beginning of this chapter, we will use the term *transformative curriculum leadership,* to refer to the professional judgment advice we will be offering throughout this book, and there are two main reasons why we employ this phrase. Though all three paradigms require curriculum judgment, the problem solving associated with the curriculum wisdom paradigm is the most subtle and sophisticated. Because predetermined test "scripts" guide standardized management decisions, the curriculum problem solving within this paradigm can be likened to creating a cut-and-dried television plot. The point of the standardized teaching is to achieve predictable results.

This is not the case for the other two paradigms. Constructivist best practices are directed toward idiosyncratic performances of understanding (Gardner, 2005); these performances involve personally expressive outcomes, described by Eisner (1994):

> Outcomes are essentially what one ends up with, intended or not, after some form of engagement. Expressive outcomes are the consequences of curriculum activities that are intentionally planned to provide a fertile field for personal purposing and experience. . . . Expressive activities precede rather than follow expressive outcomes. The tack taken with respect to the generation of expressive outcomes is to create activities that are sufficiently rich to allow for a wide, productive range of educationally valuable outcomes. (pp. 118–120)

Teaching for 3S understanding is directed toward broad idiosyncratic outcomes. Educators ask their students not only to demonstrate a deep understanding of the subject matter but also to exhibit democratic self and social understanding.

This is a challenging way to educate, requiring a deeply committed pursuit of excellence. The curriculum wisdom paradigm is based on a high professional standard. It requires inspired, voluntary effort, and it positions educators as *transformative leaders.* Because the curriculum wisdom paradigm is not the professional norm, those who teach for 3S understanding are outliers. When they reach out to others, they must seek to uplift, energize, and enlighten from a minority position. They must find ways to inspire their students as well as other curriculum stakeholders.[3]

Burns (1978) describes "transformative" leaders as individuals who encourage "principled levels of judgment" through dedicated effort (p. 455). They inspire others to higher levels of performance. Because transformative curriculum leaders care so deeply about the facilitation of a personalized 3S understanding, they affirm the "best selves" of those who are around them (Noddings, 1984). Burns (1978) contrasts transformative leadership with a more traditional understanding of leadership, with its focus on the efficient attainment of goals and not on "consciousness raising on a wide plane" (p. 43). Traditional leadership makes sense within the parameters of the standardized management paradigm. The creation and maintenance of a testing accountability system indicates a lack of trust and the need to ensure compliance. Perhaps such distrust is warranted in some circumstances with some educators, but this is not true for all educators in all situations. As already mentioned, the standardized management paradigm lacks subtlety and flexibility; it should not be surprising that the leadership associated with this paradigm is similarly limited. In contrast to leadership-for-compliance, transformative leadership is an inspirational orientation. It "is conceived . . . not in terms of control, but rather in terms of guiding others to higher levels of judgment and self-governance" (Snauwaert, 1993, p. 7).

We are also employing the term *transformative curriculum leadership* to acknowledge the deep-seated changes associated with this work. Transformation conveys a sense of fundamental reform, and the alterations associated with the enactment of the curriculum wisdom paradigm take place at three interrelated levels: the personal, the interpersonal, and the societal.

Personal Change

Though the personal changes embedded in the practice of curriculum wisdom are quite subtle, diversified, and idiosyncratic, we highlight one likely transformation for illustrative purposes. Educators may experience shifts in their professional identity as part of embracing and enacting the curriculum wisdom paradigm (Henderson & Kesson, 2004), a point dramatized in the three vignettes. All three paradigms require hard work; however, the standardized management paradigm conveys a relatively straightforward message to the curriculum worker:

> *Your job is to follow orders, not question the system. You have some flexibility in how you achieve these orders, but there are general guidelines that you must follow. These guidelines are tied to specific standardized outcomes, and these outcomes are your bottom line. If your students do not achieve these outcomes, you will suffer consequences.*

[3] This professional challenge is clearly dramatized in the film *Radio,* which was briefly described in the third vignette. It is a movie worth seeing.

Given the general nature of socialization in modern societies, this type of message, which can be characterized as "semi-professional" in its orientation (Sykes, 1996), does not place much of a strain on educators' identities.

However, consider the message associated with the curriculum wisdom paradigm, expressed as an analogy with the medical profession:

> *If medical doctors engage in the disciplined study of their patients' physical health in the context of their specialty, they have the right to exercise discretionary clinical judgment. Similarly, if educators engage in the disciplined study of their students' democratic health in the context of their subject matter expertise, they have the right to exercise discretionary curriculum judgment.*

Educators were raised by medical doctors or other professionals who think that good judgments are made case by case and are informed by disciplined study should not find this message too difficult to understand. However, educators who were raised to follow the orders of their superiors may find this message difficult to digest. They may need to reflect deeply on the nature of their professional identity.

Interpersonal Change

Changes at the interpersonal level are as complex as changes at the personal level, and again for illustrative purposes, we provide an example of this type of transformation. The enactment of the curriculum wisdom paradigm is informed by a *power with* orientation, which has a particular manifestation in the classroom. In many traditional classrooms, teacher-student relations are embedded in a *power over* orientation. This use of power is characterized by command, control, and competition for scarce goods like "A" and "B" grades, teacher approval, and other rewards. Such *power over* relationships can limit communication, inhibit empathy, and foster a sense of powerlessness (Kreisberg, 1992).

Educating for 3S understanding requires teachers to establish a *power with* working relationship, summarized by Kreisberg (1992):

> Power with is manifest in relationships of co-agency. These relationships are characterized by people finding ways to satisfy their desires and to fulfill their interests without imposing on one another. The relationship of co-agency is one in which there is equality: situations in which individuals and groups fulfill their desires by acting together. It is jointly developing capacity. The possibility for power with lies in the reality of human inter-connectedness within communities. . . . (pp. 85–86)

In this type of working relationship, teachers and students respect one another. Students' autonomy and initiative is encouraged in a context of responsible, constructivist learning transactions. The instruction is flexible and creative, and the teacher encourages the students to ask such critical questions as:

- How does this lesson enhance my subject matter understanding?

- Am I cultivating a responsible sense of personal agency?

- Am I learning to fulfill my dreams in a generous spirit, so that I can celebrate my personal victories in a context of celebrating the personal victories of others?

- Am I learning to work with my peers, so as to not allow our differences to interfere with our collaborative meaning making?

- Am I acquiring a sense of interdependence, a feeling that I am connected to others in many significant ways?

Because power is a pervasive feature of human affairs, a shift in power relations in the classroom is closely linked to, and perhaps dependent upon, changes outside the classroom, including the organization of the workday, the prioritization of money, and the use of time (Hargreaves, 1994, 2003). There is a reason why the concept of *power* is a central topic in curriculum studies (Martusewicz & Reynolds, 1994). It is a pivotal dimension of educational work. Changes in power relations can influence the daily work life of curriculum stakeholders in many subtle and significant ways.

Societal Change

The curriculum leadership advice in this book is ultimately directed toward fundamental changes in society. To embrace a love of curriculum wisdom is to continually ask deep-seated questions about "good" living. Curriculum wisdom is a demanding professional norm that links self-examination with social critique. As Kekes (1995) notes, Socrates felt that moral wisdom was the greatest of the human virtues. He explains:

> A just and honorable life is lived according to virtue, and Socrates recognizes five virtues required by such a life: temperance, courage, piety, justice, and . . . moral wisdom. He held that these virtues are related to each other more intimately than parts are related to a whole, . . . although "wisdom is the greatest of the parts" [Plato, 1961, p. 329], . . . because no action can be virtuous unless it is based on the knowledge moral wisdom gives." (pp. 32, 37)

The love of democratic wisdom requires a soul-searching honesty directed toward public virtue. Do my judgments embody the democratic good life? Am I truly open to diverse others? Do I listen carefully to people with whom I disagree, and am I willing to talk with them, or at least to "agree to disagree"? Am I willing to challenge social policies and institutions that I feel are undemocratic? As an educator, am I committed to facilitating a meaningful educational journey for each of my students? Am I concerned about their personal dreams of excellence? Am I comfortable with the inherent pluralism and idiosyncrasies of the democratic good life?

Such wide-ranging social and cultural questions bring forth the philosophical side of curriculum work. Philosophy literally means the "love of wisdom," and a fundamental premise of the curriculum wisdom paradigm is that democracy is a moral way of living.[4]

---

[4] Because you may be reading this book in the context of a college or university course, it may interest you to note that a teacher with a Ph.D. degree possesses a doctorate literally in the love of wisdom.

Democracy is not just a form of government that can be contrasted with other forms of government such as oligarchy, aristocracy, and theocracy. Philosophically speaking, it is a "good" life orientation. In 1939, on the eve of World War II, American philosopher John Dewey contemplated the challenges that democratic societies faced from a communist Soviet Union and a fascist Germany:

> The democratic road is the hard one to take. It is the road which places the greatest burden of responsibility upon the greatest number of human beings. Backsets and deviations occur and will continue to occur. But that which is its own weakness at particular times is its strength in the long course of human history. Just because the cause of democratic freedom is the cause of the fullest possible realization of human potentialities, the latter when they are suppressed and opposed will in time rebel and demand an opportunity for manifestation. We have advanced far enough to say that democracy is a way of life. We have yet to realize that it is a way of personal life and one which provides a moral standard for personal conduct. (Dewey, 1939/1989, pp. 100–101)

Democracy understood as a moral standard for personal conduct is the basic philosophical idea that guides this book. Snauwaert (1993) describes this orientation as a developmental understanding of democracy: "From the perspective of this [democratic] tradition, human development rather than efficiency is the ultimate standard upon which systems of governance should be chosen and evaluated" (p. 5). Dewey (1938/1963) describes his democratic faith as an "end in view." An end in view is different from a precise belief. It is an organizing ideal that forever remains open to diverse perspectives. Carlson (1997) characterizes Dewey's democratic end in view as "fuzzy" utopianism. A Deweyan democrat does not bring ideological closure to his/her "faith," knowing full well that the notion of democracy as a moral way of living requires continuous, disciplined study.

In this spirit of open-ended inquiry, Greene (1988) notes that perspectives on human freedom can never "be finished or complete. There is always more. There is always possibility. And this is where the space opens for the pursuit of freedom" (p. 128). As she philosophically examines the connections between democracy and education, she presents a complex, layered understanding of human liberation: "Freedom cannot be conceived apart from a matrix of social, economic, cultural, and psychological conditions" (Greene, 1988, p. 80). She further explains that this understanding of human freedom demands a sophisticated practical wisdom informed by a multidimensional critical awareness. She notes that such progressive and pragmatic individuals as Oliver Wendell Holmes, Thorstein Veblen, Vernon Louis Parrington, William James, John Dewey, Lincoln Steffens, Charles Beard, and Jane Addams "shared a profound faith in hypothetical and empirical inquiries; and they shared an understanding of the transactional relationships between living human beings and their environments" (Greene, 1988, p. 42). She argues that the "consequences of free action . . . are to a large degree unpredictable" (p. 46). Engaging in our best practical intelligence is "the price we must pay" for democratic pluralism (p. 46).

Greene (1988) advances a subtle "dialectical" understanding of human freedom through a balancing of critique and celebration. Her critique focuses on "oppression or exploitation or segregation or neglect" (Greene, 1988, p. 9). Through disciplined critical work, people can establish distance from their psychological and/or social shackles; they can responsibly express "the right not to be interfered with or coerced or compelled to do what [one] did not choose to do" (Greene, 1988, p. 16). This is the *freedom from* side of the dialectic. It is an essential feature of democratic living. Brooks (2005) reinforces this important critical point:

> The United States is a country based on the idea that a person's birth does not determine his or her destiny. Our favorite stories involve immigrants climbing from obscurity to success. Our amazing work ethic is predicated on the assumption that enterprise and effort lead to ascent. "I hold the value of life is to improve one's condition," Lincoln declared.
>
> The problem is that in every generation conditions emerge that threaten to close down opportunity and retard social mobility. Each generation has to reopen the pathways to success. Today, for example, we may still believe American society is uniquely dynamic, but we're deceiving ourselves. European societies, which seem more class-driven and less open, have just as much social mobility as the United States does. And there are some indications that it is becoming harder and harder for people to climb the ladder of success. (p. 11)

Greene celebrates human freedom through expressions of responsible, authentic self-direction. This is the *freedom to* side of her dialectic, and it refers to the ultimate fruition of democratic emancipation: "freedom shows itself or comes into being when individuals come together in a particular way, when they are authentically present to one another (without masks, pretenses, badges of office), when they have a project they can mutually pursue" (Greene, 1988, p. 16). Authentic, responsible self-direction is directed toward a "carnival" of creative human expression (Sidorkin, 1999), which culminates in a robust cultural renaissance that replaces unimaginative standardization. Over 2,000 years ago, the great Greek leader Pericles celebrated the democratic freedoms in the city–state of Athens with these words: "Yet ours is no workaday city only. No other city provides so many recreations for the spirit—contests and sacrifices all the year round, and beauty in our public buildings to cheer the spirit and delight the eye day by day. . . . We are lovers of beauty without extravagance" (Cahill, 2003, pp. 241–242).

Greene's (1988) analysis of this dialectic of freedom is comprehensive and diversified. She describes a variety of forms of oppression, exploitation, segregation, and neglect in American society. Those forms are associated not only with racial, gender, and class relations, but also with more subtle forms such as "constraining family rituals," "bureaucratic supervisory systems," and, ironically, even static images of freedom in the media that serve the interests of the wealthy and powerful (Greene, 1988, p. 17). She recognizes that struggles against freedom's constraints must be broad based and multileveled. Greene's (1988) presentation of authentic expressions of democratic freedom is equally sophisticated. Tapping into American history, she draws on the writings of Thomas Jefferson, Walt Whitman, Mark Twain, Horace Mann, Ralph Waldo Emerson, and many others. She summarizes her understanding of human freedom by acknowledging the intimate relationship between personal and social emancipation:

> This book arises out of a lifetime's preoccupation with quest, with pursuit. On the one hand, the quest has been deeply personal: that of a woman striving to affirm the feminine as wife, mother, and friend, while reaching, always reaching, beyond the limits imposed by the obligations of a woman's life. On the other hand, it has been in some sense deeply public as well: that of a person struggling to connect the undertaking of education, with which she has been so long involved, to the making and remaking of a public space, a space of dialogue and possibility. (Greene, 1988, p. xi)

CURRICULUM AS CURRERE

There are two sides to this book. We are not offering just curriculum problem-solving advice; we are also inviting you to undertake your own personal, public quest. We are encouraging you to engage in your own emancipation. To embrace a love of curriculum wisdom is to embark on a journey of self-discovery. Teaching for 3S understanding requires a balanced subject, self, and social inquiry. This requires an autobiographical examination that is embedded in academic and historical knowing. Pinar (2004) calls this type of disciplined professional study *currere*, which is the infinitive form of the Latin noun *curriculum*. He explains:

> To support the systematic study of self-reflexivity within the processes of education, I devised the method of *currere*. The method of *currere*—the Latin infinitive form of curriculum means to run the course, or, in the gerund form, the running of the course— provides a strategy for students of curriculum to study the relations between academic knowledge and life history in the interest of self-understanding and social reconstruction. . . . The method of *currere* reconceptualized curriculum from course objectives to complicated conversation with oneself (as a "private" intellectual), an ongoing project of self-understanding in which one becomes mobilized for engaged pedagogical action—as a private-and-public intellectual—with others in the social reconstruction of the public sphere. (pp. 35, 37)

Transformative Curriculum Leadership is a method book in two senses of the term. We are providing guidance on a complex method of curriculum problem solving. That is, we are presenting advice on four decision-making processes informed by two fundamental challenges. We are also illustrating the method of currere. Each chapter includes a relevant component of the currere narrative composed by Rosemary Gornik, the coauthor of this book. Rosie is the assistant superintendent of a public school district in northeast Ohio.

We present Rosie's currere narrative, rather than a teacher's, for three reasons. Rosie is teacher centered in her leadership approach, and we want the teacher readers of this book to feel that central administrative support for their professional development efforts is possible. She also exemplifies the collaborative nature of transformative curriculum leadership. She does not overly identify with her administrative role; she is, first and foremost, an educator who possesses a love of democratic wisdom and who reaches out to other educators in this spirit. Finally, and perhaps most importantly, she is deeply committed to enacting the curriculum wisdom paradigm. She is realistic about its challenges and excited about its possibilities. You will shortly meet Rosie Gornik, and you will come to know her well as you read this book.

We incorporate the currere method into this book because we acknowledge that educators who choose to facilitate their students' personalized journeys of understanding cannot do so without undertaking a similar journey of understanding. Simply stated, teaching for holistic understanding requires a journey of self-understanding as a democratic historical agent. The curriculum wisdom paradigm is a personally demanding frame of reference. It advances a multifaceted problematic that requires multiple modes of address (Ellsworth, 1997), and it advances a democratic *way of being* an educator. This should not be surprising, given that democracy is a moral way of living.

Given this text's dual advice/narrative design, there are at least three ways it can be approached. Read the book from start to finish, study the advice sections first and then go back and read the narrative sections, or read the narratives first and then go back and study the advice. Whatever your study approach, you will notice that we attempt to keep our problem-solving advice as straightforward as possible but then allow for the subtleties and ambiguities of the curriculum wisdom paradigm to emerge in the currere narratives.

A purpose of this book is to encourage you to become a "connoisseur" of democratic education—a professional who understands the nuances of educational growth in societies with democratic values (Eisner, 1994; Henderson, 2005). Rosie Gornik is cultivating her connoisseurship voice, and we want you to do the same. There is a reason why John Dewey calls education "the supreme art" (Dewey 1897/1997, p. 23). How does a society become a "deep democracy" (Green, 1999) without the daily efforts of dedicated educators? Welcome to this book's curriculum frame of reference. Welcome to the journey of understanding that accompanies a love of curriculum wisdom. Welcome to the visionary work of transformative curriculum leadership!

At an earlier point in this chapter, we introduced the star image, Figure 1.1, which provides a schematic overview of the problem-solving cycle that is the organizing referent for the curriculum wisdom paradigm. We told you that this image will appear at the beginning of each chapter and that the topic under discussion will be highlighted. Due to the centrality of *currere narratives* in curriculum wisdom work, the star image in Figure 1.2 incorporates this term four times. We want you to appreciate the importance of narrative expressions of self-understanding in the problem-solving process advanced by this book. Although the *currere narrative* term will not appear in the book's repeating star image, keep in mind that a journey of self-understanding, which is clarified and expressed though currere narratives, is integral to curriculum problem solving.

Currere Narrative

Early one day in late October, my students piled into the classroom. There was much chatter and sharing of stories. Some student behaviors were just this side of out of control. Darius exploded into the room.

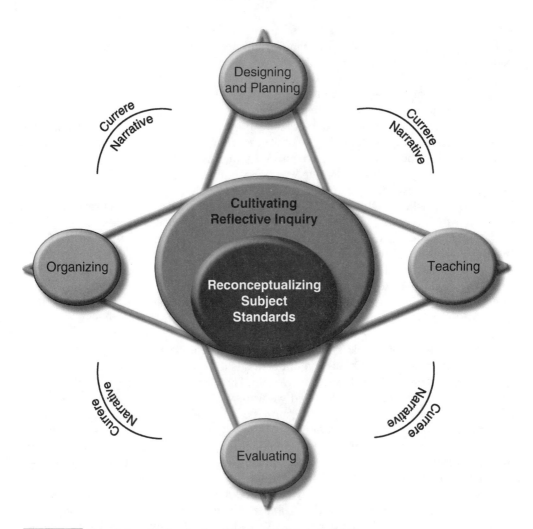

Figure 1.2 | Sustaining the Curriculum Wisdom Problem Solving

"Hey, did you watch *Mod Squad* on television last night?" he squealed. "Wasn't that cool when that guy got shot?"

"I like the way James is sitting in his seat, ready to start his day," I chided. Reluctantly, Darius took his cue.

"I watched *The Brady Bunch* and *Sanford and Son,*" Angela yelled from across the room as she slammed the top of her desk. The bang evoked a collective groan from several startled students. The noise filled the room.

"I like the way Leroy hung up his coat and has his book on his desk ready to go," I bellowed above the din, nervously rushing to close my classroom door. A new teacher in a classroom within earshot of the principal's office must be careful, I thought.

It would be 8 minutes before I was able to get the class settled down to our routine for the day. Not bad, I thought. With a smile in my heart, and just maybe a shadow of one on my face, I knew I was a teacher who could handle students. I had it together, I told myself. I smugly noted that 8 minutes to rally classroom control was an improvement over my earlier 15-minute record.

Life was sweet. It was the fall of 1973. Nature was ablaze, with trees of red, gold, and brown heralding the peak of her maturity. In much the same way, I was ripe. Graduating from college the previous spring with a degree in elementary education was a life-dream and something I had always wanted to accomplish. Now, here I was teaching fourth and fifth graders in a combination class in a small, public school district in the southern part of a midwestern state. In the fullness of age 22, I had landed my first teaching job. This harvest was more significant because many others in my class were waiting tables, working retail, or settling for substitute teacher status. In a word, I was ecstatic. The whopping $7,300 annual salary did not matter. Money was not the reason I chose to teach. I had dreamed of this teaching opportunity for most of my life, and the time had finally arrived. Filled with all the idealism of youth, I had a room full of students who needed me and the thought of influencing their lives stirred my heart and mind. Life was sweet indeed.

My small elementary school was typical in many ways. The K–5 structure housed traditional, graded classrooms and two or three sections of each grade. We served approximately 400 students. Mine was a combination class of fourth and fifth graders because of an odd number of students in those grades. I had so much to learn but was a quick study and a willing participant. I suffered the typical classroom management issues that many of us experience in our first few months. "Never smile before Christmas," was the admonition of my supportive and more experienced colleagues. "The kids will walk all over you," they said. While I did not like the message and worried about the dynamic that it might set up in my classroom, I tried to follow the advice. Could "smiling before Christmas" really be a chink in my armor? They must know what they are talking about, I thought. Who was I to challenge the wisdom of the many who have gone before me? I took my responsibilities seriously and did my best to comply, with a smile lurking beneath a thin veil of authority.

On this particular morning there was one student who, in spite of repeated warnings, continued to challenge me. Every other student was working quietly, yet Renard was being disruptive and distracting attention from our bell work.

"I watched *Sanford and Son*, too," he yelled as he ran across the room toward Angela's desk. Legs flying and arms in the air, Renard began to roll around on the floor, kicking chairs and laughing. His sweater vest and bell-bottom pants collected dust from the floor. Renard was holding court.

"Renard, take your seat or I will have to put your name on the board," I said. He continued to thrash, now under the desk.

"Renard," I called out. "Take your seat or you will miss lunch recess today." Angela's chair toppled as he tripped the leg with his foot. "Renard! Stop that this instant," I demanded. Renard persisted.

I had prided myself on making a limited number of student referrals to the office. Sending students to the office was a personal and professional failure, not to mention downright embarrassment. In spite of my steely resolve never to abdicate my authority or wound my pride by sending a student to the office, the "oh my gosh, I am going to kill this kid" meter in my head blew a gasket. That kid crossed the line. This was not the first, the 10th, or the 20th time this student had caused problems. He and I were in a power struggle, and I knew I needed to assert my authority, pull rank, and send him to the office. I needed to draw the line in the sand and set an example for him and the other students. More importantly, he was denying the 27 other students the right to my time and attention. He had to go.

"Out!" I shrieked at him, my arms waving and pointing toward the door.

"Out!" I yelled again, "and don't come back until you, Principal Davis, and I talk about your behavior."

My decision to send Renard to the office that day ranks with hard-wired memories of Kennedy's assassination, news of my brother-in-law's death, and my mom's cancer diagnosis. Every minute detail of that experience lurks under the razor-thin layer of my consciousness: Renard's tattered sweater vest, which hung around his knees; his hair piled high enough to nest a giant pick; my paisley dress that strained across my too-full stomach from yet another failed "Twiggy-inspired" diet; my toes pinched into too-small and too-high platform shoes that made my gait wobbly and unstable; the stink of too much Old English splashed on the face of the middle-aged principal. Thirty-two years later, my heart pounds, my palms shine, and my stomach seizes.

While I knew Renard had issues on the playground, at lunch, and on the bus, I was unaware of one small but important detail: My referral to the office resulted in the accumulation of enough referrals that launched him to the next level of discipline in the hierarchy of consequences. The term *progressive discipline* was new to my professional vocabulary. Unbeknownst to me, my referral was the tipping point on Renard's discipline scorecard. We hit a grand slam, and it was not good.

Within minutes of sending him out of the classroom and to the office, I learned that the next consequence for this 10-year-old child was a paddling from the principal! That fateful referral launched a cascade of bureaucratic events that whirled out of my control. Gone were opportunities for missing recess, calls to the parents, and isolation from other students. Gone were possibilities for more creative responses to his antics. My relationship with Renard was falling through my grasp.

Just when I thought things could not have been worse, I learned that not only was he going to receive five swats with a thick paddle riddled with holes, but also that I was required to be the "adult" witness in the room!

Salt formed in my watering mouth. My ears pounded with the beat of my heart. My senses registered unfamiliar impressions in a surreal slow motion. I was instructed by the secretary to report to the office during my next planning period, so the deed could be done.

In an act of desperation, I grabbed the teacher next door and asked her to watch my students while I went to the office. I found the principal sitting at his desk, coolly signing papers in what seemed to be a bizarre activity just before an execution. I mustered what energy I could and lobbied hard. I attempted to convince him that a paddling was not necessary; I minimized Renard's behavior, suggesting that I place him on a behavior contract that might improve things; I told him that I was the problem and needed one more chance to bring this kid around. Nothing would dissuade this principal from his mission to follow the rules of the code of conduct. My shoulders slumped; I slowly walked back to my classroom. In 15 minutes, my planning period would begin.

The principal led the two of us into a small hallway, away from the view of others. Without a word, the ritual began. Watching, I became more upset with each blow. With each collision, I felt a growing weakness in my knees and a rising sense of nausea. Renard stared at me, looking over his shoulder crying, using his eyes to silently beg me to help him. His eyes pierced me. By strike four, I could not contain myself any longer and had to reach for the wall to steady myself, platform shoes notwithstanding. I started to cry, urging the principal that it was enough. In a flash of an instant, the principal whirled around, glared at me, and yelled at me to be silent. He delivered the last blow to the student and sent him crying wildly out of the hallway to take a seat in the outer office. I barely remember what happened in the moments that followed or the words the principal used, but his message was loud and clear: "Never do that again!" He warned that it was my professional responsibility to hold my emotions in check, follow the rules of the discipline code, and never, under any circumstances, show my emotions to students. I stuffed the tears, swallowed the bile, and left.

When I reached my classroom door, 20 minutes of my planning period remained. Bitter, silent tears flowed. A sickening sense of horror enveloped my head as I wondered how I could have been involved in such an assault on another human being, much less a 10-year-old child. I knew I wanted to teach in the public schools, and was darn lucky to have this job. I wanted to keep my job and knew that my response to this situation would affect my future employment. A newbie with a 1-year contract, I could ill afford to have this incident find its way into my annual performance evaluation.

Yet, I asked myself, what did I stand for as a teacher? Is this what teaching was all about? Couldn't we ask questions about all this, I wondered? Couldn't we get in a room and ask each other if this was in the best interest of children? Couldn't we problem solve in a way that considered the merits of our decisions and purposefully decide *who* was benefiting from our decisions and *how* they were benefiting? What were our assumptions about paddling students? Corporal punishment was standard in the late 1960s and the early 1970s and would not be deemed illegal until many years later. Had this principal taken time to examine or articulate those assumptions? He was also living his story and doing his job as best he understood it. Was paddling as a practice politically correct and ethical? What kind of change might we expect in Renard's behavior? Was it the kind of change we wanted? Could we probe into the impact of our discipline policies and programs on student motivation? Would these decisions foster Renard's generosity, compassion, and benevolence? Couldn't we try to name our vision of human possibility?

While it would take many, many years before I would be able to articulate these questions, the veil of naiveté dropped from my eyes that day. At that moment, amid the confusion and sadness, the seeds of a new consciousness were germinating and an unfolding awareness about my identity as a teacher and as a professional was being forged. Those 10-year-old eyes spoke volumes to me that day and stirred an awakening in me that would serve as a rudder in my life and in my journey as an educator. Somehow this little boy became more than just another student. He represented the children I hoped to have someday and indeed every child ever born . . . he represented me. Not to worry, Mr. Principal, I will never do that again. I learned my lesson, although maybe not one he thinks. Little did he know that my version of "never do that again" involved a steely resolve to find a better way. I did not know exactly what that was, but I knew I would never find myself in that position again.

As I look back on the last 30-plus years, I realize finding a better way would involve a lot of searching, a lot of questioning and critical thought, a lot of reading and many complicated conversations that just might imagine a better future. Over time, the message in that little boy's eyes has come to represent my platform for my professional work and my professional identity. That message in those dark eyes would guide how I design programs in accordance with that platform, how I translate that platform into instructional plans, how my teaching and leading are informed, how I evaluate the results of my teaching and leading, and how I communicate with a wide range of curriculum stakeholders.

And so, dear reader, this is a book about hope, a desire accompanied by expectation. What do we as authors and educators desire and hope for? What is our expectation? The answers to these questions will emerge throughout these chapters. This is a book for practitioners who are ready to explore the relationships between schools and society with conversations that are open ended, critically aware, and imaginative. This is a book for practitioners who are ready to use the value of the standards-based education and the content standards to move students beyond the immediate and temporary to the long-term and enduring American dream of democratization and self-realization. This is a book that just might help us learn to provide educational experiences for students who integrate "academic knowledge and life history in the interest of self-understanding" (Pinar, 2004, p. 35) and building a better society.

At issue is the fact that this hope cannot be reduced to a sound bite, packaged as a formula condensed to a worksheet for implementation in your classroom tomorrow. You are invited into what we have come to know as an "extraordinarily complicated conversation" (Pinar et al., 1995, p. 848), which could transform the spectator-like academic content standards into real-life autobiographies that not only tell the stories of the past and enable the student to situate the "self" in the present, fostering a meaningful existence, but also increase the likelihood of a brighter future. All the discrete subjects, such as English or mathematics, tend to focus on teaching strategies within single teaching fields. Much like an autobiographical account, the complicated conversation aspires to deal with the "overall educational significance of the curriculum (content standards), focusing especially upon interdisciplinary themes—such as gender or multiculturalism or the ecological crisis—as well as relations among the curriculum, the individual, society and history" (Pinar, 2004, p. 21).

Staying with the concept of a complicated conversation, you are invited to view a kind of "curriculum real-world," a reality peek into my life as an educator, past and present, as I attempt to envision a future navigating the rocky waters within my school district, my county, my state, and my country. In the popular "real-world" television programs, viewers witness the unfolding dramas, conversations, and stories of individuals as a camera chronicles myriad experiences about work, relationships, difference, conflict, and love.

Within the pages of this book, I will share with you my real-world experiences and many "extraordinarily complicated conversations" I hold regularly with myself and others about curriculum designing and planning, teaching, curriculum evaluation, organizing, and communicating with curriculum stakeholders.

Lest you think that the real world of curriculum designing, planning, teaching, and evaluating is not interesting enough for a voyeuristic peek, you just might change your mind. The stories in these chapters are true, with the names and settings slightly altered to protect the anonymity of those involved. We think that by the end of this reading, you might come to realize that curriculum work, done wisely, is intensely dramatic and grounded in human, soul-searching, private, and public autobiographical issues.

This book is about "discovering and articulating, for (myself) and with others, the educational significance of the school subjects for self and society in the ever-changing historical moment" (Pinar, 2004, p. 16). Throughout these chapters, I will share with you my own understanding of what it means to teach, to study, and to become educated. In order to convey to the reader my understanding of this curriculum theory, I will use a form of autobiographical truth telling that articulates my lived educational experiences.

Through the use of narrative in the remaining chapters, I will provide a critical and passionate look at my experiences as a teacher, elementary principal, and executive director of instruction and assistant superintendent. In this real-world look, we come to view curriculum not as a series of objectives for which there are countless tests and accountability that measure "achievement," but rather as an authentic, and personal, moral yearning for the public good. As Jardine (1990/1997) puts it, "It is not accumulated curricular knowledge that we most deeply offer our children in educating them. It is not their mastery of requisite skills or their grade-point average, but literally their ability to live, their ability to be on an Earth that will sustain their lives" (pp. 216–217). What could be more real-world than that!

The reflective inquiry outlined in chapter 3 is designed to help you develop a capacity for curriculum work as disciplined autobiographical study. What I have learned from my own reflective inquiries over the past 10 years is that our work as educators is pragmatic. Daily, we deal the real challenges and opportunities of helping students develop as human beings . . . to learn and tell their story, finding their place in the world of science, math, and social studies. I have an ever-present sense of our incredible responsibility and the resultant sacred quality of our work. I remain humbled each day by the power we have individually and collectively to harm, humor, hurt, humiliate, or heal our students, colleagues, and parents. A look, a glance, a word, a smile can be an instrument of growth or a weapon of destruction. Our goal is to have you witness the manner in which I enact reflective inquiries, testing them in the real world. While the reflective inquiries in chapter 3 provide a sort of map that has been useful to me as I make decisions, the subtleties of this work defy a formula or a prescription.

Chapter 3 provides a map for the reflective inquiry journey, but the "answers" to the curriculum dilemmas we face each day are as unique as the students we serve. As you know, even the best curriculum materials, which may endure, must be modified each year to meet the changing needs of students in your classrooms. Professionals in every field from medicine to law know the fundamentals of their practice, and the best among them stand ready to make modifications to meet the individual needs of the client. Reflective inquiry will help you cultivate the ability to play with contradictory intellectual perspectives. In the process, your responses to all these unique curriculum dilemmas will be sharpened and subtler.

Lest you think that I somehow have elevated myself to perfection, think again. While I work diligently, each and every day I fail; I succeed; I disappoint myself and others; I amaze myself and others; I acquiesce to more powerful forces; I confront difficult realities; I give up; I persevere. The point of this work is that I embrace the journey and all my humanness in the process. Yes, this is visionary work, but the long-term perspective gives me the courage, boldness, and bravery to sustain my efforts, in spite of intermittent setbacks. It is with this deep sense of responsibility and discipline that I persist, and in the overall impact I think I am acting in transformative ways and making a difference in the lives of those I touch. I wish I knew all this before I met Renard, but at least I learned my lesson. And I continue to learn my professional lessons.

REFERENCES

Bobbitt, F. (1918). *The curriculum.* Boston: Houghton Mifflin.

Bobbitt, F. (1924). *How to make a curriculum.* Boston: Houghton Mifflin.

Bobbitt, F. (2004). Scientific method in curriculum making. (Selections from *The curriculum*). In D. J. Flinders and S. J. Thornton (Eds.), *The curriculum studies reader* (2nd ed.), pp. 9–16. New York: Routledge Falmer. (Original work published 1918)

Brooks, D. (2005). Bush must topple barriers to class mobility. *The Plain Dealer,* Section B, p. 11.

Brooks, J. G., & Brooks, M. G. (1993). *In search of understanding: The case for constructivist classrooms.* Alexandria, VA: Association for Supervision and Curriculum Development.

Brown, T. M. (1988). How fields change: A critique of the "Kuhnian" view. In W. F. Pinar (Ed.), *Contemporary curriculum discourses* (pp. 16–30). Scottsdale, AZ: Gorsuch Scarisbrick.

Burns, J. M. (1978). *Leadership.* New York: Harper & Row.

Cahill, T. (2003). *Sailing the wine-dark sea: Why the Greeks matter.* New York: Nan A. Talese/Doubleday.

Carlson, D. (1997). *Making progress: Education and culture in new times.* New York: Teachers College Press.

Cuban, L. (2003). *Why is it so hard to get good schools?* New York: Teachers College Press.

Dewey, J. (1963). *Experience and education.* New York: Macmillan. (Original work published 1938)

Dewey, J. (1989). *Freedom and culture.* Buffalo, NY: Prometheus. (Original work published 1939)

Dewey, J. (1997). My pedagogic creed. In D. J. Flinders & S. J. Thornton (Eds.), *The curriculum studies reader* (pp. 17–23). New York: Routledge. (Original work published 1897)

Eisner, E. W. (1994). *The educational imagination: On the design and evaluation of school programs* (3rd ed.). New York: Macmillan.

Eisner, E. W. (2004). Artistry and pedagogy in curriculum. *Journal of Curriculum and Pedagogy, 1* (2), 13–14.

Ellsworth, E. (1997). *Teaching positions: Difference, pedagogy, and the power of address.* New York: Teachers College Press.

Gardner, H. (2000). *The disciplined mind: Beyond facts and standardized tests, the K–12 education that every child deserves.* New York: Penguin Books.

Green, J. M. (1999). *Deep democracy: Community, diversity, and transformation.* Lanham, MD: Rowman & Littlefield.

Greene, M. (1988). *The dialectic of freedom.* New York: Teachers College Press.

Hargreaves, A. (1994). *Changing teachers, changing times: Teachers' work and culture in the postmodern age.* New York: Teachers College Press.

Hargreaves, A. (2003). *Teaching in the knowledge society: Education in the age of insecurity.* New York: Teachers College Press.

Henderson, J. G. (1996). *Reflective teaching: The study of your constructivist practices* (2nd ed.). Upper Saddle River, NJ: Merrill/Prentice Hall.

Henderson, J. G. (2005). Standing on Elliot Eisner's shoulders. In B. Uhrmacher & J. Matthews (Eds.), *Intricate palette: Working the ideas of Elliot Eisner* (pp. 53–62). Upper Saddle River, NJ: Merrill/Prentice Hall.

Henderson, J. G., & Kesson, K. R. (2004). *Curriculum wisdom: Educational decisions in democratic societies.* Upper Saddle River, NJ: Merrill/Prentice Hall.

Jardine, D. W. (1997). "To dwell with a boundless heart": On the integrated curriculum and the recovery of the earth. In D. J. Flinders & S. J. Thornton (Eds.), *The curriculum studies reader* (pp. 213–223). New York: Routledge. (Original work published 1990)

Kekes, J. (1995). *Moral wisdom and good lives.* Ithaca, NY: Cornell University Press.

Kreisberg, S. (1992). *Transforming power: Domination, empowerment, and education.* Albany: State University of New York Press.

Kuhn, T. S. (1962). *The structure of scientific revolutions.* Chicago: University of Chicago Press.

Kuhn, T. S. (1977). *The essential tension.* Chicago: University of Chicago Press.

Macdonald, J. B., & Purpel, D. E. (1987). Curriculum and planning: Visions and metaphors. *Journal of Curriculum and Supervision, 2* (2), 178–192.

Martusewicz, R. A., & Reynolds, W. M. (1994). (Eds.). *Inside/out: Contemporary critical perspectives in education.* New York: St. Martin's Press.

Noddings, N. (1984). *Caring: A feminine approach to ethics and moral education.* Berkeley: University of California Press.

Pinar, W. F. (2004). *What is curriculum theory?* Mahwah, NJ: Lawrence Erlbaum Associates.

Plato. (1961). *Protagoras.* In E. Hamilton & H. Cairns, (Ed.), *Plato: The collected dialogues.* Princeton, NJ: Princeton University Press.

Pinar, W. F., Reynolds, W. M., Slattery, P., & Taubman, P. M. (1995). *Understanding curriculum: An introduction to the study of historical and contemporary curriculum discourses.* New York: Lang.

Robinson, D. N. (1990). Wisdom through the ages. In R. J. Sternberg (Ed.), *Wisdom: Its nature, origins, and development* (pp. 13–24). New York: Cambridge University Press.

Schwab, J. J. (1969). The practical: A language for curriculum. *School Review 78* (1), 1–23.

Schwab, J. J. (1978). *Science, curriculum, and liberal education: Selected essays* (I. Westbury & N. J. Wilkof, Eds.). Chicago: University of Chicago Press.

Sidorkin, A. M. (1999). *Beyond discourse: Education, the self, and dialogue.* Albany: State University of New York Press.

Snauwaert, D. T. (1993). *Democracy, education, and governance: A developmental conception.* Albany: State University of New York Press.

Sykes, G. (1996). Reform of and as professional development. *Phi Delta Kappan, 77,* 465–467.

Zemelman, S., Daniels, H., & Hyde, A. (1993). *Best practice: New standards for teaching and learning in America's schools.* Portsmouth, NH: Heinemann.

TWO FUNDAMENTAL CHALLENGES

In this section of the book, we introduce two fundamental challenges central to transformative curriculum leadership. You can neither elevate your curriculum judgment, nor collaborate with others on the elevation of their curriculum judgment, without addressing these challenges. These challenges can be compared to problematic adventures that must be undertaken in a spirit of continuing education. They require a willingness to undertake a journey of self-understanding as a democratic educator. They require a desire to approach curriculum work as a democratic "currere."

Teachers, administrators, and other educators are hired to work within the confines of a particular policy environment; in our current historical context, the standardized management paradigm is the dominant orientation for educational policy decisions. Therefore, most educators must work with a conception of standards that emerges out of this paradigm and that is then handed "down" to them. In general, they have little choice on this matter. However, if these educators are to begin to function as transformative curriculum leaders, they must not passively submit to this historical condition. They must reconceptualize these received standards in more holistic terms. They must create curriculum goals that articulate their students' specific journeys of *S*ubject matter understanding integrated with democratic *S*elf and *S*ocial understanding. That is, they must construct 3S *holistic understanding goals.* As part of this work of rethinking the received standards, they must also consider how they will infer that their students have embarked on their individual journeys of understanding and how they will judge the quality of these journeys. In effect, they must consider their students' *performances of understanding,* and they must delineate *criteria for judgment.* These three topics serve as the fundamental challenge of chapter 2.

The work of reconceptualizing subject standards is assisted by the curriculum study of 3S education. We will characterize this study as *inquiry* to convey the disciplined, open-ended, and action-oriented questioning that we have in mind. Furthermore, the enactment of the reconceptualized subject standards requires ongoing reflective practice. Transformative curriculum leaders must continually deliberate over the consequences and the underlying assumptions of their standard-based actions. Combining the principles of reflective practice and curriculum study, we can say that the work of transformative curriculum leadership requires a *reflective inquiry.* Educators must develop their capacity to ask and pursue a wide range of questions as an integral component of their curriculum problem solving. Cultivating this reflective inquiry is the fundamental challenge addressed in chapter 3.

As you read chapters 2 and 3, keep in mind that these two fundamental challenges are central to the decision-making processes that we will discuss in section II of this book. As depicted by the star image at the beginning of each chapter, the curriculum wisdom problem-solving cycle incorporates the section I challenges and the section II processes. Transformative curriculum leaders elevate their curriculum judgments through the integration of these fundamental challenges and decision-making processes.

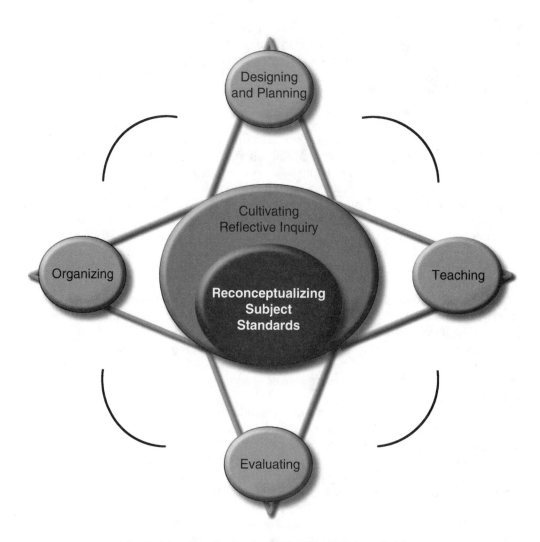

Sustaining the Curriculum Wisdom Problem Solving

CHAPTER 2

RECONCEPTUALIZING SUBJECT STANDARDS

Those who see education as a way to make the world a better place often turn to curriculum improvement as a means to achieve their vision, whether they want to build a brave new world, sustain the world they have, or return to a former golden age.
        (Walker, 2003, p. 213)

Let's think about the manner in which curriculum improvement can be a means for a vision about a society in which citizens are open to continual dialogue about their core beliefs; a society in which they consciously choose *not* to be comfortable, nonquestioning true believers; a society in which citizens accept the give-and-take of differing points of view because they possess a balanced outlook on life with a full appreciation of subtleties, ironies, and ambiguities; a place where critical maturity is cultivated, celebrating democratic, multicultural principles, activities, and institutions (Henderson & Hawthorne, 1995).

Are you thinking that this vision is too lofty, unrealistic, or unattainable? Do you believe that this vision has little or nothing to do with what goes on daily in your classroom? Does this vision even make sense to you, given the stresses in schools today? If this vision creates a demand for insights that reach beyond your meaning-making system, keep in mind that the very act of asking questions about what you may not understand is one important step toward clarity. As stated earlier, insights that alter your meaning-making system may be generated by the very act of asking the questions and making the inquiry.

Before we ask questions, let's find some comfort in the world we know the most completely: *the subject matter in classrooms under the standardized management paradigm* mentioned in chapter 1. We will build upon the benefits of the standardized management paradigm and use it as a toehold for the s-t-r-e-t-c-h to transformative teaching for 3S understanding, and we hope to move a little closer to realizing the vision mentioned above. In much the same way that good teachers know how to find useful information in even the most naive or underdeveloped student response, standardized management can be mined for its advantages to education. Good teachers know that a student's answer contains information that reveals the internal logic of his/her understanding, and they will use that information as a starting point to build the student's comprehension of the material. We can do the same here. Let's use the paradigm as a path.

RECEIVED SUBJECT MATTER STANDARDS

Eisner (2002) reminds us that the formulation of curriculum objectives and "received" standards was an effort to describe what a student is to know and/or be able to do with respect to a standardized body of content at the end of a designated period. In the early

1920s in the United States, Franklin Bobbitt (1924) described more than 700 instructional objectives outlining what students were expected to learn as a way of making curriculum planning rational. By the 1950s and 1960s, these objectives were operationalized by specifying conditions that would make it possible to measure their achievement. "The current push towards standards is, in part, an effort to specify in operational terms the desired outcomes of curriculum and instruction" (Eisner, 2002, p. 160).

Within the standardized management paradigm, the purpose of educational accountability is to improve student learning of important academic content. In virtually every state in the Union, from Ohio with its content-area "Strands, Benchmarks and Grade-level Indicators," to Louisiana, with its "Benchmarks, Standards, and Focus," to Texas, with its "Essential Knowledge Skills," to California, with its "Goals, Strands, and Content Standards," the principles of high-quality assessment and accountability include at least three components: (1) setting appropriate targets based on a balanced curriculum, assessing a wide-range of subjects and attainable standards; (2) administering assessments, which are aligned and symmetrical with shared district/school/teacher accountability for overlapping incentives and consequences using state criteria; and (3) providing all students the opportunity to learn in schools with adequate resources using ongoing and multiple measures.

Most would agree that assessment of student achievement based on curricular goals and objectives is important for sound educational decision-making (Eisner, 2002; Gardner, 1999). As in any other profession, educators need to know baseline information about the "client," which in education is the student. We need to know the student's skill set in order to plan and adjust classroom instruction for the entire class and provide more personalized instruction based on a student's individual need. Congruence between the written curriculum (what we say we teach), the enacted curriculum (what we actually teach), the assessed curriculum (what we measure), and the experienced curriculum (what students actually learn) is also essential for achievement. Ohio's Academic Content Standards, for example, outline overarching goals and themes, indicating what all students should know and be able to do. These standards are then redefined into benchmarks and grade-level indicators. The benchmarks provide checkpoints that help educators monitor student progress toward academic content standards. Grade-Level Indicators provide teachers with detailed information on these benchmarks. All three are intended to provide educators with a *set of common expectations* from which to base math, language arts, science, or social science curricula. This is a standardization theme in almost every state in the country and indeed in every province and country in the world.

WHICH WAY DO WE GO?

I mentioned in my introductory currere narrative in chapter 1 that I began teaching in the early 1970s. During that time, it was not uncommon for teachers to choose from between two and three sets of instructional materials for the same subject. As a first-grade teacher, for example, I had three separate sets of basal readers. When I asked which to use for instruction, I was told to choose. While I loved the autonomy and believe I selected the best materials for my students that year according to my interpretation, I learned that my other grade-level colleagues had selected the other series. As a result, each first-grade teacher was using different materials to teach reading. If a course of study existed, we did not have a copy. In addition, as first-grade teachers, we were not aware of the kindergarten academic expectations, much less what might be expected in the first grade. This lack of congruence was present throughout my elementary school and many other elementary schools in Ohio. The lack of congruence was amplified in high schools across the state because high school curricula did not provide a coherent, aligned, and strong curricular experience for students.

A Step on the Path in the Right Direction

The fact that disciplinary subject area specialists in our country have outlined what a "literate" person should know and be able to do in the areas of math, science, language arts, and social studies is an important step in the right direction. Gardner (1999) believes educators can use subject matter objectives to show students how one thinks and acts in the manner of a scientist, a geometer, an artist, or an historian, for example. These objectives emphasize not only content standards, but also process standards outlining ways of knowing and inquiry for the future. For too long, teachers have not been given the necessary guidance for academic literacy in these subject areas. For too long, the curriculum experiences of each child depended upon which teacher he or she had in any given year. For too long, the curriculum consisted of the table of contents in the textbook adopted for a grade level. The textbook became the syllabus. Without a coherent set of rigorous objectives, educating students was random at best and as variable as the personality, skills, and knowledge of the individual teacher.

As a principal from the mid-1980s through the mid-'90s, I was puzzled by what teachers were teaching, classroom to classroom and grade to grade. Certainly, they taught from the materials in adopted textbooks, but content was listed as topics without the backbone of deeper and broader curricular objectives, in spite of what Franklin Bobbitt may have published in 1924. Walker (2003) cites research that from one-half to over 90 percent of what happens in classrooms involves published instructional materials like textbooks. Even though I discussed lesson plans with teachers and observed in their classrooms, three fourth-grade teachers, for example, would be teaching different topics, at different points, in different ways, for different lengths of time. Textbook companies, in the business to sell as many books as possible, are often little more than a compendium of short topical paragraphs with little depth on the concept. The curriculum has become "an inch deep and a mile wide." While I *fully embrace* that teachers should have input into building the overall platform and vision of the curriculum with the freedom to select and plan activities, schedule and pace the activities throughout the year, motivate and evaluate students (Walker, 2003), and while I delight in the variety of ways that teachers make curricular adjustments based upon what they know about their students, without some framework, timeline, or professional expectation the right hand does not know what the left hand is doing. "There are many great teachers—but the lack of coordination among classes and the absence of accountability to those 'outside the door' is lamentable. The lack of coordination and accountability regularly results in cases where students who move from one school to another discover almost no overlap between the two institutions' offerings" (Gardner, 1999, p. 117).

A Partial Solution

The accountability movement and standardized management have spawned dialogue among teachers and educators that rarely occurred until now. The sanctity of the class-room was always preserved and professional conversations rarely happened because schools were (are) not structurally arranged to ensure professional interactions and dia-logue. In my experience, the culture of isolation, so endemic to teaching, is slowly thawing as teachers are now collaborating in new ways around curriculum mapping (Jacobs, 1997; Wiggins & McTighe, 1998) and Lesson Study (Stigler & Hiebert, 1999), for example.

Many teachers are embracing more of a "systems approach" to their material, developing a greater understanding of grade-level expectations for students in previous and subsequent grades. Great teachers have always been great, irrespective of the accountability movement, and we need to protect the freedom of those teachers who ask students to demonstrate a deep understanding of subject matter and exhibit democrati-cally responsible self and social understandings. However, adequate or marginal teach-ers needing external intervention are at long last being sufficiently guided and coached. For those teachers, what gets measured gets done. External pressure is not everyone's motor, but for some teachers pressure from an outside force is one important way to get them to start taking professional responsibility for their students. I am sure you can name a teacher or two in your building who does little more than pull a paycheck, flying below the principal's radar. Over the years, I have felt intense frustration teaching side by side with weak teachers who allowed their professional identities to be shaped by the external authority of the principal. I have endured working with educators who are unable to imagine fundamentally different arrangements that would make schools a bet-ter place for students. I have an ever-present sense that our students have one chance to be 6 years old, or 10 or 15, and I must honor the time they spend with me. One year with a weak or marginal teacher has a huge impact on not only a student, but also on every teacher who has the student in the future (Sanders & Horn, 1994).

Now that we have "mined" the benefits of the standardized management para-digm, we will go for the s-t-r-e-t-c-h to transformative teaching for 3S understanding, and perhaps draw a little closer to realizing the vision mentioned in the first paragraph of this chapter.

THE PATH HAS A FORK IN THE ROAD . . . AND WE NEED TO TAKE IT!

Eisner (2002) reminds us that:

> reforms in education harbor an implicit conception of human nature; so do govern-ments and so does religion. What needs to be scrutinized is the conception of human nature residing deep within the reform. Reforms in education that are born out of suspicion and distrust for professionals typically lead to policies and practices that monitor, mandate, measure, and manage; policies that seek to prescribe and control that do not distinguish between training and education. (pp. 174–175)

Dennis Ferraro, a former high school teacher and current director of educational research at the Bill and Melinda Gates Foundation, captures what most educators know and believe about teaching when he asserts that our goal is not to produce high test scores, but rather to create "good" people living a "good" life. In this country, that aspiration is normative and based on the democratic values of personal responsibility, respect, hard work, and justice, to name a few.

The *American Evaluation Association* (AEA) supports systems of assessment and accountability that help education. The association, however, opposes the use of paper–pencil tests as the sole or primary criterion for making decisions and believes the limits of this kind of testing carry serious negative consequences for students, educators, and schools. In its position statement on high-stakes testing in pre-K–12 education, the AEA states that the simplistic application of a single test or test batteries to make high-stakes decisions about individuals and groups impedes rather than improves student learning. In the view of the AEA, high-stakes testing violates the principle of "do no harm" because it leads to underserving or misserving all students, especially the most needy and vulnerable. To read this statement in its entirety, go to www.eval.org. You are strongly encouraged to download it, make copies, and share it with your colleagues. Then ask the principal to put this on the agenda for discussion at the next faculty meeting. You should get a spirited reaction.

How shall we interpret the quality of education of those students who score well on a paper–pencil test? Have they employed knowledge effectively in diverse, authentic, and realistically messy contexts? Have they revealed a personalized, thoughtful, and coherent grasp of subjects, demonstrating the ability to think for themselves? Are they wide awake, willing to welcome new insights, refining core beliefs through conversations with diverse others? Have they demonstrated the ability to effectively and sensitively interpret texts and the ability to read between the lines? Have they extended or applied what is known in novel ways to become more cognitively, emotionally, physically, aesthetically, and spiritually attuned to themselves and others?

As curriculum workers, we try to consider the implications of our decisions with respect to such criteria as "good conduct" and "enduring values"; we think about the relationship between educational means and ends and ask ourselves whether the testing (means) justifies the scores (ends). We feel compelled to be simultaneously immediate and visionary, yet the current emphasis on the immediate shackles our best work. So what do we do next? Proceed with caution.

CAUTION: POTENTIAL OBSTACLES ON THE PROBLEM-SOLVING PATH

While there may be undeniable appeal in the notion of clear and unambiguous expectations, Eisner (2002) cautions us to ask whether a nation as diverse as ours is well served by conceptualized subjects that are exempted from that diversity. To be sure, students need to learn their basic skills. Providing opportunities for "gatekeeper skills" ensures that "students are minimally equipped to pursue more schooling, frame and express their thoughts and participate in their local and national communities" (Hess, 2004, p. 4). We are painfully aware that each year, more than a million children leave high school without mastering the basic skills (Hess, 2004) and that an ever-widening achievement gap exists in the United States between White students and students of color. We know that every student should be literate and numerate so that the gates of opportunity may be opened. This is the strength of subject matter understanding and an integral part of students' journey of 3S understanding. As stated in chapter 1, we will not become so preoccupied with self and/or social learning that we lose sight of our subject matter teaching responsibilities. While the dominant standardized management paradigm has appeal because of its simplicity of purpose, straightforward approach to accountability, and direct intervention for substandard teaching, many educators are being crushed under its weight. These mainstream methods may be used as part of our repertoire if professional judgment indicates, but they are not ends in themselves. Democratic subject matter and self and social understanding allow us to be simultaneously immediate and visionary.

UNDERSTANDING STUDENT UNDERSTANDING

Let's ponder, for a moment, what student understanding "looks like." One important step for you as a transformative educator is to be able to describe what a student actually does to demonstrate that he or she understands the disciplinary subject matter beyond what is measured on paper–pencil assessments. A further challenge is for you to be able to anticipate the expressive performances of understanding, which imply that the student's holistic 3S journey of understanding is under way. How do you know students really understand the subject matter material and are able to use that content to integrate "academic knowledge and life history in the interest of self-understanding" (Pinar, 2004, p. 35) and building a better society? What criteria will you use to judge the quality of students' expressions? What do you need from students to confirm their understandings, and how do you plan for it? Wiggins and McTighe (1998) concede that while many teachers talk about wanting to teach for deeper understanding, most soon discover how difficult it is to specify what understanding looks like. Gardner (1999) notes that "understanding is itself a complex process that is not well understood" (p. 179).

Wiggins and McTighe (1998) implore us to ask the following (pp. 23–25): "What would you accept as evidence that students have attained the desired understanding? What knowledge is worth understanding? What kind of achievement target is 'understanding,' and how does it differ from other targets or standards? What are matters of understanding in any achievement target?" They posit that understanding is not a single concept but rather a family of interrelated abilities, which they organize into a framework of "Six Facets of Understanding": explanation, interpretation, application, perspective, empathy, and self-knowledge. In effect, they are providing guidance on six ways that students can demonstrate their understanding of the subject matter. Students can explain their responses or justify their course of action; interpret as many salient facts and points of view as possible; apply knowledge using simulations or real applications with an overarching purpose, audience, and setting in mind; take a perspective, by grasping the importance or unimportance of an idea, and assess the degree of sufficiency of answers, not just their correctness; empathize with others using a robust intellectual imagination; and/or self-assess their past and present work.

Gardner (1991) points out even the best students in the best schools do not "understand" very much curricular content. He states that while these students perform exceptionally well in classroom exercises and end-of-unit tests, when asked to explain relatively simple phenomena, often more than half fail to give the appropriate explanation or end up reporting the same answers as classmates or younger students who never studied the content in the first place. Gardner (1999) also notes that students "understand a concept, skill, theory, or domain of knowledge to the extent that he or she can apply it appropriately in a new situation" (p. 119). Memorizing formulae or definitions and applying them rigidly lulls the student into a false sense of security when consideration of multiple factors or subtleties are required. Studying the American Revolution using British and French texts, for example, or grappling with the notion that some Americans in the 1940s and 1950s considered the Ku Klux Klan a peace-keeping organization, requires students to provide complex explanations with multiperspective insights, which go well beyond memorization. Gardner (1999) believes that education should instill in students an understanding of "major disciplinary ways of thinking . . . to see how one thinks and acts in the manner of a scientist, a geometer, an artist, an historian" (pp. 117–118) and suggests a "pathway for understanding, inspired by a set of essential questions" (p. 216). He calls for a manageable number of distinct curricular pathways, and he favors the "Understanding Pathway," which is inspired by the Socratic pursuit of understanding the most fundamental questions of existence around the topics of "the true, the beautiful, and the good" (p. 226). He believes an education aimed toward understanding is best suited for a world that is constantly changing. "Only those who can demonstrate their continued utility in a knowledge-suffused society can expect to reap the rewards of that society indefinitely" (Gardner, 1999, p. 49).

Now that you have pondered what student understanding "looks like," another important step in your transformative teaching journey is to release the power of standards that actually facilitate that understanding.

TRANSFORMATIVE STANDARDS

There are many ways that standards can be interpreted. Standards are not for standardization, but to be used as criteria for judging. A thorough understanding of these interpretations will help us introduce, explain, and clarify our notion of transformative standards coming out of the wisdom paradigm. Our transformative standards will be compared to and contrasted with the "received" standards coming out of the dominant standardized management paradigm and with the constructivist standards coming out of the constructivist best practice paradigm.

While educators know the importance of improving student learning of academic content, many also know that an emphasis on that alone is not enough. Many educators work diligently to provide students with curriculum experiences that foster a deeper and more enduring understanding of subject matter. Teachers who believe that their singular professional goal is student achievement as measured on episodic, standardized tests will find the "received" standards to be all they need to reach that goal. On the other hand, teachers who embrace a professional goal of fostering a deeper and more enduring student understanding of subject matter will most likely find the received standards to be limited. They will need to think differently about what a student is to know and/or be able to do. Most likely these teachers are aligned with the constructivist best practice paradigm and will treat their students as active meaning makers. As such these teachers will need to rework the received standards to "manage the large amounts of content, especially discrete factual knowledge and basics skills by clustering the specifics under two broader conceptual umbrellas containing big ideas and core tasks" (Wiggins & McTighe, 2005, p. 63). By taking this step, teachers aligned with this paradigm will be able to provide experiences for students that allow them to demonstrate a deep and personal understanding of subject matter.

Teachers who embrace the wisdom paradigm and the professional goal to inspire the sustained practice of curriculum judgments that are attuned to student performances of subject matter understanding that are embedded in democratic self and social understanding will need to think *very* differently about what a student is to know and/or be able to do. These teachers most likely will find the received standards to be limit*ed* and the constructivist best practices reworking of the standards too limit*ing*. Teachers embracing the wisdom paradigm will reconceptualize the standards to integrate subject matter learning into democratic self and social learning. Content knowledge is important; personally meaningful content knowledge is more important; and content knowledge that is embedded in democratic self and social understanding is enduring and wise. By reconceptualizing the standards, teachers will be making practical and thoughtful judgments directed toward subtle matters of goodness. By reconceptualizing the standards, teachers will embrace more qualitative dimensions of educational judgments such as values, aesthetics, justice, and meaning. Going beyond "what works," teachers *reframe* the problem from "how do we get kids to pass tests" to "how do we help teachers elevate their curriculum judgments to include moral decisions that touch the core of what it means to be human, to live in community with others, to find meaning and purpose, and to create a more just and peaceful world" (Henderson & Kesson, 2004, p. 45).

Paradigmatic Tensions: Framing Our Work

In chapter 1 you learned that we are using the paradigm concept to convey the fundamental differences in professional orientation. Based upon what you have read in this book, have you situated yourself within one (or more) of these paradigms? Are you more aligned with Robert in vignette 1; or Diane in vignette 2; or Liz and Harry in vignette 3? By virtue of this orientation, whether you realize it or not, each day you are framing and justifying the curricular and student problems you encounter, and then stating how these problems should be studied and resolved.

As you engage in designing and planning each day, you are attempting to make the *best* judgments about: (1) your educational goals for each lesson/unit; (2) the student performances, which will reveal whether the student has grasped or understands the educational goals for the lesson/unit; and (3) the criteria for judging the quality of the student performance of knowledge or understanding of the educational goals for each lesson/unit. The professional orientation within which you operate has huge implications for how you frame, justify, study, and resolve your work problems. Again, the best decision is determined by your professional orientation: standardized management paradigm; constructivist best practice paradigm; or the wisdom paradigm. Let's look at what *best* looks like in each of these three paradigms and how the orientation affects the role of teacher judgment.

Dominant Standardized Management Orientation

Educators who are ideologically aligned with the standardized management paradigm will embrace the "received" standards. In this instance, the teacher's *best educational goal* is student achievement of standardized factual knowledge and skills. Within this paradigm, there is an emphasis on a set of predetermined skill-based and content-based subject learning. The *best student performance* will be based on an episodic standardized test measuring knowledge and skills that are testable with a large population. These performance standards are conceived in a general, conceptual way so they can be tested. The *best criteria for judging* that performance will be achievement verified and based on standardized criteria for test scores to rank, classify, promote, place, or fail students. "Learning cooperative and compliant behaviors in the context of a competitive educational meritocracy" (Henderson & Hawthorne, 2000, p. 5) is prevalent. Teacher judgment is irrelevant and even repressed because decisions about students are reduced to a metric, based on counting numbers. Problem solving is limited because the teacher is working from a script, and quality is measured with test scores. Counting is a substitute for judgment, and teachers "accept superficial evidence as proof of learning" (Gardner, 1999, p. 108).

Constructivist Best Practice Orientation

Under the constructivist best practice paradigm, there is a fundamental shift in orientation from the dominant standardized management paradigm. In this instance, the best educational goal is student demonstration of personally meaningful subject matter. Here, the teacher uses the received standards and translates or "constructs" them into a "set of design standards for achieving quality control in curriculum and assessment designs" (Wiggins & McTighe, 2005, p. 5). Student subject matter *knowledge* is distinguished from student subject matter *understanding* and teacher voice or judgment emerges. Wiggins and McTighe (2005) refer to understanding as the result of facts acquiring meaning for the learner. Under this paradigm, the best student performances are demonstrations of a more enduring understanding of the meaning of the facts and, therefore, the ability to apply, analyze, synthesize, and evaluate the information. The best student performances are about "transfer; in other words, to be truly *able*, requires the ability to transfer what we have learned to new and sometimes confusing settings. The ability to transfer our knowledge and skill effectively involves the capacity to take what we know and use it creatively, flexibly, fluently, and in different problems or settings, on our own" (Wiggins & McTighe, 2005, p. 40, emphasis added). This ability is essential because teachers can help students learn only a limited number of ideas, facts, and skills in a given field of study. Developing the students' ability to transfer their limited learning to other settings in a meaningful way is the essence of the constructivist, best practice orientation.

The *best criteria for judging* the quality of student performances under the constructive best practices is based on a rubric using facets of understanding such as explanation, interpretation, application, perspective, empathy, and self-knowledge (Wiggins & McTighe, 1998, 2005) in which students actively make sense of subject matter's meaning by making personal connections between past experiences and the content they are studying. Less prescriptive than the dominant standardized management paradigm, the constructivist best practice orientation is guided not by standardized test measures, but by more authentic student performances of understanding. Clear and appropriate criteria specify the degree of understanding for making judgments about the depth of the student's subject matter understanding, with regular and ongoing feedback. Teacher judgment is essential. These criteria are consistent, fair, and published. The rubric "describes degrees of quality, proficiency or understanding along a continuum" (Wiggins & McTighe, 2005, p. 173).

Curriculum Wisdom Orientation

Under the curriculum wisdom paradigm, the *best educational goal* is student demonstration of subject matter understanding that is integrated in personally meaningful democratic self and social understanding. The teacher and the student are engaged in a process of reconceptualizing the received standards into *understanding goals*. The teacher "infuse[s] critical and creative thinking into subject matter instruction, in which students analyze, critique, defend, question, and explore alternative points of view (Henderson & Hawthorne, 2000, p. 6). The teacher constantly clarifies what is to be done with and for students in the classroom. The teacher is "sensitive to the flow of events and to the student's engagement in those events in order to make adjustments and, indeed to invent activities that are appropriate for the students (Eisner, 2002, p. 152). The received standards are reconceptualized as "aids, as heuristics for debate and planning. They are not [should not be] regarded as contracts or prescriptions that override local judgments" (Eisner, 2002, p. 173). These reconceptualized standards would exist among many possible interpretations. The role of the teacher is more "emergent rather than prescriptive [and] the stakes for pedagogical innovation are higher and the demands greater" (Eisner, 2002, p. 152).

The *best student performance* under the curriculum wisdom paradigm is the demonstration of subject matter understanding through expressive and idiosyncratic performances that are integrated with self and social understandings. The *best criteria for judging* the quality of the performances are based on a plurality of understandings. Evaluation focuses not only on what was intended, but on the unintended outcomes as well (Eisner, 2002). It is here that we have the most powerful insights into what the student has actually learned. "Students learn both more and less than they are taught" (Eisner, 2002, p. 70). They need to be in classrooms, in which they are free to choose and free to act in personally and socially responsible ways, and free from psychological constraints so they can realize their "best selves" (Noddings, 1984). Both process and products are evaluated based on criteria, which the student gradually internalizes, becoming personally responsible for his or her own learning.

Table 2.1 may help you gain a deeper understanding of reconceptualizing received standards into constructivist standards, and constructivist standards into holistic, transformative standards.

Table 2.1 RECONCEPTUALIZING STANDARDS			
Standards as	**Received Standards**	**Constructivist Standards**	**Transformative Standards**
Educational goals	Student achievement of standardized factual knowledge and skills	Student demonstration of personally meaningful subject matter understanding	Student demonstration of subject matter understanding that is holistically integrated in personally meaningful democratic self and social understanding
Student performances	Standardized, episodic test performances— knowledge and skills that are testable with a large population	Students provide evidence of enduring subject matter understanding by demonstrating that they can transfer personally meaningful knowledge and skills to new situations, i.e., portfiolio	Expressive performances of holistic and enduring subject matter understanding integrated with self and social understanding
Criteria for judgment	Standardized test criteria based on a predetermined metric based on counting	Facets of understanding criteria for performance	Judgment criteria are based on a plurality of understandings
		Regular feedback is available for midcourse adjustments based on a published rubric	Idiosyncratic demonstrations of subject matter, self and social understanding
			Both process and products are assessed and evaluated based on criteria in a rubric the student gradually internalizes

Paradigm Lines Are Blurred

Keep in mind that an important premise of this book is to *reframe* the problem that includes "How do we get kids to pass tests?" and "How do we help teachers elevate their curriculum judgments?" Lest we convey a rigid demarcation between the three orientations outlined in this text, we note an interesting dynamic. While the paradigm is a powerful tool for framing the problem, teachers operating out of the wisdom paradigm have available all of the tools used in the standard management and constructivist best practices paradigms. In fact, the teacher may even use one or more of these tools case by case. Teachers operating out of the wisdom paradigm have the problem-solving agility to make the best pragmatic judgment in a particular situation, for a particular amount of time, for a particular group of students.

This may not hold true for teachers operating out of the standardized management paradigm. Depending upon the strength of the ideological grip, the teacher operating out of the standardized management paradigm may not have access to the problem-solving tools of teachers operating out of the constructivist best practices paradigm and the wisdom paradigm; problem solving cultivated out of the constructivist best practices paradigm and wisdom paradigm may not make sense or hold any relevance for the teacher (Gornik, 2002). Teachers operating out of the standardized management paradigm may see only the value in received standards, standardized tests, and one-size-fits-all curriculum.

Paradoxically, the same judgment made from a curriculum wisdom frame of reference compared to a standardized management frame of reference will alter the quality of the student's experience completely. For example, you may decide that students need to quickly recall the major battles of the Civil War. What you have students *do* with that information and how you judge the depth of their understanding is where the quality of the experience is altered. Teachers framing the curriculum experience out of the standardized management paradigm may use a timed, paper–pencil, fill-in-the-blank test to measure the students' knowledge of the content. This metric will be recorded in a gradebook or on a report card, and then the teacher will move on to the next subject objective.

Teachers *re*framing the experience through a curriculum wisdom orientation may use a timed, paper–pencil, fill-in-the-blank test to measure the students' knowledge of the content and then provide opportunities for students to express their deep understanding with a wide, productive range of educationally valuable outcomes that uses these discrete facts in authentic ways. This wide range of outcomes could include, for example, writing and performing a newscast about the Civil War in which the student might demonstrate his or her journey of understanding by a growing ability to (1) honor differences in others, (2) resist the temptation to use logic based on habit or custom, and (3) recognize role of power in human interactions. In order for the student to express this outcome, knowledge of the major battles of the Civil War would be evident in the performance, and the quality of the performance would be judged based on criteria that included an understanding of the subject matter, as well as a more idiosyncratic and growing understanding of the democratic self and society.

Reconceptualing the subject matter is an important step to realizing the vision at the beginning of this chapter. Unless we challenge and reconceptualize the received standards, the teachers' curriculum judgments will not matter because the received standards collapse the experience into a straightforward logic. There is no broader purpose. The subtleties of cultivating a disciplined mind, acquiring a love of learning, the flexibility to meet the individual needs of students or demonstrating a deeper understanding of the subject matter are irrelevant. Before you try your hand at reconceptualizing received standards into holistic understanding goals, we need to gain a deep sense of the meaning of democratic self understanding and democratic social understanding.

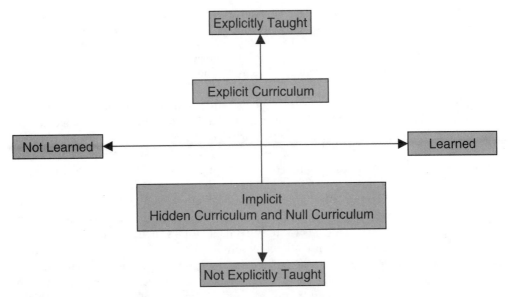

Figure 2.1 **Implicit and Explicit Aspects of the Curriculum**

The Hidden and Null Curricula

What teachers choose to leave out of the curriculum is no less important than what they choose to include. Those choices are based on a number of factors, including personal beliefs, personal and professional background, knowledge of subject matter, time, and available materials. Marsh and Willis (2003) expose the hidden curriculum as "parts of the curriculum that are unplanned or even unplannable [that] seem to exert a more subtle but far greater influence over what students learn than the curriculum itself" (p. 11).

As authors of this text, we suggest Figure 2.1 as a way to conceptualize the implicit and explicit aspects of curriculum. The upper half represents the aspect of the explicit curriculum. This aspect contains those things that we formally teach and that are either learned or not learned by the student. This aspect is often what is codified in a country's or province's standards. What is formally taught is often found in plan books, courses of study, and textbooks.

The lower half represents the aspect of curriculum that is not explicitly stated, but potentially learned by students nonetheless. This hidden curriculum is extremely powerful and contains a large body of knowledge learned by students, such as social and academic groupings and how to follow the rules in the game of schooling. We need to reflectively examine the appropriateness and significance of what students are learning in the hidden curriculum. Here, the hidden curriculum often forms student values, attitudes, and assumptions about race, class, gender, ethnicity, and disability.

The implicit curriculum also includes what is *not* taught. Eisner (1994) characterizes the conscious or unconscious avoidance of certain instructional topics as the null curriculum, which he describes:

It is my thesis that what schools do not teach may be as important as what they do teach. Ignorance is not simply a neutral void; it has important effects on the kinds of options one is able to consider, the alternatives that one can examine, and the perspectives from which one can view a situation or problems. The absence of a set of considerations or perspectives or the inability to use certain processes for appraising a context biases the evidence one is able to take into account. A parochial perspective or simplistic analysis is the inevitable progeny of ignorance. (p. 158)

The lower half also represents the aspects of the null curriculum. The null curriculum is also linked to the hidden curriculum and contains elements of knowledge that are conspicuous by their absence. They may be learned or not and often contain beliefs about such social dynamics as premarital sex, homosexuality, and lifestyle preference. The null curriculum also may embody implicit political, spiritual and psychological ideologies. Students may learn or not learn what is in both the hidden and null curricula.

If we embrace the power of the hidden and null curricula, how do we harness their influence? How do we unearth the implicit, subtle, yet powerful forces therein? Greene (1988) implores us to invite students to study explicitly topics such as oppression, exploitation, social injustices, sexism, authentic communities, and interdependence with others. Studying these topics may bring to the surface one interpretation of democratic morality as the affirmation of a generous and generative life. A generative educational experience allows the continuous "development and fulfillment of self" (Dewey, 1934/1958, p. 302), which is inhibited by oppression, exploitation, and so on. Garrison (1997) writes, "Those who are in love with life desire to grow. Those who love to grow, love and care for others, and let others care for them" (p. 52). "In educational work this love is enacted in teaching–learning relationships. Teachers realize the beauty of their professional selves by facilitating the unique beauty of their students' selves" (Henderson & Kesson, 2004, pp. 10–11).

Students' Democratic Freedom

Maxine Greene (1988), in her philosophical essay *The Dialectic of Freedom*, notes that when oppression or exploitation or segregation or neglect is seen as "natural" or "given," there is little stirring in the name of freedom. "A teacher in search of his/her own freedom may be the only kind of teacher who can arouse young persons to go in search of their own" (p. 14). She cautions that "ordinary life provides distractions and comforts for those who might be expected to go in search" (p. 15). Have you succumbed to the distractions and comforts of life? Are you prepared to be aware of and confront the implicit injustices potentially lurking in the hidden and null curricula? I struggle with this every day.

Freedom from . . . Freedom to . . .

Greene's (1988) focal interest is in human freedom and the capacity to surpass the given and to look at things as if they could otherwise be. She draws the distinction between the struggles to be "free from" limitations, oppression, alienation, and coercion, and the "freedom to" come together as authentic individuals around projects they can mutually pursue. "Negative freedom [freedom from] is the right not to be interfered with or coerced or compelled to do what they did not choose to do" (p. 16). Greene asserts, "because of the general preoccupation with negative freedom in American social history, [stories] are not viewed as accounts of people gaining—simply through their coming together—the power to act and the power to choose" (p. 76). We are asked to educate students for positive freedom; the freedom to "articulate connections between the individual search for freedom and appearing before others in an open place, a public and political sphere" (p. 116).

Freedom from . . . Freedom to . . . Self and Social Understanding

In the spirit of Greene's (1988) challenge to educate for positive freedom, we need to develop standards that include democratic self and social understanding. This work is centered on the freedom necessary for the making and remaking of a public space for dialogue and possibility:

- As individuals and as members of groups, we are "free from" certain impositions in a society with democratic ideals (negative freedom).

- As individuals and members of groups, we are "free to" be and do, in a society with democratic ideals (positive freedom).

You are encouraged to reflect alone and with others on the many ways in which you may be educating for negative freedom or positive freedom, or perhaps you are not educating for freedom at all. You and your colleagues may find yourselves at the creative edge of your consciousness, because reflecting in this manner may evoke the "complicated conversation" we referred to earlier. We hope you will recognize the debate and the sensitive nature of this type of self and social understanding. You may also leave this reflection more convinced of the power of teaching for negative and positive freedoms and the reasons why we as educators often elect to leave it in the background. The story below illustrates the power of the hidden and null curricula and demonstrates why it should be foregrounded.

In the late 1990s, one of our high school students committed suicide. The note left was a gut-wrenching account of the ridicule suffered at the hands of classmates, here and in previous districts, that did not understand her. This student was a transgendered person. Born with all the physical characteristics of the female gender, the forces within compelled her to seek a male identity. She so carefully masked her female identity with hairstyles and clothing that many teachers, upon the news of her death, were not aware she was biologically female. Exhausted by the fight to fit in, belong, and be understood, ending her broken life made more sense than living a half-life.

We were all devastated. I felt overcome with sadness and frustration trying to make sense of the senseless. As a school district, how could we have helped prevent this? Did the components of the hidden and null curricula contribute to her decision to end her life? What if we had had curriculum experiences that actually served as a guide for a student's safe and healthy journey of subject matter, self, and social understanding? What if we had designed opportunities for students to use their subject matter knowledge to more fully understand themselves and others? What if we had had learning experiences that provided opportunities for students to dialogue with diverse others to construct knowledge? What if we had reinforced a disposition in students to honor diversity and then included expressions of such as part of their assessments in school? What if we had been set up to use the curriculum as a vehicle to guide her journey and the journey of those who ridiculed her? Would we come together as a group of concerned educators and parents and decide to reject a school culture of intolerance to differences? Could we make this a teachable moment, at her parents' request, to "tune in" and pay attention to the subtleties of student life in our schools? A vision of this 3S journey of understanding is that the students and indeed all stakeholders, would recognize that in a pluralistic society, no one cultural element is the norm and that every person must be considered important and be treated with respect.

Not too long after this horrible loss, parents of another student who had graduated from our high school several years earlier attended a board of education meeting. Their purpose was to share their daughter's high school story as a transgendered person. They displayed photos of their daughter in high school and photos of her now, as a man, married and living a happy and productive life. They felt great pain over the suicide of the young student and related a similar despair experienced by their daughter at the hands of intolerant classmates. While their daughter was fortunate enough to have parents who saw the signs and helped her work through the transition, she nonetheless suffered unnecessary pain. Could we, they implored, "wake up" and pay attention to the subtext in our high school, or, as Greene (1988) calls it, "reawaken the consciousness of possibility" (p. 23)?

I wish I could report that everyone in attendance that night embraced the challenge, but they did not. Some were threatened and angry that these parents would hold the schools in any way culpable for this. Some made private jokes, snickering at the "bizarre" life this person was leading. Some felt powerless to do anything differently, expressing fatalism that the scope of the problem was just too big to address. Some expressed complete apathy, fully accepting that life is tough and that's "just the way it is." One person confided great concern, but did not want the others to know her feelings because she feared their ridicule. The political and personal stakes were just too high.

Greene (1988) cautions that when people are "cynical about reform, despairing of bringing about change in the world, they are no longer able to imagine alternative possibilities" (p. 20). Unfortunately, that is where we left it. While I will never know the exact impact of that student's suicide on so many in our schools, I do know that we as a district did not pick up the challenge. Once the buzz in the community died down, we acceded to the "givens" and life went on.

I am not proud to be reporting this. I ache that I am somehow complicit in the apathy. It is here that this work becomes very difficult, almost overwhelming. How much easier it would be to skim the surface in the safety of the technical, standardized management paradigm. I assuage my "Catholic guilt" by focusing on issues that seem more manageable. After all, I tell myself, you eat an elephant one bite at a time. Here I must be Teflon, not Velcro, in order to cope and hope for tomorrow. While I did not confront this intolerance head-on, it just may be that fools rush in where angels fear to tread. For now, I pledge to take action, to look for more subtle opportunities to attack the intolerance. To that end, we have provided significant opportunities for teachers to engage in professional development around relationship building . . . with students, parents, and colleagues. The district is in the midst of a district diversity and strategic plan, and respect for differences is a major component of the plan. I will stay awake and consciously move forward ever hopeful that what I do will make a difference, if nothing else than through my example. But I still wonder, what if . . . ?

WHERE THE RUBBER MEETS THE ROAD

Now that you have worked to refine your understanding of what it means to educate students in this way, try your hand at constructing a reconceptualized set of standards that *holistically* balance the disciplinary subject matter standards with democratic self and social understanding. These holistic standards form one essential component of 3S visionary designing and planning, which you will learn more about in chapter 4. Below, you will find an overview or a kind of "starter kit" for this challenging curriculum work. You will note three areas to consider when reconceptualizing received standards.

Reconceptualizing Received Standards

1. Creating holistic standards of understanding
   a. Six facets of understanding (Wiggins & McTighe, 1998)
   b. Democratic self and social understanding
      - Hidden and null curricula
      - Freedom from . . . Freedom to . . .

2. Articulating illustrative expressive performances of understanding
   a. Infer that the holistic journeys of understanding are under way through expressive performances (Gardner and Eisner)
   b. Deliberative practice

3. Articulating judgment criteria
   a. Treat standards as criteria for judgment (Eisner and Dewey)
   b. Deliberative practice

The recursive nature of these considerations is illustrated in Figure 2.2. Read several of the received standards and try your skill at reworking them in a way that will encourage students to become proactive members of the mathematics community or the science community and also encourage them to advance humanity's age-old struggle with liberation (Henderson & Hawthorne, 1995). This may necessitate the blending of several benchmarks or grade-level indicators (depending on your state, province, or country) that will form the foundation of essential understandings related to self-worth, identity, a disciplined mind, authenticity, and self-actualization during the learning process. What big ideas are presented in the standards (Wiggins & McTighe, 1998)? How might they be clustered for their similarities or paradoxes? What are some of the essential understandings? What are the ways the standard(s) could be contextualized and embedded in a real-life situation? How might the standards be used to engage students in exploring and deepening their understanding of important ideas? Does the standard address subject matter learning in a context of democratic self and social learning?

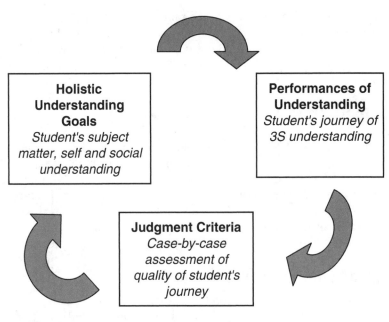

Figure 2.2 Reconceptualizing Received Standards

If not, how might you reconceptualize the language in the standard to reflect these dimensions? What might be the unacknowledged attitudes, assumptions, and beliefs buried in the standard? What embedded codes of conduct or conventions for social relationships exert a subtler, but far greater, influence over what students learn than the official standard itself (Marsh & Willis, 2003)? Is there a lack of 3S balance because of unconsciousness about the nature of the self and social learning embedded in the subject matter (Henderson & Kesson, 2004)? What are students learning about social relations from the standards? What are they learning about the value of competition and the relevance of cooperation and collaboration? What are the opportunities for complementary standards from other subject area disciplines? Currently, the received standards have become so "particularized" (Eisner, 2002) and numerous that if a teacher were to teach each objective as a discrete lesson, the designated instructional period would exceed a typical kindergarten through 12th grade timeframe and require an additional 10 years to complete. Reeves (2002) notes that most states have adopted a cumulative approach to standards and over the years have added layers of content and specificity. Teachers then, are faced with the problem of figuring out how to do more in the same amount of time and with the same amount of resources. His solution is for educators to develop what he calls "power standards." Power standards are created by applying some criteria for prioritization and discernment that give teachers and students the opportunity to focus on standards that are "most important" for academic success. In my district, we have tried to manage the morass of standards by developing interdisciplinary 3S understanding units that combine several grade-level indicators using pacing charts and curriculum maps.

Our experience has been that when teachers reconceptualize the subject matter in this holistic way, they experience the curriculum as an "extraordinarily complicated conversation" (Pinar et al., 1995). Students and teachers alike make sense of subject matter in diverse ways, and each person's democratic self and social understanding is equally diversified and idiosyncratic. Throughout the conversation, most teachers come to realize that curriculum work done wisely is a journey of discovery, intensely dramatic and grounded in soul-searching, private and public autobiographical issues, their own and their students'. Most importantly, teachers come to comprehend the power of reflective inquiry as a means to elevate their curriculum judgments and use the content standards to move students beyond the immediate and temporary to the long-term and enduring American dream of self-realization and liberation. Remember: The ability to secure meaning in the course of our experience is a basic human need (Eisner, 1994).

By reconceptualizing the standards to include a holistic balance between subject matter understanding, self understanding, and social understanding, we are advancing a rigorous professional goal. We heed Eisner's (2002) warning about tightly conceptualized subjects in such a diverse nation. By reconceptualizing the standards to include performances of 3S understanding with criteria for judging the quality of the students' journey, we believe that students will be more fully equipped to live in and contribute to our democratic society. Under the received standards, students learn to read; within the holistic standards, students learn to read *and* read to learn about the democratic self and society through the subject matter. Under the received standards, students learn to write; within the holistic standards, students learn to write *and* write to learn about the democratic self and society through the subject matter. Under the received standards, students learn to compute; within holistic standards, students learn to compute *and* compute to learn about the democratic self and society through the subject matter. Eisner (2005) calls this "pedagogical improvisation in the service of meaningful teaching and learning." The attempt to transform subject matter into instances of democratic living (Henderson & Kesson, 2004) is the heart of curriculum wisdom.

A DISCIPLINED JOURNEY FOR ALL OF US

We need to think deeply about what we do with and for our students. "External forms of democracy are more easily imitated than its underlying values" (Gardner, 1999, p. 46). Our prelesson, in-lesson, and postlesson reflections must include a disciplined inquiry into and curiosity about the relationship between the educational experiences we provide for our students and human freedom (Henderson & Kesson, 2004). At the risk of overdoing the metaphor, inquiry paves the problem-solving path for us to be transformative teachers who treat their students as if they have minds of their own, encouraging them to use their mental capacities to build more sophisticated democratic understandings.

What is at issue is your capacity to use your own inquiry, experience, intuition, context, imagination, and desire to guide your curriculum problem solving and decision making. In the next currere narrative, I will share my story of waking up from the Land of Nod and of the powerful forces operating to shape my consciousness and my identity. I ask you to consider your story to examine the parts of your life, which may be mechanical, bound by convention, and shaped by habit or custom. In order for you to treat your students as if they have minds of their own, encouraging them to use their mental capacities to build more sophisticated understandings, you must believe that *you* have a mind of your own with the mental capacities and intellectual maturity to question social conditioning. Remember: The values, beliefs, and assumptions that guide your actions often bypass conscious intelligence. The exercise of conscious, disciplined, reflective inquiry will help you cultivate curriculum wisdom as you facilitate students' active ability to create meaning out of the subject matter. Transformative teachers are on their own personal and professional inquiry journey and are good company along the way for their students on a very similar path.

Currere Narrative

For the better part of my early life, asking questions about what seemed to be a fixed world was not a part of my consciousness. Just like a fish does not know it lives in water, I was not aware of the powerful forces operating to shape my consciousness and my identity or my role in it. The notion that the environment is designed and invented by my presence was not yet on my radar screen. While the roots of the past continue to occupy space deep within my being, I have spent the last 30 years working to gain a greater consciousness of my "self," my decisions, and the world around me. The concept that "organisms do not experience environments; they create them" (Lewontin, 1991, p. 35) would have been blasphemy in the 1950s. Small wonder that this potentially heretical idea, which makes central my role in codetermining my world, would become the hopeful foundation upon which my consciousness, creativity, and very being would find liberation and transformation.

I am one of nine children, born into a Slovenian and very Catholic family. Bound by the Catholic belief that artificial contraception defiled procreation, which the faithful believed was the only reason for sex, my parents practiced rhythm or what is now termed "natural family planning." They had one son, then five daughters, and then three more sons. Is it any wonder that Catholics are known for rhythm and bingo, and when one doesn't work . . . BINGO! Born in 1951, I was the sixth born and the youngest in a string of five daughters. My father and mother were first-generation Slovenians whose parents immigrated to the United States in the early 1900s. My grandfather and grandmother, filled with gratitude as Catholic, Slovenian American citizens, yearned to share their good fortune with others still in Yugoslavia. They became rather well known in the local area because of their work, planning, and creativity with other immigrants seeking citizenship in the United States.

My parents were also good people. They did their best, in my opinion, under the circumstances within their historical context. In spite of a fair amount of noise and more than a little confusion, there was love in our home. My parents fostered a strong Catholic ethic. Our lives were punctuated with traditional rituals such as 40-hour devotions, novenas, and weekly confessions. We fasted before Communion at Mass on Sundays, never ate meat on Fridays, and some of us more successfully than others endured no television and no desserts during the long, 40-day Lenten season. Images of my sisters and I kneeling on birdseed, reading the lives of the saints, and reciting the rosary to share in the suffering from noon to 3:00 p.m. on Good Friday afternoon tickle my memory. Education, music, and sports dominated our waking hours. I have fond memories of weekend camping trips, with endless hikes in breathtaking beauty, river swimming, and learning a deep respect for nature. We were exposed to every sport imaginable; a disciplined body was second only to a disciplined mind. Music theory, piano, and voice were provided and strongly encouraged. Educational achievement was expected, as well as attendance at college. "When you go to college" permeated our discussions; "if" was never in the room. This dynamic was particularly significant during the 1950s and 1960s. With five girls, the general culture promoted marriage and babies as the ultimate life choice for females, but this would not be our story. "Use your brain," "make a difference," and "distinguish yourself" were in the air. My father was especially known for the mantra "How bad do you want it?" These words were propelled at us as we struggled with anything from stretching for an impossible tennis shot to straining to sing a note in the octave above upper C to studying for a test.

There was also another dominant ethos in our home. Docile compliance to the rules of adults was expected, coupled with the discipline of always putting others first. The essence of a joyful life we were taught, was available if we put Jesus first, then Others, and then, and only then, You. JOY . . . *Jesus, Others, You*. The hallmark of our existence was captured in these phrases: "Just say okay" (don't argue with me); "Bend over backwards" (to get along with your brothers and sisters); "Never allow yourself the pleasure of showing your displeasure" (your individual needs were always secondary to the collective good of the group). Influenced by a greater desire to avoid pain than to experience joy, I operated under the assumption that what I needed did not matter as much as the needs of others. With that many people growing up under one roof, disciplined conformity was the rule of the day.

I was very socialized to "cope" with the "reality" of any situation. When I found myself in situations at home or at school that were so untenable, my first response was to talk myself out of the pain. The extent of my problem-solving techniques was bound up in discovering and doing what the other person wanted. . . . "Voila! The solution." I was spared the conflict, the turmoil, the thinking, the tangled, messy consequences, and the intimacy necessary for finding common ground. No reflective inquiry here. I found a comforting sense of balance by being in alignment with the values created by others in my environment. That was my modus operandi. The "best" way for me to live in my house as a child growing up was to go along to get along. Compliance kept me out of the controversy when it erupted, and erupt it did if for no other reason than 11 people, nine kids born between 1943 and 1959, were all living in a four-bedroom house. My birth order offered the benefit of observing in wallflower safety, the consequences my older siblings experienced. When my sister arrived home late from a date, or another "talked back" in search of her voice to make a point, I thought to myself, "Whoa, I guess I won't try *that!*"

I watched the dramas unfold and was shaped. My own adolescent efforts to assert my independence, once quashed, forced a humble submission. The path of least resistance was so much easier. I hated conflict and, as an off-the-chart extrovert, feared the isolation of living in any way outside the safety of the tribe. As a result, the subtleties of my own capacity to question were systematically pushed out of my consciousness and subjugated to keep everyone else happy.

While I believe my parents did their best and I remain grateful for all they sacrificed and afforded, over time I knew I needed to wake up from my sleepwalk. The Land of Nod was not the best place to stay. I had to wake up to the fact that life behaves in messy ways. All systems, family systems and even your own classroom system, are continuously exploring, bent on discovering what works as each member asserts and seeks meaning. Structures emerge, change, and disappear, all the while attracted to order, organizing into new relationships so that more life can flourish with greater stability (Wheatley & Kellner-Rogers, 1996). Small wonder that the same teacher can teach the same subject matter in the same school in a completely different environment period to period. Likewise, the same parents can raise children in the same house with a multiplicity of reactions. Relationships in homes and classrooms are central because we live in a world shaped by our interactions with it. Yet the systemwide stability depends on the ability of its members to change and paradoxically will maintain itself only if change is occurring somewhere in it at all times.

When my parents divorced after 31 years of marriage, I did not have the complexity of mind to understand these concepts. Taking my lessons from chaos theory and quantum physics, I now realize that as conditions change, individuals experiment with new possibilities. In my family (and probably most families), change was the only constant. An infant was introduced into our family mix, on average, every 24 months! With each passing day, each one of us was changing from preschooler to school age to young adult; from puberty to menstruation to acne. The combinations also included my mom's cycles from pregnancy, to birth to lactation and eventual menopause to my dad's aging and testapause. Toss in the historical context of the ending of World War II, the baby boom, *Ozzie and Harriet, Father Knows Best*, and the losses suffered as a result of Kennedy's and King's assassinations, the civil rights movement, and the war in Vietnam and one realizes the incredible influences on our behaviors and our lives. I know my older siblings experienced a very different mom and dad than I did; my three younger brothers also knew two very different parents than the rest of us. Our family system was in the constant state of flux, and we acted as if it were in a constant state. I realize now that as conditions change, if even one in the system fails to respond, the entire system suffers. Those incapable of change may disappear and the downfall will affect the lives of everyone in the web; the system becomes moribund because without interior change it "sinks into the death grip of equilibrium" (Wheatley, 1966, p. 33) no longer able to participate in co-evolution. Life requires that we change because unless we do, we cannot explore other possibilities. "This broad paradox of stability and freedom is the stage on which co-evolution dances" (Wheatley, 1996, p. 33).

I cannot begin to name the exact interplay of all the forces that acted upon my parents' decision to divorce in 1973, but life expands and thrives by linking together. We reconstituted ourselves as a "family" because organization wants to happen, but this took a new form; the disorder was a source for a new order, even though it happened in a disorderly way. And once again, we as organisms did not experience our environment; we created it, and new relationships created new capacities. My beliefs have changed over the years, and I now realize that every change we make in ourselves changes many others. As adults, my siblings and I are each free to choose our paths, no longer held captive by our past habits or unexamined thoughts to codetermine once again, the current environment. The operative word is "choose."

Given my experiences, I do believe that my critical thinking skills were seriously inhibited and underdeveloped. Incubating deep within, however, was my proverbial "line in the sand," my push-back point, where I finally said, "Enough." Nascent consciousness notwithstanding, this journey has been slow and fraught with uncertainties. Rubbing the sleep from my eyes, my yearnings for growth and expression were protractedly pointing me to a new kind of evolving equilibrium, even if it meant conflict with others. For all the reasons that I let the forces of the environment shape me, including my chronological age, emotional development, and birth order, before long my own internal authority became very important to me. I soon began to find it impossible to fulfill the expectations of others without disappointing myself. Relationships became difficult because my efforts to sustain one relationship unwittingly had the potential to injure another relationship. The seductive and mind-numbing comfort of living within the rules of the social surround that "held" me began to suffocate more and support less. Laboring through another kind of birth, I was soon better able to eclipse those forces. I began to know these forces as separate from my "self," able to direct and author my own life. I was reaching a new threshold of consciousness (Kegan, 1994). I did not want other people to make up my inner circumstances.

My passion for life as mother, teacher, leader, and perennial student became needs requiring expression. I could not see the force, but I knew it was there, like the wind. Embracing the notion that organisms do not experience environments but are created by them, was a critical shift in my consciousness. My self-generated, and self-sustaining, *action*, in relationship with others, required that I take full responsibility for the conditions of my world and stop holding others responsible for what was right or wrong with my life. While this transformation was terrifying in one sense, I found it predominately liberating and empowering. The power to choose and take action made me the author of my world, rather than reading from someone's predetermined script. What a relief! With more study, reflection, questioning, and experience, I now believe that every living organism acts to develop and preserve itself (Wheatley & Kellner-Rogers, 1996). Every unique behavior exhibited by me, by my siblings and my parents within that environment, had a survival value (Branden, 1994) and was choreographed to codetermine the family environment in support of his or her distinctive identity.

And this is what this book is about. A kind of curriculum theory that encourages you to wake up and start asking questions about what may have been a taken-for-granted reality in your classroom, school, and life. A curriculum theory that embraces the "self," encouraging all of us, students, educators, parents, and the broader community to participate actively in our own evolution. A curriculum theory that asks you to be receptive to new information, even if it is unsettling, and to reexamine old assumptions; to persevere in the attempt to understand, in spite of confusion; a commitment to learning and growth as a *way of life* always seeking to expand your awareness to understand the world around you and to want all this for your students as much as you want it for yourself.

What are the networks of values, beliefs, and assumptions that make up your world? Do you raise critical questions about what is going on with students, particularly about matters of personal fairness and social justice? Do you encourage the unique perspectives of students and colleagues, honoring differing viewpoints? Do you engage in honest self-examination that challenges personal assumptions and commitments? Do you know what you take for granted? What is your professional identity? What do you stand for? Those values, beliefs, and assumptions that are not identified overtly are more difficult to call into question because they often bypass our conscious intelligence. Branden (1994) reminds us that we all possess implicit beliefs about nature, reality, human beings, relationships, and good and evil that reflect the values of a historical time and place. A measure of our intellectual maturity, however, is one's capacity to question. Questioning is mental work and, as you have learned from my life, does not happen instinctively or automatically (Branden, 1994). So, what is your story? What parts of your life are mechanical but may need to be more on purpose? Are you up to this personal and professional challenge to lead a life of inquiry, purposefully cultivating a democratic character in your*self* and your students? If you were writing this memoir, what would you name as the powerful forces of your past and present life that shape your consciousness? Have you absorbed the values of the tribe? Have you unwittingly surrendered your judgment to an external authority? Do you have what Dewey (1938/1963) calls a more effective source of authority? Just as important, what is the quality of the environment in your classroom? How are you fostering open and honest dialogue with and among your students? Are you encouraging each student's sense of autonomy within collaborative inquiry? Is it possible that you have unwittingly created a dynamic in your classroom that promotes the same mind-numbing compliance that you rail against in your life? You and only you can answer these questions, which mark the first step on your journey.

As Levoy (1997) points out, our lives are not measured in grand sweeps, but rather in small gestures. The most significant epiphanies in our lives generally occur as a result of an accumulated effect after months and even years of grappling with unanswered questions, so be gentle with yourself. Pay attention. While all this may seem like a tall order, my experience with my doctoral research is that this work is generative. In what I call "generative reciprocity," the data suggest that insights teachers needed for meeting the mental demand of living a life of inquiry for continuous growth cannot be taught or memorized. The act of practicing reflective inquiry, however, may develop the consciousness that gives rise to the insights to meet the demand. In other words, asking questions creates a demand on us for insights that may reach beyond our meaning-making system. Insights that alter our meaning-making system may be generated by the act of asking the questions (Gornik, 2002). You will learn more about practicing reflective inquiry in the next chapter.

As you read this book, I ask that you pay attention to what troubles you. Take note of the ideas that may make you uncomfortable. Is 3S understanding too challenging? Do you feel buried by the challenge of fostering democratic goodness with a curriculum wisdom mind-set? Does a disciplined liberation of the mind, body, and spirit seem like too much work? A friend of mine discussing this work with me asked incredulously, "If this is so hard and so complicated, why do you do it?" He was certain that teachers reading this book would abandon these notions because it was just too damn hard. I believe, as Eisner

(1994) states, that the ability to secure meaning in the course of our experience is a basic human need. We all want to lead meaningful lives and are drawn to growth and change. Experiencing "cognitive dissonance" (Festinger, 1957) or "productive disequilibria" (Lord, 1994) is cause for celebration. A healthy dose of dissonance, as a state of mind, is perhaps more fertile and growth producing than the mind that is unchallenged. In the Zen wisdom tradition, the pain is the path.

Yes, life is messy, but if we stay awake, it is not beyond thoughtful action. Let's do this together for our students, for one another, for our "selves." You will not uncover this work, but rather discover it through your daily inquiries. In the next chapter, we invite you to continue your exploration using a kind of map for your personal/professional journey. This map is designed to help you cultivate your reflective inquiry capacity for disciplined judgments to meet the challenges of transformative teaching. You will learn about a reflective practice that is carefully integrated with democratic curriculum studies. Our term for this integration is *reflective inquiry*. Let's get started.

REFERENCES

Bobbitt, F. (1924). *How to make a curriculum.* Boston: Houghton Mifflin.

Branden, N. (1994). *The six pillars of self esteem.* New York: Bantam Books

Branden, N. (1996). *Taking responsibility.* New York: Simon & Schuster.

Dewey, J. (1958). *Art as experience.* New York: Capricorn Books. (Original work published 1934)

Dewey, J. (1963). *Experience as education.* New York: Macmillan. (Original work published 1938)

Eisner, E. (1994). *The educational imagination: On the design and evaluation of school programs* (3rd ed.). New York: Macmillan.

Eisner, E. (2002). *The arts and the creation of the mind.* New Haven and London: Yale University Press.

Eisner, E. (2005, June 13). The satisfaction of teaching. *Stanford University School of Education News.* Retrieved May 31, 2006, from http://ed.stanford.edu/suse/news-bureau/displayRecord.php?tablename=susenews&id=119

Festinger, L. (1957). *Theory of cognitive dissonance.* Stanford, CA : Stanford University Press.

Gardner, H. (1991). *The unschooled mind: How children think and how schools should teach.* New York: Basic Books.

Gardner, H. (1999). *The disciplined mind: Beyond facts standardized tests, the K–12 education that every child deserves.* New York: Simon & Schuster.

Garrison, J. (1997). *Dewey and eros: Wisdom and desire in the art of teaching.* New York: Teachers College Press.

Gornik, R. (2002). *Teacher inquiry capacity: A case study.* Unpublished doctoral dissertation, Kent State University.

Greene, M. (1988). *The dialectic of freedom.* New York: Teachers College Press.

Henderson, J. G. (2001). *Reflective teaching: Professional artistry through inquiry* (3rd ed.). Upper Saddle River, NJ: Merrill/Prentice Hall.

Henderson, J. G., & Hawthorne, R. D. (1995). *Transformative curriculum leadership* (1st ed.). Upper Saddle River, NJ: Merrill/Prentice Hall.

Henderson, J. G., & Hawthorne, R. D. (2000). *Transformative curriculum leadership* (2nd ed.). Upper Saddle River, NJ: Merrill/Prentice Hall.

Henderson, J. G., & Kesson, K. R. (2004). *Curriculum wisdom: Educational decisions in democratic societies.* Upper Saddle River, NJ: Merrill/Prentice Hall.

Hess, F. M. (2004). *Common sense school reform.* New York: Palgrave Macmillan.

Jacobs, H. H. (1997). *Mapping the big picture: Integrating curriculum and assessment K–12.* Alexandria, VA: Association for Supervision and Curriculum Development.

Kegan, R. (1994). *In over our heads: The mental demands of modern life.* Cambridge, MA: Harvard University Press.

Levoy, G. (1997). *Callings: Finding and following an authentic life.* New York: Three Rivers Press.

Lewontin, R. C. (1991). *Biology as ideology: The doctrine of DNA.* New York: HarperCollins.

Lord, B. (1994). Teachers' professional development: Critical colleagueship and the role of professional communities. In N. Cobb (Ed.), *The future of education: Perspectives on national standards in America* (pp. 175–204). New York: College Entrance Examination Board.

Marsh, C. J., & Willis, G. (2003). *Curriculum: Alternative approaches, ongoing issues* (3rd ed.). Upper Saddle River, NJ: Merrill/Prentice Hall.

Moore, T. (1992). *Care of the soul.* New York: HarperCollins.

Noddings, N. (1984). *Caring: A feminine approach to ethics and moral education.* Berkley: University of California Press.

Pinar, W. F., Reynolds, W. M., Slattery, P., & Taubman, P. M. (1995). *Understanding curriculum: An introduction to the study of historical and contemporary curriculum discourses.* New York: Peter Lang.

Pinar, W. F., (2004). *What is curriculum theory?* Mahwah, New Jersey: Erlbaum Associates.

Pinar, W. F. (2005). The problem with curriculum and pedagogy. *Journal of Curriculum and Pedagogy, 2*(1), 67–82.

Reeves, D. B. (2002). *Making standards work: How to implement standards-based assessments in the classroom, school, and district.* Englewood, CO: Advanced Learning Press.

Sanders, W. L., & Horn, S. (1994). The Tennessee Value-Added Assessment System (TVAAS): Mixed-model methodology in educational assessment. *Journal of Personnel Evaluation in Education, 8,* 299–311.

Stigler, J. W., & Hiebert, J. (1999). *The teaching gap.* New York: The Free Press.

Walker, D. F. (2003). *Fundamentals of curriculum: Passion and professionalism* (2nd ed.). Mahwah, NJ: Lawrence Erlbaum Associates.

Wiggins, G., & McTighe, J. (1998). *Understanding by design* (1st ed.). Alexandria, VA: Association for Supervision and Curriculum Development.

Wiggins, G., & McTighe, J. (2005). *Understanding by design* (2nd ed.). Alexandria, VA: Association for Supervision and CurriculumDevelopment.

Wheatley, M. J. (1994). *Leadership and the new science: Learning about organization from an orderly universe.* San Francisco: Berrett-Koehler.

Wheatley, M. J., & Kellner-Rogers, M. (1996). *A simpler way.* San Francisco: Berrett-Koehler.

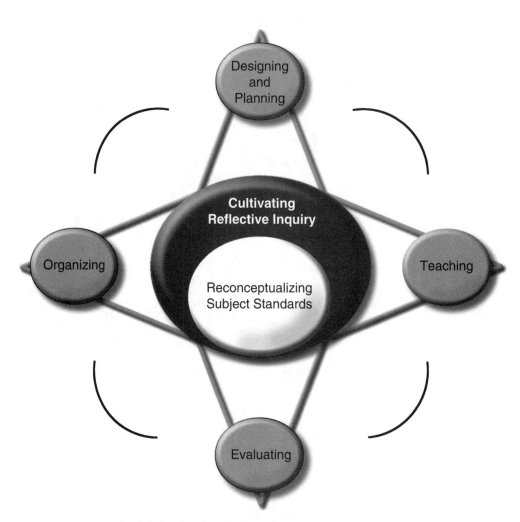

Sustaining the Curriculum Wisdom Problem Solving

CHAPTER 3

CULTIVATING REFLECTIVE INQUIRY

Introducing reflective inquiry during our early fieldwork would make a world of difference in how we view what is happening in the classroom. It would be invaluable, perhaps changing our perspectives a bit, such as providing a wider angle to look at teaching and learning. The more I practice reflective inquiry, the more natural it feels.

(Shari, Early Childhood Education preservice teacher [Thomas, 2005])

Before we begin our discussion on cultivating reflective inquiry, let us review the focus of this book. *Transformative Curriculum Leadership* (TCL) is about elevating curriculum-based teaching judgments through responsible professional autonomy, and this more sophisticated judgment is embedded in fundamental changes at the personal, interpersonal and societal levels. As we presented in Table 1.1 of chapter 1, the identical Table 3.1 summarizes three paradigms that influence curriculum problem solving. Although the *standardized management* paradigm is the most influential because of the current educational policy environment, many educators and other curriculum stakeholders are committed to the *constructivist best practice* orientation. They understand the value of teaching for active subject matter understanding. In Gardner's (2000) language, they understand the many advantages of cultivating "disciplined minds." One goal of this book is to invite these constructivist educators to transition to the *curriculum wisdom* paradigm, which can be understood as a deepening of the constructivist best practice paradigm. There are, of course, a smaller percentage of educators and other curriculum stakeholders who intuitively, tacitly, or consciously embrace wisdom problem solving. They understand the value of teaching for an active subject matter understanding that is embedded in democratic understanding. They are committed to this "doubled" problem solving: the attempt to solve immediate learning problems in constructivist ways while also tackling the problem of teaching for responsible democratic living (Henderson & Kesson, 2004). They are aware that a society with democratic ideals must find practical ways to actively engage students in making sense of those ideals.

When we introduced Table 1.1 in chapter 1, we noted that the "Organizing Problem" heading refers to how learning problems are framed and, consequently, shape the curriculum problem solving, while the "Problem-Solving Cycle" heading refers to how educators move through the general problem solving iterations of setting goals, deciding how to act, experiencing the consequences of specific actions, reflecting on these consequences, and revisiting and, if necessary, resetting goals. Notice how "reflective practice" is a central feature in each of the three curriculum problem-solving paradigms. In effect, reflection is a key component of curriculum problem solving—no matter how that problem solving is practiced. To discuss the way educators reflect on their practices is to acknowledge that reflection is embedded in a continuous educational problem solving.

Table 3.1 EDUCATIONAL PARADIGMS		
Educational Paradigm	**Organizing Problem**	**Problem-Solving Cycle**
Standardized management	Student performances on standardized tests	Goal-setting, decision-making, and reflecting activities aligned to high-stakes standardized tests
Constructivist best practice	Student performances of subject matter understanding	Goal-setting, decision-making, and reflecting activities that facilitate students' subject matter meaning making
Curriculum wisdom	Student performances of subject matter understanding embedded in democratic self and social understanding	Goal-setting, decision-making, and reflecting activities that facilitate students' subject matter meaning making in a context of active democratic learning

INTRODUCING REFLECTIVE INQUIRY

We will introduce a special kind of reflective practice in this chapter. It is a reflective practice that is integrated with democratic curriculum inquiry and our term for this integration will be a *multifaceted reflective inquiry*. We use the term *inquiry* instead of study[1] in recognition of the action-oriented nature of curriculum problem solving, and because the reflective inquiry we will be introducing is multifaceted, you will notice that we use a singular noun, *reflective inquiry,* to refer to a complex set of questions. As you will learn in this chapter, we will advance a multifaceted reflective inquiry because democratic education has too many dimensions to be studied through a unidimensional methodology. It requires the practice of a complex, multimodal inquiry (Henderson & Kesson, 2004).

Another way to explain this important methodological principle speaks to the organic connection between reflective inquiry "means" and the democratic "end in view" (Dewey, 1938/1963). We are concerned about the integration of reflection in problem solving with democratic curriculum inquiry because 3S education requires such a close linkage. Though many educators may separate the tradition of curriculum studies from educational practice,[2] we challenge this custom. Simply put, 3S education is informed by democratic curriculum inquiry. In effect, it requires two types of integration. To teach for a subject matter understanding that is integrated with democratic self and social understanding, educators must integrate democratic curriculum inquiry into their reflective problem solving. If they don't practice this latter integration, which is the topic of this chapter, they will not be in a position to practice the former integration, which is the topic of chapter 2.

---

[1] Scholars in the general field of curriculum studies may use terms *inquiry* and *study* interchangeably. However, we will not do so for the reason just stated.

[2] We will present an historical account of North American curriculum studies in chapter 9.

This chapter is organized into six additional sections. After completing our introduction of reflective inquiry, we will explore the nature of reflective practice in education with the assistance of selected literature. Next, we will provide a brief introduction to democratic curriculum inquiry and the subsequent "marriage" of reflective practice and democratic curriculum inquiry. To facilitate this marriage of reflective practice and democratic curriculum inquiry, we will provide a kind of map or scaffolding of seven reflective inquiries. This map includes a set of personal questions that can be integrated into daily curriculum wisdom problem solving. To further emphasize the importance of reflective inquiry in wisdom problem solving, we will then present another view of the standardized management, constructivist best practice, and curriculum wisdom paradigms. We will then introduce an imaginary personal account of a teacher practicing reflective inquiry. We hope that this fictional narrative, which is based on years of research-based experience, will help you envision how you might cultivate your reflective inquiry capacities. There are, certainly, many personal, idiosyncratic ways to practice reflective inquiry, so keep in mind that this imaginary account is simply an illustration on how to proceed. As part of this narrative, we present another comparison of the three paradigms—this time through the use of contrasting questions. We conclude our discussion of reflective inquiry as a fundamental challenge of wisdom problem solving with a look ahead to the book's remaining chapters.

MORE ON REFLECTIVE INQUIRY

There is no precise protocol for reflective inquiry. However, Schwab (1971, 1997) does provide theoretical language for reflection in the curriculum problem-solving cycle. He calls for curriculum work that is positioned at the intersection of *practical arts*, which are concerned with deliberative choice and action, and *eclectic arts*, which are concerned with the diversified study of educational problems. In effect, Schwab argues that good curriculum work is characterized by the marriage of practical and eclectic artistry, and this is precisely the focus of this chapter. We will further examine Schwab's theory of artful deliberation in curriculum work in chapter 9; however, our attention now is on the practice of reflective inquiry.

We can anticipate a question that you might have at this point in the chapter: "How in the world, with all that is on my plate, do I go about reconceptualizing the received standards into transformative standards with the assistance of a reflective inquiry?" Fear not; we will guide you step by step as we focus on introducing the professional challenge of participating in a gradual, self-sustaining, and generative growth. Franke, Carpenter, Fennema, Ansell, and Behrend (1998) write, "For change to become generative, teachers must engage in practices that serve as a basis for their continued learning;" (p. 67) and this is exactly how we will proceed in this chapter. We will be providing practical guidance for your continuing professional education.

What do we know about human "understanding"? How do we know when we or others "understand" something? In chapter 2 we focused on the fundamental challenge of understanding students' understanding. As you grapple with this doubled understanding, consider Dewey's (1910/1997) insights into human understanding:

> To grasp a meaning, to understand, to identify a thing in a situation in which it is important, are thus equivalent terms; they express the nerves of our intellectual life. Without

them there is (a) lack of intellectual content, or (b) intellectual confusion and perplexity, or else (c) intellectual perversion—nonsense, insanity. [Therefore,] [s]omething already understood in one situation has been transferred and applied to what is strange and perplexing in another, and thereby the latter has become plain and familiar, i.e., understood. (pp. 117–118)

Dewey's view of human understanding can be applied to the questions proposed in chapter 2. As you may recall, these questions move us beyond knowledge "regurgitated" on a paper–pencil test and ask us to consider an essential question: How do I know my students really got it? With a focus on subject, self, and social understanding, let's review the questions:

1. Have they employed knowledge effectively in diverse, authentic, and realistically messy contexts?

2. Have they revealed personalized, thoughtful, and coherent grasp of subjects demonstrating the ability to think for themselves?

3. Are they wide awake, willing to welcome new insights, refining core beliefs through conversations with diverse others?

4. Have they demonstrated the ability to effectively and sensitively interpret texts and the ability to read between the lines?

5. Have they extended or applied what is known in novel ways to become more cognitively, emotionally, physically, aesthetically, and spiritually attuned to themselves and others?

Addressing these concerns about student understanding requires the practice of a democratic curriculum inquiry that is integrated into a continuous reflective practice. Specific questions must be woven into 3S designing, planning, teaching, evaluating, and organizing decisions, and the best approach to this professional challenge is to proceed holistically and humbly, not literally and ideologically. However, before turning to this marriage of reflective practice and democratic curriculum inquiry, let's first explore the nature of reflective practice in education.

REFLECTIVE PRACTICE IN EDUCATION

As a catalyst for helping us understand reflective practice, let's call upon some people who have written extensively about the basics of reflection and then examine some studies that explore its practice. We might even describe this section of the chapter as a further introduction to one of the "engagement" partners in the proposed "marriage" of reflective practice and democratic curriculum inquiry.

We begin with influential literature on the related topics of reflective thinking, reflection-on-action and reflection-in-action, and reflective practice characteristics. In his *How We*

Think, Dewey (1910/1997) notes the importance of disciplined uncertainty in reflective thinking and describes it as (a) a state of perplexity, hesitation, doubt; and (b) an act of search or investigation directed toward bringing to light further facts that corroborate or nullify the suggested belief (p. 9). He also suggests that reflective thought is consecutive, not merely a sequence. He says, "Reflection involves not simply a sequence of ideas, but . . . a consecutive ordering in such a way that each determines the next as its proper outcome, while each in turn leans back on its predecessors. The successive portions of the reflective thought grow out of one another and support one another. . . . The stream or flow becomes a train, chain, or thread" (pp. 2–3). In believing that reflective thought requires both a conscious and voluntary effort, Dewey presents such effort as "[a]ctive, persistent, and careful consideration of any belief or supposed form of knowledge in the light of the grounds that support it, and the future conclusions to which it tends" (p. 6).

While Dewey focuses on key cognitive features of reflection, Schön (1983) advances the distinction between reflection-in-action and reflection-on-action. This distinction enables him to explore the dynamic nature of reflection. Teachers and their students reframe problems and reshape situations in specific, idiosyncratic, and fluid ways. They engage in a series of "moves, discovered consequences, implications, appreciations, and further moves" (p. 131), and this constant movement produces unintended changes that give situations new meanings to investigate. To maximize reflection-in-action, Schön asks professionals to move beyond responses such as "He doesn't know his facts" or "She hasn't learned to think critically" to a place where students have voice and can reason. This change in our behavior/reaction enables us to become curious about behavior rather than judging behavior. Schön suggests that if we begin by describing our understandings of our observations, we can restructure what we see. This type of dynamic reflection promotes continued dialogue and interaction between teachers and their students.

Rodgers's (2002) work supplements both Schön (1983) and Dewey (1910/1997) by outlining four key characteristics of reflective practice:

1. Reflection is a meaning-making cycle that moves a learner from one experience into the next with deeper understanding of its relationships with and connections to other experiences and ideas. It is the thread that makes continuity of learning possible, and ensures the progress of the individual and, ultimately, society. It is a means to essentially moral ends.

2. Reflection is a systematic, rigorous, disciplined way of thinking, with its roots in scientific inquiry.

3. Reflection needs to happen in community, in interaction with others.

4. Reflection requires attitudes that value the personal and intellectual growth of oneself and of others. (p. 845)

With reference to Rodgers's first point, we have found that the personal meaning making often provides the context for reflective inquiry, and this is one reason why we have integrated Rosie's currere narratives into all the chapters of this book. You will notice that many of her personal stories incorporate reflective inquiry, and so we hope that her autobiographical currere narratives inspire your own reflective inquiries. Engaging in self-reflection and collecting student feedback related to classroom instruction will also prompt us to critically examine the degree of student involvement in the learning process and to adjust our instructional practices accordingly (Artzt & Armour-Thomas, 1999).

Let's now turn to some studies that focus on the importance of collaboration in reflective practice. Garet, Porter, Desimone, Birman, and Yoon (2001) study teachers engaged in collegial collaboration and dialogic exchanges or what they called *active learning* related to teaching and learning. Teachers observed expert teachers, were observed by colleagues, and engaged in discourse about the observations. The collected feedback then provided an opportunity for further discussions related to the goals of the lesson, teaching strategies, student tasks, and student learning. Furthermore, collaborative, collegial dialogue that reflected on problems and worked toward solutions provided the catalyst for improved goals for student learning.

Do you think you would gain such detailed knowledge about your students if you only reflect by yourself? Probably not. As we have noted in our earlier chapters, reflective practice is often not best done in isolation. Moreover, this is truly collaborative work. Not only did Garet and colleagues report rich findings for teacher growth and student learning, but they also found that reflective teachers applied educational principles and techniques to reach their goals. Furthermore, this cycle has been known to result in the examination of the hows and the whys at the practical and critical levels of teaching.

Reflective practices are intended to revisit one's teaching methods *and* prompt collaborative conversations about the impact of our teaching on students' learning. This notion is supported by Hollingsworth (1992), who reports that teachers' learning is supported within collaborative conversations in several ways, such as through commitments to relational processes, through focused learning on common practiced-based concerns, by asking broad questions and reflecting upon feedback, by valuing experiences and emotions as knowledge, by valuing biographical differences, by developing a supported critical perspective, and by reinforcing learning to teach as a process. In sum, Sparks-Langer, Simmons, Pasch, Colton, and Starko (1990) suggest that technical, practical, and critical reflective practices encourage teachers to consider teaching methods, means and ends, and moral and ethical issues.

Through reflective practice, teachers should be able to transcend everyday experiences to imagine the possibilities of what ought to be rather than the way things are. In turn, such thinking presents the opportunity for teachers to evolve into *transformative intellectuals* who are capable of examining the ways in which schooling and one's own teaching contribute, or fail to contribute, to a just and humane society (Giroux, 1988). It is expected such a transformation will shape teachers' practice, their thinking about their practice, and their worldview about teaching.

DEMOCRATIC CURRICULUM INQUIRY

As we noted at the beginning of this chapter, reflective inquiry results from the integration of reflective practice and democratic curriculum inquiry in the context of ongoing wisdom problem solving. This marriage requires two partners: reflective practice, which we have just discussed, and democratic curriculum inquiry, which we will discuss next.

Pinar (2005) states, "study is the site of education. Not instruction, not learning, but study constitutes the process of education" (p. 70). Furthermore, he contends, "While I disclaim the aspiration for 'control,' I embrace study's capacity to contest conformity" (p. 69). Pinar argues that both teachers and their students must engage in disciplined study; otherwise, they are not practicing education. Without disciplined study, education devolves into narrow training, and teachers become simple-minded test proctors. Pinar summarizes his curriculum argument with a key insight into 3S education, and we hope you will keep this insight in mind as you study this chapter and contemplate how you will cultivate your reflective inquiries: "While one's truths—academic knowledge grounded in lived, that is, subjective and social experience—cannot be taught . . . they can be acquired through the struggle of study, for which every individual has the capacity, but not necessarily the will . . ." (p. 79).

While Pinar's (2005) essay hints at the vital relationship between teachers' disciplined study and students' disciplined study, Barth (1990) explores this relationship through numerous illustrations, personal narratives, and supportive research, and he uses the term *inquiry,* which is also our preferred term. A thesis in his book is the close correlation between teachers' inquiry growth and students' growth. He writes:

> Too often teachers do what they did today because that is what they did yesterday or because that is what they think others expect them to do. Just as potters cannot teach others to craft in clay without setting their own hands to work at the wheel, so teachers cannot fully teach others the excitement, the difficulty, the patience, and the satisfaction that accompany learning without themselves engaging in the messy, frustrating, and rewarding "clay" of learning. Inquiry for teachers can take place both in and out of the view of students, but to teacher and student alike there must be continuous evidence that it is occurring. For when teachers observe, examine, question, and reflect on their ideas and develop new practices that lead toward their ideals, students are alive. When teachers stop growing, so do their students. (pp. 49–50)

Like Barth, we celebrate teachers who are engaged in continuous inquiry, but we want this inquiry to be carefully integrated into their reflective practices. Furthermore, we are not interested in just any kind of inquiry. Our focus is on democratic curriculum inquiry. In our paradigmatic language, our focus is on a disciplined inquiry into 3S education in the context of wisdom problem solving; therefore, democratic curriculum inquiry recommendations are embedded in our reflective inquiry map, which is introduced in the next section.

REFLECTIVE INQUIRY MAP

We now introduce a *reflective inquiry* map, which is designed to facilitate your personalized integration of reflective practice and democratic curriculum inquiry. After each of the seven inquiries is discussed, you will find a set of personalized questions that require deep introspection and that can enhance your work with facilitating students' 3S understanding. These questions provide a starting point for understanding the reflective inquiries in relation to your actions before, during, and after teaching and learning occur. They also invite you to engage in ongoing reflective inquiry self-assessment such as identifying strengths and working on weaknesses. The seven reflective inquiries follow. Please note that these reflective inquiries are not listed in any particular order. They are not to be considered hierarchical. One reflective inquiry is not more important than the others. As you engage in the problem-solving cycles, you will find that these inquiries overlap and blur; often one is in the foreground, and then almost imperceptibly slips to the background, subtly related to another that emerges. For purposes of clarity, these inquiries are explained separately, but in practice blend into a coherent whole. We use the map metaphor as a guide or scaffolding for your and your students' journey of understanding.

Reflective Disciplinary Inquiry

Reflective disciplinary inquiry is the study of your subject matter discipline in the context of curriculum problem solving. Shulman (1987) provides insight into reflective disciplinary inquiry. He closely examines the sources of knowledge for teaching, how these sources are conceptualized, the processes of pedagogical reasoning and action, and the implications for teaching policy and educational reform. In fact, his work is so highly regarded that it provides the theoretical framework for the National Board Certification guidelines. Shulman argues that teachers have a tremendous responsibility to their students; "[t]his responsibility places special demands on the teacher's own depth of understanding of the structures of the subject matter, as well as on the teacher's attitudes toward and enthusiasms for what is being taught and learned" (p. 9). We agree with Shulman when he states that teachers should have a deep understanding of their subject matter. After all, this is one of the Ss in our 3S formulation. However, we take his work a step further by recommending that understanding of subject matter content should be integrated with democratic self and social understandings as well.

Gardner (2000) further informs reflective disciplinary inquiry by recommending that teachers who are committed to cultivating their students' subject matter understanding use: (1) multiple entry points to rich topics such as vivid and dramatic narratives, timelines of events, logical "if/then" scenarios, existential invitations (raising deep questions about existence), aesthetic examinations of works of art, hands-on projects (working with materials), field-trip experiences, and cooperative peer learning activities; (2) powerful analogies and metaphors; and (3) multiple representations of core ideas through the use of multiple intelligences (spatial, kinesthetic, interpersonal, linguistic, rhythmic, naturalist, intrapersonal, and mathematical). Gardner states that there is no distinct order for these three approaches to teaching for understanding. More importantly,

> [t]he teacher's job resembles that of a master orchestrator, who keeps the whole score in mind and yet can home in on particular passages and players. He or she should come up with questions, units, and performances of understanding that fit together comfortably, engage the students, and, ultimately, aid the vast majority of them to achieve deeper understandings of the topic. Within that broad prospect, the teacher can and should be encouraged to be as versatile as possible. (p. 209)

Wiggins and McTighe (2001) also provide a useful framework for *reflective disciplinary inquiry*. Using their "Six Facets of Understanding," teachers can help their students deepen their understanding of subject matter. The six facets are referred to throughout this text because of the practical guidance Wiggins and McTighe offer. The six facets are:

1. explanation—sophisticated and apt explanations and theories, which provide knowledgeable and justified accounts of events, actions, and ideas

2. interpretation—interpretations, narrative, and translation that provide meaning

3. application—ability to use knowledge effectively in new situations and diverse contexts

4. perspective—critical and insightful points of view

5. empathy—the ability to get inside another person's feelings and worldviews

6. self-knowledge—the wisdom to know one's ignorance and how one's patterns of thought and action inform as well as prejudice understanding (pp. 44–62).

Reflective Disciplinary Inquiry Questions to Ponder

- How do I go about assessing the educational materials I use to plan for instruction?

- How are the educational materials I use representative of the student diversity in the classroom?

- How does the plethora of educational literature inform my content selections and instructional practices? How might I contribute to this literature?

- What needs do I have for enhanced understanding of my subject matter understanding?

- What needs do my students have for enhanced understanding of their subject matter understanding?

- What connections am I making with my deep subject matter understanding to democratic self and social understandings?

- What connections are my students making with their deep subject matter understanding to democratic self and social understandings?

The second of the seven reflective inquiries—*reflective poetic inquiry*—is explained next.

Reflective Poetic Inquiry

Reflective poetic inquiry is concerned with the soulful, expressive aspects of creation in the context of curriculum wisdom problem solving. There is a focus on the aesthetics of constructivist learning—the bringing together of structure, content, and form to create beauty and meaning. There is a receptivity to educational eros, passion, and holism, and there is an underlying sense of surrender, care, and fulfillment. There is an emphasis on self-discovery, inventive play, experimentation, and the romance of acquiring new understanding. Through poetic *making*, the expressive self, in all of its complexity, is revealed. In *Art as Experience*, John Dewey brilliantly explores how ordinary experience can become a profoundly aesthetic event. This occurs through the cultivation of a qualitative intelligence grounded in deep perception. Dewey (1934/1958) writes: "Perception replaces bare recognition. There is an act of reconstructive doing, and consciousness becomes fresh and alive. . . . To think effectively in terms of relations of qualities is as severe a demand upon thought as to think in terms of symbols, verbal and mathematical" (pp. 53, 46). Through this qualitative thinking, the ordinary becomes the sacred; the prosaic becomes the profound; and the fragmented becomes whole. Reflective poetic inquiry, thus, begins with the perceptive and culminates with the creative.

Through reflective poetic inquiry, we examine why we are called to facilitate students' 3S understanding. Pinar (2004) heeds this sense of professional calling when he invites educators to "articulate relations among the school subjects, society, and self-formation" (p. 191) by distancing themselves from the standardized management of education. He expounds:

> That curriculum has become so formalized and abstract, so often distant from the everyday sense of conversation signals . . . how profoundly the process of education has been institutionalized and bureaucratized. Instead of employing school knowledge to complicate our understanding of ourselves and the society in which we live, teachers are forced to "instruct" students to mime others' (textbook authors') conversations, ensuring that countless classrooms are filled with forms of ventriloquism rather than intellectual exploration, wonder, and awe. (Huebner, 1999, p. 186)

Decisions informed by reflective poetic inquiry are made by considering not just the instrumental solving of a problem but also the multifaceted effects of a solution. Does the solution add order, harmony, or well-being for the participants? Asking aesthetic questions can generate a deeper involvement with questions of meaning and enable the conceptual movement from perceived part to imaginative whole.

Reflective poetic inquiry transforms teaching from a role or a function into a calling. Palmer (1999) invites us to explore this calling along three distinct but interrelated pathways: intellectual (the way we think about teaching and learning, content and students), emotional (the way we and our students feel as we are teaching and learning), and spiritual (personally connecting with the world around us). When we engage in reflective poetic inquiry, we become attuned to the spiritual dimensions of educational work. Why is democratic morality so compelling? What is the eros embedded in the synergistic interplay of diverse voices? Why is democracy a loving way? Why does democratic living require spiritual maturity? Palmer (1999) continues:

> Teaching, like any truly human activity, emerges from one's inwardness, for better or worse. As I teach, I project the condition of my soul onto my students, my subject, and our way of being together. The entanglements I experience in the classroom are often no more or less than the convolutions of my inner life. Viewed from this angle, teaching holds a mirror to the soul. If I am willing to look in the mirror, and not run from what I see, I have a chance to gain self-knowledge—and knowing myself is as crucial to good teaching as knowing my students and my subject." (p. 1)

Palmer (1999) also reminds us that focusing on our inner selves "is not exactly a conventional approach to problem-solving in education!" In the dominant paradigm, "[w]e are trained to deal with educational dilemmas by adopting new techniques or changing the curriculum—not by deepening our own sense of identity and integrity" (p. 2).

Reflective Poetic Inquiry Questions to Ponder

- Do I provide/engage in meaningful learning opportunities?

- Have I awakened a passion for teaching/learning?

- Am I willing to discuss my values and beliefs? How do I act on these values and beliefs? Do my actions align with my values and beliefs? How is my teaching reflecting my beliefs?

- What does it mean to be a teacher?

- In what ways do I engage in professional dialogue with colleagues?

- Am I willing to discuss my professional values and beliefs? If not, why not?

Reflective Critical Inquiry

Reflective critical inquiry addresses social and economic inequities in the context of curriculum wisdom problem solving (Henderson, 2001). It challenges all habits, customs, and deeply embedded structures through the exercise of a critical intelligence that is geared to asking penetrating, unsettling questions and thinking deeply about social justice and personal fairness of actions. This line of questioning considers the "overt, tacit, and covert power relations between people" (Henderson, 2001, p. 22). Reflective critical inquiry is not only the examination of the structural obstacles, but it is also the artful deliberation on how these deep-seated barriers can be overcome. Van Manen (1977) writes, "The critical approach to curriculum seeks to establish interpersonal and social conditions necessary for genuine self-understanding, emancipatory learning, and critical consciousness" (p. 221).

When critical inquiry is integrated into reflective practice, it is often called *praxis.* Lather (1991) describes praxis as educational practice that is explicitly committed to critiquing the status quo and building a more just society. As critically informed teachers, we refine and enact our passion for justice and fair play. Sirotnik (1991) writes, "Critical inquiry begins with the answer 'No!' and continues with a process of informed reflection and actions guided by explicit, normative considerations" (p. 245). When we are critical, we don't believe everything we are told, and we don't rely on pleasing appearances. We ask penetrating, unsettling questions, and we think in a visionary way about the possible consequences of our actions. Cherryholmes (1999) provides insight into a critically informed, pragmatic approach to educational practice:

> Pragmatism looks to consequences that we endlessly bump up against. We respond to and live with outcomes all day, every day. These results come from our actions and those of others. They also come from events beyond our control. Pragmatists anticipate outcomes. They look to imagined and actual outcomes. . . . Pragmatists conceptualize the world where we, all of us, are constantly thrown forward as the present approaches but never quite reaches the future. Pragmatism is a discourse that attempts to bridge where we are with where we might end up. The future, the other unknown side of this bridge, can certainly be forbidding. There is little, if anything, that we can say with confidence about it. The temptation is to look backward. Pragmatism resists this siren's song by accepting the challenge to look ahead. (p. 3)

When we are pragmatic in Cherryholmes's critical visionary sense, we continually wonder if we are seeing things correctly. We pursue deeply penetrating questions because we want to get to "the truth of the matter." Because of our critical commitments, we are as willing to challenge our own beliefs and practices as we are those of others. We understand that there are no sacred cows in education and that whatever has been constructed can be questioned, modified, and even significantly altered.

Public schooling was created, in part, to help maintain society's freedoms (Greene, 1988), but freedom is a tricky subject with many subtle considerations. We may believe that all citizens in our country are endowed with freedom and that we live in an "equal opportunity" society. We may also believe that our country's Constitution provides all citizens with the power to overcome any obstacles standing in their way—what Greene (1988) calls an absence of interference. However, ask many African Americans and Native Americans in the United States whether they view themselves as "free." Then think about society's deeply embedded structures. Do you think they're fair? Do you think all citizens have an equal opportunity to realize their potential? When you ask such questions as part of your curriculum wisdom problem solving, you are engaging in reflective critical inquiry.

Greene (1988) helps us understand that social imagination is an integral part of our critically informed work. She writes that educators must cultivate their "capacity to surpass the given and look at things as if they were otherwise" (p. 5). She argues that teachers should help their students think deeply about the value of democratic living. Teaching "is an undertaking oriented to empowering persons to become different, to think critically and creatively, to pursue meanings, to make increasing sense of their actually lived worlds" (Greene, 1986, p. 72). As critical educators, we must help our students see both the overt and the covert obstacles in front of them, to understand these obstacles, and, ultimately, to see beyond them to a better life.

Kincheloe (1999) points out the wide range of considerations associated with an awareness of power relations in education. He writes that critical inquiry "is especially concerned with how democracy is subverted, domination takes place, and human relations are shaped in schools, in other cultural sites of pedagogy, and in everyday life" (p. 71). He adds that critical consciousness helps an educator understand "how and why his or her political opinions, worker role, religious beliefs, gender role, and racial self image are shaped by dominant perspectives" (pp. 71–72).

Like many teachers, you may think, "My job is simply to teach." If this is your position, ask yourself this question: *If teachers work only as subject matter specialists, how will students experience the joys and responsibilities of democratic living?* Shor (1993) notes the challenges of critically informed teaching:

> After long years in traditional schools, teachers become conditioned to lecture, to assert their authority, to transfer official information and skills, as the proper way for professionals to do their work. It is not easy for them to share decision-making in the classroom, to negotiate the curriculum, to pose problems based in student thought and language, to lead a dialogue where student expression has an impact on the course of study, and to learn with and from students. (p. 29)

Reflective Critical Inquiry Questions to Ponder

- How do I achieve congruence between the *written curriculum* (what we say we teach), the *enacted curriculum* (what we actually teach), the *assessed curriculum* (what we measure), the *hidden curriculum* (what is not explicitly stated yet is learned by students, such as social and academic groupings, following the rules in the game of schooling), and the *null curriculum* (what may or may not be learned yet often contains beliefs about social dynamics such as premarital sex, homosexuality, and lifestyle preference)?

- Why am I not doing what needs to be done?
- What impact do the values of the community have on the classroom? the school?
- Are questions asked without fear?
- Is the environment a place where people can grow together?
- In what ways am I reaching out to colleagues?
- Who is silenced? Why?

Reflective Multiperspective Inquiry

Reflective multiperspective inquiry explores the diverse perspectives on the democracy and education relationship in the context of curriculum wisdom problem solving. This reflective inquiry recognizes and embraces the existence of many plausible and illuminating interpretations of the same stories and human events. Henderson (2001) suggests that engaging in multiperspective inquiry requires teachers to listen carefully to explore diverse viewpoints, confront basic beliefs/dogma, and challenge their own and others' egocentric tendencies. It examines how to establish (coconstruct) public agreements and how to cultivate inclusive conversations.

According to Henderson and Kesson (2004), reflective multiperspective inquiry reaches across differences and encourages dialogue with diverse others to construct understanding. Furthermore, this inquiry reminds us that, "while people might engage in shared experiences, their perceptions of their experiences are shaped differently by their perspectives and constructed out of their racial, class, ethnic, sexual, gendered, age, and ability-related identities" (p. 54).

Reflective multiperspective inquiry invites us to look at our students as individuals with distinctive styles and voices, which are important features of teaching and learning. When individual expression is discouraged, inhibited, or suppressed in the classroom, much of the passion of education is lost. Greene (1986) calls upon educators to honor and cultivate personal identity:

> I would like to think of teachers moving the young into their own interpretations of their lives and their lived worlds, opening wider and wider perspectives as they do so. . . . I would like to see teachers tapping the spectrum of intelligences, encouraging multiple readings of written texts and readings of the world. . . . Such a project demands the capacity to unveil and disclose. It demands the exercise of imagination enlivened by works of art, by situations of speaking and making. . . . Perhaps we can invent ways of freeing people to feel and express indignation, to break through the opaqueness, to refuse the silences. We need to teach in such a way as to arouse passion now and then. . . . (p. 441)

Teaching for 3S understanding requires this sensitivity to individual perspectives. As Sidorkin (1999) writes, "democracy implies lengthy discussions, ability to listen, compromise, see things through the eyes of the other" (p. 66). In other words, conformity is not an option when teaching for democratic 3S understanding. If teachers do not develop their capacity to "confirm" the unique voices of their students in caring ways (Noddings, 1984), they are simply not in a position to teach democratic 3S living.

Reflective multiperspective inquiry invites teachers to become comfortable with ambiguity and uncertainty in their classrooms. Henderson (2001) writes: "They must continuously stretch their minds, refine their beliefs, and acknowledge the multifaceted nature of their instructional practices. They must recognize that everything in life is not black and white and that much of education is cloaked in shades of gray" (p. 73).

Reflective Multiperspective Inquiry Questions to Ponder

- Do I see things through the eyes of other cultures, races, genders, ages, and socioeconomic classes?

- Do I explore problems from a variety of perspectives? Do I support and accept the potential solutions of others? Do I present and accept more than one solution?

- How do I accommodate diverse learning styles?

- During small and large group dialogic exchanges, what evidence is apparent that (1) people in the group are listening and (2) everyone had an opportunity to share?

- Am I sensitive to everyone's voice?

- Do I facilitate dialogue on issues/topics?

- Are there observable behaviors of exclusiveness? If so, how are these behaviors addressed?

Reflective Ethical Inquiry

Reflective ethical inquiry addresses the democratic ethics of curriculum wisdom problem solving. The focus is on congruence between ideals and actions—on "walking the talk" of one's deepest democratic beliefs. Through this reflective inquiry, teachers ask themselves: "Am I doing no harm, and am I promoting democratic well being?" The challenge is to facilitate students' experience of democratic education. As Dewey (1939/1963) points out, education should not be a vague, disengaged promise of democracy, it should be the real thing. Student learning should occur in the democratic here-and-now. Teachers do this by actively cultivating the values associated with the democratic good life. These are the values that transcend individual and group identity interests.

Reflective ethical inquiry focuses on students' distinctive learning styles, interests, strengths, and areas of growth. This sensitivity is central to wise democratic problem solving. If teachers do not work in this sensitive, collaborative way, their students will experience "curriculum" as disconnected subjects, predetermined knowledge and skills, and systems of meaning that have no relation to their world (Greene, 1988, 1997). Under such fragmented curricular conditions, there is little opportunity for well-integrated cognitive, social, and emotional development. There is little opportunity for 3S education. Greene (1997) wants students to actively engage in logical thinking, to resolve moral dilemmas, and to master interpersonal rules. She wants teachers to collaborate with their students in the clarification of their own interests and projects, and, in turn, to guide their meaning making of the world around them. This is an inclusive classroom ethic in which as many interpretations as possible about the world and the multiple ways of being in the world are incorporated into the curriculum. Working in this democratically inclusive way, teachers nurture the emergence of diverse personal awareness and voice. After all, students are breathing, conscious human beings and,

> consciousness, being intentional, throws itself outward *towards* the world. It is always consciousness *of* something—a phenomenon, another person, an object in the world: Reflecting upon himself as a conscious object, the individual—the learner, perhaps—reflects upon his relation to the world, his manner of comporting himself with respect to it, the changing perspectives through which the world presents it to him. (Greene, 1997, p. 140)

Reflective ethical inquiry is personally and professionally challenging and potentially risky. Most educational institutions have created curriculum mission statements that contain lofty articulations of the relationship between democracy and education. But how many educators take these mission statements seriously? How many educators are even aware that their institutions possess such statements? In fact, how many of these democratic education mission statements are simply gathering dust in some central administrator's file? Educators who engage in reflective ethical inquiry challenge this moral–ethical numbness. In paradigmatic terms, they strive, to the best of their ability, to be exemplars of the democratic good life. They readily embrace Pinar's (2004) challenge to create "a public sphere, a public sphere not yet born, a future that cannot be discerned in, or even thought from, the present. So conceived, the classroom becomes simultaneously a civic square and a room of one's own" (pp. 37–38).

Reflective Ethical Inquiry Questions to Ponder

- Am I functioning as a public educator, as a public intellect?
- Am I careful not to function primarily in the dominant paradigm?
- Is what I am doing enhancing the quality of life or the quality of learning for the group or individual?
- What evidence is there that demonstrates I am working in the standardized management paradigm, the constructivist best practice paradigm, and the curriculum wisdom paradigm?
- How am I going about reconceptualizing the problem to work in the curriculum wisdom paradigm?
- What are my biases?

Reflective Politial Inquiry

Reflective political inquiry considers the negotiation of power across the standardized management, constructivist best practice, and wisdom paradigms. This inquiry examines local political realities and how they can be negotiated in ways that are consistent with democratic ideals. Reflective political inquiry is attuned to the fact that people think in different ways. Walker (2003) notes, "[b]ecause the struggle to shape curriculum is a struggle over our cultural identity, the public will never turn it over entirely to professionals. . . . [C]urriculum issues are inherently political, and so people will always fight about them" (p. 19). For this reason, reflective political inquiry is an essential mode of questioning in curriculum wisdom problem solving. Through this inquiry, educators find ways to foster reciprocal dialogue among members of the "community" in a context of respecting diverse perspectives and opinions.

According to Freire (1987), all forms of schooling are political, even if teachers are not consciously aware of this aspect of their work. Decisions about curriculum, about teaching and who teaches, and about standardized tests are all political. Teachers must consider the political power relations in their classrooms, schools, and communities. Shor (1993) writes:

> Education is politics because it is one place where individuals and society are constructed. Because human beings and their society are developed in one direction or another through education, the learning process cannot avoid being political. (p. 28)

Working with Freire's ideas, Bartolome (1995) describes the importance of teachers' political awareness in their classrooms as *political clarity:*

> Political clarity refers to the process by which individuals achieve a deepening awareness of the sociopolitical and economic realities that shape their lives and their capacity to recreate them. In addition, it refers to the process by which individuals come to better understand possible linkages between macro-level political economic and social variables and subordinate groups' academic performances at the micro-level classroom. It requires links between sociocultural structures and schooling. (p. 43)

When educators engage in reflective political inquiry, they recognize the importance of negotiating across differences and even allowing for collective dissent. They understand that politics is the art of the possible. They value civility, but not at the price of forcing a false consensus. They acknowledge the potential "wisdom of the crowds," as summarized by Surowiecki (2005):

> Diversity and independence are important because the best collective decisions are the product of disagreement and contest, not consensus or compromise. An intelligent group, especially when confronted with cognition problems, does not ask its members to modify their positions in order to let the group reach a decision everyone can be happy with. Instead, it figures out how to use mechanisms . . . to aggregate and produce collective judgments that represent not what any one person in the group thinks but rather, in some sense, what they all think. Paradoxically, the best way for a group to be smart is for each person in it to think and act as independently as possible. (pp. xix–xx)

Surowiecki precisely captures the spirit of reflective political inquiry in the context of democratic curriculum wisdom problem solving. It is an attunement to the synergistic interplay of diverse voices. It is the search for ways to achieve truth through a contest of perspectives from a "power with" (Kreisberg, 1992) frame of reference.

Reflective Political Inquiry Questions to Ponder

- How do I negotiate with people working out of different orientations?

- How do I involve students in curriculum decision making?

- How do I provide an environment that encourages openness, exploration, and the freedom to ask?

- How do I provide an atmosphere where people can grow together through collaborative problem solving?

- In what ways do I examine why things are the way they are and how they could be?

- In what ways have I included the voices of the stakeholders in the broader "community"?

- Am I ready to welcome constructive criticism as a way to grow? Do I view suggestions as a threat or a motivator?

- Do I encourage productive dissent?

Other Reflective Inquiries

We conclude this scaffolding of reflective inquiry in curriculum wisdom problem solving by acknowledging that you may identify other relevant questions, explorations, or investigations. In the spirit of open-minded and open-hearted inquiry (Dewey, 1910/1997), we invite your creative input into the map we have constructed:

- What other relevant explorations and investigations might guide my inquiry into 3S education?

- What other relevant explorations and investigations might inform the facilitation of my students' 3S holistic, constructivist learning?

- What other relevant explorations and investigations might inform my designing, planning, evaluating, and organizing decisions?

- What other relevant explorations and investigations might inform my transformative curriculum leadership work with other professionals and with local stakeholder groups?

- What other relevant explorations and investigations might inform my emergent currere understanding and narratives?

The reflective inquiry map is designed to cultivate your understanding of democratic education. Certainly, you cannot teach for 3S understanding without cultivating your own 3S understanding in the context of your day-to-day curriculum problem solving.

The marriage of reflective practice and democratic curriculum inquiry is developmentally challenging but not impossible. We hope you will be one of the educators who is willing to take on this exciting professional challenge. If you are, we commend your strong commitment to your continuing education. Without your efforts to facilitate your students' deep understanding, there is little hope that we will become a deep democracy.

A VIEW OF THE THREE PARADIGMS

We have created a view of the standardized management, constructivist best practice, and curriculum wisdom paradigms to further clarify the vital importance of reflective inquiry in curriculum wisdom problem solving. Take a look at Figure 3.1. It provides a way to understand the qualitative shifts among the three curriculum problem solving orientations.

In the standardized management (SM) paradigm (top of Figure 3.1), the received standards from state mandates and/or other sources serve as the curriculum problem solving organizer. The curriculum decision making (CDM) is generally limited to planning and teaching deliberations. In this paradigm, educators' actions and experiences are aligned with policy mandates. The cultivation of currere understanding, that is, the self-understanding of the democratic educator, is unnecessary and may, in fact, be a distraction or even detrimental to this other-directed problem solving cycle. The actions may not be based on personal experiences but, rather, on top-down directives. There is an equally limited reflective practice; if reflective inquiry exists at all, it is constrained, spotty at best, and not well integrated into the educators' decision-making processes. The reflective inquiries are depicted as faint and shadowy.

In the constructivist best practice (CBP) paradigm (middle of Figure 3.1), performances of subject matter understanding serve as the organizer for the curriculum problem solving. Systemic curriculum decision making (CDM) extends beyond planning and teaching to include designing, evaluating, and organizing deliberations. Constructivist educators' actions are necessarily based on transactional experiences with their students because teaching for understanding requires constant fine tuning. Though the currere understanding of the democratic educator has not yet emerged, a certain degree of self-insight has been generated through educators' personal subject matter meaning making. Though comprehensive reflective inquiry is not yet practiced, there is an integration of reflection in subject matter disciplines. There is reflective disciplinary inquiry, but the other reflective inquiries are not consciously practiced.

In the curriculum wisdom (CW) paradigm (bottom of Figure 3.1), performances of subject matter understanding embedded in democratic self and social understanding serve as the organizer for the curriculum problem solving. Similar to the CBP paradigm, but missing in the SM paradigm, systemic curriculum decision making (CDM) includes designing, planning, teaching, evaluating, and organizing; in this case, however, the decision making is grounded in rigorous deliberation. Acting and experiencing are deeply interconnected in the context of the personal, interpersonal, and social nuances of 3S educational work. A robust currere understanding, modeled by Rosie Gornik in this book, begins to emerge. Efforts are made to enact a comprehensive, multimodal reflective inquiry in the spirit of this chapter's map or scaffolding. As a result, all six reflective inquiries, plus the open category of other inquiries, are highlighted.

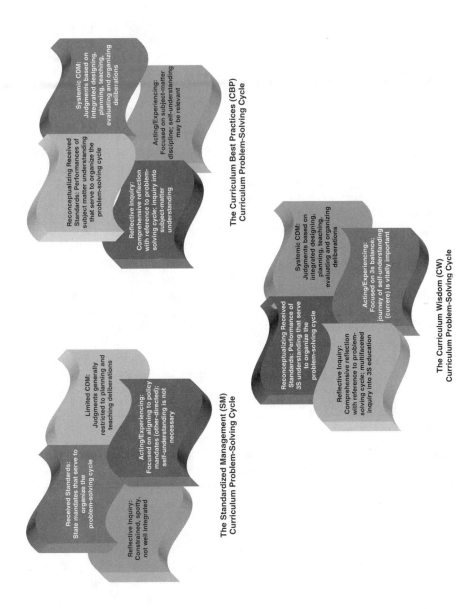

Figure 3.1 Curriculum Problem-Solving Orientations

An Imagined Personal Account of Practicing Reflective Inquiry

The Giver by Lowry (1993) is a magnificent story that introduces the reader to a unique world with unsettling echoes of our own. The story evokes penetrating questions about how we live together in a society. What must we give up, for example, in order to live in peace? How much should the individual lose of himself or herself for the collective good? Can we ignore and minimize physical and emotional pain in our lives to live happier existences? These ideas, combined with an ending that can be interpreted in at least two ways, can lead to a classroom experience that challenges, provokes, and perhaps disturbs.

As I engage in reflective inquiry about this curriculum project, I am faced with a number of important planning, teaching, and evaluating decisions. Because I am framing this curriculum "problem" out of the wisdom paradigm, the problem-solving cycle I use to make these decisions will have specific features associated with the facilitation of a particular 3S understanding. I know that in any problem solving, there is a fairly predictable cycle of discovery, which includes setting goals, deciding how to act, experiencing the consequences of specific actions, reflecting on these consequences, and revisiting and, if necessary, resetting goals. Problem solving for the wisdom paradigm, however, requires reflective inquiry as a key feature. Reflective inquiry is necessary because I know at the outset that I want to integrate the subject matter learning into democratic self and social learning. As I plan, teach, and evaluate using *The Giver* as my curriculum resource, I want to be sure to consider what my students will learn about the possibilities of a freedom-loving society, and the quality of human life realized through a holistic, disciplined, and personalized journey of understanding. I want to give my students active meaning making experiences that cultivate a personal responsibility for lifelong learning, a generosity for diverse others, and a commitment to fair play and social justice.

If these are my goals, how will I proceed? The last time I taught using this book I took the safe way out. I followed the received standard and interpreted it literally through the standardized management paradigm.

Received Standard

Write responses to novels, stories, poems, and plays that provide an interpretation, a critique, or a reflection and support judgments with specific references to the text.[3]

I was worried about some of the underlying concepts in the book. I did not want to address personal and societal issues I felt unable to handle. As we have said, teachers who facilitate their students' journeys of understanding must cultivate their own journey of understanding. At the close of the unit, I felt disappointed in myself. I lost the chance to explore how an ordinary experience can become a profound event. The opportunity to help my students grow and mature as they grappled with the social and moral issues presented in the story was gone. I knew I had missed teachable moments when a student's aged pet had to be "put down" because of intense pain while his elderly grandma lived in

[3] *Source:* Ohio Department of Education. (2002). *Ohio Academic Content Standards K–12 English Language Arts.* Columbus, OH: Author.

a vegetative state in a nursing home. What kind of discussion would have ensued if I had been ready to discuss his question: "My mom wants to know why we put dogs to sleep when they are suffering, and we are not allowed to do that for people."

Full of resolve to make a more sophisticated judgment the next time; judgments that addressed fundamental changes at the personal, interpersonal, and societal levels, I reset my goals. I felt a tremendous responsibility to my students and therefore needed to embrace the responsibility of my own depth of understanding of the structures of the subject matter. As a result, I read everything I could about the subject (disciplinary inquiry) including euthanasia (ethical inquiry), diversity (multiperspective inquiry), and utopian communities (critical political inquiries). I studied the Shakers in the 18th century and the Fruitlands, led by the father of Louisa May Alcott, Bronson, in the mid-19th century. I wondered about the principles that guided these communities and the assumptions behind those principles. I studied the Amish, Native American tribes, and Hasidic Jewish communities to learn more about groups that seek to maintain an identity outside the mainstream culture. I needed to be able and ready to discuss my own habits and deeply embedded beliefs (critical inquiry). I embraced Pinar's (2004) notion that "study is the site of education. Not instruction, not learning, but study constitutes the process of education . . ." (p. 70). I would explore the importance of "memory," the relationship between pain and pleasure.

I sought the guidance of the teachers on my team who had taught using this book. We discussed many of these ideas and the "best" way to problem solve this issue and attempted to anticipate the consequences of my approach. We would share currere narratives about *The Giver,* knowing that collaborative, collegial dialogue that reflected on problems and worked toward solutions provided the catalyst for improved goals for student learning. This work is ultimately very pragmatic, and the pragmatist looks to consequences that we endlessly bump up against. We respond to and live with outcomes every day as a result of our actions and those of others. Pragmatists anticipate outcomes, and that is what I needed to do. I learned so much from my colleagues about what to do and in some cases, what not to do. I let the parents know that we would be reading this book, and I provided information about the topics we would be discussing. I explained how this work relates to their child's growth and development as a human being in a democratic society. I attempted to make them aware that a society with democratic ideals must find practical ways to actively engage students in making sense of those ideals.

Most importantly, I reconceptualized the received standard in a manner that enabled the students to write responses to a novel that provide an interpretation, a critique, or a reflection and support judgments, and the impact on self (student) and the broader community in which she or he lives.

With this reconceptualized standard, I would follow Gardner's (2000) advice on how to cultivate my students' disciplinary subject matter learning: (1) multiple entry

---

Reconceptualized Standard

Write responses to a novel and provide an interpretation, a critique, or a reflection, support your judgments with the class readings and other related readings, and include in your responses the impact on self (you) and your community.

points to rich topics such as vivid and dramatic narratives, timelines of events, logical "if/then" scenarios, existential invitations (raising deep questions about existence), aesthetic examinations of works of art, hands-on projects (working with materials), field-trip experiences, and cooperative peer learning activities; (2) powerful analogies and metaphors; and (3) multiple representations of core ideas through the use of multiple intelligences (spatial, kinesthetic, interpersonal, linguistic, rhythmic, naturalist, intrapersonal, and mathematical).

I would seek to have my students learn about the possibilities of a freedom-loving society and the quality of human life realized through a holistic, disciplined, and personalized journey of understanding. I want to give my students active meaning-making experiences that cultivate a personal responsibility for lifelong learning, a generosity for diverse others, and a commitment to fair play and social justice with a deepening awareness of the sociopolitical and economic realities that shape their lives and their capacity to re-create them . . . even as seventh graders. These systemic planning, teaching, evaluating, and organizing *decisions* would be the result of my wisdom problem-solving cycle, which includes reconceptualizing received standards, acting based on a focused 3S balance, and reflective inquiry.

Comparing the Three Paradigms Through Contrasting Questions

Table 3.2 offers insights into the power of the curriculum wisdom paradigm, by contrasting illustrative questions associated with that problem-solving orientation with illustrative questions associated with the standardized management and constructivist best practice orientations. You will notice questions generated out of the curriculum and teaching deliberations just described.

With reference to the Ohio state standard, students will be required to support their responses with examples from the text. With reference to the constructivist standard, students will be asked to demonstrate subject matter understanding through specific, idiosyncratic performances; with reference to the wisdom standard, students will be asked to demonstrate subject matter understanding embedded in democratic self and social understanding. As you can see, judgment criteria becomes increasingly subtle and sophisticated across the three paradigms.

Furthermore, while working through the Table 3.2 questions, I will consider how to provide opportunities for students to:

1. Employ knowledge effectively in diverse, authentic, and realistically messy contexts.

2. Reveal a personalized, thoughtful, and coherent grasp of subjects, demonstrating the ability to think for themselves.

3. Remain wide awake, willing to welcome new insights, and refine core beliefs through conversations with diverse others.

4. Demonstrate the ability to effectively and sensitively interpret texts and the ability to read between the lines.

5. Extend or apply what is known in novel ways to become more cognitively, emotionally, physically, aesthetically, and spiritually attuned to themselves and others.

Table 3.2 THE POWER OF THE CURRICULUM WISDOM PARADIGM

Reflective Inquiry	Received Standard?	Constructivist Standard?	Curriculum Wisdom Standard?
Disciplinary	What are the names of the ceremonies that Jonas experiences as he progresses through his young life and what are the specific "qualities" of each ceremony?	What is the significance of each of the ceremonies that Jonas experiences throughout his young life and what impact do they each have on Jonas?	How do these ceremonies affect Jonas, his family, and the broader community? Why would you or would you not want to become a member of this community?
Poetic	What role does each member of Jonas's family have in the community?	What is the significance of each of the roles within the community? What role would you prefer if you were a member of this community? Why is this so?	What is the role of community in the 21st century? What roles do you, your family members, your friends have in the communities in which you live?
Critical	What are the rules Jonas's community must live by? What happens if they do not carefully, closely abide by the rules?	How would you describe the community in which Jonas and his family live? How is it similar/different from the one in which you live?	How would you describe the social interactions, the economic circumstances, and political relations among the members of this community? Where does Jonas fit into these dynamics? How would you fit into these dynamics?
Multiperspective	What happens to make Jonas curious about the changes in his surroundings? What does he notice is beginning to occur daily? What does he realize his friends and family are missing out on? Who else knows what is going on and why this is happening to Jonas?	What influence does color have on our world?	What would happen if we suddenly lived in a world without color? Once you consider this question yourself, ask a few of your friends or family members this question and examine how your responses are similar and different.

(Continued)

Table 3.2 (Continued)			
Reflective Inquiry	**Received Standard?**	**Constructivist Standard?**	**Curriculum Wisdom Standard?**
Ethical	Once Jonas learns what is happening around him, how does he react?	How would you react to being "chosen" to live in a world that is completely different from the one you know well?	What advice would you give Jonas as he considers what he should do regarding his future? What impact will his decisions and actions have on his family and on the broader community?
Political	Who is ultimately responsible for the coming together and disassembling of the community? What happens to this person?	You have called together members of the community for a meeting to share what you have learned, what might you anticipate their reactions to be? What will be your next steps?	Although we might agree that this is a very civil community, because all rules must be followed, how are issues related to equity and diversity addressed? If they were addressed in our society in manner in which they were addressed in *The Giver*, what might be some possible outcomes?
Other			

As I practice my personalized reflective inquiry, I realize that I am pushing against my own developmental readiness. The integration of reflective practice with democratic curriculum inquiry is quite challenging, and there are moments when I experience an internal dissonance. So many questions! So much tolerance for ambiguity! So much required sensitivity to nuance and shades of gray! So much attention to holistic complexities! So much constant deliberation! There are times when I feel my head will explode. Am I really capable of such inquiry openness? Do I really want to be on a journey of understanding? Why don't I just settle for the habitual and the customary? What's wrong with buying into ideological scripts? What's wrong with just memorizing my lines and functioning as a true believer? What's wrong with a little mental laziness? Who needs personal voice or the complexities associated with the interplay of diverse voices? Maybe I just want to be a "regular" person who comfortably fits into the crowd. Maybe I don't want to think and feel for myself any more. Do I really want to heed my calling to work as a committed democratic educator? But if I don't heed this calling, what are the personal consequences? How

Walker, D. F. (2003). *Fundamentals of curriculum: Passion and professionalism* (2nd ed.). Mahwah, NJ: Lawrence Erlbaum Associates.

Wiggins, G., & McTighe, J. (2001). *Understanding by design.* (Special ed.). Upper Saddle River, NJ: Merrill/Prentice Hall.

SECTION II

FOUR INTERRELATED DECISION-MAKING PROCESSES

We introduce four interrelated curriculum decision-making processes in this section. Wisdom-oriented educators deliberate over the basic designs or blueprints of their teaching-learning programs. They don't unthinkingly follow the publisher's guidelines for a particular curriculum package or textbook. Instead, they develop a rationale, what we will call a curriculum platform, for appropriate educational programming and then translate this rationale into specific program, course, and unit/lesson level plans. Though there may be a separation of designing and planning decisions in the dominant standardized management paradigm, constructivist best practice and curriculum wisdom decision making cannot be conducted in this way. It's not possible to teach for understanding, whether focused only on subject matter learning or more holistically focused on subject matter learning integrated with democratic self and social learning, without integrating designing and planning. For this reason, we treat designing and planning as one organic decision-making process; this process will be our focus in chapter 4.

Ultimately, designing/planning decisions must be incorporated into artful teaching decisions; otherwise, the curriculum and teaching deliberations are disconnected. This discontinuity, which can frequently occur in a standardized management work, has no place in curriculum wisdom problem solving. Teaching for democratic self and social understanding in the context of facilitating subject matter understanding requires a curriculum-based teaching. As we point out in the book's introductory chapter, *3S education* is a complicated curriculum *and* teaching goal. Our focus in chapter 5 is on the moment-to-moment teaching decisions that result from the enactment of 3S designing/planning.

Making decisions on how to evaluate educational practices is a complex topic, particularly in the context of 3S education. Because wisdom educators are so heavily invested in designing/planning and teaching decisions, they have much to evaluate. They must make value judgments on the quality of their work in all aspects of the problem-solving cycle, including the conceptualization of the 3S standards, the systemic decision making, the emergent currere understanding, and the cultivation of reflective inquiry. This comprehensive approach to evaluation will be the focus of chapter 6; as we introduce this decision-making process, we will note that it is quite different from the more fragmented, disconnected evaluations that are generally part of the standardized management paradigm.

Finally, though wisdom educators may find some "wiggle room" in their workday to engage in the designing/planning, teaching, and evaluating decision-making processes introduced in chapters 4–6, they will most likely feel that their judgments are quite constrained by the dominant paradigm. Therefore, it is natural for them to begin to think about how they might organize their workday and their work year to better support their transformative curriculum leadership efforts. What daily and yearly work structures must they address, and how should they proceed? We will offer recommendations on how to deliberate over such questions in chapter 7.

As you read the four chapters in this section, you will notice the interrelated nature of all the four decision-making processes. We are advancing a particular ecological approach to curriculum-based teaching. You will also notice how the two fundamental challenges in section I are deeply embedded in each process, and each chapter in this section begins with the star image that we introduced in chapter 1 to remind you of these complex interactions. We want to constantly remind you that the work of transformative curriculum leadership involves complex problem solving and deliberative decision making in chapters 4 through 7 there is only one component of that problem solving. Without a commitment to this comprehensive deliberation, there is no elevated judgment.

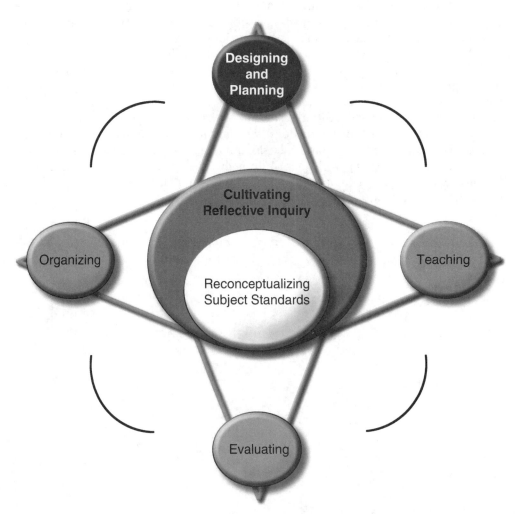

Sustaining the Curriculum Wisdom Problem Solving

CHAPTER 4

DESIGNING AND PLANNING FOR 3S EDUCATION

What children study and learn in school makes a difference in their lives. Curriculum improvement offers an opportunity to enhance the lives of many thousands of students. As a result of learning different things they will develop different abilities and interests, commit to different values, pursue different careers and live different lives. Their very identity will be shaped by what they study . . . the curriculum also shapes the Americans' identity as a people.

(Walker, 2003, p. 13)

Now that you have been introduced to two fundamental challenges of this work (reconceptualizing "received" standards and cultivating reflective inquiry), take a deep and cleansing breath. We encourage you to allow yourself to be challenged by what you are reading. Pinar et al. (1995) remind us:

> *The educational possibility for curriculum theory is to help you reflect more profoundly, and not without humor on occasion, on your individual, specific situation.* Be patient with material that is difficult to grasp; be patient with yourself. Tolerate material that seems irrelevant or just "way out." You are not obligated to agree with what you read, or, for that matter, to remember it. You *are* obligated as an educator to consider material, which you may not like immediately, and to formulate some response, however negative. Your obligation is to reflect in your own situation, to formulate language to describe and understand the situation more carefully, more precisely, more fully. (p. 9; emphasis in original).

That said, we hope you feel fortified with new information and skills learned in chapters 2 and 3. Now we will integrate those skills in service of our work with the four decision-making processes, which comprise this section of the book. In this chapter we will deal specifically with *designing and planning* for students' 3S understanding. What is a design and how does it relate to a plan? We borrow a metaphor used in this text's second edition, by James Henderson and Richard Hawthorne (2000), to provide insight.

DESIGNING AND PLANNING

A design provides an image of what is to be developed, much like an architect gives clients a drawing of the house to be built. Typically, an architect interviews clients to learn what they mean by a comfortable and functional home. For example, what kinds of activities will take place in the house: formal parties for adults or informal gatherings for small children? What kinds of space do the clients prefer: open, flowing spaces, clearly defined spaces for specific functions, spaces integrated with external surroundings? What aesthetic qualities do clients want to enjoy? In both curriculum and architectural design, questions concern an evolving vision of the life to be lived, the defining features of the program or house, an overall structure connecting spaces yet allowing for flow, and a set of technical and aesthetic expectations (standards).

Just as an architectural design guides the development of house plans for a client and guides contractors as they build a house, a curriculum design guides teachers' and students' classroom curriculum planning. Curriculum planning ranges from deciding what will happen in the classroom tomorrow through a lesson plan, to developing a four-week integrated unit with other teachers, to planning a course, which might last a semester or year, to planning a full program, under which many courses may exist.

To that end, the designing and planning decisions you make will affect four interrelated levels of specificity: *platform* designing; *program* planning; *course* planning; *unit/lesson* planning. The planning decisions for program, course, and unit/lesson will be guided by aims, criteria, assumptions, principles, key ideas, and shared beliefs outlined in what is called a *curriculum visionary platform design.* At the level of platform, designing is the primary activity. The platform design becomes pivotal because it informs all the planning for program, course, and unit/lesson. The aim of this chapter is to help you begin to design a visionary platform, which serves as a decision-making tool in support of planning for students' 3S understanding. Your judgments for all four designing and planning levels will be deliberated within a supportive learning community and shaped through personalized, ongoing reflective inquiry using the seven reflective inquiries as you proceed on your journey of understanding. Walker (2003) states that a principled approach to curriculum improvement is practical reasoning. "In practical reasoning, decision-makers consider what action, if any, is best for this situation all things considered" (p. 214). Consideration of possible actions is called deliberation, and it is the core of practical reasoning. As decision makers, we must strive for the best informed and most thoroughly considered decision, taking into account all the most promising alternatives in light of the best available knowledge. When we engage in deliberations, we pay attention to our working assumptions, the consequences of our actions, and our continuing inquiry into democratic education. The challenge is to engage in deliberative decision making. We now carry this challenge forward into the context of designing and planning decisions.

GENERAL FEATURES OF DESIGNING AND PLANNING DELIBERATIONS

Both designing and planning are deliberative. Good deliberation is an art, takes time and resources, and is an important first step in decision making. Gail McCutcheon (1999) defines deliberation as a process of socially constructing knowledge about the curriculum to solve practical problems (p. 36). Walker (2003) notes the following features of curriculum deliberation:

1. The deliberating body's purpose is to agree on a course of action they will take on as curricular problem.

2. Discussion centers on particular courses of action not general principles, ideas, or theories.

3. The group insists on principled reasons for choosing one course of action over another.

4. In evaluating a possible course of action, the group weighs competing considerations of very different orders drawn from different realms of discourse.

5. The group considers the issue resolved when they find a course of action that will resolve their problem better than other actions that they have considered. (pp. 219–220)

A Deliberative Ideal

Reaching a sound resolution to practical problems is artful, indeed. Walker (2003) reminds us that ideally, good deliberations will lead to a better course of action relative to certain values and beliefs. An ideal deliberative body must:

1. construe the problem in the most defensible way;

2. consider all the most promising alternative courses of action;

3. consider in full the merits of each alternative, taking into account all relevant knowledge and using valid arguments to examine the bearing of this knowledge on the issue;

4. include the points of view and values of all interested parties to the decision; and

5. reach a fair and balanced judgment. (p. 235)

Curriculum deliberations will always fall short of this ideal because to reach it, participants would need complete knowledge and perfect justice. Because this is unlikely, Walker (2003) suggests that deliberative bodies collaborate, build a sound platform based on research theory and experience, study examples closely, be constructively self-critical, consult experts, make artful use of knowledge through argumentation, manage conflicts of belief and value, and consider alternative points of view as well as the context. Building on this ideal, deliberations for transformative curriculum leadership are guided by a love of wisdom, which will result in elevated judgments grounded in moral insights essential to facilitating a student's 3S journey of understanding.

A Deliberative Ideal for Elevated Judgments

Recognizing the challenges inherent in any deliberative effort, we offer some practical guidance for your reflective inquiries. In order to be better positioned to make practical decisions guided by of a love of wisdom and oriented toward the expansion of deep democracy (Henderson & Kesson, 2004), we encourage you to integrate Walker's (2003) deliberative ideal with the reflective inquiry questioning from chapter 3. By integrating reflective inquiry questioning with Walker's deliberative ideal, you will know as an individual or a group that you have elevated your judgments in all your decision making.

THE INTERPLAY OF DESIGNING AND PLANNING

Designing and planning are intimately related. The curriculum platform design conveys the overall direction and priorities of the program, course, and unit/lessons. Key to the relationship of designing and planning is the role of students. "The platform design constructed by a group of community members and professional educators provides a vision of the curriculum to be planned and experienced" (Henderson & Hawthorne, 2000, p. 82). With this vision in mind, teachers engage in practical problem solving about who is going to do what, how they will do it, and when and where (Walker, 1971). You can imagine the differences in the vision and the subsequent problem solving depending upon the paradigm in which you are situated. Educators designing and planning out of the dominant management paradigm will most likely focus on the problem of standardized test performances enforced by state accountability mandates, envisioning, for example, an environment that is designed for students to pass all standardized tests. Educators designing and planning out of the constructivist best practice paradigm will most likely focus on the problem of performances of subject matter understanding informed by traditions of disciplinary knowing, envisioning an environment that is designed to treat students as active meaning makers demonstrating public and idiosyncratic demonstrations of that meaning.

Throughout the remainder of this chapter, we will give you advice on designing and planning out of the wisdom paradigm. This problem solving is disciplined by an artful deliberation in which students and educators are called upon to exercise ever more sophisticated forms of intelligence, and within which currere narrative stories are told so students and teachers will consider the following question: "What does curriculum have to do with my life?" "Just as the platform design is intended to influence curriculum planning by teachers and their students, the context and lives of students and teachers, in turn, influence design work" (Henderson & Hawthorne, 2000, p. 83). In transformative curriculum work, students are informed about key aspects of the platform design and when it is developmentally appropriate, they are directly involved in translating the platform design into specific plans and enactments in their classroom contexts.

To grasp the relationship between platform designing and program, course, and unit/lesson planning, an apt visual is to imagine the relationship between each sculpted figure in the Russian matryoshka nesting doll; each is intimately related to the others. The one after houses the one before in every increasing size (scope). Deliberations begin with the platform design, and all planning decisions about program, course, and unit/lesson are related. Decisions made and problems solved at the unit/lesson level, for example, cannot be made in isolation from course, program, and platform goals. Figure 4.1 is another representation of this process. This image locates unit/lesson planning at the center of all the other planning. The essential work of teachers and students (unit/lesson planning and enactments) encompasses all course and program planning, as well as the

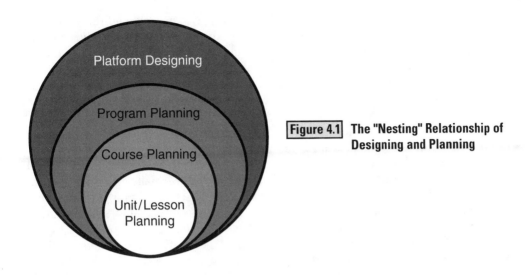

Platform Designing

Program Planning

Course Planning

Unit/Lesson Planning

Figure 4.1 The "Nesting" Relationship of Designing and Planning

spirit of the platform design. Designing and planning are an educator's occupational tools. Let's look more closely at each of these four designing and planning levels for guidance on how to make informed judgments grounded in moral insight and oriented toward the expansion of deep democracy (Henderson & Kesson, 2004).

Platform Designing: Who, What, Why, How

A district or school's curriculum leadership committee engages in deliberations for designing a *platform*. This committee is typically made up of teachers, parents, community members, central office colleagues, students (when appropriate), and university colleagues (if available). The key purpose for involving faculty members in the platform design work is to create common ground for curriculum planning and enactment. The size of the committee will vary depending upon the size of the school/district and the scope and diversity of the people to be represented. This platform, while not prescriptive, becomes a public, common referent for teachers, classrooms, parents, and the community. It coherently states aims, basic assumptions, and the forms of teaching and learning. The intent of this broad representation of voices is to open entrenched interests and controls over the curriculum and related matters so that the committee can deliberate on all the important issues. We must remember that the members of this committee are equal. The university professor is not necessarily the expert and the teacher, the client. These relationships are more collaborative. Pinar et al. (1995) point out that contemplation must not be reserved for the privileged.

A platform is a set of key shared understandings and ideas explicitly written by a deliberative body to guide those deliberations (Walker, 2003). "This set of ideas constitutes a platform that expresses [their] shared beliefs and values and guides [their] deliberations in the same way that a political platform can guide party members in deciding on what political initiatives to support" (p. 237). The platform consists of the aims and assumptions about the teaching–learning relationship and principles that direct and justify program, course, and unit/lesson planning. The platform design should affirm what is centrally important and stimulate teaching artistry, and therefore matters of policy will also need to be considered. In the United States, curriculum policy is controlled at the national, state, district, school, and classroom levels (Walker, 2003). The platform designing committee members must have a full understanding of the implications of these policies as they proceed with their deliberations. Unless the committee is destined to engage in advocacy for change at the national and state levels, the members will need to know and comply with the legal, policy "nonnegotiables" in order to conduct their deliberations.

It is here, however, that transformative curriculum leaders can use policy statements to their strategic advantage. In this country, most state and local policy manuals extol the virtues of democracy. Our research has proven that virtually every state and district in the United States makes some reference to "students contributing to and participating in a democracy or democratic society," yet most if not all states and districts do not express democratic virtues in everyday work with children and teachers. We wonder why we use the mission statements that declare public education to be a democratically inspired institution, and then drop it when we teach. We are freedom loving, but we do not apply this in the classroom. Because policy symbolizes and expresses cultural values, we suggest that transformative curriculum leaders use the policy statements, which refer to these democratic values and include these virtues in their platform design.

The district platform designing committee will influence such things as the philosophy, curricular aims, and assumptions about the teaching–learning relationship. The platform designing committee might discuss the conceptual vision, including the description of possible scenarios about how students will be treated and how teachers and parents will be supported. There is much to be considered, because ostensibly this platform design committee will attempt to capture curricular problem solving from the perspective of the democratic "good" life. They will attempt to define the quality of life within the district, schools, and classrooms. Henderson and Kesson (2004) remind us that democracy is an interpretive term. Because it has many meanings that are not anchored in any specific moral doctrine, the decision-making process must necessarily be multifaceted. They suggest 5Cs of wise curriculum judgments: collaboration (there is too much for one person to know and consider, and everyone has a voice), caring (practicing an ethic of care), character (soul-searching honesty), challenge (disciplined life of inquiry; embracing ambiguity; wisdom is fragile, even fleeting), and calling (what may have begun as ordinary is now inspired) (p. 12–15). The platform design then might outline these characteristics so that the program, course, and unit/lesson planning committee will consider these 5Cs in all their decisions.

We concede that while many national and state policies such as No Child Left Behind and each state's standard curricula are in a standardized management lockdown, we believe that there is a fair amount of "wiggle room" (Cuban, 2003, p. 35) within which to work. In spite of the "nonnegotiables," the platform designing committee can make significant improvements by reframing the problems from "How do we get kids to pass the tests?" to "How do we get kids to pass the tests *and* how do we help teachers elevate their curriculum judgments to include moral decisions that touch the core of what it means to be human, to live in community with others, to find meaning and purpose, and to create a more just and peaceful world?" (Henderson & Kesson, 2004, p. 45). This is a critical point in the platform design and the aims, assumptions, shared beliefs, and values, such as the 5Cs, will have a tremendous influence over the quality of life for people in the district, schools, and classroom.

Integrating the seven reflective inquiries, the committee might grapple with the questions "Why do we exist?" and "What do we hope to become?" (DuFour, 1998, p. 62). The first question challenges members to reflect on the essential purpose of public school and the reason for its existence. The focus is not on what the group can do better, but rather on what and why it is doing it in the first place. Reflecting on the second question will give committee members a sense of direction or a kind of blueprint for an evolving vision. More importantly, as stated above, this platform then serves as a decision-making tool that supports students' 3S understanding. Making this platform explicit is very important to this work. Sergiovanni and Starrat (2001) state, "unless teachers . . . uncover their platform, they will not establish a base of mutual understanding that is necessary to ground their collaborative effort" (p. 70). Platform statements are shared with all stakeholders and serve as a public frame of reference for teachers' and students' program, course, and unit/lesson planning.

The purpose of platform deliberations is to formulate the site-specific educational platform, which sets forth the central beliefs, understandings of what is, and the vision of what ought to be in the curriculum development process (Macdonald & Purpel, 1987; Walker, 1971). If teaching is a moral undertaking, it can be judged by "how we make ethical choices in situations that provoke deliberation and that culminate in a value judgment" (Cuffaro, 1995, p. 53). Through platform deliberations an overall design is set for more specific planning. These deliberations are essential because it is through deliberating that we make informed and wise curriculum judgments, as opposed to decisions by default based on habit or custom. Making wise judgments about curricular issues is an important aspect of professional growth. Dewey (1934) reminds us "a judgment as an act of controlled inquiry demands a rich background and a disciplined insight" (p. 300). In addition, the platform is then used to inform the community, board of education, and all stakeholders what is worth learning and what teaching approaches are congruent with that learning.

As the committee members begin their platform deliberations, they engage in seven parallel activities using the reflective inquiry map found in chapter 3 for guidance. Using these questions, the members will be able to refine their general aims of student learning, their central assumptions about the relationship between teaching and learning, and the overall flow of programs, courses, and unit/lesson plans. We build upon the second edition of Henderson and Hawthorne's book (2000) and expand to include the following:

1. They describe and analyze curriculum as it is currently expressed in plans and policies, teachers' thoughts and images, and materials used; as it is enacted and experienced in classrooms; and as it is reflected in student perceptions and learning.

2. They share personal currere narratives about particularly meaningful and exciting curriculum experiences and reflect on recurring assumptions, beliefs, and values about living fully in a democratic society.

3. They analyze projections about the economic, ethical, cultural, political, technological, and interpersonal future of the nations and the region and consider the implications of those projections.

4. They examine received state and national standards and discuss considerations for reconceptualizing those standards to include holistic, understanding goals. These

reconceptualized standards are informed by Greene's (1988) *freedom from . . . freedom to . . . dialectic* and Eisner's *hidden/null curricula* considerations.

5. They consider likely student performances, which are demonstrations of the journey of 3S understanding; outstanding curriculum plans developed by other groups.

6. They analyze judgment criteria for case-by-case assessments of the quality of the students' journeys.

7. They plan and provide leadership in districtwide community forums about the proposed platform and outline procedures for evaluating the quality of their platform design.

Out of these deliberations comes the curriculum design platform that directs and justifies program, course, and unit/lesson planning. "The platform is the soul of the curriculum, clearly showing what kinds of learning are valued and why" (Henderson & Hawthorne, 2000, p. 86). Figure 4.2 illustrates this dynamic process of deliberative questioning for platform designing.

| Figure 4.2 | **3S Deliberative Questioning for Platform Designing**

Hidden Curricula

Critical Reflective Inquiry

Other Reflective Inquiry

Ethical Reflective Inquiry

Shared beliefs, values, aims, and assumptions about the teaching— learning relationship

Freedom from . . .

Freedom to . . .

Multiperspective Reflective Inquiry

Political Reflective Inquiry

Poetic Reflective Inquiry

Null Curricula

As the members deliberate on the importance of the received state and national standards, their potential platform becomes more evident. When people explain why a particular standard, reconceived or not, is essential, they open their beliefs and priorities to scrutiny and debate. "Fundamental differences and commonalities become evident; assumptions about knowledge, democratic values and the essence of being human are shaken, examined reaffirmed, revised and revoked" (Henderson & Hawthorne, 2000, p. 100). As the committee examines futurist projections, it may recognize that many decisions and actions are based on personal assumptions. One assumption, for example, is that in this country by 2017, non-White students will outnumber White students. If a person or community's personal assumption denies this projection, the common curriculum will not include diversity competence. Reconceptualized, holistic, understanding goals and futurist projections are interrelated and the committee should balance these considerations as they deliberate.

The platform, which is usually 8–10 pages in length, is most useful when written in straightforward language that community members and teachers can understand and assumes that both are capable of translating the platform into meaningful classroom experiences based on their own understandings of students. This will include preparation for tomorrow, the next six weeks, or the entire school year. Selection of materials, allocation of time, essential questions, student engagement, and assessment features are all guided by the images, criteria, and possibilities established in the platform design. In all levels of transformative curriculum designing and planning, teachers apply democratic principles and use equity, multiplicity of views, and open-mindedness as moral references in the decision-making process.

The platform designing committee will then host several districtwide and schoolwide faculty, parent, and community sessions in which currere narratives about meaningful learning experiences can be shared. After several people have shared their currere narratives, the facilitator can ask the group to reflect on the stories. What themes, issues, or criteria emerge? What do people seem to argue about? Appointing a recorder, who will keep notes for analysis, is essential. Be certain that all parties at each currere session are aware of and agree to the recorder's activities. Guide Sheet #1 may be used by the committee to collect and analyze currere narrative accounts for the purposes of describing and understanding the real worlds of students and teachers and for elevating the quality of their judgment through deliberative questioning.

Once the radically new curriculum platform has been forged, the members of the committee will find it valuable to bring together the entire faculty, as well as parents and community members to consider the platform and the conceptual vision. These community forums will have several purposes (Henderson & Hawthorne, 2000):

1. To solicit additional ideas about the aims, assumptions, and major structural features of the conceptual vision.

2. To assess how well the platform and the vision convey an image of the design to those not involved in developing them.

3. To deliberate the pros and cons of the platform [design].

4. To build community support for the educational agenda conveyed in the platform [design]

5. To create networks of advocates who can help communicate the platform [design] to others. (p. 103)

3S Deliberative Questioning Platform Designing Guide Sheet #1

Questions to Consider During Platform Deliberations

1. What do our and other currere narratives suggest about knowledge we think is most worth learning? Does this knowledge culminate in a profound order, harmony, or well-being for students and teachers? (Poetic inquiry)

2. What kinds of thinking do we want today's youth to master and use easily as adults? Will this knowledge move our social world toward more equity and social justice? (Critical inquiry)

3. What kind of school/classroom (5Cs) environment keeps students free from limitations, oppression, alienation, and coercion? Does this environment recognize and affirm the rights of people of color, gays, lesbians, women, minority religious groups, and others? (Political inquiry)

4. What kind of school/classroom (5Cs) environment allows students to be free to come together as authentic individuals? Does this environment recognize competing interests? (Ethical inquiry)

5. What did teachers and other adults do when we were children to show that they valued children? Were teachers and students free to express sensitivity to each other's needs? (Multiperspective inquiry)

6. What kinds of experiences did we cite as most meaningful? What made them meaningful? How did these experiences support subject matter knowledge? (Disciplinary inquiry)

7. What metaphors best capture the qualities of the intellectual and interpersonal climates described? What kinds of understandings and capacities will enable a person to live a full, democratic life today and in the future? (Critical inquiry and poetic inquiry)

8. What assumptions about children, learning, knowledge, power, teaching, and caring relationships operated during our discussions? (Political inquiry)

9. What values, attitudes, and assumptions about race, class, gender, ethnicity, and disability are embedded in the hidden or null curricula? (Ethical and multiperspective inquiry)

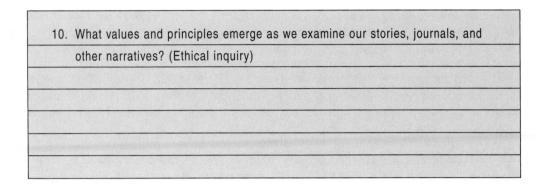

10. What values and principles emerge as we examine our stories, journals, and other narratives? (Ethical inquiry)

The change process is complex, and curriculum platform designing and planning is a sensitive activity in many communities. DuFour (1998) points out that one of the most damaging myths that educators often learn is that the change process, if managed well, will proceed smoothly. Sarason (1995) exposes this myth:

> The decision to undertake change more often than not is accompanied by a kind of optimism and rosy view of the future that, temporarily at least, obscures the predictable turmoil ahead. But that turmoil cannot be avoided and how well it is coped with separates the boys from the men, the girls from the women. It is . . . rough stuff. . . . There are breakthroughs, but also brick walls. (p. vii)

Do not expect a vote of thanks for your efforts; assume that your work will be challenged. Fully embrace the journey, yours and others', and trust in the process. "To be pragmatically wise, one must adopt an approach to decision making and problem solving that recognizes the inherent unpredictability of situations, admits the possibility of error, understands each moment is different from the one preceding it, is carefully attentive to the present circumstances and works to transcend fragmentary thinking" (Henderson & Kesson, 2004, p. 46). We must be aware of the consequences of our actions and not allow the ends to dictate the means. We must be alert to the implications of these consequences for our democratic way of life. We hope you will find some measure of guidance in the inquiry map to assist you on this journey.

Program, Course, and Unit/Lesson Planning

Now let us turn our attention to the task of program, course, and unit/lesson planning. In chapter 2 you tried your hand at constructing a reconceptualized set of standards that holistically balance the disciplinary subject matter standards with democratic self and social understanding. In order to create holistic understanding goals, recall that you considered three interpretations of curriculum standards (not necessarily in this order): (1) your educational goals; (2) the student performances, which will reveal whether the student knows/has grasped or understands the educational goals; and (3) the criteria for judging the quality of the student performance of knowledge or understanding of the educational goals. Recall also, that we are *reframing* the problem from "How do we get kids to pass tests?" to "How do we get kids to pass tests *and* how do we help teachers elevate their curriculum judgments to include moral decisions that touch the core of what it means to be human, to live in community with others, to find meaning and purpose, and to create a more just and peaceful world?" (Henderson & Kesson, 2004, p. 45). Please forgive our repetitions. Our experience has been that the gravitational pull of the dominant paradigm for some is so fierce that reminders and repetitions for reframing the problem are helpful.

The holistic, understanding goals balance subject matter, self, and social goals so that kids will be able to pass the tests *and* find meaning and purpose, as well as to create a more just and peaceful world. These three recursive considerations were illustrated in Figure 2.2 in chapter 2. In this chapter, we extend our curricular planning work to include program, course, and unit/lessons, which will now be based on the reconceptualized, holistic understanding goals. This new set of standards is vitally important because in your planning you will be making practical and thoughtful judgments directed toward subtle matters of goodness. Your programs, courses, and unit/lesson judgments will include the qualitative dimensions of values, justice, aesthetics, and personal meaning coming out of the platform design. Keep in mind that a student's identity will be shaped by what he or she studies (Walker, 2003). Figure 4.3 is a reconfiguration of Figure 2.2 from chapter 2. It now includes the addition of the generative learning experiences.

Remember, under the wisdom paradigm, the *best educational goal* is student demonstration of subject matter understanding that is integrated in personally meaningful democratic self and social understanding. Your program, course, and unit/lesson planning would include the teacher constantly engaged in clarifying what is to be done with and for students in the classroom. The teacher would be "sensitive to the flow of events and to the student's engagement in those events in order to make adjustments and, indeed to invent activities that are appropriate for the students" (Eisner, 2002, p. 152). The new holistic understanding goals would not be considered contracts or prescriptions that override local judgments of the specific planning committees. These holistic understanding goals would exist among many possible interpretations. The role of the teacher would be more emergent rather than prescriptive (Eisner, 2002).

As your planning proceeds, the *best student performance* under the wisdom paradigm would be the demonstration of subject matter understanding through expressive and idiosyncratic performances that are integrated with self and social understandings. The *best criteria for judging* the quality of the performances would be based on a plurality of understandings. The *best generative learning experiences* will include lessons that use discrete subject matter skills and facts to focus on democratic concepts, principles, and processes of the self and the society. Wiggins and McTighe (2005), recommend that daily planning must consider the desired results and the students' targeted performances. We embrace this constructivist best practice notion. Viewed through the lens of the wisdom paradigm however, "desired results" and "targeted performance" are now regarded as expressive performances of holistic enduring subject matter understanding integrated with self and social understanding. Lesson planning would be

Figure 4.3 **3S Visionary Designing and Planning**

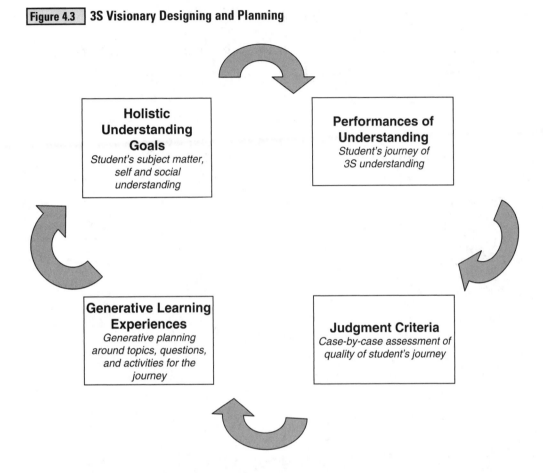

purposefully generative and crafted around topics, questions, and activities for the student's 3S journey of understanding.

Deliberative questioning, with sensitivity to the hidden/null and freedom from/freedom to dynamic, would pervade and guide every program, course, and unit/lesson planning decision. The 3S Visionary Designing and Planning Template has been created to offer guidance for your work. Depending upon the planning level of specificity (program, course, or unit/lesson), your work will focus on one or more parts of the template. However, *every* part of the template will need to be considered for every planning program, course, or unit/lesson decision (Remember the nesting dolls). The template is designed to focus and guide the deliberative questioning to elevate your curriculum designing and planning decisions.

Program Planning: Who, What, Why, How

A subset of the district or school's curriculum leadership committee engages in deliberations for planning a *program*. Sometimes the program is referred to as the curricular framework.

3S Visionary Designing and Planning Template

Reconceptualizing the Received Standards Into Transformative Standards
Student's Subject Matter, Self, and Social Understanding

Received Standards:

Reflective Inquiries: (Remember Freedom from . . . Freedom to Hidden/Null Curriculum Considerations)

Disciplinary Mode:

Poetic Mode:

Critical Mode:

Multiperspective Mode:

Ethical Mode:

Political Mode:

Other Mode(s):

Holistic Subject Matter, Self, and Social Standard:

Expressive Performance
Student's journey of 3S Understanding

Possible Expressive Performances:

Judgment Criteria
Case-by-case assessment of quality of student's journey of 3S understanding

Facets of Understanding:	Rubrics:

Learning Experiences
Generative planning around topics, questions, and activities for the journey

This planning committee will discuss such matters as high school graduation requirements, selection of textbooks, the big ideas, enduring understandings, and essential
questions (Wiggins & McTighe, 1998, 2005) outlined in the received content standards.
The committee will discuss and how these will recur within and throughout the K–12
experience, minimum competencies at each grade, district testing, professional development for teachers, program and course approval, content, organizational structures, time
allotments, and so on. This committee is typically made up of teachers, parents, central office
colleagues, and students (when appropriate). The size of the committee will vary depending
upon the size of the school/district and the scope and diversity of the people to be represented. The program plan will defer to the vision about the teaching–learning relationship
laid out in the platform design, but it will contain more refined conceptual and operational
details. The program planning committee carefully reads and understands the platform
design aims, assumptions, and rationale. The committee then deliberates and organizes
people to conduct seven major tasks:

1. Collect and analyze currere narratives and curriculum maps to understand the
   real classroom worlds of students and teachers.

2. Examine state and national standards and continue the work of the *platform* committee to reconceptualize the received state and national standards into holistic,
   understanding goals, which support the platform. (See 3S Visionary Planning
   Template)

3. Develop a curriculum framework (big ideas, enduring understandings, and essential questions) (Wiggins & McTighe, 1998, 2005), which supports the platform and
   conceptualize courses within the framework, which supports the platform.

4. Determine a conceptual vision for resource allocations, entrance requirements,
   graduation requirements, content, choice of curriculum materials, and organizational structures, which support the platform.

5. Brainstorm likely student performances of understanding, which are demonstrations of the journey of 3S understanding, which support the platform. (See 3S
   Visionary Designing and Planning Template)

6. Brainstorm and analyze judgment criteria for case-by-case assessments of the
   quality of the students' journeys, which support the platform. (See 3S Visionary
   Designing and Planning Template)

7. Plan and provide leadership in schoolwide community forums about the proposed
   program design(s).

A program plan typically covers a full year. The committee is free, however, to imagine other possibilities. Life in schools would be quite different if we reconceptualized the
received content standards and engaged students in experiences that helped them grow personally, *and* academically, over a year or longer. The quality of this growth could be evaluated in a number of ways from expressive student performances of understanding to some
form of measurement on standardized tests, if that was considered to be the wise judgment.

Learning should be the constant and time the variable in all designing and planning. Schools and classrooms would be transformed if our daily, purposeful goal was to develop our students' meaning-making capabilities. Meaning making capabilities would be enhanced by having them join us in the complicated conversations, using the subject matter to tell their own personal stories, thereby composing an identity that defines their personal "good life." In the telling of stories then, we shape the ongoing creation of the world. "Personal stories are not merely a way of telling someone about one's life; they are the means by which identities may be fashioned" (Rosenwald & Ochberg, 1992, p. 1). One of the freedoms we enjoy in our democratic society is the opportunity to pursue personal and fulfilling interests, yet in schools every day we treat kids in ways that foster conformity and uniformity. As Eisner (2002) so nicely states, "the curriculum is a mind-altering device" (p. 148). What might happen if schools were set up to allow students, teachers, and parents to tell their stories? Guide Sheet #2 on the next page will assist a program planning committee with its work.

Course Planning: Who, What, Why, How

Now let us turn our attention to a greater refinement of the program—planning for a specific *course*. A subset of the district or school's curriculum leadership committee engages in deliberations for planning a course. The course design will hold elements of the vision laid out for the overall program, but it will contain more refined conceptual and operational details. The course designing and planning committee carefully reads the platform aims, assumptions, and rationale, as well as the plan of the program committee. The course planning committee will discuss such matters as assignments of students and teachers to class, the big ideas, enduring understandings, and essential questions (Wiggins & McTighe, 1998, 2005) outlined in the received content standards and how these will recur within and throughout the semester-long or year-long experience, selection of supplementary curricular materials, elective course offerings, scheduling, initiatives, professional development for teachers, and assessments. This committee is typically made up of teachers, administrators, central office colleagues, and students (when appropriate). The size of the committee will depend on the size of the school/district and the number of sections for each grade level or course and on the scope and diversity of the people to be represented. The committee deliberates and organizes people to conduct six major tasks. The 3S Visionary Designing and Planning Template will provide guidance.

1. Collect and analyze currere narratives and curriculum maps to understand the real classroom worlds of students and teachers.

2. Examine state and national standards and distinguish between all the possible content topics, skills, and resources; the important knowledge such as facts, concepts, strategies, and methods; and the more precise choices that anchor the course and reconceptualize the received standards into holistic, understanding goals for the course. Use the reflective inquiry map for guidance to describe progressive student-centered concerns and society-centered advocacies. (See 3S Visionary Designing and Planning Template)

3. Determine the curricular priorities (big ideas, enduring understandings, and essential questions, Wiggins & McTighe, 1998, 2005) for the course, as well as

3S Deliberative Questioning Program Planning Guide Sheet #2

Questions to Consider During Program Deliberations

1. Given the inherent complexity and uncertainty of the world, what kinds of content knowledge and understanding capacities will enable a person to live a full, democratic life today and in the future? What program of study over the K–12 experience might facilitate this kind of life? (Disciplinary and critical inquiry)

2. How do you personally define knowing and becoming and what type of organizational structures and curriculum experiences will best facilitate that becoming? (Poetic and disciplinary inquiry)

3. How do you understand adult and child human learning and development? What kinds of financial, human, and temporal resources best support that learning and development? (Ethical and political inquiry)

4. What kind of understanding goals—big ideas, enduring understandings, and essential questions (Wiggins & McTighe, 1998, 2005)—would make sense in a pluralistic, democratic society? (Multiperspective inquiry)

5. Describe likely student performances of understanding, which are demonstrations of a journey of 3S understanding. (Disciplinary, critical, ethical, political, poetic, and multiperspective inquiry)

6. Describe judgment criteria to evaluate the quality of the journey. What would be required and how would it be judged? (Disciplinary, critical, ethical, political, poetic, and multiperspective inquiry)

time allotments and syllabi, which support the understanding goals and student performances of 3S understanding.

4. Determine the likely student performances for the course and how the work should be differentiated to meet the needs of students. Plan for selection of curricular materials.

5. Determine judgment criteria for case-by-case assessments of the quality of the students' journeys for the course, using rubrics for student feedback. (See 3S Visionary Designing and Planning Template.)

6. Elevate curriculum judgments in humble and pragmatic openness.

An important component of planning any course is determining the curricular priorities. Course planning must distinguish between all the possible content topics, skills, and resources, such as facts, concepts, strategies, and methods in the received standards. A course is often specific and designed to typically last for a semester or a year. The course committee is given latitude to plan beyond this timeframe as understanding goals and student performances of 3S understanding dictate. Course planning for 3S understanding represents a balanced approach to traditional subject-centered concerns and progressive student-centered concerns and society-centered advocacies (Henderson & Kesson, 2004). This 3S frame of reference in a course offers a general test of how well a platform or program is functioning as an instance of democratic living. The course serves as a succinct referent for evaluating the quality of the curriculum judgments. Guide Sheet #3 on the next page should support your deliberations.

Unit/Lesson Planning: Who, What, Why, How

Typically, teachers plan a *unit/lesson*. Viewed through the wisdom paradigm, teachers and students would plan the units/lessons collaboratively. The number of teachers and students will depend on the size of the school and the number of sections for each grade or course, as well as on the scope and diversity of the people to be represented. Because the unit/lesson planning is responsive to the needs of a particular student or group of students, a teacher may want to customize it based on that need. The unit/lesson plan will hold elements of the vision laid out for the overall *course,* but it will contain more day-to-day details. The persons working on the unit/lesson plan will carefully read and understand the holistic, understanding goals of the course, as well as the likely expressive performances of understanding and judgment criteria. They will also understand how their planning is "nested" within design program *and* platform. Deliberation for unit/lesson planning is organized around five major tasks:

1. Write holistic, understanding goals for the unit/lesson. Use the inquiry map for guidance to describe progressive student-centered concerns and society-centered advocacies. (See 3S Visionary Designing and Planning Template)

2. Write the curricular priorities—big ideas, enduring understandings, and essential questions (Wiggins & McTighe, 1998, 2005)—as well as time allotments (anywhere from 2 to 4 weeks), which support the understanding goals and student performances of 3S understanding in the unit/lesson.

3S Deliberative Questioning Course Planning Guide Sheet #3

Questions to Consider During Course Deliberations

1. What types of thinking are students expected to bring to particular ideas and theoretical perspectives embedded in the standards? Is this thinking aesthetic, thereby receptive, loving, passionate, and holistic? (Disciplinary and poetic inquiry)

2. What are some of the curricular priorities (big ideas, enduring understandings, and essential questions)? What assumptions about knowledge, democratic values, and the essence of being human are shaken, examined, reaffirmed, or revoked? (Critical and ethical inquiry)

3. How can we explore the nature of ordinary experiences as a profoundly aesthetic event filled with students' emotional, perceptive, intuitive, and creative expressions? What might be the likely student performances for the course? (Poetic and multiperspective inquiry)

> 4. Deliberations should consider the balance between projections (demographic, economic, technological, educational, and moral) and the reconceived, holistic understanding goals. What criteria might we use to judge case-by-case student expressions of 3S journey of understanding? (Political and ethical inquiry)

3. Write the likely student performances and describe how the work should be differentiated to meet the needs of students. Plan for the selection of curricular materials in the unit/lesson.

4. Write the judgment criteria for case-by-case assessments of the quality of the students' journeys, using rubrics for student feedback. (See 3S Visionary Designing and Planning Template)

5. Elevate curriculum judgments in humble and pragmatic openness.

Planning a unit/lesson that supports 3S understanding is a challenging task. We strongly support the work of Wiggins and McTighe (1998, 2005) and suggest their methods of unit/lesson planning, with modifications. They suggest that one "strategy is to build curriculum around the questions that gave rise to the content knowledge in the first place, rather than simply teaching students the 'expert answers found in the textbooks' " (Wiggins & McTighe, 1998, pp. 26–27). The questions implicitly demand more than just a menu of random activities, which help us to focus the learning in deep subject matter and self and social understandings. Building on Wiggins and McTighe's *"Six Facets of Understanding"* (1998; 2005); 3S educators consider the relationship between good subject matter learning and good self and social learning. These six facets of understanding are:

1. *Explanation:* sophisticated and apt explanations and theories, which provide knowledgeable and justified accounts of events, actions, and ideas

2. *Interpretation:* interpretations, narratives, and translations that provide meaning

3. *Application:* ability to use knowledge effectively in new situations and diverse contexts

4. *Perspective:* critical and insightful points of view

5. *Empathy:* the ability to get inside another person's feelings and worldview

6. *Self-Knowledge:* the wisdom to know one's ignorance and how one's patterns of thought and action inform and prejudice his or her understanding (pp. 44–46)

While we recognize and are grateful for the planning and designing contributions of Wiggins and McTighe (1998, 2005) and the manner in which they have advanced constructivist best practices, the facets of understanding do not explicitly address the transformation of courses or units or lessons into instances of democratic living, nor do they advance reflective inquiry judgment as the basis for curriculum decisions.

As stated earlier, students' 3S understanding is a complex educational phenomenon that must be understood in a holistic manner and a humble spirit. Individual student meaning-making is as unique as the student herself. Students make sense of themselves, the subject matter, and the society in unique and diverse ways. The challenge surfaces as we plan to meet the individual and varied needs of students. 3S understanding assumes that curriculum is not a one-size-fits-all endeavor. Theoretically, we are able to plan according to guiding principles, and practically speaking our day-to-day enactments are specific and unique and must be "right" for a particular case. Transformative curriculum leaders must be able to plan units/lessons, which are subtle and intelligent, avoiding what might seem to be simple theoretical solutions to complex practical problems. Units and lessons cannot be planned in isolation from the course and program planning, which of course considers the platform design. Units and lessons would have too great a burden without being able to embed the big ideas of that unit into broader ideas at the course and program levels. Unit/lesson planning considers the big ideas, enduring understandings, and essential questions (Wiggins & McTighe, 1998, 2005) outlined in program and course, and finally it addresses how these will recur within and throughout the unit/lesson experience.

Unit/lesson planning must also define the actual performances that will express the student's subject matter and self and social understandings, which reflect the big ideas, enduring understandings, and essential questions. This work done collaboratively with students case by case will ensure that there are individualized and idiosyncratic opportunities to express that understanding. All the specific daily lesson plans will provide generative learning experiences, which will prepare students to express their 3S understandings. Wiggins and McTighe (2005) cite Dewey's (1916) distinction between exercises and the problems of performance. They caution teachers not to fall into the trap of the activities that are fun and even interesting but do not lead to anything intellectual. Teachers must ensure that there are clear priorities and a guiding intellectual purpose to frame the learning experience.

Finally, unit/lesson planning must also define judgment criteria for case-by-case assessments of the quality of the 3S student's journey. Rubrics are developed to provide feedback for the students and to determine what evidence is needed for judgments. Rubrics help us secure publicly credible evidence of learning that tells us so much more than test scores.

The process of designing, planning, thinking, and decision making is not neat, linear, or mechanistic (Henderson & Kesson, 2004). Many educational judgments are made on the basis of habit or custom, but during these times of rapid change educators and students alike are called upon to exercise ever more sophisticated forms of judgment and intelligence. Deliberative questioning will guide your curriculum design and planning, as each mode of inquiry has problem-solving potential and holistic interactive synergy. Table 4.1 provides an overview of this deliberative designing and planning process.

Table 4.1	DELIBERATIVE DESIGNING AND PLANNING PROCESS			
3S Understanding	**Platform Designing**			
	Who	What	Why	How
Platform	Teachers, parents, community members, central office colleagues, students, and university colleagues.	Public, common referent for teachers, classrooms, parents, and the community that coherently states aims, basic assumptions, and the relationship of teaching and learning. 8–10 pages in length.	Serves as a decision-making tool and public statement, which supports students' journey of 3S understanding at the policy level.	Public deliberations integrating seven reflective inquiries. Describe and analyze curriculum as it is currently expressed in plans and policies (currere).
3S Understanding	**Program, Course, Unit/Lesson Planning**			
	Who	What	Why	How
Program	Teachers, central office colleagues, students	Curriculum framework, which supports the platform design.Consists of course offerings, resource allocations, entrance requirements, graduation requirements. Considers choice structure,and organization of curriculum materials, as well as holistic understanding goals, performances of 3S understanding, judgment criteria, generative learning experiences.	Outlines the specific program and experiences, which support the platform design. Serves as a planning tool for course and unit/lesson planning.	Group deliberations in supportive learning community integrating seven reflective inquiries. Describe and analyze curriculum as it is currently expressed (currere).

(Continued)

Table 4.1 (*Continued*)

3S Understanding	Program, Course, Unit/Lesson Planning			
	Who	**What**	**Why**	**How**
Course	Teachers, central office colleagues, students	Specific course supporting the program. Time allotments—semester to one year long. Syllabi, holistic understanding goals, performances of 3S understanding, judgment criteria, generative learning experiences	Outlines the specific courses and experiences, which support the program plan. Serves as a planning tool for unit/lesson planning.	Group deliberations in supportive learning community integrating seven reflective inquiries. Describe and analyze curriculum as it is currently expressed (currere).
	Who	**What**	**Why**	**How**
Unit/Lesson	Teachers, students.	Units/lessons in the course. 2–4 weeks in length. Holistic standards, performances of 3S understanding, judgment criteria, generative learning experiences.	Outlines the specific units/ lessons and experiences, which support the course plan. Serves as a planning tool for 3S journey of understanding.	Deliberations in supportive learning community integrating seven reflective inquiries. Describe and analyze curriculum as it is currently expressed (currere).

THE MARRIAGE OF THEORY AND PRACTICE

Examining *Transformative Curriculum Leadership* and 3S understanding from a theoretical and practical approach helps ground curriculum design and planning choices and decisions. Curriculum designing planning and choices derived from this theory gives principled reasons for including particular subject matter content, purposes, assessments, and forms of classroom and school organizations, and so on. While some curriculum theorists believe that "no single theory can unite ideas about students (their previous knowledge, needs, abilities, interests), teachers (their beliefs, knowledge, skill, experience), the subject (key ideas, structure), and the society (its needs), into one all-encompassing set of ideas (Walker, 2003, p. 214), teaching for 3S understanding is different. Unlike other curriculum theories, this theory uniquely unites ideas about all of the practical curriculum commonplaces, including the student, the teacher, the subject matter, and the milieu. The definitions of these four commonplaces are summarized in this statement: "Someone (a teacher) is teaching something (subject matter) to someone (students) in a network of social and cultural contexts (milieu)" (Harris, 1991, pp. 297–298). Teaching for 3S understanding captures all of these commonplaces, which is precisely why the transformative curriculum leader must develop reflective inquiry capacities in new ways and guard against interpreting this theory too narrowly. "Curriculum problems happen to specific, unique, living people, institutions, and communities and a good curriculum decision must be right for a particular case" (Walker, 2003, p. 214), and the challenge of this work is to consider, with wisdom, what educational action is best for the situation when *all* things are considered. This is the essence of elevating your curriculum judgments in humble and pragmatic openness. As practical decisions are made, the experience is fed back into our visionary designing and planning in a never-ending cycle of disciplined educational effort. We must act with integrity, operating out of a deep sense of conscience, principle, and honor to translate our educational vision into creatively designed programs, meaningful student learning experiences and authentic forms of assessment. Planning is a creative and complex decision-making process, which requires your reflective inquiry judgment for your own journey of understanding as you make decisions for curriculum design and planning. Henderson and Kesson (2004) suggest:

> When we make curriculum decisions, we must think broadly about the consequences of our actions, which requires a very sophisticated intelligence. Therefore we must develop our intellectual capacities as completely as we can. In fact, as educators, we are morally bound to cultivate our intellects because our educational decisions must be directed toward courses of actions with long-term implications. While doctors are engaged in critical life and death decisions, educators are engaged in critical choices about leading a good life. At its best, our curriculum practices are informed by a broad, visionary educational agenda. To work in this way is to engage in a professional art that requires our best judgment. (p. 3)

NEGOTIATION STRATEGIES

Educators who desire to teach for 3S understanding are most likely a professional minority. They will need to be sensitive to political realities of this type of curriculum work. You are cautioned not to expect a vote of thanks for your efforts, and you should assume that your work will be challenged. In some cases, your efforts to make any kind of change will be met with resistance and even hostility. Walker (2003) cautions also that deliberation is not dialogue. "Dialogue is a form of conversation in which people try to understand one another's viewpoints, regardless of whether they agree or disagree. Dialogue requires genuine openness to the other persons' concerns" (p. 301). While dialogue with its give and take can shape the vision and help seek common ground, "dialogue is not a method for decision making. The time for dialogue is before hard decisions must be made. Deliberation is the process for decision making" (p. 301). Walker (2003) outlines six key negotiation strategies that curriculum leaders need to employ in order to meet the challenges of any curriculum improvement and, in this case, teaching for 3S understanding:

1. Achieving working agreement

2. Making principled decisions

3. Working constructively with teachers

4. Seeking substantial, lasting improvements

5. Facing conflict constructively

6. Combining curriculum work with other initiatives

We will examine each strategy more closely.

Achieving Working Agreement

Working agreement on actions is essential, even if agreement on philosophy, values, or theory is not reached. "People with utterly different philosophies of education can agree to support the same action" (Walker, 2003, p. 300). It is imperative that educators advocating for teaching for 3S understanding determine the support and opposition for this proposed curriculum action. The only way to know for certain whether a working agreement exists is to risk action and gauge a response. This can be risky indeed, and the wise curriculum leader will take time to engage the stakeholder groups in a series of forums to "float a test balloon." Engaging in dialogue is one important factor. Dialogue requires openness to the other person's concerns. The give and take of dialogue can be the beginning of shared visions, especially when conducted during informal gatherings rather than in the middle of a high-stakes curriculum initiative. Have as many conversations as possible before the proposal is initiated officially. It is advisable to build a trusting relationship with opinion leaders, faculty, and community stakeholders before treading into more divisive issues. "Two pillars of ethical action when building working agreements among people who are divided are dialogue and negotiation" (Walker, 2003, p. 303).

The currere narrative is one important kind of dialogue. Currere narratives are a natural way of sharing insights about a child, expressing concerns about a program, or just conveying a funny human event. As a basis for constructing understanding and insights, story "captures in a special fashion the richness and the nuances of meaning in human affairs. . . . The knowledge represented in story cannot . . . be reduced to abstract rules, logical propositions, or the covering laws of scientific explanation . . . story accommodates ambiguity and dilemma as central figures or themes" (Carter, 1993, p. 5). The currere narrative at the end of this chapter highlights this challenge.

Making Principled Decisions

"Theories, research and experience give us the strongest basis for our curriculum decisions" (Walker, 2003, p. 303). Case studies of successful 3S understanding enactments are the most effective information to offer and the best assurance for a favorable outcome. The gravitational pull to make decisions on the basis of custom or habit is strong, especially when the stakes are high or the politics are running deep. Often decisions are made on the path of least resistance. A principled decision in the case of 3S understanding would be guided by a love of wisdom, which will result in elevated judgments grounded in moral insights essential to facilitating a student's 3S journey of understanding.

Working Constructively with Teachers

Many teachers have deeply ambivalent attitudes toward the curriculum they are charged to implement (Walker, 2003). Some regard it as extremely important, while others have little interest in it. Teaching for 3S understanding assumes a professional way of living, and knowing, which demands a high standard for curriculum and teaching work. "To work in this way is to ultimately make a quality work decision that emerges out of a deep sense of professional calling" (Henderson & Kesson, 2004, p. 97). It has been our experience that teachers without control over their curriculum become mere performers following the script. We believe that most teachers will rise to the professional challenge when they realize that they are empowered to make wise judgments for the students in their care.

Seeking Substantial, Lasting Improvements

Walker (2003) advises curriculum leaders to align their efforts with larger forces. Many, many educators feel crushed by the overemphasis on accountability and high-stakes testing. Many more are frustrated with published ratings that emphasize high test scores, rather than a 3S balanced approach. Just because students score well on standardized test scores does not mean that they are becoming good human beings. We believe that there is a readiness nationally for a "push-back" to a more holistic educational vision and professionally compelling work that is centered on democratically wise systemic reform. "Major lasting initiatives respond to deep important trends, especially demographic, economic, and social needs . . . curriculum improvements that respond to globalization, multiculturalism, and an increasingly complex world of work stand a better chance of playing a major, lasting curriculum role" (Walker, 2003, p. 306).

Facing Conflict Constructively

Conflict is inevitable in matters of curriculum. The wise curriculum leader embraces this and understands that the problem is not conflict, but rather how we respond to the conflict. Setting a tone of openness in your interactions by listening honestly and respectfully to all views promotes civility, even when parties agree to disagree.

Combining Curriculum Work with Other Initiatives

3S understanding is the heart of everything that happens in classrooms, schools, and districts. Walker (2003, p. 307) suggests that anyone interested in curriculum improvements or change ask the following questions: "What other initiatives are underway or under discussion? How can we work in ways that also facilitate desirable curriculum changes?" We are of the opinion that many teachers are ready for this challenge because of their own need for work that makes a difference in the lives of students. The mantra here is "work smarter, not harder." Teaching for 3S understanding contains all the practices teachers engage in every day from planning to assessing, from teaching to communicating with stakeholders. The difference is the subtlety, the intelligence, and the democratically wise lens through which all these activities are viewed. Building upon the knowledge base teachers bring to the enterprise is the starting point to the s-t-r-e-t-c-h to teaching for 3S understanding.

Currere Narrative

A few years ago, the district was scheduled to revise the K–6 mathematics course of study. Using a 5-year revision cycle for each subject, it had been at least 5 years since the math course of study had been revised; it was time. Over the course of the next 24 months, I would face challenges, which truly tested my mettle as an educational leader. Applying all I knew about the change process for curriculum and teacher development, this process was as rewarding as it was stressful, conflicted as it was collaborative, and fruitful as it was frustrating.

A Little Background

The culture in the district was purposefully placed within standardized management because of low student proficiency test scores. The political reality of the day was such that the quality of the schools was judged by the number of students who passed the test. If the students did not pass the tests, the schools would be deemed deficient and property values would decline as a result of failed operating levy attempts. "Strong School, Strong Community" was the tagline.

In preparation for this revision, several teachers attended the Marilyn Burns Mathematics Workshops. A former public school mathematics teacher, Marilyn Burns worked with teachers to develop very high-quality mathematics investigations designed to deepen a student's mathematical understanding. Most if not all who had attended these workshops returned to the district full of energy and enthusiasm ready to get started on the revision process. Motivated by the reform efforts of the National Council of Teachers of Mathematics (NCTM), several K–6 teachers approached me and suggested that we look carefully at this program and consider recommending its adoption by the Board of Education. The current text at the time was relatively algorithmic in nature. We knew that the state's mathematics proficiency test included higher order mathematical reasoning and worried that our current materials and methodology would not be sufficient in preparing students. The NCTM Standards were visionary and called for constructivist practices that deemphasized rote memorization of facts/algorithms and emphasized mathematical reasoning.

This, I hoped, would be a portal through which I might be able to foster constructivist best practices in this dominant management district and begin to wind my way on the journey of 3S understanding, at least incrementally. Visions of establishing curricular priorities, big ideas, and essential questions (disciplinary inquiry) danced in my head. The possibilities of providing meaningful curricular experiences that put students' mathematical investigations and discovery at the center of the work was very exciting (ethical and poetic inquiry). Students would be asked to investigate real-world problems (multiperspective and political inquiry), which had the potential to become performances of understanding that would include the subject matter knowledge necessary to pass the tests (disciplinary inquiry). In an attempt to achieve working agreement and work constructively with teachers, several more teachers were sent to the Marilyn Burns professional development workshops. Those who attended returned with just as much enthusiasm as the others about the power of mathematical reasoning, the real-world applications, and authentic assessments.

Currere narratives were shared about what was learned about mathematical knowledge. While we did not call them currere narratives, I provided opportunities for sharing. Several teachers poignantly admitted their own lack of mathematical reasoning and expressed gratitude to have had the chance to learn more now. I pointed out that both they and their students were on an individual and collective journey of mathematical understanding (disciplinary inquiry). To be a teacher is to be a learner. I was thrilled with their enthusiasm.

Knowing that "every curriculum change demands a change from teachers" (Walker, 2003, p. 271), I was not surprised that all teachers did not embrace this new learning. Some did not want to change. Others could not or would not attend the professional development offered in the summer. I knew that they would need to learn new content and reconsider their conception of the subject from memorized algorithms to discovery investigations. Most importantly, I knew that many of our elementary teachers felt deficient in their mathematical knowledge. For some, the last formal mathematics course they had was high school geometry. This new curriculum would challenge their esteem as a professional. Still others brought forth a second set of materials, which they found to be aligned with the state's standards and in their opinion were more likely to equip the students to pass the tests.

In an effort to work constructively with teachers, we launched two pilot projects, to field test each of the programs in question, and continued to engage teachers in mathematics education professional development with their own colleagues and local university faculty. Teachers were also given stipends to attend after-school sessions, facilitated by their own colleagues who had championed the work. Teachers were encouraged to take release time to observe demonstrations lessons in other teachers' classrooms. Time for collegial conversations after the observations was provided. Professional reading material was purchased, and book studies were held by teachers, for teachers.

The pilot was conducted in two schools, one for each program. By the spring of that year, additional meetings were held to ascertain the quality of the materials and to make a selection. Pros and cons were debated and each group, not surprisingly, praised its own more familiar pilot program. Because we were expected to use standard materials across the district, we had to select one program. Parents had been complaining that there was not equity of resources from classroom to classroom, and they strongly resented that one teacher used different or "better" materials than others across the hall or across the district. Why, they wondered, did the quality of their child's experience depend so much on which teacher the student had that year? Because the district served two communities that were demographically very different, the prevailing perception was that the students in the schools with a predominantly African American population were using substandard materials as compared to the materials for the students in schools with a predominantly Caucasian population. Careful examination revealed that not to be the case, but after much deliberation it was determined that the most ethical decision was to standardize the curricular experiences with the "best" curriculum materials available (ethical, critical and political inquiry).

After working constructively with teachers and attempting to build working agreement with much dialogue, deliberation, and negotiation, we were unable to reach consensus. The teachers asked me to decide. I was under considerable pressure from each group to select the program it had used. After more deliberation and negotiation, I consulted colleagues in other districts, read reviews of curriculum materials by the NCTM and other professional organizations, and studied professional journals (disciplinary inquiry). Based on the information I gathered, I made a judgment to go with the more constructivist approach (ethical and political inquiry).

In spite of all the groundwork and the attention to the details of managing a change process, several teachers were upset with my decision. I was roundly criticized for my choice of materials. More than a few of the teacher leaders who championed this work were also highly criticized and even marginalized within their schools. The curriculum revision process became a topic for labor/management groups.

As DuFour (1998) stated, "both research and practice offer one inescapable, insightful conclusion to those considering an improvement initiative: *change is difficult*" (p. 49, emphasis in original). He goes on to say that one of the most damaging myths that change agents learn is that if the change process is managed well, things will proceed smoothly. This is an important message for those promoting transformative curriculum leadership. Walker (2003) reminds us that "reform-minded leaders have an enormous task in getting those involved to question seriously the content, purpose, and organizing framework of the educational programs they participate in and thus to give new ideas a fighting chance" (p. 315). We must not however, be dissuaded by the formidable challenges of this work, for it is through our daily efforts that our democratic society will prevail. "When we embrace democracy, we do not make our lives easier or clearer; we take on an engagement of demanding responsibilities, perplexing possibilities, and paradoxical choices (Hoffert, 2001, p. 39). Our world depends on it.

REFERENCES

Carter, K. (1993). The place of story in the study or teaching and teacher education. *Educational Researcher, 22*(1), 5–12.

Cuban, L. (2003). *Why is it so hard to get good schools?* New York: Teachers College Press.

Cuffaro, H. K. (1995). *Experimenting with the world: John Dewey and the early childhood classroom.* New York: Teachers College Press.

Dewey, J. (1916). *Democracy and education.* New York: Free Press.

Dewey, J. (1934). *Art as experience.* New York: Perigee Books.

DuFour, R., & Eaker, R. (1998). *Professional learning communities at work. Best practices for enhancing student achievement.* Alexandria, VA: Association for Supervision and Curriculum Development.

Eisner, E. (2002). *The arts and the creation of the mind.* New Haven and London: Yale University Press.

Greene, M. (1998). *The dialectic of freedom.* New York: Teachers College Press.

Harris, I. (1991). Deliberative inquiry: The arts of planning. In E. C. Short (Ed.), *Forms of curriculum inquiry* (pp. 289–307). Albany: SUNY Press.

Henderson, J. G., & Hawthorne, R. D. (2000). *Transformative curriculum leadership* (2nd ed.). Upper Saddle River, NJ: Merrill/Prentice Hall.

Henderson, J. G., & Kesson, K. R. (2004). *Curriculum wisdom: Educational decisions in democratic societies.* Upper Saddle River. NJ: Merrill/Prentice Hall.

Hoffert, R. W. (2001). Education in a political democracy. In R. Soder, J. I. Goodlad, & T. J. McMannon (Eds.), *Developing democratic character in the young* (pp. 26–44). San Francisco: Jossey-Bass.

Macdonald, J. B., & Purpel, D. E. (1987). Curriculum and planning: Visions and metaphors. *Journal of Curriculum and Supervision, 2*(2), 178–192.

McCutcheon, G. (1999). Deliberation to develop school curricula. In J. G. Henderson & K. R. Kesson (Eds.), *Understanding democratic curriculum leadership* (pp. 33–46). New York: Teachers College Press.

Pinar, W. F. (1979). What is the reconceptualization? *JCT, 1*(1), 93–104.

Pinar, W. F., Reynolds, W. M., Slattery, P., & Taubman, P. M. (1995). *Understanding curriculum: An introduction to the study of historical and contemporary curriculum discourses.* New York: Peter Lang.

Rosenwald, G. C., & Ochberg, R. L. (1992). Introduction: Life stories, cultural politics, and self-understanding. In G. C. Rosenwald & R. L. Ochberg (Eds.), *Storied lives: The cultural politics of self-understanding.* New Haven, CT: Yale University Press.

Sarason, S. (1995). Foreword. In A. Lieberman (Ed.), *The work of restructuring schools.* New York: Teachers College Press.

Sergiovanni, T. J., & Starrat, R. (2001). *Supervision: A redefinition* (6th ed.). New York: McGraw-Hill.

Walker, D. F. (1971). A study of deliberation in three curriculum projects. *Curriculum Theory Network, 7,* 118–134.

Walker, D. F. (2003). *Fundamentals of curriculum: Passion and professionalism* (2nd ed.). Mahwah, NJ: Lawrence Erlbaum Associates.

Wiggins, G., & McTighe, J. (1998). *Understanding by design* (1st ed.). Alexandria, VA: Association for Supervision and Curriculum Development.

Wiggins, G., & McTighe, J. (2005). *Understanding by design* (2nd ed.). Alexandria, VA: Association for Supervision and Curriculum Development.

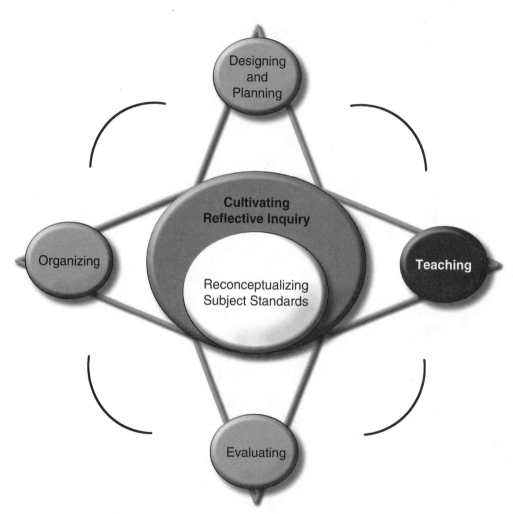

Sustaining the Curriculum Wisdom Problem Solving

CHAPTER 5

TEACHING FOR 3S
UNDERSTANDING

Teaching can be done as badly as anything else. It can be wooden, mechanical, mindless, and wholly unimaginative. But when it is sensitive, intelligent, and creative—those qualities that confer upon it the status of an art—it should, in my view, not be regarded, as it so often is by some, as an expression of unfathomable talent or luck but as example of humans exercising the highest levels of their intelligence.
(Eisner, 1994, p. 156)

Eisner's words can be so heartening for those willing to embrace the challenges and opportunities of this work. Sensitive, intelligent, and creative teaching is *not* as an expression of unfathomable talent or luck, bestowed externally or reachable only by a chosen few. By making conscious choices to exercise wise curriculum judgment that is grounded in moral insight and oriented toward the expansion of deep democracy, we can do this. Visionary? You bet! Random or based on luck? No way! Fortified with information about the basic concepts introduced earlier, we hope that you have the energy and drive to continue on this, your journey of understanding.

What does teaching for 3S understanding look like? By now you realize this is not an easy question to answer, and it certainly is not capable of being distilled into a single sound bite. As you know from the last chapter, the four decision-making processes, which you engage in every day, when viewed through the lens of 3S understanding require an inquiry-oriented reflective action on envisioning and enacting a "good" educational journey for you and your students. There is much to consider when problem solving within the wisdom paradigm. Creating a learning environment that celebrates the possibilities of human growth well beyond the emphasis on high test scores requires a caring imagination and disciplined searching (Henderson & Kesson, 2004), not unfathomable luck or talent. Teaching for 3S understanding belies a strict script or protocol, yet this chapter focuses on some pragmatic and usable tools for enacting this kind of teaching. While we can give decision-making advice as you embrace these ideas, keep in mind that your own professional growth in this area depends upon your reflective inquiry capacities. Remember the theory of "generative reciprocity," mentioned in chapter 2 (Gornik, 2002). Insights needed for teachers to meet the mental demand of living a life of inquiry for continuous growth cannot be taught or memorized. The act of practicing reflective inquiry, however, may develop the consciousness that gives rise to the insights to meet the demand. In other words, asking questions will create a demand on us for insights that may reach beyond our meaning-making system. Insights that alter our meaning-making system may be generated, however, by the very act of asking the questions.

REFLECTING-AS-ACTION

In a more technically based environment, reflective inquiry may be considered a waste of time, inefficient, unnecessary, or perhaps even indulgent or self-absorbed. With an emphasis on producing tangible and concrete outcomes, time for more reflective inquiry into the problems of the day is not reinforced in many schools. Asking questions with no easy answers about the reasons for a particular student's lack of achievement, recurrent tardiness, or excessive absence seems to fly in the face of what teachers are paid to do: Have the answers! Precious few of us may have the emotional fortitude or the political resolve to admit that we do not have "*the* answer" or that we need more time in professional dialogue with our colleagues to find the best next step, all things considered.

Recognizing reflective inquiry as a powerful and thoughtful *action step*, where deliberative questioning is foregrounded, is an important signpost on this journey. In chapter 3, we referred to the work of Schön (1983) and his distinction between *reflection-in-action* and *reflection-on-action*. We believe that this distinction enables all curriculum workers to explore the dynamic nature of reflection, which produces unintended changes spawning new meanings to investigate. Building on the work of Schön (1983), in the next section we discuss some important ways that demonstrate reflective inquiry as an action step for wise curriculum judgments, not an inefficient, passive waste of time.

Reflecting-in-Action and Reflecting-on-Action

We agree with the assumption that competent practitioners in the fields of architecture, law, education, medicine, and so forth usually know more than they can say (Schön, 1983). We further believe that competent practitioners "exhibit a kind of knowing-in-practice, most of which is tacit. Indeed practitioners themselves often reveal a capacity for reflection on their intuitive knowing in the midst of action and sometimes use this capacity to cope with the unique and uncertain conflicted situations of practice" (Schön, 1983, p. viii). "Sometimes, in the relative tranquility of postmortem, they [practitioners] think back on a project they have undertaken, a situation they have lived through, and they explore the understandings they have brought to bear on the case" (Schön, 1983, p. 61). Many of us act, consider the consequences, and make thoughtful adjustments.

In response to what Schön (1983) calls "technical rationality," a linear cause and effect, measurable, and controlled way of thinking and making judgments, he argues that there is a "high, hard ground where practitioners can make effective use of research-based theory and technique" (p. 42). In our case as educators, this entails our more technical work including received content standards, behavioral objectives, testing, assessment, and so forth. As professionals, this technical part of our work is important and comprises some important decision-making processes. Schön (1983) points out, however, that in most professions there is swampy lowland where situations are confusing and messy, often incapable of technical solutions. The difficulty is that the problems of the high ground whatever their technical interest, are often relatively unimportant to clients or to the larger society, while in the swamp are the problems of greatest human concern. Shall the practitioner stay on the high ground, where he can practice rigorously but where he is constrained to deal with problems of relatively little social import? Or shall he descend to the swamp, where he can engage the most challenging problems if he is willing to forsake technical rigor (p. 42)?

Reflecting for Action: Deliberative Questioning on Working Assumptions

When we carefully examine the decisions we make each day and the thousands of judgments we pursue to meet the needs of students and the demands of the job, there is in reality precious little that is clear-cut or formulaic for our practice. The technical precision of the steps in a lesson plan such as the stated objectives, the procedures, the materials, and the assessment are important, to be sure. Knowing your content, with meaningful and carefully planned units and authentic assessments for the year, is extremely important.

When that lesson plan is enacted, however, it is often modified to meet the needs of the students. Teachers make judgments every minute of every day in response to their students. Can you recall times when you reflected on your actions as they unfolded in the classroom or with colleagues and made midcourse adjustments based on the reaction or the consequences? Are you also reminded of a time when you reflected after the rush of the moment and may have wished you had made another choice or taken a different route? These judgments, which are usually the result of some degree of reflective inquiry, have huge consequences. Taneshia's story below illustrates the power of "reflection for action" (Hyun, in press):

The students in the ninth-grade English class were assigned to read *The Adventures of Huckleberry Finn*. Because many of the students in the class were struggling readers, the teacher made the decision to have the students read the book out loud in class, in a round-robin format. The class was composed of approximately 60 percent African American students and 40 percent Caucasian students. Many of the African American students and even more than a few Caucasian students felt very uncomfortable with the contents of the story. When the students came upon the part in the story where African Americans are referred to as *niggers,* Taneshia, an African American, felt very uncomfortable. Shy about expressing her feelings to the teacher, she suffered through what was to her a humiliating class period.

That evening, Taneshia spoke to her mother about her discomfort. Wisely, her mom suggested that Taneshia talk to the teacher on the next day before class. Expressing discomfort about hearing such a word being used to refer to their race was an important value held by both Taneshia and her mom. Taneshia felt strongly that she should not have to read such a book. The content was upsetting, and the characterization of African Americans was too offensive. She asked her mother to contact the school and demand that another book be selected for her and her classmates.

Recognizing the value of American literature as an important tool for young people to learn about historical lessons so they are not repeated, Taneshia's mom suggested that Taneshia ask the teacher to allow the students to substitute "n" for the word, rather than actually saying the word (disciplinary inquiry and critical inquiry). Removing the book from the school list was not in the best interest of the students, as long as the teacher was willing to problem-solve.

Taneshia gathered her courage and arrived early to class in the hopes of talking to the teacher. Unfortunately, the teacher was busy in the minutes before class, and the opportunity did not present itself. Taneshia and her classmates silently suffered through another read-aloud, hearing the offensive word repeatedly. Tanehsia grew more and more saddened as the story unfolded.

That evening, Taneshia shared what happened with her mom. Once again, her mother suggested she talk to the teacher privately. If time before class was not available, perhaps Taneshia could stay after class or make an appointment. The advice remained the same: Taneshia should talk to the teacher in her own words, in her own way, to make her request about changing the word and convey such an important and heartfelt emotion (ethical inquiry and multiperspective inquiry).

On the next day, time before class to talk with the teacher was once again not available. Because the next class was on the other side of campus, she did not have time to talk to the teacher after class. One more time, Taneshia was silent and sat motionless while the word was repeatedly used. Taneshia began to feel that this word was being used to describe *her*.

The next day in class, encouraged by her mother's words, Taneshia gathered her courage and raised her hand to speak. Taneshia asked the teacher whether they could speak privately in the hall. The teacher honored the request and the two headed for the door. Feeling tentative, Taneshia conveyed her feelings. She communicated how the use of that word, read out loud day after day, was very hurtful. She shared the fact that many of her classmates, White and Black, felt the same way. Could they, she asked, substitute the letter *n* for the very offensive word?

The teacher placed a hand on Taneshia's shoulder and looked her in the eye. "Taneshia," the teacher said, "*nigger* is only a word. It does not have any meaning, really; it's just part of the story and not a reference to you. You will have to get over this and just ignore it. We are almost done with the book, so it is too late to change anything. Let's get back to class." Too stunned to speak, Taneshia went back to class biting back tears of anger, frustration, and resentment.

The cascade of events that occurred in the days that followed as a result of that brief interaction between Taneshia and her teacher was incredible. When Taneshia arrived home that evening and related the events to her mom, they set in motion a formal request to have the book banned from the school's supplemental reading list. Following a very tight grievance procedure outlined in board policy about removal of a book, committees were formed, deliberations and hearings were held, and a final vote of the committee was set to determine its fate. Tanehsia's mother reasoned that had the teacher honored her daughter's request to change the word, or even to let the students read the book silently, none of this would have happened. The mother remained incredulous that a teacher could make such a calloused judgment. If the teachers at this high school were so insensitive, they could not be trusted to use a book such as *Huck Finn* in the curriculum for any purposeful gain.

If the teacher had been willing to deliberately become involved in this "messy" but crucially important issue, so much could have been learned about respect, prejudice, hope, and the possibilities for human growth (ethical inquiry, multisperspective inquiry, critical inquiry, disciplinary inquiry, political inquiry, poetic inquiry). If the teacher had had the psychological capacity to remain vulnerable to this student's historical experience holding the personal view open for scrutiny, resisting the tendency to stay with what was familiar, we all would have befitted. This was a "teachable moment" for the students *and* the teacher. This moment was passed off, in part, in the name of efficiency and, in part, because of the lack of depth in this teacher's "repertoire" for handling a situation, which required creative and caring pragmatic judgment. The teacher chose to view this situation through a more technical, clear-cut, "go–no go" process, unwilling or perhaps unable to enter the realm of inquiry, or in Schön's (1983) words, "the swampy lowland for deliberately involving [them] herself in messy, but crucially important problem(s)" (p. 43).

I do not want to leave the reader with the notion that the educators in the school district are blind to the needs of students. This district is filled with caring people who work tirelessly to meet the needs of students. No one wanted this to happen.

If we are to prevent this from occurring in the future, however, we need to ask ourselves a series of questions. What student needs are we meeting? How do we spend our time? What do we talk about? Are we so focused on meeting the test-taking and test-passing needs of students that we may have become blinded to the power and influence of the hidden and null curricula? Depending upon the curriculum problem-solving lens you use and the questions you ask, the manner in which you spend your time and the outcomes will be significantly altered.

While the story of a student's literal death is an extreme way to make this point, I believe that students metaphorically die small deaths every day. When a student's voice is silenced or her needs marginalized by practices and routines designed for mass efficiency, growth will not occur. In no way are schools totally responsible for all of our students' social challenges. We could, however, enable our students to gain a deeper understanding of themselves and society by expanding our core mission to include getting students to pass tests using the curriculum as a vehicle to engage them in the creative world of democratic ideas and feelings.

Professional specialization can have a negative effect and sometimes leads to a parochial narrowness of vision. As Schön (1983) points out, stimulated by surprise, we need to turn thought back on our actions and on the "knowing" that is implicit in action. If this teacher had had "a reflective conversation about a unique and uncertain situation" (Schön, 1983, p. 129), so much learning could have taken place and so much angst could have been avoided.

We are all to be cautioned, "as the practice becomes more repetitive and routine, and as knowing-in-practice becomes increasingly tacit and spontaneous, the practitioner may miss important opportunities to think about what he is doing" (Schön, 1983, p. 133). The reflective inquiry map in Chapter 3 will assist you in making inquiries into your own practice because it is so easy to fall into indifference. A practitioner's reflection can serve as a corrective to over learning" (Schön, 1983, p. 61). "When someone reflects-in-action, he becomes a researcher in the practice context" (p. 68). The demands of real-world practice have unique and unpredictable elements. One of the hallmarks of a professional, therefore, is the ability to take a more technical knowledge base and judge wisely, converting it into professional services that are tailored to the unique requirements of the client system. We dream of the day when educators are encouraged to describe their methods of inquiry, speak of their experience, and expose their trial and error on the route to elevated judgment and decision making.

We personally and professionally wish Schön (1983) had not characterized the space of deliberative reflection as the "swampy lowlands." If we are ever to fully realize this vision, we must embrace, even relish, opportunities for this kind of deliberation. Those advocating a more standardized management approach would point to situations such as this as reason enough to eliminate as much ambiguity from our work as possible. Opponents of teacher empowerment point to the subjectivities of professional judgment as weak or inconsistent and call for a more rigorous application of the standards. We still believe, however, there is no substitute for professional judgment. This does not mean that we advocate a flabby sort of "anything goes" liberalism. Engaging in this type of professional judgment requires a sophisticated, disciplined, highly conscious, and intellectual rigor that exceeds any amount of mind-numbing, one-size-fits-all decision making. Indeed, skimming the surface of what people need is often the easier path. Taking the time, the energy, the caring, and the creativity to reflect upon all the nuances of a situation in order to make the most informed and wise judgment in the best interest of the "whole" child takes a considerable amount of discipline and rigor and adherence to a higher professional standard. Because of the risks and the dangers involved for our democratic society as a result of too many children being "schooled" and not educated, with a focus on organizational goals and concentration on measurable outcomes rather than on growth-producing student learning (Henderson & Hawthorne, 1995), one important premise of this book is a fundamental confidence that educators, through reflection and discipline, will "surface and criticize tacit understandings that have grown up around the repetitive experiences of a specialized practice, and make new sense of the situations of uncertainty or uniqueness, which he may allow himself to experience" (Schön, 1983, p. 61).

I Already Do This . . .

At this point in the reading, you might recognize that you already reflect on your actions, and can recall times when you reflected and studied during your teaching practice to make a more informed choice. As authors we agree that most if not all teachers, every day engage in some form of designing, planning, teaching, evaluating, and communicating with colleagues and parents as stakeholders about their subject matter. Teaching for 3S understanding requires, however, a subtle and democratic expression of all these decision-making practices, with a heightened level of consciousness through the reflective inquiries you learned about in chapter 3. Here is an example:

Have you ever driven in a parking lot with large speed bumps designed to slow down cars? As the driver, if you take the speed bump at an accelerated rate, you will barely feel the bump. The shock absorbers do their job, mask the impact of the bump, and off you go. If, however, you go carefully and purposefully over the bump, you feel the rise of each wheel on the incline. You are aware of exactly where you are and know exactly when to let the car coast down the other side. Note the differences in the experience. While speeding over the bump, you "barely feel," the "shock is absorbed," and the "impact is masked." Conversely, when you slow down and *consciously* navigate the bump, you "feel the rise of each wheel," are "aware of exactly where you are," and "know exactly when to coast." Ostensibly, these are exactly the same activity (driving over the speed bump), but they are experienced differently when you make a different choice of execution.

Teaching for 3S understanding is much the same. You design, plan, teach, evaluate, and so on, but without using the wisdom problem-solving cycle, which requires reflective inquiry as a guide, you may be navigating without a moral compass. Under our current conditions, teaching for 3S understanding poses an interesting problem, which requires our careful, conscious, and purposeful attention. Bound by the conventions of the accountability movement with its emphasis on the subject matter, teachers need to think differently about teaching. The problem may be that most of us have been trained to accept realities defined by those in authority. Recall the high school laboratory experiment in which houseflies are placed in a jar with a lid, sufficiently punctured with air holes. Initially, the flies move wildly about the jar, smacking their heads and bodies against one another and the inside surface of the jar in a vain attempt at liberation. Over time, the flies settle down and adjust to the confined environment. Surprisingly, even when the lid is removed, the flies remain within the jar, seeming to have lost all interest in leaving.

We need to ask whether we have all been socialized, much like these flies. Over time, we lose consciousness about what "could be" because we have been trained to stay focused on "the way it is." Teaching cultures are elusive but powerful, and school structures have substantial implications for the way we behave within them (Eisner, 1994). Many of our beliefs about teaching are not merely idiosyncratic preferences, but the result of tacit, implicit, unconscious, entrenched cultural norms (Smyth, 1989). We may have developed habits of mind that lulled us into complacency or left us feeling so burdened by legislated testing realities that we feel unable to use subject matter understanding as a tool for a deeper understanding of the needs of the self and the society. "There are several impediments to artistry in teaching. One is habit nurtured by comfortable routine. Experienced teachers develop routines that simplify professional lives" (Eisner, 2002, p. 56). Eisner further suggests that these routines are not conducive to professional growth. He suggests, "We need to treat teaching as a form of personal research. We need to use the occasions of our performance as teachers as opportunities to learn to teach" (Eisner, 2002, p. 56). Stigler and Hiebert (1999, p. 110) encourage "lesson study." "If you want to improve teaching, the most effective place to do so is in the context of a classroom. . . . The improvements are devised within the classroom in the first place. The challenge now becomes that of identifying the kinds of changes that will improve student learning [and in our case 3S understanding] in the classroom and, once the changes are identified, of sharing this knowledge with other teachers who face similar problems or share similar goals in the classroom" (p. 111).

We need a supple imagination of what could be, with less acceptance of "what is." When some of our most powerful political leaders unabashedly admit that they "do not do nuance," it is no surprise that there is a kind of cultural gravity pulling us toward the dominant paradigm. It may take a tectonic shift for some of us to move from the dominant to a constructivist paradigm, and more still to the wisdom paradigm emphasizing expressive outcomes and productive idiosyncrasy (Eisner, 2002). What we want is a curriculum *for being* and, more importantly, a curriculum *for becoming.* Yes, we want students who are smart in subject matter, but we also want good people. Our world depends on it.

In section II, you learned about reconceptualizing the received standards in such a way as to bring into balance the subject matter, and the self and the societal aspects of understanding as criteria for making judgments about your students' expressions of democratic living. The remainder of this chapter will focus on the ways in which you, as a practitioner, may foreground the subtleties of this work in your daily practice. Let's slow down on this journey of understanding and pay attention to the speed bumps.

CREATIVE AND CARING PRAGMATISM

When you care about someone, you ask questions: "How can I help? What do you need? What do I need to know to understand your needs?" When you are creative and caring, you bring a new set of questions and perhaps your highest energy and most loving perspective to bear on your judgments and decisions. Only you know the quality of the educational experiences you provide for your students. Are your lessons creative and thinking centered, and do they promote personal understanding? Do students use their subject matter knowledge in pursuit of their own meaning making? Is there a relationship between the classroom activities and the lives they live outside of class? Do you consider the value of alternative approaches and more expressive outcomes? Are students invited to engage in the creative world of ideas and feelings? Are students treated as if they have minds of their own and encouraged to use their mental capacities to build more sophisticated understandings? Do you foreground the hidden and null curriculum in your planning?

In his June 12, 2005, commencement address to students of the Stanford University School of Education, Elliot Eisner reminds us that *ideas* provide a natural high for students and teachers. This "high" is derived from the satisfaction of puzzlements that invite the most precious of human abilities an opportunity to take wing. Imagination, he posits, is the neglected stepchild of American education. He states, "Questions invite you in. They stimulate the production of possibilities. They give you a ride. And the best ones are those that tickle the intellect and resist resolution." This kind of creative inquiry facilitates each student's individual understandings, promotes proactive problem-solving and nurtures aesthetic engagement and expression (Henderson & Hawthorne, 2000). Only you know how closely this description fits your classroom practice. Only you know how you express sensitivity to students' needs as they engage in inquiry. Do you carefully observe your students' meaning-making responses, noting successes or problems? Do you provide support when necessary? How do you share their experiences and empathize with their feelings? Is the student's role to receive and accept subject matter knowledge in docile compliance or in more fluid and vital ways (Dewey, 1902)? Are you open to learning from students, including being changed in fundamental ways as students use the subject matter to express multiple meanings?

PULLING IT ALL TOGETHER

In this decision-making chapter, what you have learned heretofore comes to bear. In the teaching, we pull together all the pieces on the 3S Visionary Designing and Planning Template found in chapter 4, to provide deeply meaningful and democratically wise curriculum experiences for students. As you build your capacity for this kind of work, you may use the Wiggins and McTighe concepts as a toehold for 3S Understanding designing, planning, teaching, and evaluating. These authors provide many useful tools for this work. A quick and easy teaching, planning, assessing, and evaluating tip advocated by Wiggins and McTighe (2005) is to ask students the following questions at any point in a lesson or unit:

- What are you doing?

- Why are you being asked to do it?

- What will it help you do?

- How does it fit with what you have learned previously?

- How will you show what you have learned?

Wiggins and McTighe also advocate the use of *essential questions* to guide students in uncovering the important ideas at the heart of each subject. In the mass of the received subject matter content standards, we need to focus our priorities. The work you did in chapter 2 on reconceptualizing the received standards is one important step to determining these essential questions. Essential questions that emerge from the reflective inquiries can be an effective way of framing an entire program, course, or unit of study. Creating your essential questions, using the reflective inquiries, positions you as a teacher to develop learning experiences and professional interactions that integrate democratic values into daily educational activities and practices. Essential questions (Wiggins & McTighe, 1998):

- Go the heart of a discipline

- Recur naturally throughout one's learning and in the history of a field

- Raise other important questions

- Provide subject/topic-specific doorways to other questions

- Have no obvious "right" answers

- Are deliberately framed to provoke and sustain student interest (pp. 29–30)

For those electing to use the Wiggins and McTighe concepts as a toehold for 3S understanding designing, planning, teaching, and evaluating, Figure 5.1 may help you see the connections between their facets of understanding and what a teacher actually "does" when she or he is engaged in this kind of work. Column 1 outlines Wiggins and McTighe's Six Facets of Understanding. Column 2 shows the corresponding reflective inquiry associated with that particular facet of understanding.

| Figure 5.1 | Six Facets of Understanding |

Facet 1. A student who really understands can explain. *She demonstrates sophisticated explanatory power and insight. She can . . .*

- Provide complex, insightful, and credible reasons—theories and principles, based on good evidence and argument—to explain or illuminate an event, fact, text, or idea; provide a systematic account, using helpful and vivid mental models.

- Make fine, subtle distinctions; aptly qualify her opinions.

- See and argue for what is central—the big ideas, pivotal moments, decisive evidence, key questions, and so on.

- Make good predictions

- Avoid or overcome common misunderstandings and superficial or simplistic views—shown, for example, by avoiding overly simplistic, hackneyed, or imprecise theories or explanations.

- Reveal a personalized, thoughtful, and coherent grasp of a subject—indicated, for example, by developing a reflective and systematic integration of what she knows effectively and cognitively.

- Substantiate or justify her views with sound argument and evidence.

A teacher who is teaching for 3S understanding will . . .

- Plan lessons that promote student inquiry, allowing students to find their own meaning that encourages them to make sense of content in their own way. (Disciplinary inquiry)

- Facilitate an atmosphere in which students generate solutions rather than only listen to answers. (Disciplinary inquiry)

- Confirm the value of alternative approaches and outcomes. (Multiperspective inquiry)

- Present meaningful, problem-posing incidents that spark student inquiry. (Critical inquiry)

- Encourage students to explore multiple solutions. (Multiperspective inquiry)

- Express sensitivity to students' need as they engage in inquiry. (Poetic inquiry)

- Carefully observe students' meaning-making responses, noting any success or problems. (Ethical inquiry)

- Ask . . . Why is that so?
  What explains such events?
  What accounts for such actions?
  To what is this connected?
  What is implied?

Facet 2. A student who really understands can interpret. *He offers powerful, meaningful interpretations, translations, and narratives. He can*

- Effectively and sensitively interpret texts, language, and situations—shown, for example, by the ability to read between the lines and offer plausible accounts of the many possible purposes and meanings of any "text" (e.g., book, situation, or human behavior).

A teacher who is teaching for 3S understanding will . . .

- Recognize and embrace the existence of many different plausible and illuminating interpretations of the same stories and human events. (Multiperspective inquiry)

- Determine how interpretations relate to the school community and the community at large. (Critical inquiry)

Figure 5.1   **(Continued)**

- Offer a meaningful and illuminating account of complex situations and people. He has the ability, for example, to provide historical and biographical background, thereby helping to make ideas more accessible and relevant.

- Address the structural basis of the problems and concerns identified. (Ethical inquiry)

- Accept challenges to one's own critical challenges. (Ethical and Political inquiry)

- Actively support imaginative problem solving. (Poetic inquiry)

- Ask . . . What does it matter?
  What does it mean?
  What does it illustrate in human experience?

Facet 3. A student who really understands can apply. *She uses knowledge in context, has know-how. She can*

- Employ her knowledge effectively in diverse, authentic, and realistically messy contexts.

- Extend or apply what she knows in a novel and effective way—that is, invent in the sense of innovate, as Piaget (1973) discusses in *To Understand Is to Invent.*

- Effectively self-adjust as she performs.

A teacher who is teaching for 3S understanding will . . .

- Question attempts to apply universally "valid" principles. (Ethical inquiry)

- Address questions in an unbiased manner for all students regardless of gender and ethnicity. (Critical inquiry)

- Decide willingness to agree to disagree. (Multiperspective and Political inquiry)

- Create a safe atmosphere where all students have an equal opportunity to grow successfully. (Disciplinary inquiry)

- Allow for personal passion and expression. (Poetic inquiry)

- Ask . . . How and where can we use this knowledge?
  How should my thinking and action be modified to meet the demands of this particular situation?

Facet 4. A student who really understands sees in perspective. *He can*

- Critique and justify a position to see it as a point of view; use skills and dispositions that embody disciplined skepticism and the testing of theories.

A teacher who is teaching for 3S understanding will . . .

- Examine biases in presenting issues. (Multiperspective inquiry)

- Know students well enough to incorporate their cultural framework into the lesson

(Continued)

Figure 5.1 **(Continued)**

- Know the history of an idea to place discussion and theory in context; know the questions or problem to which the knowledge or theory studied is an answer or solution.

- Infer the assumptions upon which an idea or theory is based.

- Know the limits as well as the power of an idea.

- See through argument or language that is biased, partisan, or ideological.

- Wisely employ both criticism and belief, an ability summarized by Peter Elbow's (1973) maxim that we are likely to better understand when we methodically "believe when others doubt and doubt when others believe."

Facet 5. A student who really understands demonstrates empathy. She has the ability to sensitively perceive. She can

- Project herself into, feel, and appreciate another situation, affect, or point of view.

- Operate on the assumption that even an apparently odd or obscure comment, text, person, or set of ideas may contain insights that justify working to understand it.

- See when incomplete or flawed views are plausible, even insightful, though perhaps somewhat incorrect or outdated.

- See and explain how an idea or theory can be all too easily misunderstood by others.

- Listen—and hear what others often do not.

(Disciplinary and Multiperspective inquiry)

- Interrogate all dogma, encouraging a healthy skepticism. (Critical inquiry)

- Communicate passion to reject all forms of covert and overt manipulations. (Ethical inquiry)

- Generate varying viewpoints or solutions to issues/problems. (Multiperspective inquiry)

- Cultivate one's own professional growth to be the best facilitator of students' growth. (Ethical inquiry)

- Ask . . . From whose point of view?
  From which vantage point?
  What is assumed or tacit that needs to be made explicit and considered?
  Is it plausible?
  What are the limits?
  So what?

A teacher who is teaching for 3S understanding will . . .

- Foster respect among students. (Ethical inquiry)

- Create evaluations that allow for diverse perspectives. (Multiperspective inquiry)

- Have the courage to "step outside the box." (Multiperspective inquiry)

- Take the time to reflect each day, contemplate, and regenerate. (Poetic inquiry)

- Actively seek ways to encourage reciprocal exchange of thoughts and feelings. (Ethical inquiry)

- Ask . . .
  How does it seem to you?
  What do they see that I don't?
  What do I need to experience if I am to understand?
  What was the person seeing, feeling, and trying to make me see and feel?

Figure 5.1   **(Continued)**

Facet 6. A student who really understands reveals self-knowledge. *He can*	A teacher who is teaching for 3S understanding will . . .
• Recognize his own prejudices and style, and how they color understanding; see and get beyond egocentrism, ethnocentrism, present-centeredness, nostalgia, and either-or thinking. • Engage in effective metacognition; recognize intellectual style, strengths, and weaknesses. • Question his own convictions; like Socrates, be able to sort out mere strong belief and habit from warranted knowledge, be intellectually honest, and admit ignorance. • Accurately self-assess and effectively self-regulate. • Accept feedback and criticism without defensiveness.	• Engage in recurring cycles of instructional study, application, observation, and reflection. (Disciplinary inquiry) • Actively work against traditions that foster elitism, tribalism, and other narrow forms of human sectarianism. (Critical inquiry) • Sense any ironies or contradictions between what is taught and how it is taught, as it relates to one's beliefs about a pluralistic, democratic society. (Critical and Ethical inquiry) • Be able to describe the democratic ethics being used in the classroom. (Ethical inquiry) • State the best way to educate for moral competency, personal ethics, character development, and citizenship. (Political and Ethical inquiry) • Cultivate a subtle, multilayered understanding of the relationship between democracy and education. (Multiperspective inquiry) • Ask . . . 　How does who I am shape my views? 　What are the limits of my understanding? 　What are my blind spots? 　What do I misunderstand because of prejudice, habit or style?

We hope this comparison of Wiggins and McTighe's Six Facets of Understanding and reflective inquiry illustrates how this work may be integrated into your classroom practices.

Dewey (1978) reminds us that in a deeper sense reflective inquiry "involves a state of doubt, hesitation, perplexity, mental difficulty, in which thinking originates, and an act of searching, hunting, inquiring, to find [solutions] that will resolve the doubt, settle and dispose of the perplexity" (p. 12). Refer to the 3S Visionary Designing and Planning Template and Guide Sheets in chapter 4 for assistance as you deepen your understanding of this kind of teaching.

Dewey also reminds us:

There is a strong temptation to assume that presenting subject matter in its perfected form provides a royal road to learning. What is more natural than to suppose that the immature can be saved time and energy, and be protected from needless error by commencing where the competent inquirers have left off? The outcome is written large in the history of education. Pupils begin their study . . . with tests in which the subject is organized into topics according to the order of the specialist. Technical concepts and their definitions are introduced at the outset. Laws are introduced at an early stage, with at best few indications of the way in which they were arrived at. . . . The pupil learns symbols without the key to their meaning. He acquires a technical body of information without ability to trace connections [to what] is familiar—often he acquires simply a vocabulary. (Dewey, 1910/1997, p. 232)

Henderson and Hawthorne (2000) outline the following precepts to illustrate the type of ethical code that teachers on their own journey of understanding strive to collaboratively establish with their colleagues:

Ethical Code on the Journey of Understanding

- I will actively seek ways to elevate, ennoble, and energize my students, my colleagues, and myself. I want all of us to see ourselves in the best possible light. I want all of us to be inspired to do our best in personally constructive and non-harmful ways.

- I will actively seek ways to encourage the reciprocal exchange of thoughts and feelings. I believe in inclusive communication and robust dialogue.

- I embrace various forms of educational collaboration. I will work to encourage all curriculum stakeholders to support one another in trusting and nonmanipulative ways.

- I will encourage all curriculum stakeholders to think for themselves—to make up their own minds on pressing educational topics and issues. Even if I disagree with others' perspectives, I will actively support the continuing construction and refinement of their own understandings on important curriculum matters.

- I will actively support imaginative problem solving. When curriculum stakeholders complain about some educational state of affairs, I will encourage them to undertake a relevant form of curriculum deliberation—to find ways to frame problems and seek creative solutions. I will exhibit impatience with protracting complaining, and I will reject all forms of overt and covert manipulation.

- I will encourage aesthetic engagement with all curriculum and teaching matters. I want curriculum stakeholders to become attuned to their deepest feelings about education. I will work to create settings in which students, teachers, and others are not too busy to explore their perceptions about educational matters, and I will encourage diverse expressions of these perceptions.

- I want people to be comfortable with humanistic insight and diverse forms of knowing. I want all curriculum stakeholders to envision and actively support the rich multiliterate and multi-intelligent possibilities of human culture.

- I will make sure that all people are treated equitably in all possible senses of that term. I will support the active cultivation of all constructive human talents, and I will not play favorites with any individual or group.

- I will actively work against all forms of overt and covert bias. I will seek to undermine conscious and embedded patterns of prejudice.

- I will actively question all attempts to apply universally "valid" principles to educational work. I will interrogate all dogmas, and I will encourage a healthy skepticism and humility about curriculum and teaching practices. The traditions I will support are associated with the play of human differences. I will actively work against traditions that foster elitism, tribalism, and other narrow forms of human sectarianism. I will also actively challenge all pat answers and final solutions. And in the spirit of open-minded inquiry, I will accept challenges to my own critical challenges.

- Finally, I will gladly submit exhibitions of my continuing reflective inquiries to a process of responsible peer review, and I expect the same of my colleagues. (pp. 62–63)

We began this chapter with a quote by Eisner (1994) about the potential for teaching to be wooden, mechanical, and mindless. We end with a quote by John Dewey (1910/1978) which captures the essence of transformative curriculum leadership and the potential of what this reform effort will do in the name of all teachers and students

> Genuine freedom, in short, is intellectual; it rests in the trained *power of thought,* in the ability to "turn things over," to look at matters deliberately, to judge whether the amount and kind of evidence requisite for decision is at hand, and if not, to tell where and how to seek such evidence. If a person's ["man's" in the original] actions are not guided by thoughtful conclusions, then they are guided by inconsiderate impulse, unbalanced appetite, caprice, or the circumstances of the moment. To cultivate unhindered, unreflective external activity is to foster enslavement, for it leaves the person at the mercy of appetite, sense and circumstance. (p. 232)

REFERENCES

Dewey, J. (1902). *The child and the curriculum.* Chicago: University of Chicago Press.

Dewey, J. (1916). *Democracy and education.* New York: Free Press.

Dewey, J. (1978). *How we think.* In J. A. Boydston, *John Dewey: The middle works. 1899–1924.* Vol. 6. 1910–1911, 177–356. Carbondale, IL: Southern Illinois University Press. (Original work published 1910)

Eisner, E. (1994). *The educational imagination: On the design and evaluation of school programs* (3rd ed.). New York: Macmillan.

Eisner, E. (2002). *The arts and the creation of the mind.* New Haven and London: Yale University Press.

Eisner, E. (2005, June 13). The satisfaction of teaching. *Stanford University School of Education News.* Retrieved May 31, 2006, from http://ed.stanford.edu/suse/news-bureau/displayRecord.php?tablename=susenews&id=119.

Elbow, P. (1973). *Writing without teachers.* New York: Oxford University Press.

Gornik, R. (2002). *Teacher inquiry capacity: A case study.* Unpublished doctoral dissertation. Kent State University.

Henderson, J. G., & Hawthorne, R. D. (1995). *Transformative curriculum leadership* (1st ed.). Upper Saddle River, NJ: Merrill/Prentice Hall.

Henderson, J. G., & Hawthorne, R. D. (2000). *Transformative curriculum leadership* (2nd ed.). Upper Saddle River, NJ: Merrill/Prentice Hall.

Henderson, J. G., & Kesson, K. R. (2004). *Curriculum wisdom: Educational decisions in democratic societies.* Upper Saddle River, NJ: Merrill/Prentice Hall.

Hyun, E. (in press). Transforming instruction into pedagogy through curriculum negotiation. *Journal of Curriculum and Pedagogy, 3*(1).

Schön, D. A. (1983). *Reflective practitioner.* New York: Basic Books.

Smyth, J. (1989). A critical pedagogy of classroom practice. *Journal of Curriculum Studies, 21*(6), 483–502.

Stigler, J. W., & Hiebert, J. (1999). *The teaching gap.* New York: The Free Press.

Wiggins, G., & McTighe, J. (1998). *Understanding by design.* Alexandria, VA: Association of Supervision and Curriculum Development.

Wiggins, G., & McTighe, J. (2005). *Understanding by design* (2nd ed.) Alexandria, VA: Association of Supervision and Curriculum Development.

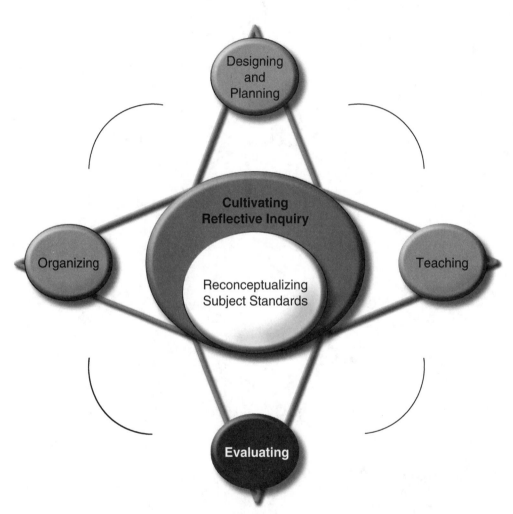

Sustaining the Curriculum Wisdom Problem Solving

CHAPTER 6

EVALUATING 3S EDUCATION

When properly conceived as an activity of teaching and learning resulting in an action-oriented self-understanding, evaluation becomes more continuous with the way we are human beings in our everyday lives. If evaluation is viewed as continuous with our ordinary ways of being engaged in the world, then we are led to consider more carefully the particular moral obligation and responsibility that we shoulder when we evaluate our own and others' actions.

(Schwandt, 2002, pp. xi–xii)

Evaluating is a central feature in curriculum problem solving. Judging the quality of our work with students is essential in any of the three paradigms. Within the standardized management paradigm, evaluating is set apart and positioned at the end of a linear process; a kind of "look back," after all is said and done. The emphasis is on a summative evaluation, which is defined by Scriven (1967) as the formal, overall appraisal of an educational program. Summative evaluation provides a more global and terminal appraisal of a program or activity, usually conducted by an external evaluator. There is a de-emphasis on ascertaining the value of daily actions or on providing opportunities for midcourse corrections through ongoing feedback.

Within the curriculum wisdom paradigm, we advocate a recursive, *formative evaluation* to ensure balanced value judgments on the quality of the 3S educational efforts. Scriven (1967) defines *formative evaluation* as assessment designed to improve ongoing programs. This evaluative approach requires disciplined critical and visionary thinking with an emphasis on case-by-case deliberations. The focus is on making midcourse corrections with reference to the "bottom line" of the work, which is the quality of students' 3S journeys of understanding. As decision makers, we strive for the best-informed and most thoroughly considered decision, taking into account all the most promising alternatives in light of the best available knowledge, with reference to the best possible program designs, the best possible instructional planning, and the best possible teaching decisions. In effect, evaluative decision making is treated as an integral, organic, and dynamic component of all designing, planning, and teaching deliberations.

Furthermore, as we attempt to transform educational courses of action into instances of democratic living, evaluating becomes more continuous and purposeful with the way we approach and experience all aspects of our everyday lives. This is why we begin this chapter with the above quote from Thomas Schwandt's *Evaluation Practice Reconsidered*. If evaluating is viewed as continuous with our ordinary ways of being engaged in the world, rather than good test-taking behaviors, then we need to consider more carefully the particular moral obligations and responsibilities that we have when we evaluate our own and others' actions.

In the context of wisdom problem solving, when we engage in curriculum deliberations, we pay attention to our working assumptions, the consequences of our actions, and our continuing inquiry into democratic education. This, too, has subtle and overt evaluative dimensions. The questions we ask affect the quality of the decisions, and the judgments we make affect the quality of the journeys. This is a simple idea, but it is not always easy to execute.

The evaluative challenge is to formatively, constructively judge the quality of our decision making, whether we are *reconceptualizing* subject standards into holistic 3S understanding goals (chapter 2), *cultivating* our reflective inquiries (chapter 3), deliberating about *designing* and *planning* (chapter 4), or deliberating about *teaching* (chapter 5). In effect, evaluative decision making permeates all of the topics that have been discussed so far in this book. In part, this should not be surprising because professional self-understanding, which is facilitated through the creation of currere narratives, is a central and critical feature of curriculum wisdom problem solving.

Evaluating 3S education is a central feature of transformative curriculum leadership. In light of this formative approach to evaluative decision making, we have organized this chapter around five important questions. These five questions will guide your evaluative process and will ascertain the quality of your deliberations and your curriculum judgments or decisions. After sharing two currere narratives that highlight the importance of evaluating in this manner, we will draw the distinction between assessing and evaluating the personal and individual quality of students' 3S journey of understanding. Then you will learn how to apply the five evaluative questions to your work with the two fundamental challenges and the four decision-making processes necessary to transformative curriculum leadership.

Keep in mind that given the holistic nature of the curriculum wisdom paradigm, evaluating will be framed around a fundamental question. When in doubt about evaluating the quality of your deliberations, decision-making processes, or curriculum judgments, refer to this question:

Have the teacher's curriculum judgments been elevated to include moral decisions that touch the core of what it means to be human, to live in community with others, to find meaning and purpose, and to create a more just and peaceful world?

WHAT IS CURRICULUM EVALUATION?

In the literature, evaluation is defined as the activity of judging the merit, worth, or significance of some human action like a policy, program, or project. Successful program development cannot occur without some form of evaluation. Curriculum program evaluation is the process of systematically determining the quality of a school program and how the program can be improved (Sanders, 2000). Curriculum evaluation depends on how educators answer at least five important questions:

- Who decides what will be assessed and evaluated?

- What questions are to be answered?

- How might data be gathered and analyzed?

- What criteria will be used to interpret and judge data?
- Who analyzes data, makes judgments, and uses judgments?

Evaluation out of the dominant standardized management (SM) paradigm will be typically preoccupied with the "right" method for producing knowledge that has not been "contaminated" by prejudices, tradition, and historical contexts. Typically the third-party evaluators have been insulated, detached, and stood apart from the programs and policies they evaluate (Schwandt, 2002). State standardized achievement exams, which narrowly focus on subject matter skills and knowledge, are often the primary measure of assessing student learning. Test scores are substituted for teacher judgment. Experts outside the classrooms are often the primary decision makers. The dominant criteria are effectiveness and efficiency to the extent that students are meeting the standards by passing the tests while spending the least amount of money. Data are used to compare schools and districts with one another based on state and national norms. For these reasons, we distinguish between assessing and evaluating. The logic of the SM paradigm is primarily concerned with assessing a student's subject matter content knowledge. The curriculum wisdom (CW) paradigm, on the other hand, assesses a student's deep understanding of subject matter content knowledge, and it is then holistically focused on evaluating who that student is becoming in the process.

DISTINGUISHING BETWEEN ASSESSING AND EVALUATING

We draw an important distinction between assessing and evaluating: *Assessing* is gathering evidence of content knowledge and skills, and *evaluating* is the case-by-case *value* judgment of the quality of the teachers' and students' 3S journey of understanding. This distinction pervades all of our work in evaluating 3S education.

We embrace Wiggins and McTighe's (2005) notion that assessing is the practice of gathering evidence of desired results. We agree also that assessing is a kind of umbrella term under which falls a scaffold of methods for gathering evidence of meeting desired results, whether the evidence is skills and knowledge or performances of understanding. Assessing for subject skills and knowledge of received content standards (SM paradigm) focuses specifically on observations, dialogues, quizzes, and tests. You may recall your own test-taking experiences in which you enter the testing room, with metaphoric blinders securely fastened to your temples, palms pressed tightly against your ears, imploring those around you not to speak or distract you in fear that the memorized facts from the night before will randomly jettison from your brain. Content knowledge memorized for a test is often forgotten once the pressure of the test has been removed. The deeper performances of understanding of those skills and knowledge (constructivist best practices [CBP] paradigm) around big ideas and essential questions (Wiggins & McTighe, 2005), would include observations, dialogues, quizzes, tests, performance tasks and projects, and "students' self-assessment gathered over time" (p. 6). In either case, the knowledge of the content must be available to the student, and the teacher must assess whether or not the student has integrated the content well enough to transfer it to new situations.

While we need to gather standardized information and agree that assessment is important, when standardized content learning morphs into a means to the end, which is assessment (Pinar, 2005), we take issue. We do not want to limit our students and ourselves to that kind of assessing only. The story of Joe is a great illustration of this "means to an end" dynamic.

Go . . . No–Go . . . That Is the Question

Joe was a second grade boy in our district who was a good, average reader. Joe did well in reading and, compared to other students in the class, was in the middle of the pack. Joe's report cards indicated that he was on schedule in meeting the standard benchmarks for reading by the end of second grade. Totally unbeknownst to him, this average boy became the poster child for a debate in our district about the qualifying criteria for receiving reading intervention services.

In our district, we use Title I funds from the federal government to support a portion of our reading intervention activities. Based on the percentage of students who qualify for free or reduced lunch, each district is awarded an amount of federal money to provide necessary interventions to increase student achievement in reading or math. Based on a needs assessment of parents and teachers, we determined that the early prevention of school failure was best addressed by providing reading interventions to students in grades one through four. Free and reduced lunch is determined by the federal poverty guidelines. For example, a household of four must earn $19,350 or less annually to qualify. Once the percentage of poverty is determined in a given district and the funds are received, federal guidelines are used to determine which students are eligible to receive the actual intervention services.

For years in our district, we used a single score on the Gates-McGinitie Test to qualify students for services. If a student scored at the 36th percentile or below on this test, she or he was eligible to receive reading intervention services. This bothered me. How, I wondered, could a single test score determine whether a child was fluent, able to comprehend the story, knew the vocabulary, could decode words, could infer meaning, or understood the concepts about print? The collapse of all these skills into one score upon which educational decisions would be made was troubling indeed. I reasoned that if my son's college batting stats could include over 15 categories of assessment including number of at bats; plate appearances; number of RBIs; number of stolen bases; number of times he was caught stealing; number of singles, doubles, and triples; number of singles, doubles, and triples with one player on base; number of singles, doubles, and triples with two players on base; number of singles, doubles, and triples with three players on base; number of fielder's choices; number of sacrifice flies; number of bunts . . . why on earth could we not accommodate a more contextual representation of a child's reading level?

Well, in the late 1990s, when the federal guidelines mandated a multicriteria approach for intervention eligibility, we added a more qualitative checklist, which was completed by the teacher in an attempt to capture the student's daily reading achievement and performance in the classroom. What was once a merely technical, clear-cut, "go/no-go" process to qualify students for services suddenly became, in Schön's (1983) words, the swampy lowland for deliberately involving ourselves in messy but crucially important problems.

In Joe's case, he scored below the 36th percentile on the test. His daily class work and the teacher's rating on the multicriteria checklist told a different story. Using a scaled scoring device that weighted these factors, it was determined that Joe did not qualify for services. However, the prevailing "wisdom" among a few significant stakeholders in the district was that Joe's score on the standardized test was more indicative of his ability to read than was his teacher's view of his daily work. Joe was a fine reader, but on that test, on that day, in that setting, he scored poorly, and so therefore he should receive services. Many others of us believed otherwise. We all "knew" that Joe was a fine reader, so I gathered those closest to the situation and we had "a reflective conversation about a unique and uncertain situation" (Schön, 1983, p. 129). I did not want to be driven by questions of technique and formal models. We reasoned that placing him in reading intervention would not only take a precious spot from a needier student, but also, and more importantly, convey to Joe an inaccurate assessment of his reading capabilities and take him away from other classroom activities. The demands of real-world practice have unique and unpredictable elements. One of the hallmarks of our profession, therefore, is the ability to take a more technical knowledge base and judge wisely, converting it into professional decisions tailored to the unique requirements of the situation. After much deliberation, the final decision was not to place Joe in reading intervention services.

I must also confess, that the story of Joe did not end there. When a few teachers in the district discovered that the qualifying score for reading intervention included their input on the multicriteria checklist, they knowingly submitted lower scores to ensure intervention services for the child. Through more deliberation, I learned that some teachers engaged in this practice motivated out of a deep sense of caring for the child. Believing that the child would benefit from reading interventions twice each day, scores were submitted to ensure eligibility. I also learned that some teachers were motivated to systematically remove poorer readers from their classrooms, believing that these students were the responsibility of someone else. Obviously neither scenario is acceptable. Teachers and principals were gathered to engage in reflective conversations so that more appropriate and professional actions could be taken.

Those advocating a more standardized management approach would point to these situations as reason enough to eliminate as much ambiguity from our work as possible. Recognizing the subjectivities of professional judgment as weak or inconsistent and calling for a more "rigorous" application of the standards, some would draw the conclusion that a strict and careful protocol designed to inoculate the school environment from contaminated or inconsistent judgment is preferred. I still believe, however, there is no substitute for professional judgment. As I said earlier, this does not mean that we advocate a flabby "anything goes" liberalism, but rather quite the opposite. Engaging in this type of professional judgment requires a sophisticated, disciplined, and intellectual rigor that exceeds any amount of mind-numbing, one-size-fits-all evaluative decision-making. Indeed, paint-by-number is the easier path. Taking the time, the energy, the caring, and the creativity to reflect upon all the nuances of a situation in order to make the most informed and wisest judgment in the best interest of the "whole" child takes a considerable amount of discipline and rigor and adherence to professional standards. Assessing, then, places a value on knowledge, rather than on a journey of understanding. A central feature of the SM paradigm is assessing for subject matter knowledge. Rob's story below offers some insight into the limited nature of assessing for subject matter knowledge only.

Rob's Story

A straight-A, honors, and advanced placement student, Rob was the kind of student who made us proud to be in education. Hard working, diligent, and committed to learning, he was a pleasure to have in class. Rob had been selected and served on the district's Curriculum Advisory Council. The Curriculum Advisory Council is composed of a variety of stakeholders, including building and central office administrators, teachers, Board of Education member representatives, parents, community members, and parents. Rob was one of four who represented the students on the council. The fundamental role of the council is to give input and provide advice to teachers and administrators as new curricula are being written and adopted.

During one of our many spirited discussions, the topic of critical thinking skills in mathematics was being debated. Some stakeholders were advocating for a deeper understanding of math with an emphasis on mathematical reasoning as a goal. This, they argued, would enable students to have the agility to apply mathematics in a variety of settings, settings that may not fit the prescribed formula or theorems. Whenever possible, they reasoned, students should have opportunities to learn mathematics through real-world contexts.

Others argued passionately that students needed to memorize math. Because of the sequential nature of mathematics, the best way to learn was in a sequential, lockstep manner. Until and unless the rules and foundation were in place, the student should not go on to higher-level mathematics.

Throughout the debate, Rob sat quietly taking it all in. Noticing his passive demeanor, I probed Rob to see how he would weigh in on all this. After all, he was our success story incarnate. In his inimitable fashion, Rob explained how he navigated his higher-level math classes and how he earned such high grades. Memorization, he admitted, was his modus operandi. He was fortunate to have a great memory for details and used this skill handily to pass math tests that required only regurgitation of algorithms and formulas. He sheepishly confessed that if the teacher changed cosigns or if the problem deviated from the formula, he was lost. He was unable to transfer his "knowledge" in novel settings. Rob faced this realization squarely one day when he was asked to tutor younger students who were struggling with algebra. He was unable to explain the reasoning behind the algorithm and therefore was unable to convey his knowledge to the younger student. The best Rob could do for the student was to tell him to memorize the material.

Being the kind of person he is, Rob took it upon himself to learn the material to better explain it to his younger friend. "If you want to learn something," he reported to the group, "try to teach it." And that is what he did. He retaught himself algebra and found examples of algebra being applied in practical applications, using real data and numbers associated with situations and problems encountered in daily life. He and his younger friend learned together. Careful not to implicate any of his teachers, Rob said he wished his teachers had emphasized reasoning over memorization, problem-solving over one right answer.

Assessing for Subject Matter Understanding

The work of Wiggins and McTighe (1998, 2005), on the other hand, is an exemplar of the constructivist best practices (CBP) paradigm. They emphasize teaching for understanding and provide useful guidance for assessing a student's subject matter understanding. They advocate alternative, authentic forms of assessment and problem-based learning that uses subject matter knowledge and skill. If we assume that students "understand" by authentic endeavors (Wiggins & McTighe, 2005), then,

> understanding is revealed in performance. Understanding is revealed as a transferability of core ideas, knowledge and skills on challenging tasks in a variety of contexts. Thus assessment for understanding must be grounded in authentic performance-based tasks. An assessment task, problem or project is authentic if it
>
> - Is realistically contextualized
>
> - Requires judgment and innovation
>
> - Asks the student to "do" the subject
>
> - Replicates key challenging situations in which adults are truly "tested" in the workplace, civic life, and in personal life
>
> - Assesses the students' ability to efficiently and effectively use a repertoire of knowledge and skill to negotiate a complex and multistage task
>
> - Allows appropriate opportunities to rehearse, practice, consult resources, get feedback, and refine performances and products
>
> An assessment approach grounded in authentic work calls for students (and teachers) to come to two important understandings: first, learning how adults in the larger world beyond the school *really* use or don't use the knowledge and skills that are taught in school; and second, learning how discrete lessons are meaningful, that is, how they lead to higher-quality performance or mastery of more important tasks. (pp. 153–155, emphasis in original)

As can be plainly seen, teaching for deeper subject matter understanding coming out of the CBP paradigm assesses content knowledge and skill as a means to a higher-quality student performance. Accepting the fact that we need to assess before we make case-by-case value judgments about the quality of a student's journey of 3S understanding, Wiggins and McTighe (1998, 2005) are enormously helpful for assessing deeper subject matter understanding, but are not particularly helpful for evaluative judgments about a student's 3S journey of understanding.

Assessing Embedded Within the Evaluating

The CW paradigm uses the best of both the SM and the CBP paradigms, and it is expanded to explicitly address the transformation or reconceptualization of subject matter content knowledge, skills, and understandings into holistic instances of democratic self and social living. Nowhere in the standardized management (SM) paradigm or the constructivist best practices paradigm are students asked to demonstrate deep subject matter understanding that fosters a democratic self and social learning. Nowhere in either of the first two paradigms are students asked to shift their orientation from an external to an internal source of authority, requiring sophisticated, context-based judgments (Henderson & Kesson, 2004). While Wiggins and McTighe (1998, 2005) provide a useful framework for conceptualizing 3S education through their "Six Facets of Understanding," the authors do not advance artful deliberation and reflective inquiry as the basis for curriculum designing and planning. This is precisely why Transformative Curriculum Leadership and the wisdom paradigm must be conceived as a way of being and a way of knowing.

It is here, then, that we use *evaluating* with reference to the holistic purpose of this work. While there is assessment going on in all three paradigms, what is missing in the first two is the evaluation; evaluating to determine the case-by-case *value* judgment of the quality of the students' 3S journey of understanding, which are personal, individual, idiosyncratic performances. The criteria for judging the quality of these performances will be as individualized as the performances themselves. Holistic evaluation is not designed to make any definitive statements, but to facilitate the *doubled* journey for students and teachers, guided by the principles of democratic ideals. We recognize the need for assessing subject matter skills and knowledge and will not shy away from that accountability; however, we embrace a higher degree of accountability with evaluative decision making, because we cannot turn a blind eye and deaf ear to the issues in students' lives that go beyond the skills and knowledge of the subject matter. The simplicity of reducing and reporting a student's subject matter knowledge and skills is a limited part of the story. We want to get away from the kind of sloppiness that comes with this narrow focus on test scores. In the grand scheme of things, from a holistic evaluative decision-making orientation, high test scores do not equate with respect of self and others; or intellectual capacities; or loving, compassionate, and caring choices; or openness to new possibilities and multiple meanings.

The curriculum wisdom (CW) paradigm challenges educators to cultivate their connoisseurship and critical capacities (Eisner, 1994) in the exercise of this artful and democratically grounded, evaluative process:

> Effective criticism, within the arts of education, is not an act independent of the powers of perception. The ability to see, to perceive what is subtle, complex, and important is its first necessary condition. The act of knowledgeable perception is, in the arts, referred to as connoisseurship. To be a connoisseur is to know how to look, to see, and to appreciate. Connoisseurship, generally defined, is the art of perception. It is essential to criticism because without the ability to perceive what is subtle and important, criticism is likely to be superficial or even empty. (p. 215)

Educators embracing the curriculum wisdom (CW) paradigm will approach their holistic, evaluative decisions through their connoisseurship and critical capacities, lest their wisdom is limited. The curriculum wisdom (CW) paradigm is not abdication of subject matter knowledge accountabilities. Skills and knowledge are not the enemy of the curriculum wisdom (CW) orientation. Quite the opposite; content skills and knowledge remain in service of the curriculum wisdom (CW) paradigm as the "stuff" used to grapple with the questions and concerns that have democratic personal and social significance.

For example, students may be asked to "describe advances and issues in Earth and space science that have important long-lasting effects on science and society" (Ohio Department of Education, 2002). Teachers have it within their purview to provide students with one of many experiences to address this grade-level indicator. Within the standardized management (SM) paradigm, students may be asked to complete and submit a work sheet that describes geological time scales and charts of exponential population growth. The teacher would assess the work sheet, enter the grade into the grade book, and move on to the next indicator.

Within the curriculum wisdom (CW) paradigm, this would be like a proverb; I hear, I forget; I see, I remember; I do, I understand. This grade-level indicator might be reconceptualized to include a more purposeful direction guided by a big idea. Wiggins and McTighe (1998, 2005) suggest that big ideas are the building material of understandings, which enable the student to connect the dots of fragmented knowledge. The reconceptualized standard might look something like this: "Describe an experience in which you were personally affected by advances and issues in Earth and space science and prepare a position paper for publication, which argues for sustaining the planet and its occupants." The students and the teacher may collaboratively discuss ways that global warming and depletion of resources are being affected by exponential population growth, for example. Each student would offer ways they have been personally affected. One student might share that she has relatives who live in New Orleans, which was devastated by two hurricanes in 2005. Hurricanes have been pounding the coast for centuries, but the force and frequency of recent hurricanes are believed to be the result of global warming. She may wonder why this happened to people she knows and loves. She may wonder whether the people in New Orleans are being punished for some unknown reason. She may want to know how such death and devastation could be avoided in the future. In order for her to grapple with these personal and meaningful questions and concerns, she needs subject matter knowledge and skills to respond intelligently. When the subject matter knowledge and skills are presented within a real-life context that is personally meaningful to the student, she will more readily and willingly learn about geologic time scales and the politics of global warming, depletion of resources, and exponential population growth because her family in New Orleans has been so affected. Her naive notions about hurricanes as a punishment are matured with accurate context information. When she is encouraged to express her subject matter knowledge and skill in public, pragmatic, and idiosyncratic performances, which foreground her holistic, personal, and social democratic journey of understanding, she and the teacher will judge the value of her expression together. Daily lesson plans provide students with the time and support to learn the subject matter content and thereby prepare the position paper for a public demonstration of understanding. Figure 6.1 captures the embedded nature of assessing subject matter knowledge within the holistic evaluation of a student's 3S journey of understanding.

Figure 6.1 The Embedded Nature of Assessing Subject Matter Knowledge

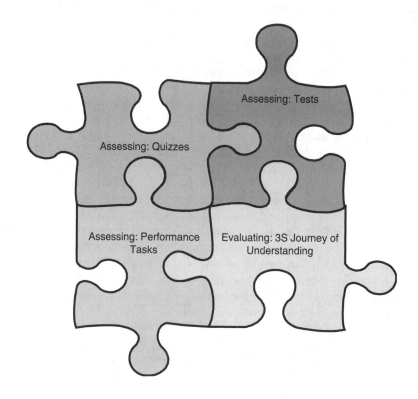

EVALUATING THE JOURNEY AND THE JUDGMENT FOR A TRANSFORMATIVE EXPERIENCE

As you have read so many times throughout this book, Transformative Curriculum Leadership is about elevating one's judgment and evolving through a journey of personal and interpersonal societal changes. This kind of leadership suggests both deep-seated change, tied to the journey of understanding, and elevated judgment for a transformed experience. In this chapter, we are not advancing another method, procedure, metric, or method for evaluation. Evaluation done in the spirit of transformative curriculum leadership means two things: that you are constantly improving your *judgment*, and in this case your *evalu*ative judgment, and also that you are on this *journey* of change. The nature of the curriculum wisdom (CW) orientation embraces the personal, contextual, case-by-case aspects of teaching and learning as judgment and journey. We believe that evaluating 3S education is impossible through a methodological lens that attempts to screen out engagement. We agree with Schwandt (2002) that through evaluation, we are in search of practical knowledge, knowledge of how to be a particular kind of person. This type of knowledge gained through evaluation is inaccessible to method. We accept the fact that there are problems in human and social life with no good solutions. We are reconciled to the idea that there are ambiguities, doubts, and moral agonies that cannot be solved through another method, legislation, or another assessment. We do not desire to impose order on the messiness of this human endeavor. Evaluating 3S education will not make sense if we conceive of this evaluation in terms of the "logic of evaluation" (Sanders, 2000), replete with "monological practice dedicated to constructing and employing methods of sound reasoning from empirical premises to evaluate conclusions" (Schwandt, 2002, p. 73).

Instead of acting like impartial judges, we suggest what Schwandt (2002) refers to as critical intelligence, in which evaluators would "seek to make their practice continuous with the work of clients and stakeholders by becoming partners in an ethically informed, reasoned conversation about essentially contested concepts like . . . education" (p. 71). This critical intelligence is the willingness and capacity to deliberate the values of various ends of a practice, and it is fundamentally an exercise on practical–moral reasoning. Evaluating 3S education requires this type of critical intelligence. "Evaluation concerned with teaching critical intelligence seeks to improve the rationality of practices in the field of . . . education . . . by enabling practitioners . . . to refine the practices for themselves" (Schwandt, 2002, p. 72). The evaluator does not intervene as a knowledge expert, working rather "as a partner enabling conversation, introducing new ideas, and facilitating examination and critique" (p. 72).

In chapter 2, we cited the American Evaluation Association (AEA) position statement on high-stakes testing in pre-K–12 education. The AEA supports systems of assessment and accountability that help education, but it opposes the use of paper–pencil tests as the sole or primary criterion for making decisions. The limits of this kind of testing, it says, carry serious negative consequences for students, educators, and schools. The simplistic application of a single test or test batteries to make high-stakes decisions about individuals and groups impedes rather than improves student learning because it leads to underserving or misserving all students, especially the most needy and vulnerable. The AEA's expectation for improved evaluation practice, on the other hand, includes the principle that important decisions should be made on the basis of multiple criteria and multiple high-quality measures. The AEA states and we agree that:

> The most serious problem with high stakes testing is its insistence that education be evaluated in a narrow way. The practice of high stakes testing in America is an effort to treat teaching and learning in a simple and fair manner, but in a world where education is hugely complex with inequitable distribution of opportunity. When we increase the standardization of education, we need challenges from multiple viewpoints as to the costs and benefits for the children in our schools. Education requires decisions as to how children, teachers, and schools will be sustained, improved, and promoted, but high stakes testing oversimplifies the decision to be made. We declare our obligations to follow the principle of "do no harm," and that requires us to examine consequences in real situations for all people affected, not just authorities. Current high stakes testing policies and practices fail to provide the mechanisms of review, meta-evaluation, and validation demanded by our professional standards. (p. 3)

Enabling conversation, introducing new ideas, and facilitating examination and critique of consequences in real situations for all people affected poses challenges. Because engagement is central to evaluating 3S education, we now revisit a few of the negotiation strategies (Walker, 2003), which you were introduced to in chapter 5. Not everyone will agree with this visionary curriculum. The ability to negotiate is an important component of this work and will be integrated within the evaluative process, which you will be introduced to shortly. These negotiation strategies are listed again for your review:

1. Achieving working agreement

2. Making principled decisions

3. Working constructively with teachers

4. Seeking substantial, lasting improvement

5. Facing conflict constructively

6. Combining curriculum work with other initiatives

Now that we have clarified evaluating as a central feature of the curriculum wisdom (CW) problem-solving cycle, proposed a definition of evaluation from a transformative point of view, and offered a distinction between assessing and evaluation with assessing being embedded in evaluation, in the next section we will provide a five-question scaffold for evaluative decision making about the two fundamental challenges and four decision making processes, which are key in transformative curriculum leadership.

SCAFFOLDING FOR EVALUATIVE DECISION MAKING

Curriculum evaluation depends on how educators answer at least five important questions: Who decides what will be assessed and evaluated? What questions are to be answered? How might data be gathered and analyzed? What criteria will be used to interpret and judge data? Who analyzes data, makes judgments, and uses judgments? Borrowing from Henderson and Hawthorne (2000) and Henderson and Kesson (2004), let's examine both how these evaluative questions might be addressed through the wisdom paradigm/transformative approach and the relationships between and among the people doing the evaluating.

How Are We Doing?

With a sense of adventure on this journey of understanding, let's explore and ask ourselves how we are doing with reconceptualizing subject standards into holistic understanding goals; how we are doing with cultivating our reflective inquiry capacity using the seven reflective inquiries; how we are doing with our designing and planning; how we are doing with our expressive performances of understanding, criteria for judging the quality of the 3S journey of understanding, and the generative learning experiences; and how we are doing with our teach*ing*. When you strip it all away, this is essentially what we want to know when we evaluate anything . . . just how are we doing?

As stated in chapter 1, whether you are grappling with the two fundamental challenges or the four decision-making processes, it is not possible to precisely demarcate where one ends and another begins. For purposes of clarity, we have separated and grouped the fundamental challenges from the decision-making process and attempt to provide evaluative guidance by offering suggested responses to the five evaluative questions in each area. The holistic nature of this kind of curriculum evaluation will be really apparent. The suggested responses to these five basic questions are just that, suggestions, and not intended to be used as a script or a step-by-step formula for 3S evaluative decision making.

Quick Reminder: Two Things

It is also important to remember that assessing is embedded in evaluating. *Assessing* is gathering evidence of students' content knowledge and skills, and *evaluating* is the case-by-case value judgment of the quality of the students' 3S journey of understanding. Depending upon which process we are evaluating, assessing will either be foregrounded or backgrounded. This is a subtle but important distinction. Also, when in doubt about evaluating the quality of your deliberations, decision-making processes, or curriculum judgments, refer to this question to keep you on track:

> *Have the teacher's curriculum judgments been elevated to include moral decisions that touch the core of what it means to be human, to live in community with others, to find meaning and purpose, and to create a more just and peaceful world?*

EVALUATING TWO FUNDAMENTAL CHALLENGES FOR 3S EDUCATION

> *Who decides what will be assessed and evaluated?* Teachers, students, parents, and administrators all have a stake in what aspects of the reconceptualized standards, reflective inquiry capacity, and learning communities will be evaluated. However, a smaller group of faculty members, administrators, and students who worked on the program, course, or unit/lesson planning may be involved to deal specifically with the expressive performances of understanding and the criteria for judgment.

> *What questions are to be answered?* To what extent was the hidden/null curriculum and "freedom from . . . freedom to" dialectic considered? Were deliberations open, honest, and inclusive of all perspectives? Do the reconceptualized standards address subject matter learning in a context of democratic self and social learning? What are the conditions under which 3S understanding takes place? How do teachers engage in collegial collaboration and dialogic exchanges

related to teaching and learning? Do teachers' reflective practices address teaching methods and prompt collaborative conversations about the impact of teaching on students' learning? Does reflective inquiry result in a problem-solving process for making wise curriculum judgments related to students' 3S understandings? To what extent do our reflective inquiries encourage students and teachers to become aware of the aesthetic and spiritual dimensions of their work? What is the evidence that teachers are relying less on habit or custom and more on critical intellect as they think deeply about the consequences of their actions? Do teachers explore diverse points of view, confront basic beliefs, and negotiate through multiperspective conversations? What is the evidence that teachers challenge existing practices and ethically ground their actions to create safe classrooms where students will flourish and experience democratic ideals? Are educators able to negotiate with people working out of a different frame of reference? Is there evidence of other relevant explorations and investigations, which guide teaching and student learning?

How might data be gathered and analyzed? Gathering data to describe the holistic transformative standards could involve currere narratives about the actual deliberations, as well as currere narratives from students about their expressive performances of 3S understanding, classroom observations, students' performances of 3S understanding, educators' performances of 3S understanding, portfolios, quizzes, local tests, and standardized tests. Gathering data to describe the quality of our reflective inquiry capacities and the manner in which we are building professional and stakeholder learning communities could involve currere narratives about the actual reflective inquiry used to guide planning and problem solving, as well as currere narratives from students about their reflective inquiry as a guide for deep 3S understanding. Classroom observations, students' performances of 3S understanding, educators' performances of 3S understanding, and portfolios could also be gathered and analyzed.

What criteria will be used to interpret and judge data? Criteria are statements that describe sought-after qualities and, within the curriculum wisdom (CW) paradigm, require consideration and interpretation. The criteria to interpret and judge the collected data could include indicators such as 3S balance, clarity, complex and creative thinking, idiosyncratic demonstrations of holistic subject matter, self and social understandings, bias-free testing, developmental appropriateness, and facets of understanding (Wiggins & McTighe, 1998, 2005). The reflective inquiries, students' and teachers' complex and creative thinking, evidence of the seven reflective inquiries in students' and teachers' work, idiosyncratic demonstrations of holistic subject matter, and self and social understandings are evident.

Who analyzes data, makes judgments, and uses judgments? Teachers, students, parents, administrators, and all stakeholders have a stake in the analysis of the data for making judgments about the reconceptualized standards, reflective inquiries, and learning communities.

EVALUATING PLATFORM DESIGNING AND PLANNING FOR 3S EDUCATION

Evaluating our platform and planning decisions will foreground *assessing,* which is embedded in *evaluating.* Assessing is gathering evidence of students' deep understanding of subject content knowledge and skills, and our planning decisions for program, course, and unit/lessons will surface here. Assessing for subject skills and knowledge of the reconceptualized holistic understanding goals includes asking students to demonstrate deep subject matter understanding that fosters a progressive self and social learning around big ideas and essential questions (Wiggins & McTighe, 2005). This would include observations, dialogues, quizzes, tests, performance tasks and projects, and students' self-assessment gathered over time. Alternative, authentic forms of assessment and problem-based learning that uses subject matter knowledge and skill would include tasks that are realistically contextualized, require judgment and innovation, replicate key challenging situations in which adults are truly "tested" in the workplace, civic life, and in personal life etc (Wiggins & McTighe, 2005). Included in evaluating the designing and planning would be an evaluation of the expressive outcomes, the criteria for judging the quality of the 3S journey of understanding, and the generative learning experiences.

> *Who decides what will be assessed and evaluated?* Teachers, students, parents, community members, Board of Education members, university professors, and administrators all have a stake in evaluating the platform designing and planning for students' 3S understanding. However, a smaller group of faculty members, administrators, and students who worked on the program, course, or unit/lesson planning may be involved in this task to share specific information about the expressive performances of understanding and the criteria for judgment and the generative learning experiences. Members of the smaller group need to evaluate the work in process and in retrospect. The group generates questions that will focus the inquiry; identifies or creates data gathering tools and processes; establishes criteria or indicators; gathers data; reports the data to the larger platform group and the faculty at large; and leads the process of analyzing, interpreting, and making judgments. Just as in the actual design work, the evaluating group should include people with various roles, genders, and perspectives. Specific training may be needed to develop this process. Because platform designing and program, course, and unit/lesson planning are just slightly different expressions of curriculum development, many of our considerations about platform design also apply to evaluating the planning. The challenge is that teachers' problem solving and thinking are often private activities. One measure of the efficacy of the planning is the extent to which teachers worked in collaborative groups and engaged in artful deliberations.
>
> *What questions are to be answered?* What problems and issues did the deliberations focus on, that is, reconceptualized standards, performances of understanding, and judgment criteria for evaluating the quality of the student's 3S journey of understanding? How did the group engage the faculty and community at large in

the sharing of currere narratives and in the renderings of the future for today's students? How was the draft design shared with other faculty members and the community? In what ways were others' interpretations and reactions to the draft obtained and used? What assumptions and principles related to inclusion of special students were considered and used? In what ways were teacher–student relationships portrayed? Did cultivating our reflective inquiry capacities deepen these relationships? In what ways and to what extent were matters of equity, diversity, justice, and inclusion of all students considered? How were alternative views sought and considered? How were conflicts resolved? Whose interests were and were not represented? In what ways were teacher–student relationships enacted? Did cultivating our reflective inquiry capacities deepen these relationships? How are teachers interpreting the purposes, rationale, and key features of the platform design? How are teachers interpreting the interests and readiness of their students to engage in personally meaningful and democratically wise expressions of their understandings? Were subject matter knowledge and skills presented within real-life contexts that were personally meaningful to the student? Were expressions of that knowledge and skill appreciated in a variety of idiosyncratic expressions and performances that foreground the student's personal and social democratic journey of understanding? Were observations, dialogues, quizzes, tests, performance tasks and projects, and students' self-assessment gathered over time used to assess students' subject matter knowledge? How were alternative, authentic forms of assessment and problem-based learning used to assess subject matter knowledge and skill? Were students asked to shift their orientation from an external to an internal source of authority, requiring sophisticated, context-based judgments? What was evaluated to determine the case-by-case value judgment of the quality of the students' 3S journey of understanding? How would we evaluate the doubled journey for students and teachers? How did educators cultivate their connoisseurship and critical capacities?

How might data be gathered and analyzed? Gathering data to describe the platform design, course, and unit/lesson planning group's deliberations involves observing and recording each of the meetings. Walker (2003) developed an observation system for capturing types of problems, options, and arguments within the deliberations. Currere narratives of teachers, students, faculty, and parents about their experience with the results of the platform design as it impacted the program, course, and unit/lesson work would provide fertile data. These raw data will identify whether or not the design group's aims, assumptions, beliefs, and values were upheld in the translations to the classroom.

What criteria will be used to interpret and judge data? Criteria are statements that describe sought-after qualities and, within the curriculum wisdom (CW) paradigm, require consideration and interpretation. Consideration of this criterion involves the capacity to make a deliberative judgment about the nature and qualities of student engagements based on one's observation of hundreds of cases of engagement and an implicit set of indicators that distinguish comprehensive, elegant, complex, balanced, or deep forms of engagements from average and below-average forms

(Eisner, 1998). Some criteria could be technical or logical. Others could be drawn from principles of pedagogy and still others from ethical, political, social, cultural, and aesthetic sources. Appropriateness and authenticity of the problem-based activities are best evaluated with the use of rubrics. The criteria for judging the quality of student performances should be as individualized as the performances themselves.

Who analyzes data, makes judgments, and uses judgments? Teachers, students, parents, community members, Board of Education members, university professors, and administrators all have a stake in analyzing data, making judgments, and using judgments about the platform design for students' 3S understanding. Faculty members, administrators, and students who worked on the program, course, or unit/lesson planning may be involved here.

EVALUATING TEACHING FOR 3S UNDERSTANDING

The quality of the teaching–learning relationship is the heart of Transformative Curriculum Leadership. The teaching–learning relationship touches all four of the decision-making processes in chapters 4 through 7, as well as the two fundamental challenges in chapters 2 and 3. *Nothing* is more important than the relationship between the teacher and the student, and the reconceptualized standards are key here. It follows, that evaluating the teaching–learning relationship will also have far-reaching implications into every other area. We are after holistic evaluating because we are after holistic understanding. Teaching must match evaluation and vice-versa. We need to be engaged holistically in transformative goals, performances of understanding, and judgment criteria. A performance of understanding, or what Eisner (2002) calls an expressive outcome, is the outcome a student realizes whether or not that outcome was specifically sought. In the earlier example, the student researching global warming and exponential population growth and her teacher knew exactly what specific content knowledge and skills would be demonstrated. However, the exact depth or scope of the student's personal meaning making probably surfaced during and after the public demonstration of the subject matter self and social understandings. This kind of learning defies a preordained, precise list of objectives, because of its personal, intuitive, and emergent qualities. Stake (1974, in Eisner, 2002) calls this *responsive evaluation* in contrast to preordinate evaluation. Eisner (2002) clarifies this distinction: "The evaluation process connected to expressive outcomes is applied after the fact instead of attempting to match outcomes with intentions" (p. 161). Within the wisdom paradigm, curriculum activities "can be intentionally planned that are likely to yield an unpredictable and heterogeneous array of outcomes" (p. 161). Rubrics can be written to establish criteria for judging the quality of the student's 3S journey of understanding, and Wiggins and McTighe's (1998, 2005) Six Facets of Understanding are a good starting point.

Criteria are statements that describe sought-after qualities, which require consideration and interpretation. Consideration of these criteria involves the capacity to make a deliberative judgment about the nature and qualities of student engagements. Criteria could be technical or logical and drawn from principles of pedagogy, and still others could come from ethical, political, social, cultural, and aesthetic sources. Students should know these in advance of the commencement of their work. However, as stated earlier, the exact depth or scope of the student's personal meaning making will probably surface during and after the public demonstration of the subject matter self and social understandings. The teacher's judgment criteria will have been set and shared with students, perhaps outlined in rubric. The teacher's final evaluation, however, will be suspended because of personal, intuitive, and emergent qualities of the student's performance of understanding. The teacher and the student remain open to unanticipated outcomes, signaling deeper subject matter and self, and social understanding. The curriculum wisdom (CW) orientation fosters evaluative judgment because it encourages us, even demands that we continue to learn how to teach. There is no substitute for teacher judgment.

Who decides what will be assessed and evaluated? Teachers, students, parents, community members, Board of Education members, university professors, and administrators all have a stake in evaluating teaching for students' 3S understanding. However, a smaller group of faculty members, administrators, and students who actually worked on the course or unit/lesson planning may be involved in this task to share specific information about the expressive performances of understanding and the criteria for judgment and the generative learning experiences. Teachers and students primarily will evaluate their own working relationship. The challenge is that teachers' problem solving and thinking are often private activities. One measure of the efficacy of the teaching is the extent to which teachers worked in collaborative groups and engaged in deliberation such as lesson study.

What questions are to be answered? Are teachers planning lessons that promote student inquiry? Are students allowed to find their own meanings? In what ways do students make sense of subject matter knowledge and skills? Do students have a firm grasp of the basic subject matter knowledge and skills? In what ways is student–student, student–teacher, or student–parent collaborative problem-solving occurring? How aesthetically are teachers aware of the physical and emotional work environment? How are the expressive outcomes of the student and the teacher celebrated? In what ways are the issues of ethics, diversity, equity, and civility manifested in the classroom and the school? Are teacher and student inquiries fostering the eradication of overt and covert forms of bias related to gender, race, class, sexual orientation, and other significant human differences? In what ways are students' active meaning-making experiences extending into lifelong habits of inquiry? Do teachers problem-solve together? In what ways are the varying degrees of the teacher's, developmental readiness accepted? *Have the teacher's curriculum judgments been elevated to include moral decisions that touch the core of what it means to be human, to live in community with others, to find meaning and purpose, and to create a more just and peaceful world?*

How might data be gathered and analyzed? Gathering data to describe the teaching–learning relationship involves gathering currere narratives of teachers, students, faculty, and parents about their experience. These raw data will identify whether or not the design groups' aims, assumptions, beliefs, and values were upheld in the translations to the classroom. Observations, dialogues, quizzes, tests, performance tasks and projects, and students' self-assessment will be gathered over time. Collecting and analyzing generative lesson plan would reveal support for students' 3S journey of understanding. Alignment of the performances of understanding to the reconceptualized standards and the criteria for judging the quality of the performances is essential. Alternative, authentic forms of assessment and problem-based learning are another source. Case-by-case value judgments about the quality of a student's journey of 3S understanding could be gathered and analyzed.

What criteria will be used to interpret and judge data? Standardized tests have established norms that indicate the average score and the percentiles above and below the mean. The state, district, and school can establish their own criteria for success on tests. Rubrics can be written to establish criteria for judging the quality of the student's 3S journey of understanding. Wiggins and McTighe's (1998, 2005) Six Facets of Understanding is a good starting point. Appropriateness and authenticity of the problem-based activities are best assessed and evaluated with the use of rubrics. Criteria are statements that describe sought-after qualities and, within the curriculum wisdom (CW) paradigm, require consideration and interpretation. Consideration of this criterion involves the capacity to make a deliberative judgment about the nature and qualities of student engagements. Criteria could be technical or logical. Others could be drawn from principles of pedagogy and still others from ethical, political, social, cultural, and aesthetic sources. The criteria for judging the quality of student performances should be as individualized as the performances themselves.

Who analyzes data, makes judgments, and uses judgments? Teachers, students, parents, community members, and administrators all have a stake in analyzing data, making judgments, and using judgments about the teaching–learning relationship for students' 3S understanding. Students must be active agents in analyzing and judging their own learning. Teachers individually and collectively analyze data to identify who is learning what and what are the achievement differences related to gender, special needs, race, and socioeconomic status. Parents and community members receive published "report cards" from the state department of education, ranking standardized test data. Community forums allow students to provide additional data on the personal and societal impact of their performances of understanding.

ACCOUNTABLE AND RESPONSIBLE

In our view, the standardized management (SM) paradigm is most prevalent in the area of assessment and evaluation. Assessment seems to be the point of intensification within this paradigm for educators. Teachers lament that the testing movement has forced them to bowl over children's personalities, turning a blind eye and a deaf ear to the subtext of kids' lives in the name of memorizing discrete facts for the test. There is no time, they report, for caring in a way that confirms a student's best self (Noddings, 1984). Please note, as stated earlier, that we embrace accountability and have carefully "mined" this approach for what it offers educators: academic dialogue, collaboration in a culture of isolation around curriculum mapping (Jacobs, 1997), Understanding by Design (Wiggins & McTighe, 1998, 2005), and Lesson Study (Stigler & Hiebert, 1999), for example. We recognize that as a result of the accountability movement, many teachers are embracing a more "systems approach" to their material, developing a greater understanding of grade-level expectations for students in previous and subsequent grades. Adequate or marginal teachers needing external intervention are, at long last, being sufficiently guided and coached. Students need and deserve to learn their basic skills. Providing opportunities for "gatekeeper skills" ensures that "students are minimally equipped to pursue more schooling, frame and express their thoughts and participate in their local and national communities" (Hess, 2004, p. 4). Additionally, we are painfully aware that each year, more than a million children leave high school without mastering the basic skills (Hess, 2004) and that an ever-widening achievement gap exists in the United States between White students and students of color. We know that every student should be literate and numerate so that the gates of opportunity may be opened.

While this is all well and good, the accountability movement within the standardized management (SM) paradigm robs teachers of opportunities to be accountable to and responsible for an even higher standard. It is a standard that leads to curriculum improvement, which can be a means for a vision about a society where citizens are open to continuous dialogue over their core beliefs; a society in which they consciously choose *not* to be comfortable, nonquestioning true believers; a society in which citizens accept the give and take of differing points of view because they possess a balanced outlook on life with a full appreciation of subtleties, ironies, and ambiguities; and a place where critical maturity is cultivated, celebrating democratic, multicultural principles, activities, and institutions (Henderson & Hawthorne, 1995). Eisner (2002) reminds us that reforms in education harbor an implicit conception of human nature; so do governments and so does religion. The conception of human nature residing deep within the current accountability movement relegates students and teachers to a role of bystander, rather than to a role of active citizens of a vibrant democracy. The accountability movement, with its emphasis on standardized testing alone, fosters a culture of competition, suspicion, and distrust for professionals, which have led to "policies and practices that monitor, mandate, measure, and manage; policies that seek to prescribe and control that do not distinguish between training and education" (pp. 174–175).

Given the right environment, we believe that Transformative Curriculum Leadership will produce high test scores *and* create "good" people living a democratically wise "good" life. Accountability is built into the curriculum wisdom (CW) paradigm and serves an essential component of our responsibility, but it is not limited to the accountability in the standardized management (SM) paradigm. Accountability within the curriculum wisdom (CW) paradigm uses assessing in a more holistic manner that leads to the case-by-case value judgment of a student's 3S journey of understanding. We want to be responsible for kids effectively using knowledge in diverse, authentic, and realistically messy contexts. We want to be responsible for students revealing a personalized, thoughtful, and coherent grasp of subjects and demonstrating the ability to think for themselves. We want to be responsible for students who are wide awake, willing to welcome new insights, refining core beliefs through conversations with diverse others. We want to be responsible for students who have demonstrated the ability to effectively and sensitively interpret texts with the ability to read between the lines. We want to be responsible for students who have extended or applied what is known in novel ways to become more cognitively, emotionally, physically, aesthetically, and spiritually attuned to themselves and others.

During our evaluative deliberations, we must consider the implications of our decisions with respect to such criteria as "good conduct" and "enduring values." The evaluative focus is on the enduring values of democratically good living, not the values of good test-taking behavior. "The key point is that the tests would inform curriculum judgment, not be used as a substitute for judgment (Henderson & Kesson, 2004, p. 93). We must think about the relationship between educational means and ends and ask ourselves whether the testing (means) justifies the scores (ends) and return to the basic evaluative question: Have the teacher's curriculum judgments been elevated to include moral decisions that touch the core of what it means to be human, to live in community with others, to find meaning and purpose, and to create a more just and peaceful world?

NEGOTIATE, NEGOTIATE, NEGOTIATE

Given the nature of this kind of curriculum leadership, one can readily see the virtue of skillful negotiations throughout the evaluative decision-making process. The involved stakeholders are rarely of one mind. Walker (2003) recognizes that complete consensus in any area is near impossible, and he encourages working agreement on actions. This is not just about telling stories. Informal, often polite talk among people who enjoy one another does not necessarily raise consciousness about our practice or surface critical questions for problem solving. Making principled curriculum decisions based upon democratic morality is essential. As Dewey (1939/1989, p. 100) reminds us, "The democratic road is the hard one to take. It is the road which places the greatest burden of responsibility upon the greatest number of human beings." Principled curriculum decisions help us realize democracy as a "way of personal life and one which provides a moral standard for personal conduct" (Dewey 1939/1989, p. 101). This requires working constructively with teachers. Building teachers' trust is achieved by demonstrating excellence quietly and modestly (Walker, 2003). Respecting the full range of educational beliefs and traditions held by teachers, while looking for innovations that will help teachers meet the needs of their students is an important first step. Meeting the needs of students is where most teachers derive their greatest satisfaction.

As a transformative curriculum leader, you may concur that in some situations, for some students, for some amount of time that a standardized management practice may be appropriate. Timed math tests, to increase students' agility with addition and subtraction facts, for example, may seem like a drill-and-kill method. However, if this activity is holistically embedded for a greater purpose, it can be an important strategy for giving students access to projects and performances that they otherwise would not be able to embrace.

You recognize at the same time, however, that you are working out of a different frame of reference. It may be that you have to comply, in spite of your judgment to incorporate more of the evaluative decision making. You may be constrained for a variety of reasons and you do not want to burn bridges, so you go along to get along. Keep in mind that we are *always* trying to invite people into a wisdom frame of reference. We must stay vigilantly in pursuit of "wiggle room" (Cuban, 2003, p. 3) to maintain a sense of integrity about this kind of curriculum leadership.

If we are seeking substantial, lasting improvement, we must learn how to face conflict constructively. Walker (2003) draws an important distinction between conflict and controversy. He concedes that conflict is inevitable, but with skilled deliberation controversy can usually be avoided. If and when deep differences of beliefs and values exist between stakeholders, curriculum leaders should take great pains to keep the lines of communication open.

GOOD COMPANY FOR THE JOURNEY

By now, you may be deciding not to join us on the journey. Staying home may be looking better and better with each chapter you read. You may feel so bogged down in assessing, even alternative authentic assessing, that you cannot imagine how in the world you will find time for deeper evaluative judgments.

Before you take your boots off and flop into the nearest recliner, we need to keep in mind that whether we know it or not, we make evaluative decisions every day. Regardless of whether what we evaluate is reported and published as part of the "measured" data for ranking the quality of the students, school, or district, we are still evaluating. We must keep the focus on what students are learning, not defending this curriculum wisdom orientation. If nothing else, if you cannot find wiggle room for evaluative decision making in your current setting, you are encouraged to continue to work on building your own reflective inquiry capacity. This important step will actually move you along your own journey of understanding, which in the long run will affect your deliberations, your practice, and most importantly your relationship with your students.

Districts that had beaten the "report card" rap by having students score well on standardized tests seemed to be in a better position to focus on the curriculum wisdom (CW) paradigm. Believing that these districts had met the prescribed levels of accountability on state mandates tests, finding more wiggle room for engaging students and teachers was a greater possibility. We have come to believe, however, that the curriculum wisdom orientation may be the very approach that will ensure that students perform well on subject matter standardized tests, for it is within the very personal that meaning surfaces and real learning takes place.

In the next chapter, you will learn about organizing the teacher workday to find the wiggle room and to increase the likelihood of realizing a vision of schooling grounded in human development, creativity, justice, caring, equity, and community. You will learn about heightening your awareness of the value, strength, and potential of ourselves and others and overcoming the limits that we impose, often unconsciously, on our own capacities. In an earlier narrative, I spoke about the power to choose; the power to take action that allows us to be the author of our worlds, rather than reading from someone's script; the power to wake up and start asking questions about what may have been a taken-for-granted reality in your classroom, school, and life; and the power to participate actively in our own evolution.

Through the work of Dr. David Cooperrider of Case Western Reserve University, you will learn about Appreciative Inquiry, an approach to change that suggests we look for what works in an organization. Appreciative inquiry suggests that we pay special attention to "the best of the past and present" in order to "ignite the collective imagination of what might be" (Cooperrider & Srivastva, 1987). The tangible result of appreciative inquiry is a series of statements that describe where a school wants to be, based on high moments of where it has been. Because these statements are, in essence, currere narratives grounded in real experiences and history, stakeholders know how to repeat their success. Using Appreciative Inquiry, participants determine where they already see evidence of students' 3S journeys of understanding and then how these can be repeated and expanded. By stirring up memories of energizing moments in which students and teachers experienced the liberty that makes self-government possible, they are filled with a sense of commitment and confidence to repeat what works. In the words of Robert Lewis Stevenson, "Speak only that which you choose to have come into manifestation now and continuously."

Put your boots back on, grab your backpack, and let's continue on the journey. Hope springs eternal.

REFERENCES

Cooperrider, D. L., & Srivastva, S. (1987). Appreciative inquiry in organizational life. *Research in Organizational Change and Development, 1,* 129–169.

Cuban, L. (2003). *Why is it so hard to get good schools?* New York: Teachers College Press.

Dewey, J. (1989). *Freedom and culture.* Buffalo, NY: Prometheus. (Original work published 1939)

Eisner, E. (1994). *The educational imagination: On the design and evaluation of school programs* (3rd ed.). New York: Macmillan College Publishing.

Eisner, E. (1998). *The enlightened eye: Qualitative inquiry and the enhancement of educational practice.* Upper Saddle River, NJ: Merrill/Prentice Hall.

Eisner, E. (2002). *The arts and the creation of the mind.* New Haven and London: Yale University Press.

Henderson, J. G., & Hawthorne, R. D. (1995). *Transformative curriculum leadership* (1st ed.). Upper Saddle River, NJ: Merrill/Prentice Hall.

Henderson, J. G., & Hawthorne, R. D. (2000). *Transformative curriculum leadership* (2nd ed.). Upper Saddle River, NJ: Merrill/Prentice Hall.

Henderson, J. G., & Kesson, K. R. (2004). *Curriculum wisdom: Educational decisions in democratic societies.* Upper Saddle River, NJ: Merrill/Prentice Hall.

Hess, F. M. (2004). *Common sense school reform.* New York: Palgrave Macmillan.

Jacobs, H. H. (1997). *Mapping the big picture: Integrating curriculum and assessment K–12.* Alexandria, VA: Association for Supervision and Curriculum Development.

Noddings, N. (1984). *Caring: A feminine approach to ethics and moral education.* Berkeley: University of California Press.

Ohio Department of Education (2002). *Ohio Academic Content Standards K–12 English Language Arts.* Columbus, OH: Author.

Pinar, W. F. (2005). The problem with curriculum and pedagogy. *Journal of Curriculum and Pedagogy, 2*(1), 67–82.

Sanders, J. R. (2000). *Evaluating school programs: An educator's guide* (2nd ed.). Thousand Oaks, CA: Corwin Press.

Schön, D. A. (1983). *Reflective practitioner.* New York Basic Books.

Schwandt, T. A. (2002). *Evaluation practice reconsidered.* New York: Peter Lang.

Scriven, M. (1967). The methodology of evaluation. In R. Iyler, R. Gagné, & M. Scriven, *Perspectives of curriculum evaluation* (pp. 39–83). Chicago: Rand McNally.

Stigler, J. W., & Hiebert, J. (1999). *The teaching gap.* New York: The Free Press.

Walker, D. F. (2003). *Fundamentals of curriculum: Passion and professionalism* (2nd ed.). Mahwah, NJ: Lawrence Erlbaum Associates.

Wiggins, G., & McTighe, J. (1998). *Understanding by design* (1st ed.). Alexandria, VA: Association for Supervision and Curriculum Development.

Wiggins, G., & McTighe, J. (2005). *Understanding by design* (2nd ed.). Alexandria, VA: Association for Supervision and Curriculum Development.

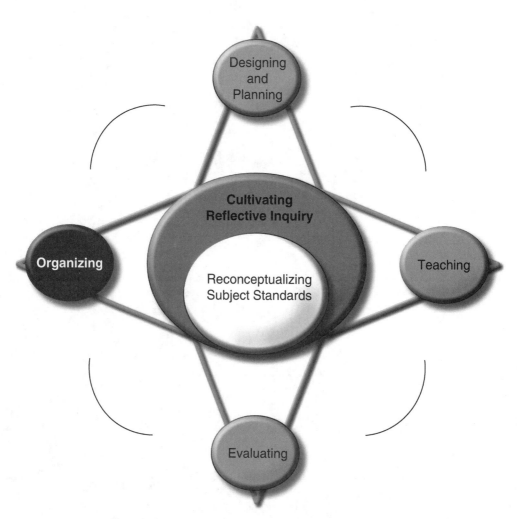

Sustaining the Curriculum Wisdom Problem Solving

CHAPTER 7

ORGANIZING FOR 3S EDUCATION

Organizing is a deep impulse. The history of life is a history of organization, disorganization, and reorganization. Life is attracted to order. Life opens to more possibilities through new patterns of connection. There is an innate striving in all forms of matter to organize into relationships. When we work with organizing-as-process rather than organization-as-object, it changes what we do. Processes do their own work. Our task is to provide what they need to begin their work. Behind all our organizing is the desire to accomplish, to create something more. In this desire, we mimic the world. Life organizes to discover new varieties, different capacities. We reach out to others to create a new being. We reach out to grow the world into new possibilities.
   (Wheatley & Kellner-Rogers, 1996, pp. 28–37)

We begin chapter 7 with this quotation because it offers an image of *organizing* that we believe creates conditions within which 3S education will flourish. Organizing for 3S education requires us to think differently about the culture of schools and the ways we have been affected by the schools *we* have created. 3S education is designed to energize and provoke growth in students and teachers. It is literally a life-giving, galvanizing, educational course to be run. Henderson and Kesson (2004, p. 1) cite Doll, who states, "Curriculum is . . . a coursing, as in an electric current. The curriculum should tap into this intense current within, that which courses through the inner person, that which electrifies or gives life to a person's energy source." Organizing for 3S education requires us to develop a different understanding of how we organize for human endeavor (Wheatley & Kellner-Rogers, 1996).

   The existing structure in schools supports the organizing problem of the standardized management (SM) paradigm: how to get kids to pass the test. Let's not be surprised that the structures we created in schools to support this work are hierarchical, predictable, rule-bound, role-bound, and based on bureaucratic routines. Think back to chapter 1 and the discussion about the power of the paradigm. For decades, educational scholars have advanced a professional orientation that is straightforward and based on administrators managing teachers into positions of paralyzing conformity through the creation of an accountability system geared to student learning achievement as measured by carefully selected standardized tests. When the organizing problem is passing tests, the organizing structure needs to support that goal. When the only tool you have is a hammer, everything looks like a nail.

   The tension that transformative educators experience when advancing the curriculum wisdom (CW) paradigm is not surprising; in a nutshell, classrooms and schools are simply not organized for students and teachers to experience a good educational journey, knowing democracy as a way of life and a moral standard for personal conduct.

   Without a doubt, however, there is a certain amount of wiggle room, and notable currere narratives depicting successful 3S journeys of understandings for students and educators are being shared. Tension does exist if for no other reason than that transformative educators are not speaking the same language of those aligned with the standardized management (SM) paradigm, the organizing problem is different, and the structural solutions are worlds apart. We emphasize again the value of employing Walker's (2003) six key negotiation strategies to bring these worlds together, to meet the challenges of organizing for 3S understanding. These strategies are: (1) achieving working agreement; (2) making principled decisions; (3) working constructively with teachers; (4) seeking substantial, lasting improvement; (5) facing conflict constructively; and (6) combining curriculum work with other initiatives. We also emphasize that in efforts to change the organizing problem from passing tests to student performances of subject matter understanding embedded in a democratic self and social understanding, organizing structures in schools will need to change.

Given the challenges of this reform work, we hope to accomplish the following in this chapter:

- Provide concrete suggestions for advancing the curriculum wisdom (CW) paradigm in the short term by recognizing and supporting wiggle room and those educators who are finding creative ways to take advantage of it;

- Provide concrete suggestions for advancing the curriculum wisdom (CW) paradigm in the long term by strategic, systemic "reculturing" (Fullan, 2001) to establish professional standards for deepening;

- Expose you to a new way of thinking about organizing, and a new way of thinking about how life organizes itself, so that the curriculum wisdom (CW) paradigm may be embedded in the school culture.

ORGANIZING AS PROCESS

What might happen if we considered organizing the school day, week, and year as a process to discover new possibilities through new patterns of connection? If we worked with organizing-as-process, rather than organization-as-object, how would it change what we do with students, parents, and one another? What if we challenged the standardized management orientation and considered the possibility that the classroom and school environment is *invented by our presence in it,* rather than a predetermined setting insulated from change? What if we could embrace the notion that processes do their own work, and our task is to provide what they need to begin their work? If behind all our organizing is the desire to accomplish, to create something more, and if life organizes to discover new varieties and different capacities, who would make curriculum decisions? How would instructional tasks be assigned, who would hold the power and how would it be used, and who would decide how money and time are allocated?

As in all the chapters throughout this text, we invite you into this inquiry. It will be through the creative use of our collective imaginations to re-create a school culture within which 3S education will flourish and be sustained, moving from an esoteric vision to pragmatic reality. Fullan (2001) calls this "reculturing" and regards it as the sine qua non of progress. Reculturing "means producing the capacity to seek, critically assess, and selectively incorporate new ideas and practices—all the time inside the organization as well as outside it" (p. 44). We believe that when teachers engage in the curriculum wisdom (CW) problem-solving cycle, this reculturing will naturally occur. Reculturing would include the curriculum wisdom orientation as a constructive alternative to the Tyler Rationale, a rationale that oversimplifies and dominates current educational programming. The capacity to engage in deep deliberations would be evidenced by reconceptualizing received standards into 3S holistic goals, performances, and criteria; systemic decision-making around integrated designing, planning teaching, evaluating, organizing, and communicating deliberations; acting/experience and the emergence of currere understanding; and reflective inquiry as reflection integrated with disciplined curriculum inquiry. 3S education calls upon students, teachers, and, indeed, all stakeholders, to question implicit and explicit beliefs, to live more consciously, and to challenge our worldviews. As we have grown in our own understanding of what it means to be on this journey of 3S education, we continue to play with new ideas and keep attending to our beliefs.

THE POWER OF PERSONAL/PROFESSIONAL BELIEFS

Views about what is most important in education, such as who makes the curriculum decisions, how the school day is organized, what forms of leadership are used, who has the power, how funds will be spent, what is expected of children, and what the understandings of and reactions are to people of different ethnic or racial heritage, stem from an individual's beliefs (Pajares, 1992). Our experiences have an enormous impact on our current belief system, and they influence decisions on everything from how we organize our time to which textbooks we use to how students are organized for instruction. "School culture is the invisible, taken-for granted flow of beliefs and assumptions [that] give meaning to what people say and do. It shapes how they interpret hundreds of daily transactions. This deeper structure of life in organizations is reflected and transmitted through symbolic language and expressive action. Culture consists of the stable, underlying social meanings that shape beliefs and behavior over time" (Deal & Peterson, 1990, p. 7).

The concept of schools having distinct cultures is not new. Parents, teachers, administrators, and other stakeholders have always sensed something powerful but undefined about their schools. "This ephemeral, taken-for-granted aspect of schools is often overlooked and consequently is usually absent from discussion about school reform" (Deal & Peterson, 1999, p. 2). Sometimes climate or ethos has been used to capture this elusive force. "School cultures are complex webs of traditions and rituals that have been built up over time as teachers, students, parents and administrators work together and deal with crises and accomplishments. Cultural patterns are highly enduring, have a powerful impact on performance, and shape the ways people think, act, and feel" (Deal & Peterson, 1999, p. 4). Garmston and Wellman (1999) cite a classic story that captures the power of this issue:

> A little girl, watching her mother prepare a ham for the oven, wanted to know why her mommy was cutting the end off before placing it in the roasting pan. "I don't really know," her mother replied. "That's the way my mommy did it."

So the little girl went to see her grandmother and asked her why *she* cut the end of the ham off before putting it in the roasting pan. "I don't really know," her grandmother replied. "That's the way my mommy did it."

So the little girl went to see her great-grandmother and asked her why *she* cut the end of the ham off before putting it in the roasting pan. "Well," the old woman exclaimed, stretching her arms wide, "I grew up on the prairie in a little sod house, and our hams were *this* big." Bringing her hands closer together, she finished: And our oven was *this big.* We had to cut the end off the ham to fit it in the oven. (p. 10; emphasis in original)

The assumption is that we are all affected by the organization *we* have created in schools, and that this organizing (what we do [cut the ham] and how we do it [or not]) was created as a result of underlying social meanings that shape beliefs and behavior over time. In this case, standardized management prevails.

Beliefs and Experiences Shape the Organizing Structure

In our work with educators, we find that many see the relevance of 3S education, resonate deeply with the beauty of the vision, and are ready to embrace the challenge. Most, however, are filled with reservations when faced with obstacles, which they perceive to be well beyond their control (Henderson & Kesson, 2004). We refer to these obstacles as structural challenges and recognize that they "emerge in many subtle ways and at many different sites: within the school; between the school and the community; in the educational bureaucracy; in the unions; in the larger political economy; at the levels of local, state, and federal governments; and in university teacher and administrator preparation programs" (p. 82). We believe that these constraints are susceptible to transformation through persistent and steady exercise of wise curriculum judgments. This is what we refer to as wiggle room, and find great hope in its power to make a difference. Wiggle room can grow in a school to a "tipping point" (Gladwell, 2002). "The Tipping Point is the moment of critical mass, the threshold, the boiling point . . . a place where the unexpected becomes expected, where radical change is more than a possibility. It is—contrary to all our expectations—a certainty" (pp. 12–14). As transformative curriculum leaders, we must search for people and situations in which 3S education is occurring and do our best to cultivate these practices.

Embedding and *sustaining* (Fullan, 2001) 3S education in the culture requires new ways to think about what does, and does not, work in schools. We agree with Einstein, who is often quoted as saying: No problem can be solved from the same consciousness that created it. The consciousness that created the organizing structure for the standardized management (SM) paradigm is different from the consciousness needed to create the organizing structure for the curriculum wisdom (CW) paradigm. We need a new kind of consciousness about how organizing happens in schools, in order for us to honor the fundamental relationship between democracy and education. Through this new consciousness and belief system, public education will emerge as a portal through which we may address the pressing social problems, which inhibit the full development of individuals and a more democratic society. Elmore (1995) points out that changing what happens in schools revolves around changing norms, knowledge, and skills at the individual and organizational levels.

"So much of human behavior is habitual. And behind every habit is a belief—about people, life, the world" (Wheatley & Kellner-Rogers, 1996, p. 2). Organizing for the standardized management (SM) paradigm depends upon routine behaviors. When these behaviors are locked into the system, they are defined, finite, predictable, measurable, and replicable. Organizing in this manner is seductively simple, because educational quality is based on how many kids pass the tests. The nature of the human being is considered to be passive and automatic. Once the person is programmed, each would continue to follow the rules inscribed in the program. Organizing for this paradigm is attractive and indeed makes "sense," because all decision making is focused on getting kids to pass tests. The adage "When in doubt, read the directions" comes to mind. Dissect curriculum into granular bits, provide short cycle assessments to determine mastery, and move on. Done!

As educators and transformative curriculum leaders, we "work from the premise that if we can know our beliefs, we can then act with greater consciousness about our behaviors" (Wheatley & Kellner-Rogers, 1996, p. 4). We believe that human beings create their own realities through symbolic and mental processes, and because of this, expanding our consciousness is a human option (Cooperrider & Srivastva, 1987). In an earlier chapter, we learned from Branden (1994) that

> *Nature has given us an extraordinary responsibility: the option of turning the search-light of consciousness brighter or dimmer.* This is the option of seeking awareness or not bothering to seek it or actively avoiding it. The option of thinking or not thinking; this is the root of our freedom and our responsibility. (p. 31, emphasis in original)

Human beings, then, create their own realities through engagements with others and events (Wheatley, 1994). "We inhabit a world that is always subjective and shaped by our interactions with it. Our world is impossible to pin down, constantly changing and infinitely more interesting than we ever imagined" (p. 8), and our *subjectivities and interactions are influenced and shaped by our beliefs.* And so, one more time we need to make the choice to seek awareness. We need to become aware of the powerful metaphors that shape our beliefs. "Educators are caught between the tensions of being guardians of the past and preparing students for an unknown and unknowable future" (Garmston & Wellman, 1999, p. 1). Raising our consciousness and seeking awareness will help us embrace this irony in productive and responsible ways.

Metaphors Shape Beliefs

Wheatley (1994) reminds us that we live and work in schools designed from mechanistic, Newtonian images of the universe. We have confined students, teachers, and parents into narrow roles, as though "they were cogs in the machinery of production" (p. 12). "We manage by separating things into parts, we believe that influence occurs as a direct result of force exerted from one person to another, we engage in complex planning for work that we keep expecting to be predictable, and we search continually for better methods of objectively perceiving the world" (Wheatley, 1994, p. 6). Centuries ago, when the world was seen as a machine set in motion by God, the concept that machines wear down, decay, and fall apart entered our consciousness. Progress, then, became the result of our energy, force, will, and momentum to reverse the decay. In schools, we have become hooked on prediction, order, and analysis of the SM paradigm, believing that to be accountable we must gather extensive numerical data and use those data to drive our decision making. In this world, number is king. Knowledge has been dissected into discrete subjects, and discrete subjects are further broken down into minute factoids. This world is filled with boundaries, so every person knows his or her place. We admonish ourselves to just work harder or longer or smarter, so then students will achieve, teachers will do their jobs, parents will stop complaining, and communities will pass levies to fund schools.

Furthermore, in classical physics, one studies a world of things and how connections work across *separations*. "In this world of things, there are well-defined edges; it is possible to tell where one stops and the other begins, to observe something without interfering with its identity or functioning" (Wheatley, 1994, pp. 28–29). It is easy to recognize the SM paradigm within this description. We are of the opinion that Ralph Tyler (1949), an influential curriculum scholar, was heavily persuaded by these powerful organizational metaphors when he developed a rationale to provide curriculum practitioners with the tools needed for educational programming. Tyler argues that curriculum workers should systematically ask themselves four questions:

1. What educational purposes should the school seek to attain?

2. How can learning experiences be selected that are likely to be useful in attaining these objectives?

3. How can learning experiences be organized for effective instruction?

4. How can the effectiveness of learning experiences be evaluated? (p. 1)

While these questions provide simple and straightforward insights into organizing for instruction, he does "not address the relationship between democracy and education and any moral or ethical depth, and it is too easily adapted to system-wide implementation strategies that can inhibit or constrain the enactment of curriculum wisdom" (Henderson & Kesson, 2004, p. 20). Idiosyncratic expressions of democratic subject self and social understanding are not likely if these are the boundaries. Tyler seemed compelled to separate curriculum and teaching decision making. Curriculum in this view is regarded as specific products, frameworks, materials, and textbooks with little mention of curriculum at the process or experiential levels. It is as if curriculum were studied as a world of separate things and it became the job of the curriculum worker to figure out how these discrete things connected across separations.

Wheatley (1994), quoting Dana Zohar in *The Quantum Self,* writes: "The whole corpus of classical physics and the technology that rests on it is about the separateness of things, about constituents parts and how they influence each other across their separateness" (p. 28). Wheatley goes on to say, "the 'thing' view of the world, therefore leads to a belief in scientific objectivity . . . working well in a world of you-me, inside-outside, here-thereness" (p. 29). Intentionally or not, most schools operate from a worldview that has been derived from the natural sciences. These are powerful images and have most likely deeply affected teacher beliefs and therefore the culture in schools today. "It is important to remember that the current system and ways of organizing schools produce the current results. The deep structure of North American schools and the ways of organizing and operating them has remained fairly stable throughout this century" (Garmston & Wellman, 1999). Our challenge, then, is to reculture schools within the wisdom paradigm.

Change the Metaphor to Change the Belief and Alter the Organizing Structure

Early in the 20th century, quantum mechanics began to answer questions and to make discoveries that Newtonian laws could not, and the path was opened for a new way to comprehend the universe (Wheatley, 1994). "In the quantum world, relationships are not just interesting; to many physicists, they are *all* there is to reality" (p. 32, emphasis in original). In this relational universe, no longer can we study anything as separate from ourselves. Garmston and Wellman (1999) explain, "The celebrated revolution in physics called quantum mechanics clarifies essential distinctions between matter and energy and simultaneously blurs the lines between them. The very term quantum mechanics means bundles of energy (quantum) in motion (mechanics). Energy becomes an avenue to attainment" (pp. 4–5). The school environment then, is created and invented by our presence in it. "None of us exists independent of our relationships with others. Different settings and people evoke some qualities from us and leave others dormant. In each of these relationships, we are different and new in some ways" (Wheatley, 1994, p. 34).

Imagine how the culture of a school would change if students, parents, and educators operated within a belief system about organizing that was connected, generative, and life sustaining, rather than fragmented, fearful, and inclined to fall apart. As educators and transformative curriculum leaders, we embrace this life-sustaining view of schools. Creating a learning environment in classrooms and schools that celebrates the possibilities of human growth through 3S education will occur much more naturally and with less stress in these creative organizations. "In a creative organization, everyone in the organization feels compelled to be alert, seeking out new measures, new events to observe. Everyone questions whether there is more to notice" (Wheatley & Kellner-Rogers, 1996, p. 26). Not surprisingly under these conditions, the hidden and null curricula surface. Values, attitudes, and assumptions about race, class, gender, ethnicity, and disability are explored in the classroom as an essential element of the curriculum and democratic morality. The powerful veneer of oppression or exploitation will no longer seem "natural" or "given" (Greene, 1988) and will likely find voice through students *and* teachers. "As we measure our measures, we create the conditions for much greater creativity. Our consciousness expands as we become willing to question even our process of observation. Consciousness and creativity are inextricably linked in this always discovering world" (Wheatley & Kellner-Rogers, 1996, p. 26). In a more natural way, human freedom and the capacity to surpass the given and to look at things as if they could otherwise be (Greene, 1988) is released. Within these conditions, students, teachers, and indeed all stakeholders experience the "freedom to" come together as authentic individuals around 3S projects they can mutually pursue. They are "free from" limitations, oppression, alienation, and coercion with an energy and power that is not confined to functions and levels. In the SM paradigm, number is king. Within the CW paradigm, relationships are everything.

PRIMACY OF RELATIONSHIPS

We believe in the primacy of relationships in schools, and we have set out to focus on the deep longings each of us has for democratic community, purpose, and meaning. Tyler's rationale that curriculum workers systematically ask themselves four straightforward questions does not address the relationship between democracy and education and any moral or ethical depth. Within the CW paradigm on the other hand, organizing is generated by relationships, connectedness, and elevated judgments to assure that students and teachers' idiosyncratic expressions of democratic subject self and social understanding. These relationships, connections, and judgments are more likely when we organize to do the following:

1. Reconceptualize received standards into 3S holistic goals, performances, and criteria

2. Ensure systematic decision making within integrated designing, planning, teaching, evaluating, organizing, and communicating deliberations

3. Act upon and experience the complicated conversation through the emergence of currere understanding

4. Engage in reflective inquiry as reflection integrated with disciplined curriculum study.

Organizing is derived out of a joy of learning that comes from a deep sensibility of voice. The quantum world offers a much more hopeful and relational metaphor for the beliefs we bring to schools in the shaping of culture. Teaching and organizing for 3S understanding requires comprehensive, collaborative decision making. It requires skillfully deliberated and well-integrated designing, planning, teaching, evaluating, organizing, and communicating decisions. It is holistic, systemic work, not fragmented parts. What new or different images might we use to support 3S education? How can we understand human nature differently and more optimistically? The following features capture some of the norms necessary for organizing 3S education and the power of relationships in shaping human behavior in schools. These have been paraphrased from Wheatley (1994) and Wheatley and Kellner-Rogers (1996):

- We evoke a potential that is already present.
- Everything is in a constant process of discovery and creating.
- Life uses dense webs of relationships and trial and error to find what works.
- We need to stop describing tasks and instead facilitate a process.
- Any one solution is temporary; there are no permanently right answers.

- The capacity to keep changing, to find what works now is what keeps us alive.

- We will need better skills in listening, communicating, and facilitating groups to build relationships.

- The era of the rugged individual has been replaced by the era of the team player.

- Life is attracted to order, a life-sustaining system.

- Life organizes to preserve its identity; self-creation is so strong that an organism will change to maintain its identity.

- Everything that happens influences everything else.

- Small changes in one part of the school amplify to create large-systems change.

- There are no unaffected outsiders; all participate in creating conditions of their interdependence.

- Improvisation is an essential skill.

- People are intelligent, creative, adaptive, self-organizing, and meaning seeking.

- Schools are living systems. They are intelligent, creative, adaptive, self-organizing, and meaning seeking.

- Power is energy that needs to flow through schools, not be confined to functions and levels.

- Power is positively or negatively charged by the quality of the relationship.

- Love in schools is the most potent force available.

Imagine for a Moment

Imagine for a moment that your school culture was organized around these norms. How would things be different? Could the school culture tolerate an emphasis on subject matter knowledge alone, if the people and the school were creative, adaptive, and self-organizing? Would one score on a single test be acceptable if improvisation were an essential skill? If there were no unaffected outsiders and all participated in creating conditions of their interdependence, would teachers be working in isolation? What role would the parents and the community occupy? How would power be experienced if it were considered to be energy that flowed through schools and not confined to functions and levels? Who would have power and how would it be used? How would decisions be made if we all had better skills in listening, communicating, and facilitating groups to build relationships? What kind of consciousness would be necessary if you knew that everything you did and said in some way influenced everything and everyone else, inside and outside your school? If small changes you made in your classroom amplified across the school and district to create large system changes, what would you do differently? If we stopped describing tasks and instead facilitated a process, imagine how much more clarity we could bring to the task of reconceptualizing the received subject standards into holistic understanding goals. Facilitating students' educational journeys would evoke a potential that is already present and uniquely expressed. Currere narratives would be a fertile source of information and learning for students, teachers, and all stakeholders. These narratives would cultivate a deepening understanding of curriculum as complicated conversation and shape the direction of designing and planning, teaching and evaluating. Life is attracted to order, details would be tended to, and shared governance, mutuality, and reciprocity would sustain meaningful life and provide adaptive order. Time for cultivating reflective inquiry capacity using the seven reflective inquiries would be built into the workweek. Reflective inquiry would be an essential skill and professional development would include opportunities for reflection integrated with disciplined curriculum inquiry. Evidence of deep deliberations for all decisions would be encouraged and celebrated. The highest and most celebrated professional standard would be evidenced by reconceptualizing received standards into 3S holistic goals, performances, and criteria; systemic decision making around integrated designing, planning, teaching, evaluating, organizing, and communicating deliberations; acting/experience and the emergence of currere understanding; and reflective inquiry as reflection integrated with disciplined curriculum study. Building a professional learning community within which to conduct decision making about designing and planning, teaching, evaluating, and organizing for 3S education would be motivated out of love and recognized as the most potent force available. "As we change our images of the world, as we leave behind the machine, we welcome ourselves back. We recover a world that is supportive of human endeavor" (Wheatley & Kellner-Rogers, 1996, p. 6) and in this case the inextricable link between education and democracy. If we are ever to move 3S education from an impossible dream to a viable reality, then we need to develop schools (and the students, parents, and educators in them) in a way that imagines these possibilities and emphasizes what works.

ORGANIZATION DEVELOPMENT

Organizing for curriculum work defined as teaching for disciplinary subject matter understanding that is integrated with disciplined democratic self and social understanding is a demanding professional ideal, but not an impossible dream. In order for this ideal to become a reality, we need to organize and develop ourselves in ways that support this kind of education. *Organization development* (OD) is understood as specific collaborative activities that build a local work culture that nurtures curriculum and professional development activities. Burdened with the machine metaphor, traditional OD processes emphasize problem-solving processes that separate and dissect pieces of a system (Hammond, 1998). Looking for gaps and needs, traditional OD helps leaders solve their problems by focusing on deficiencies. The fundamental question is "What kind of problems are you having?" Even within action–research, inquiry is a matter of following standardized rules of problem solving; knowledge is the result of good method (Cooperrider & Srivastva, 1987). The basic idea behind the model is that events proceed as planned and thus a problem is a deviation from the plan that needs to be fixed. At the quantum level, a deviation from the plan can be considered an opportunity. Action research begins with an identified problem; data are gathered for a diagnosis to produce a solution that will need to be evaluated. In problem solving, David Cooperrider and Suresh Srivastva (1987) state that something is fragmented, and the function of problem solving is to integrate or stabilize the workings of the status quo. In his review of the field, Staw (1984) points out that most organizational research is biased to serve managerial interests rather than explore broader human and/or social purposes. Within this model, the researcher must adopt the role of the objective third party, with three intervention tasks: generate valid organizational data; enable others to make free and informed choices on the basis of these data; and help the organization generate internal commitment to their choices (Argyris, 1970). Here organizational life is problematic and organizing is best understood as a sequence of problems, causes, and solutions among people and events and things. "Thus the ultimate aim and product of action–research is the production of institutions that have a high capacity to perceive, formulate, and solve an endless stream of problems" (Cooperrider & Srivastva, 1987, p. 42).

Within the curriculum wisdom (CW) paradigm, we borrow from what Cooperrider and Srivastva (1987) call Appreciative Inquiry. AI is an organization development strategy based on the premise that schools change in the direction in which they inquire. Building your reflective inquiry capacity is key here. Therefore, a school that inquires into problems will keep finding problems, but a school, which attempts to appreciate what is best in itself, will discover more and more of that which is good. These discoveries can be used to build a new future where the "best" becomes more common. Table 7.1 (Hammond, 1998) shows these distinctions.

Now that we have examined the power of personal and professional beliefs, the impact of metaphors on our worldviews and expectations for organizing, and the primacy of relationships for 3S education, let us now turn our attention to some concrete suggestions for cultivating 3S education in your school or district.

Table 7.1 **TRADITIONAL ORGANIZATION DEVELOPMENT VERSUS APPRECIATIVE INQUIRY PROCESSES**	
Traditional Organization Development Process	**Appreciative Inquiry Process**
Define the problem	Search for solutions that already exist by appreciating the best of "what is"
Analyze the causes	Envision what might be
Fix what's broken	Amplify what is working
Focus on decay	Focus on life-giving forces
What problems are you having?	What is working well around here?
Action planning treatment	Innovating what will be

FINDING THOSE FINDING WIGGLE ROOM

One essential assumption of Appreciative Inquiry, which is enormously helpful for finding wiggle room, is emphasizing *what works* in any organization. Emphasizing what works is powerful because what we focus on becomes reality. As a beginning step to organizing for 3S education, whether you are a teacher or a building or central office administrator, we suggest that you sit down with a piece of paper, and think about the students, teachers, administrators, or parents in your district. Use the employee roster to make sure you have not missed the opportunity to reflect about each teacher. Think carefully about those who seem to embody democratic curriculum wisdom. Next to the name, write down specific examples of how each has exemplified this journey of democratic subject matter and self and social understanding. The goal is to emphasize what works in reference to 3S education in your school setting, and by focusing on people and specific examples, we think you will begin to see the many and creative ways that 3S education is occurring. We think you will see how life uses a dense web of relationships, and trial and error to see what works. While every transformative curriculum leader's journey will be, and should be, unique, keep in mind that all educational work has a moral dimension. In the course of human interactions, each one of us is making thousands of decisions every day that affect the lives of others. Perhaps some of the people on your list have acted "in ways that promote the common good for all members of their community, avoiding limited interpretations of educational achievement, self worth and civil behavior" (Henderson & Hawthorne, 2000, p. 187). Perhaps some have a keen sense of the big picture. They envision a school that liberates both children and adults to become caring, imaginative, responsible, lifelong learners who are informed, participating members of a democratic society. Even if your evidence is sparse, write it down. You might have a person in mind who understands the systemic nature of successful school reform. You know this because they work with others at every level of school organization. Motivated by a love for people, others may find meaning, purpose, and joy in the work of others. Some may make connections and work with others to question program design, evaluation of adult and student work, organizational structures, and relations between the school and community. Others operate in an honest and straightforward manner, working with others to build a professional learning community through systemic and deliberative decision-making. Another still may go public, sharing currere narratives, challenging policies, organizational structures, procedures, hierarchical relationships, and the value placed on conformity, efficiency, ease, or convenience. They regularly dialogue, holding complicated conversations about educating students with boards of education, teachers' associations, volunteer organizations, and governance committees "to break through into the public space . . . to testify and speak voluntarily for ourselves" (Greene, 1995, p. 170). Others may undertake specific reform projects, either broadly or narrowly conceived and on any scale, from serving on curriculum committees, to eliminating a tightly scripted textbook, to engaging in disciplined curriculum inquiry, to the development of a schoolwide discipline plan that cultivates the inherent worth of every child. Another source of these kinds of descriptors may be found in the Code of Ethics in chapter 5.

Once you have the list of names and the descriptions of each contribution, refer to the list of features on pages 180–181, which capture some of the norms necessary for organizing 3S education. See whether you can assign an organizing norm for each description you have written about each person. We think this is a necessary step because you will begin to recognize the organizing circumstances within which this particular exemplar of curriculum wisdom occurred. Once you describe the occurrence and then articulate the organizing cultural norm that enables it to occur, the likelihood increases that you will be able to grow these opportunities elsewhere in the school or district.

It bears repeating that every transformative curriculum leader's journey will be, and should be, unique. These descriptors are not meant to be a definitive list of qualities or projects. As you tune in to this energy in your school, you will find an infinite list of examples, for they will be as unique as the people you are describing. Remember, this is *a* first step to organizing for 3S education, not the only one and perhaps not the first one. This will help you, however, by focusing on what works and expanding that energy in an appreciative manner. Guide Sheet #4 will assist you with this activity.

GROWING WIGGLE ROOM

Law of Attraction: What You Pay Attention to, Grows

Now that you have your list of people, with clarifying examples of 3S education in action, send a note of recognition and gratitude to each person for his or her contribution. A form letter will not suffice, as every example will be unique. Of course, you will want to be clear in your description, taking care to avoid jargon, such as "3S education," "Transformative Curriculum Leadership," or "a dense web of relationships." This kind of leadership is invitational, and your selection of words will make all the difference. You will, however, want to make a clear and distinct connection *between each person's behavior, choice, or action and its inextricable link to democracy in education.* Making this connection clear distinguishes this note from other notes of friendship or appreciation.

As you become more aware of demonstrated evidence of 3S education in your school or district, keep a running list in your file. In essence you are planting the seeds for building a collective sense of responsibility for democratic student learning. You will be tapping into "the law of attraction" (Cooperrider & Srivastva, 1987; Northrup, 2005), the most basic law governing the flow of energy and matter throughout the universe. The law of attraction is the concept that *like attracts like*. "The law of attraction also holds that thoughts held over time become their physical equivalents" (Northrup, 2005, p. 347). What we focus on becomes reality because "the environment is invented by our presence in it" (Wheatley & Kellner-Rogers, 1996, p. 24). We would venture to say that most of the people on this roster operate from a fundamental belief that they have a fair amount of influence over what happens in their classrooms and their lives. They may not know about the law of attraction or think about being a co-creator of the environment. They probably operate with a sense of authorship about their lives and do not think of themselves as corks in the river, bobbing and weaving directed solely by the current. Each one, in some way, has taken responsibility for what happens in his or her setting and has engaged in the demanding, practical, and intellectual task of providing democratically inspired curriculum for the students. This is their professional identity; it is who they are. Notice how one's belief system is manifested in the real world. Thoughts held over time become their physical equivalents.

Finding Those Finding Wiggle Room
Guide Sheet #4

Emphasizing What Works

On the table below, identify students, teachers, administrators, parents, and community members who have exemplified this journey of democratic subject matter and self and social understanding. In the appropriate column, write a brief explanation of what the person did to exemplify this 3S understanding.

Then write the number of the organizing feature or norm (see below) that was manifested in each example.

Name _____ Date_____

Name and Number of Organizing Feature	Educational Visionary: Communicating the Big Picture	Systemic Reformer: Great Problem Solver	Fosters Collaborative Efforts	Publicly Articulates an Educational Moral Position	Makes Connections: Speaks Their Own Authentic Voice	Engages in Supportive Dialogue	Undertakes Specific Reform Projects	Other

Organizing Feature

1. We evoke a potential that is already present.

2. Everything is in a constant process of discovery and creating.

3. Life uses dense webs of relationships and trial and error to find what works.

4. We need to stop describing tasks and instead facilitate a process.

5. Any one solution is temporary; there are no permanently right answers.

6. The capacity to keep changing, to find what works now, is what keeps us alive.

7. We will need better skills in listening, communicating, and facilitating groups to build relationships.

8. The era of the rugged individual has been replaced by the era of the team player.

9. Life is attracted to order; it is a life sustaining system.

10. Life organizes to preserve its identity; self-creation is so strong that an organism will change to maintain its identity

11. Everything that happens influences everything else.

12. Small changes in one part of the school amplify to create large-systems change.

13. There are no unaffected outsiders; all participate in creating conditions of their interdependence.

14. Improvisation is an essential skill.

15. People are intelligent, creative, adaptive, self-organizing and meaning seeking.

16. Schools are living systems. They too are intelligent, creative, adaptive, self-organizing, and meaning seeking.

17. Power is energy that needs to flow through schools, not be confined to functions and levels.

18. Power is positively or negatively charged by the quality of the relationship.

19. Love in schools is the most potent force available.

Gathering Like-Minded People

Once you are certain that each person has received your note, go back to your list. If you are a teacher or an administrator, make a follow-up call and invite them for a cup of coffee at some point beyond the school day. Convey that you have noticed teachers in the district doing curricular projects with students that go beyond the standardized test by involving students in ways that seem to be personally and socially significant. Suggest that you would like to gather in a small group to discuss and reflect upon their work and share ideas. Growing wiggle room requires getting these like-minded people in the same room to talk, reflect, and discuss. Depending upon the size of your school or district, it is possible that this meeting may be the first time they have met each other. If the group consists of elementary and high school educators, they have probably been operating on parallel tracks, with no opportunity for intersection. Even if they have had exposure to one another by having served on curriculum committee, for example, or informally through extracurricular activities, this meeting may be a first. This may be the first time someone has made arrangements for teachers to meet for the purpose of discussing something other than standardized curriculum and testing requirements. When these intellectually energized people are put in the same room to discuss their inspired projects and their beloved students, the synergy will likely be electrifying. Furthermore, providing "space" for this kind of sharing and collective sense of responsibility to care for students in this manner creates a bond between and among the group members. You may notice that organizing for 3S education includes what you learned in chapters 3 about cultivating your reflective inquiry. You may want to return to this chapters for additional deliberative advice.

Working with a group of transformative curriculum leaders is an exciting professional experience, because often these teacher leaders are passionate, caring, and creative. The specifics of what might happen at the meeting you have called are unpredictable, and they should be. Most likely, the people at this meeting will be happy to be there and ready to share. "Teachers who strive to achieve ambitious learning goals such as deep conceptual understanding, problem solving, or expressive fluency and power often experience extra tensions" (Walker, 2003, p. 250). Because they work beyond the standardized management paradigm, they may feel marginalized from other staff members. We think that most will find support and perhaps solace in this group, knowing that they are in the company of teachers who share their sense of calling and values for democratically moral expressions of curriculum. We imagine that currere narratives may be shared, and we hope that a sense of collegiality will be established based on a shared sense of vision. Garmston and Wellman (1999) suggest three focusing questions for dialogue:

- Who are we? (leads to the issue of identity)

- Why are we doing this? (unquestioned assumptions surface)

- Why are we doing this this way? (open new ways of seeing school practices) (pp. 9–11)

Engaging in this kind of professional and visionary dialogue can be renewing. Ideas and projects will be shared, and what may surface is a kind of professional knowledge base essential for the exercise of wise curriculum judgments grounded in moral insight and oriented toward the expansion of deep democracy (Henderson & Kesson, 2004). Issues of time, money, and power will be the likely subtext of the dialogue, yet the stories will demonstrate creative ways within which these inherent, potential, structural, and political obstacles were overcome. Evidence will be reported, such as two fourth-grade teachers collaborating to infuse environmental awareness into their mandated unit on the factors of production, which included an interview with the district's supervisor of food services to discuss the "environmental friendliness" of serving food on Styrofoam plates; high school social studies and language art teachers aligning the pacing of their curriculum in a way that has students reading literature from the period of history being studied, with authentic expressions of understanding being demonstrated; a first-grade teacher who at the request of a student helped her write a letter to the principal asking why all students had to stay in for recess as a consequence for a noisy cafeteria, when only a few first-graders were responsible for the noise; a science teacher who uses the Tuskegee Syphilis Experiment as the foundation for a unit on microorganisms and bacteria and ethics in science, with students being asked to formulate their own ethics statement for scientific experimentation, which included the impact of that statement on scientific advancement. (You may recall that the Public Health Service, working with the Tuskegee Institute, began the study in 1932. Nearly 400 poor Black men with syphilis from Macon County, Alabama, were enrolled in the study. They were never told they had syphilis, nor were they ever treated for it. According to the Centers for Disease Control, the men were told they were being treated for "bad blood," a local term used to describe several illnesses, including syphilis, anemia, and fatigue. For participating in the study, the men were given free medical exams, free meals, and free burial insurance.

At the start of the study, there was no proven treatment for syphilis. But even after penicillin became a standard cure for the disease in 1947, the medicine was withheld from the men. The Tuskegee scientists wanted to continue to study how the disease spreads and kills. The experiment lasted four decades, until public health workers leaked the story to the media. By then, dozens of the men had died, and many wives and children had been infected. In 1973, the National Association for the Advancement of Colored People (NAACP) filed a class-action lawsuit. A $9 million settlement was divided among the study's participants. Free health care was given to the men who were still living, and to infected wives, widows, and children. In 1997, President Clinton delivered an apology, saying what the government had done was deeply, profoundly, and morally wrong.)

In subsequent gatherings, ask each person to bring a colleague who they believe embodies this kind of curriculum wisdom. As more currere narratives are shared, the bond between and among the participants will deepen. Stories of lessons that promote student inquiry and idiosyncratic expressions of understanding abound. Examples of allowing for diverse thinking among students will surface. Projects that encourage student–student, student–teacher, or student–parent collaborative problem solving in open and honest dialogue may be discussed. Perspectives on dealing with issues of ethics, diversity, equity, and civility in the classroom and school may be shared. Puzzling over ways to highlight the relationship between knowledge and power in subject, self, and social learning may galvanize the group, prompting them to want to expand their vision and broaden their influence. The list of projects is limited only by the imaginations of the teachers and students in the classroom, but an important energy is gathering with each story. Momentum may build with the group as they discover the wiggle room that is available, and teachers, albeit on a small scale, are able to have a fairly substantial impact.

Small Changes Amplify to Create Large-Systems Change

In whatever way this happens, an important step has been taken by putting people in the same room to dialogue. It is possible that over time the group may see the need to organize more purposefully to establish an environment within which to grow 3S education in a more sustainable manner. Eventually, the group may want to take further action steps to have a wider, more systemic impact. Using their creativity and imaginations, they will see ever-expanding opportunities to bring this type of curriculum experience to students. They will begin to experience the dynamic that small changes in one part of the school amplify to create large-systems change. While sharing currere narratives with others is edifying and establishing this kind of professional identity is rewarding, it is likely that they will have evoked a potential that is already present, and the school will need to change to accommodate this new information. These "productive disturbance(s) are [is] likely to happen when guided by a moral purpose and when the process creates and channels new tensions while working on complex problems" (Fullan, 2001, p. 110). Keep in mind that schools are living systems. Schools, like people, are intelligent, creative, adaptive, self-organizing, and meaning seeking. "Self-organization develops through meaningful adult interactions about students, student work, and the purposes and processes of schooling" (Garmston & Wellman, 1999, p. 8).

Lest this sounds like a simple "let it happen" kind of experience, organizing for 3S education requires knowledge of group dynamics, power relations, and a repertoire of skills for organization and human development. There is much to consider when problem-solving from the perspective of the democratic "good" life. Fullan (2000) calls for "reculturing," a more systemic "changing the way we do things around here" (p. 43). He believes that "leading in a culture of change means creating a culture (not just structure) of change. It does not mean adopting innovations, one after another; it does mean producing the capacity to seek, critically assess, and selectively incorporate new ideas and practices—all the time, inside the organization as well as outside it" (p. 44). Fullan refers to reculturing as a contact sport that involves hard, intensive work, which takes time and persistence. He reminds leaders to be enthusiastic, hopeful, and filled with energy. In his framework for leadership, leaders must cultivate a moral purpose, understand change, build relationships, create and share knowledge, and provide a sense of coherence as fresh solutions are found.

The decision-making processes must be multifaceted and will require disciplined, deep deliberations. Garmston and Wellman (1999) point out that schools are nonlinear dynamical systems in which cause and effect are not tightly linked. They are shaped by a blend of regularity and irregularity and patterns of stability and instability. Critical choice-points present new possibilities and new forms of order. Instability permits creative life in school systems. The self-organizing interactions between people develop feedback loops that recur and amplify across the scale of the organization (p. 8).

Self-organization will occur, and it is the task of the transformative curriculum leader to understand the patterns and influence the patterns through collaboration, reflective inquiry, and disciplined decision making in a spirit of democratic morality. The remainder of this chapter will give advice on skills and strategies for organizing for 3S education when growing wiggle room evokes the need for a systemic change by galvanizing the group toward a more compelling opportunity. The remainder of this chapter will address the "adaptive" (Garmston & Wellman, 2004) skills needed for organizing 3S education in more systemic and sustainable ways.

ORGANIZING 3S EDUCATION

A common theme among educators who embrace the curriculum wisdom (CW) paradigm is a sense of moral responsibility for making a long-lasting difference in the lives of students. This sense of moral responsibility is so strong that teachers feel drawn to others who share the same. The natural outgrowth of building a collective sense of responsibility for democratic student learning is the establishment of a professional learning community (Dufour, 1998; Senge, 1990). Louis, Marks, and Kruse (1996) have identified four components of professional learning communities: shared norms and values; collective focus on student learning; deprivatized practice; and reflective dialogue. In their research, they found that when teachers take collective responsibility for students, the students have a greater sense of personal efficacy. Teaching for 3S understanding requires this kind of learning community with an emphasis on shared democratic norms and values; a collective focus on each student's 3S journey of understanding, which views students as dynamic meaning makers; teachers who learn from one another in a collaborative manner celebrating the possibilities of human growth; and reflective inquiry, which is reflection integrated with democratic curriculum inquiry.

Garmston and Wellman (1999) offer suggestions for developing professional learning communities and suggest that schools must be adaptive "to change form in concert with clarifying identity" (p. 5). Educators must cultivate organizational and professional capacities for adaptivity, which include a shared vision of a "good" educational journey for *all* students and teachers. "Healthy schools and organizations hold a vision for themselves of how they wish to operate in the world. This is a vision of values and goals in action" (pp. 20–21). One important part of this vision is to encourage and facilitate wise curriculum decision making. *Organizational* capacities for adaptivity include vision and goal focus, systems thinking, interpreting and using qualitative and quantitative data, maintaining collaborative cultures, and gathering and focusing resources. "Values and goals point out resources needs. Systems thinking frames where to target resources. Data use and interpretation sets up essential feedback loops that reflect whether and how goals are being achieved. Collaboration is the glue that allows groups to agree upon and work toward the goals" (Garmston & Wellman, 1999, pp. 23–24).

Professional capacities for adaptivity include collegial interaction; cognitive processes for instruction; knowledge and structure of the discipline; self-knowledge, values, standards, and beliefs; repertoire of teaching skills; and knowing about students and how they learn (Garmston & Wellman, 1999). There is no substitute for knowledge of self/beliefs, knowledge of your students and how they learn, and knowledge of your subject matter content. When this knowledge is shared in a collegial and collaborative environment, with democratic ideals as a moral compass, 3S education will likely flourish. Garmston and Wellman (1999) posit that simple rules govern complex behavior in groups and suggest the following "rules" for members to follow:

1. *Take care of me.* It is each group member's groundedness, resourcefulness, and energy that develops the synergy that makes high-performing groups possible.

2. *Take care of us.* It is our interdependence, interactions, and caring for each other and the group that motivates us to want to continue to work together.

3. *Take care of our values.* It is our values that drive our goals, clarity about who we are, how we want to be together, and what we will accomplish for students. (p. 31; emphasis in original)

We encourage you to read *The Adaptive School* by Robert Garmston and Bruce Wellman (1999) for a complete sourcebook for developing collaborative groups. While these authors do not specifically mention the curriculum wisdom (CW) paradigm, they offer helpful guidance about conducting successful meetings, facilitating group meetings, using tools for developing collaborative groups, using conflict as a resource, and working with unmanageable problems. By using democratic ideals as a normative referent, you will gain the knowledge you need to address the two fundamental challenges addressed in chapters 2 and 3—reconceptualizing received standards and cultivating your reflective inquiry capacity, which are so vital to sustaining the decision making processes for organizing 3S education.

Organizing the Work Week

Walker (2003) cites Cohen (1988) and Cuban (1993), who point to four causes for the enduring success of conventional classroom practices: confining frames, public expectations, ingrained habits and ideas, and the usefulness of conventional teaching strategies for teachers. "The conventional classroom organization persists not because it is effective, but because it is cheap, familiar, robust, and versatile. Competing forms of classroom organization that are more effective . . . will need to be as cheap, robust, and versatile if they are to challenge the dominance of the conventional classroom in American schooling" (p. 252). Given the wiggle room available for 3S education in the current setting, some 3S projects are cheap, robust, and versatile. If we hope to grow and sustain 3S education, however, teachers will need the following (Walker, 2003):

1. An opportunity to study the change and its implications for classroom practice

2. A voice in the deliberations leading to a decision to undertake the change

3. Incentives to undertake the change effort in their classrooms

4. An opportunity to learn what students will be expected to learn

5. An opportunity to master the new teaching skills required by the change

6. Access to resources, temporary access to resources for making the transition, and continuing access to the resources required by the new practice

7. Ways to check the quality of their realization of the new pattern

8. Continuing support to work out the bugs in the new pattern and to resolve conflicts between the new pattern and what remains of the former one

Weekly collaborative time for teachers to meet in grade level or subject area groups is essential. Walker (2003) notes that an essential starting point for curriculum change is talking about what the student actually does. Teachers need to dialogue and learn about all parts of the 3S Visionary Designing and Planning Template found in chapter 4. They need to learn how to reconceptualize the received standards into holistic goals, taking into consideration the hidden and null curricula, as well as what students should be free from and free to do; they need to dialogue about students' expressive performances of 3S understanding; they need to develop rubrics for determining the judgment criteria for the case by case evaluation of quality of student's journey of 3S understanding; and they need time need to collaborate on the development of generative learning experiences around topics, questions, and activities for the journey. Once these new approaches have been established, Walker (2003) recommends that teachers be given the opportunity to teach collaboratively for support and confidence. Additional collaborative time could then be made available to discuss student work, using the scoring rubric that describes the judgment criteria. "The specificity that student work brings enables teachers to engage in productive discussions of curriculum issues that might otherwise be too general to be helpful" (p. 272). Lesson study (Stigler & Hiebert, 1999) is another suggestion. "The premise behind lesson study is simple: If you want to improve teaching, the most effective place to do so is in the context of a classroom lesson" (p. 111). Lesson study is a problem-solving process in which the teachers:

- Define the problem that will motivate and direct the work of the lesson-study group.

- Plan the lesson once the learning goal has been chosen.

- Teach the lesson at a time when other group members will observe (sometimes the lesson is videotaped for later analysis and discussion).

- Evaluate the lesson and reflect on its effect as a form of self-improvement activity.

- Revise the lesson based on input from observations and input of others; teach the revised lesson.

- Teach the lesson again, usually by another teacher but in the presence of the entire department.

- Evaluate and reflect again.

- Share the results in the form of a report [or currere narrative]. (pp. 112–115)

It bears repeating that lesson study can be done within the SM paradigm, the CBP paradigm, and the CW paradigm. It should not be surprising that the route this activity will take will depend upon the stated problem that will motivate and direct the work of the lesson study group: Is the lesson designed to get kids to pass the test, demonstrate deeper subject matter understanding, or facilitate a student's 3S journey of understanding? This will make all the difference!

It has been our experience that in many settings, common planning time before, during, or after the workday is available for many teachers. Many schools require regular staff meetings. Instead of passing along information that can be read in a memo, staff meetings could be used for collaborative planning. Many states offer "waiver days," which count as a school day for teachers, but students do not attend to provide time for teachers to meet. Some schools do a compressed schedule and design a late start or an early release for students, allowing time for teachers to meet. Some schools budget for curriculum writing days and count these as professional development for writing curricular activities. The point is that in many schools, professional development, collaborative curriculum writing, unit development, and lesson planning are already taking place. What is at issue is the paradigm though which all this occurs. The theme throughout this book has been that *depending upon one's orientation, the same expenditure of time, in the same setting, with the same teachers can look very, very different.* Negotiating with decision makers to change *what* teachers are doing is pivotal.

Organizing the Work Year

While the development of holistic goals, expressive outcomes, judgment criteria, and generative activities will constitute an important step in this reform effort, cultivating one's reflective inquiry capacity requires a different mind-set. Course, unit, and lesson planning can happen within the workweek and work month. Cultivating one's reflective inquiry capacity, however, requires dedicated time in a retreat or workshop for an extended period in a relaxed and collegial environment. We strongly believe that the rapid pace in schools and classrooms does not provide an environment within which reflective inquiry may grow. Keep in mind that we have defined reflective inquiry as reflection integrated with democratic curriculum inquiry. Within the classroom, as you are being pulled in a number of directions, democratic curriculum inquiry is probably not on your radar screen. We quote extensively from Henderson and Kesson (2004) to convey why this is so:

To be pragmatically wise, one must adopt an approach to decision making and problem solving that recognizes the inherent unpredictability of situations and admits the possibility of error, understands each moment is different from the one preceding it, is attentive to present circumstances, and works to transcend fragmentary thinking. We must be careful observers of the consequences of our actions, and we must be alert to the implications of these consequences for our democratic way of life. Central to this notion is the importance of not allowing the ends to dictate the means: How we arrive at a destination is as important as the fact that we do arrive. We can coerce students into memorizing facts for a standardized test, and we can offer extrinsic rewards for achievement. Students may indeed raise their test scores, but if in the process they have lost their intellectual curiosity, become passive learners, and internalized the lesson of submission to an external authority, what have we done for the cause of democracy? Pragmatic wisdom calls for congruence between the means and the ends and the ends-in-view must be consistent with the criteria of deep democracy. All of this requires the cultivation of a sophisticated form of intelligence. (p. 46)

Cultivating this sophisticated form of intelligence is part of the teacher's journey of 3S understanding. By working through the inquiry map, the teacher will be grappling with the gnarly and messy contextual aspects of the curriculum. She or he will be establishing her or his professional identity and embracing the responsibility for the quality of the student's journey of understanding. Within the work year, then, we recommend 1 to 2 days of retreat at the beginning of the year and at least 1 day at the end of the school year for this purpose. The benefits will outweigh the time and money spent.

Making the Change from Within

We believe that organizing for 3S understanding may occur naturally by using the current organizational school structures and changing what you do within them. The following list is a starting point. Imagine the possibility of negotiating with decision makers to change *what* students, teachers, administrators, parents, and community members are doing as a functioning member of the group. Remember, *depending upon one's orientation, the same expenditure of time/money, in the same setting, with the same teachers can look very, very different.* The possibilities are endless.

- Local professional development committee
- Graduate studies
- Professional development budgets
- Curriculum writing projects
- Course of study revision committees

- Character education

- Conflict mediation

- School clubs

- Speakers bureau

- Business advisory councils

- Curriculum advisory councils

- Pupil services advisory councils

- Department coordinators or chairpersons

- PTA or PTO

- Board of Education—local and state

Negotiating the change from within will require knowledge of power relations, the politics of building consensus, and the productive use of politics. Being political does not mean that you are unethical, destructive, or harmful. Speaking strongly for a position and attempting to influence others' understandings can be done in caring and ethical ways. "Being political can mean taking a stand, enabling others to take a stand, and using the democratic process or deliberation and due process as you and your colleagues examine and formulate positions" (Henderson & Hawthorne, 2000, p. 173). This is essentially about communicating with stakeholders to convey the importance of enacting 3S education. If 3S education is to be sustained, we need to advocate for the robust professionalism that is associated with this work. We want to communicate with parents, community members, and all stakeholders that it is in their natural interest to have democratically wise designing, planning, teaching, evaluating, and organizing curriculum decision making. We need to communicate that these decisions will ultimately yield much better results for student learning dedicated to a life of continuous growth.

REFERENCES

Argyris, C. (1970). *Intervention theory and methods.* Reading: MA: Addison-Wesley.

Branden, N. (1994). *The six pillars of self esteem.* New York: Bantam Books.

Cohen, D. (1988). Teaching practice: Plus que ca change. In P. W. Jackson (Ed.), *Contributing to educational change: Perspectives on research and practice* (pp. 27–84). Berkeley, CA: McCutchan.

Cooperrider, D. L., & Srivastva, S. (1987). Appreciative inquiry in organizational life. *Research in Organizational Change and Development, 1,* 129–169.

Cuban, L. (1993). *How teachers taught: Constancy and change in American classrooms 1890–1980.* New York: Longman.

Deal, T., & Peterson, K. (1990). *The principal's role in shaping school culture.* Washington, DC: U.S. Department of Education, Office of Education Research and Improvement.

Deal, T., & Peterson, K. (1999). *Shaping school culture: The heart of leadership.* San Francisco: Jossey-Bass.

DuFour, R., & Eaker, R. (1998). *Professional learning communities at work. Best practices for enhancing student achievement.*

Alexandria, VA: Association for Supervision and Curriculum Development.

Elmore, R. (1995). Structural reform and educational practice. *Educational Researcher, 24*(9), 23–26.

Fullan, M. (2001). *Leading in a culture of change.* San Francisco: Jossey-Bass.

Garmston, R. J., & Wellman, B. M. (1999). *The adaptive school: A sourcebook for developing collaborative groups.* Norwood, MA: Christopher-Gordon.

Gladwell, M. (2002). *The tipping point.* New York: Back Bay Books/Little, Brown and Company.

Greene, M. (1988). *The dialectic of freedom.* New York: Teachers College Press.

Greene, M. (1995). *Releasing the imagination: Essays on education, the arts, and social change.* San Francisco: Jossey-Bass.

Hammond, S. (1998). *The thin book of appreciative inquiry.* Plano, TX: Thin Book Publishing.

Henderson, J. G., & Hawthorne, R. D. (2000). *Transformative curriculum leadership* (2nd ed.). Upper Saddle River, NJ: Merrill/Prentice Hall.

Henderson, J. G., & Kesson, K. R. (2004). *Curriculum wisdom: Educational decisions in democratic societies.* Upper Saddle River, NJ: Merrill/Prentice Hall.

Louis, K. S., Marks, H. M., & Kruse, S. (1996). Teachers' professional community in restructuring schools. *American Educational Research Journal, 33*(4), 757–798.

Northrup, C. (2005). *Mother–daughter wisdom.* New York: Bantam Dell.

Pajares, M. F. (1992). Teachers' beliefs and educational research: Cleaning up a messy construct. *Review of Educational Research, 62*(3), 307–332.

Senge, P. (1990). *The fifth discipline field book.* New York: Bantam Doubleday Dell.

Staw, B. (1984). Organizational behavior: A review and reformulation of the field's outcome variables. *Annual Review of Psychology,* 3S, 62–66.

Stigler, J. W., & Hiebert, J. (1999). *The teaching gap.* New York: The Free Press.

Tyler, R. W. (1949). *Basic principles of curriculum and instruction.* Chicago: University of Chicago Press.

Walker, D. F. (2003). *Fundamentals of curriculum: Passion and professionalism* (2nd ed.). Mahwah, NJ: Lawrence Erlbaum Associates.

Wheatley, M. J. (1994). *Leadership and the new science: Learning about organization from an orderly universe.* San Francisco: Berrett-Koehler.

Wheatley, M. J., & Kellner-Rogers, M. (1996). *A simpler way.* San Francisco: Berrett-Koehler.

SUSTAINING THE CURRICULUM WISDOM PROBLEM SOLVING

In general, educators will not be able to sustain the practice of curriculum wisdom problem solving without the support of local professional and stakeholder learning communities. Think a moment about why this is so. The educators are continually working through problem-solving cycles of setting 3S standards, enacting systemic decision-making processes, cultivating currere insights, and practicing reflective inquiry. This is not solitary work, and there is much to learn. Teachers and administrators must work closely together, encouraging disciplined professional development and deep deliberations while celebrating strengths and balancing weaknesses. All involved, including the students, are positioned as authentic learners who are grappling with challenging holistic standards. This places a premium on establishing a mutually supportive, continuing education work environment. Everyone involved must respect the emergence of diverse identity, voice, and expression, and they must do so out of a deep sense of interdependence.

Furthermore, influential curriculum stakeholders such as parents and community leaders must acquire an appreciation for 3S education. They must learn the value of curriculum wisdom problem solving and the proper ways to support the day-to-day details of this work. They must learn to function as advocates for a high professional standard, and they must understand the difference between collaborative support and destructive interference. As we pointed out in chapter 1, there are parallels between clinical judgment in medicine and curriculum wisdom judgment in education. We wrote:

> If medical doctors engage in the disciplined study of their patients' physical health in the context of their specialty, they have the right to exercise discretionary clinical judgment. Similarly, if educators engage in the disciplined study of their students' democratic health in the context of their subject matter expertise, they have the right to exercise discretionary curriculum judgment.

Curriculum stakeholders must learn how to respond to educators' wisdom judgments in the same way that they would respond to medical doctors' clinical judgments. They will also need to learn how to constructively contribute to the inevitable negotiations between proponents of the three curriculum problem-solving paradigms.

Building local professional and stakeholder learning communities will be the topic of chapter 8. Chapter 9 addresses another important avenue for sustaining transformative curriculum leadership. Educators committed to curriculum wisdom problem solving may want to entertain ways to engage with the broader public sphere. They may want to consider working with other transformative curriculum leaders in projects that extend beyond their local settings. If such large-scale collegial networking and community building could be enacted, it would be a valuable source of support for sustaining wisdom problem solving. We explore this visionary, futuristic topic in chapter 9.

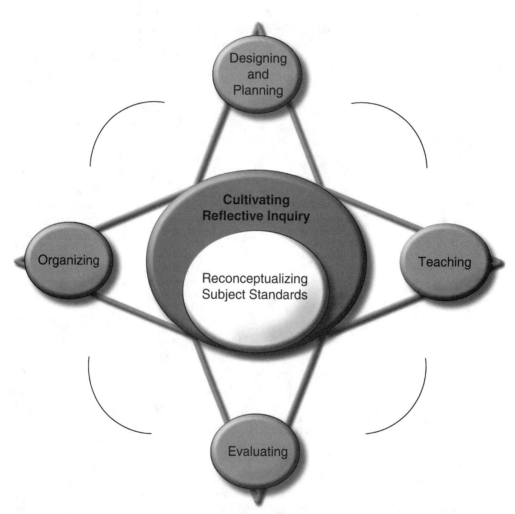

Sustaining the Curriculum Wisdom Problem Solving

CHAPTER 8

BUILDING LOCAL LEARNING COMMUNITIES

A disciplinary community emerges when a group of individuals who are engaged in similar disciplined inquiries achieve a relative consensus about the nature of the "problem" they are addressing and how this problem should be tackled. . . . Curriculum-based public intellectuals, by definition, cultivate an open, inclusive public around a compelling vision of "educating for the good life," and then establish a trusting, reciprocal and collaborative working relationship with this identified group.

(Henderson & Kesson, 2001, pp. 3–4)

As you may have recognized an important subtext and essential condition for the two fundamental challenges and the four decision-making processes advocated in this book is collaboration with others. The artful and deep deliberation that lies at the heart of curriculum wisdom problem solving requires this collaboration within the context of a local learning community. As teachers and other educators make curriculum decisions, finding common ground through a disciplined examination and articulation of the educational path for the democratic "good life" for each child, all stakeholders need to be an essential part of the community that emerges to support the work. When a group of individuals (teachers, educators, and all other stakeholders) who are engaged in similar disciplined inquiries (what is the educational path to the democratic good life?) achieves a relative consensus about the nature of the "problem" they are addressing (what is the "best" way to educate children for the democratic good life, according to their interpretation?) and how this problem should be tackled (integration of subject matter understanding with democratic self and social understanding—3S education), they must cultivate an open, inclusive community and then establish a trusting, reciprocal, and collaborative working relationship with the group. The learning community is born.

In this chapter we will examine two kinds of local learning communities: *professional learning communities* and *stakeholder learning communities*. Transformative Curriculum Leadership (TCL) requires that we work to build a specific type of professional learning community, composed of teachers, administrators, and other educators, as well as a specific type of stakeholder learning community, composed of parents, community members, and others. While the role and therefore the agenda of each of these learning communities may be different, the common purpose is to encourage and support wise curriculum decision making in societies with democratic ideals. These TCL local learning communities are essential to sustaining this work. In the next section we will explore what it means to build the first of two local learning communities: a professional learning community.

BUILDING TCL PROFESSIONAL LEARNING COMMUNITIES

Transformative Curriculum Leadership is centered on the notion that "quality teaching requires strong professional learning communities. Collegial interchange, not isolation, must become the norm for teachers. Communities of learning composed of teachers, administrators, and other educators, can no longer be considered utopian; they must become the building blocks that establish a new foundation for America's schools" (National Commission on Teaching, 2003, p. 17). We caution the reader to recognize that congenial or polite discussion with others does not comprise a professional learning community. TCL professional learning communities are committed to having the "complicated conversations," which result from the integration of problem-solving reflection with democratic curriculum inquiry as presented in chapter 3. Democratically oriented reflective inquiry is critical to the deepening deliberation that lies at the heart of curriculum wisdom problem solving. Simply put, 3S education requires sophisticated curriculum deliberation within a professional learning community that will support and sustain these deliberations.

According to Furman (1998), a "[professional learning] community is a community of difference. It is based on the ethics of acceptance of others with respect, justice, and appreciation of peaceful cooperation within difference. It is inspired by the metaphor of an interconnected, interdependent web of persons engaged in global community" (p. 312). However, Nias (1995) cautions that a professional learning community "should not be mistakenly viewed as conflict-free or cozy. . . . [A professional learning community is] built upon a belief in the value of openness, tempered by a respect for individual and collective security" (p. 9).

As you begin to build a TCL professional learning community, you will begin to experience the social, intellectual, and developmental/psychological aspects involved in the collaborative process. A learning "community," according to Grossman, Wineberg, and Woolworth (2001), develops a distribution of social and intellectual work. Grossman's ideas are paraphrased in the following list:

- Presenting new ways of thinking and reasoning collectively as well as new ways of interacting interpersonally

- Learning from colleagues, which requires both a shift in perspective and the ability to listen hard to other adults, especially as these adults struggle to formulate thoughts in response to challenging intellectual content

- Taking up others' points, pressing for clarification, and expressing what they have heard in an effort to understand the issues raised

- Providing a safe milieu in which individuals are free to voice uncertainty, explore ideas, state and retract opinions, and press for clarity while affirming the potential value of a speaker's contribution

- Learning to see difference as a resource rather than a liability

The psychological/developmental aspects must also be considered in a professional learning community willing to hold the "complicated conversations" so necessary for curriculum wisdom problem solving. The currere narratives play a significant role in the psychological/developmental aspects of this work because the language we use connects experience to understanding, and the meaning of that experience is generated as each person tells the story (Josselson, 1995). The story is the effort to grapple with the complexities of the situation. In a TCL professional learning community, the currere narrative is an important part of the wisdom problem-solving cycle. As we tell our story and transform our experiences into personal understanding, our identities as human beings are actually being shaped (Josselson, 1995). Just as knowledge is socially constructed, the self is socially constructed through language and maintained on the stories we tell (Gergen, 1991). Human development in this view is an interactive process between you and your work environment. You shape and are shaped by the environment from the stories you tell. You have experienced Rosie's stories or currere narratives in this text as one example.

The agenda for building a TCL professional learning community requires educators to deliberate over a series of questions. How do I go about beginning this challenging work, because I recognize that such a profound challenge should not begin with me working in isolation? In what ways can this professional learning community support my curriculum-based teaching judgments at the personal, interpersonal, and societal levels? What do I need from others to do this work, if I am situated in the standardized management orientation? If I am committed to the constructivist best practice orientation, what might my role be in the learning community? How will this professional learning community invite constructivist educators to transition to the curriculum wisdom paradigm? If I am already deeply committed to this kind of curriculum wisdom, what is my role in sustaining the work? In what ways will this professional learning community support my efforts to enact the curriculum wisdom problem-solving cycle, replete with reconceptualized standards, systemic decision-making processes, acting and experiencing with currere narratives and robust reflective inquiry? Through this professional learning community, will I find practical ways to engage students in making sense of democratic ideals? The following vignette may help illustrate how to begin to address these questions.

Differentiated Readiness

Think for a moment about the teachers in your building and imagine that you are with them in a faculty meeting to discuss the quality of a bullying prevention program that the faculty and staff recently put in place. The bullying program was a result of feedback from parents and guardians about a growing problem on the playground and the buses. A few older students were taking advantage of younger or more vulnerable students and terrorizing others. The older students were White and the younger students were Hispanic. Race was an issue. The process for developing the program involved a broad base of participants, including students, teachers, bus drivers, recess monitors, parents, and administrators. Data were gathered to gain a full understanding of the scope of the problem, including the number of referrals, who was involved, the frequency, and where these incidents took place. Research was done on successful programs in other districts locally and statewide. By all accounts, the program was a success as evidenced by a reduction in the number of incident referrals, parent and guardian complaints, and teacher concerns.

At the faculty meeting, after teachers have had the opportunity to discuss the outcomes and consequences of their bullying prevention programming efforts, you ask the teachers whether they have any ideas for infusing the guiding principles of bullying prevention into the curriculum. You have distinguished yourself as an informal teacher–leader in the school. You are the unofficial "go-to person," as a result of your curriculum knowledge, effective teaching strategies, and ability to relate to even the most challenging students. Many rookie and veteran teachers have been known to seek your counsel.

You explain to the group that in your experience, these programs have an all-too-short shelf life. You relate a few stories about how similar programs in the past fizzled and died away when the teacher pushing the program was transferred to another building, or when the parent or guardian who championed the initiative relocated. A further problem for sustaining a program such as this is the incredible turnover in recess monitors and bus drivers. Sure, they were involved in the development of the program, but in the last two weeks the recess monitor who was an advocate for the program quit and one of the bus drivers was put in a different run. Who would bring their replacements up to speed, and how? Because student turnover was an issue, how would the faculty ensure that new students and their parents understood the expectations? Add-on programs can have a tendency to fragment the experiences for children.

Most of the teachers nod their heads in agreement. After a period of silence, you express the opinion that an opportunity may have been missed to use the received content standards in a way that could help students grow, not only in subject matter understanding, but also in ways to help learn more about themselves and others while getting along in a school community. Is there, you ask, a way to look at our content standards in a different way?

You toss out to the group that when you examined the social studies content standards you noticed that the idea of living in community with others is a recurring and spiraling concept in almost every grade. Kindergarten begins with the family and communities, and by the time students reach high school the content standards include the global and international communities. You also share that the science content standards contain many references to the value of ecological habitats in which organisms flourish. From kindergarten through high school, students are taught that living things need diversity in the environment to flourish. Every living and nonliving thing in an environment contributes to the well-being of life in interdependent and symbiotic ways. You reason further that by talking about community and interdependence in light of the school's bullying program, students will more likely gain a deep understanding of these concepts, increasing the possibility that they will transfer this information to the context of their daily lives. Putting this into the curriculum increases the probability that students will come to understand important subject matter content and learn about the school's behavioral expectations at the same time. Why develop add-on programs when the curriculum can provide just what we need to help students become better democratic citizens? We may need to think about the received standards in a little different manner, but the benefits could be amazing. You suggest that education is not preparation for life; education is life (Dewey, 1916/1966). Is there, you ask again, a way to look at our subject-area content standards in a way for students to learn the subject matter in meaningful ways so they can learn about themselves, others, and how to get along?

During the silence after the question, you look around the room. You notice a variety of revealing body language (rolling eyes, blank stares, raised eyebrows), which if translated into words might include such comments as: "What the heck is she talking about? I have no idea what she means by that. The content standards are the content standards, pure and simple. Besides, if she thinks I have time to do anything but prepare the students to pass those tests, she is crazy." Here's another: "Oh my gosh, here she goes again. Does she think she is the principal or something? Can't we ever be happy with what we have done? The bullying prevention program was a success. Why on earth are we adding this to our plates? This is just one more pressure added to an already pressure-filled day." And another: "Well, I already do a number of project-based learning activities with my students in an attempt to have them gain a deeper understanding of the subject matter. I get the idea of using some of this in the curriculum, but why is it so important to have the kids learn about themselves? I teach the cognitive curriculum, not the affective part. We should have the guidance counselor do this. Getting along with others is important, but I will take that part more seriously when and if stuff like that is on the test and published to parents and the community." And finally: "That is a very interesting question. In our classroom discussions last week, we were learning about the value of diversity in a community (social studies content standard) as well as the interdependence of ecology for organisms in a habitat (science content standards). It never occurred to me that I could have used that content by applying it to bullying, a concept that is so real and so 'now' to our students. My guess is they would have understood the subject matter much more deeply if I had used it within the context of their lives on the bus and on the playground. I am not sure why we need to bring democracy into this, but her idea has merit. I wonder what the other possibilities are to use the curriculum in this way."

The reality in any professional learning community, TCL or otherwise, is that each teacher is at a different point in his or her career. Some are first-year teachers; others are seasoned veterans. The challenge of offering *any* professional learning opportunities to *any* group, in any setting, is tending to the variety of learning needs and knowledge base each brings to the table. In the same way that curriculum for children and young adults is not one size fits all, educators within the professional learning community will have *differentiated needs*.

Differentiated Needs in a TCL Professional Learning Community

In a TCL learning community, another significant variable is added to the mix of differentiated needs: how each teacher has constructed her or his professional identity. In addition to the number of years taught, gender, race, age, subject area certification/licensure, grade assignment, and background experiences, each teacher makes sense of daily experiences in different ways (Kegan, 1982, 1994). Some will follow the rules to the letter of the law, feeling comfortable living within the bounds of traditions. Their professional identities are shaped by being good at what others (usually this in authority) tell them to do. Teachers who make sense this way often feel uncomfortable when someone disagrees with them, and they will go along in the name of harmonious relationships.

Other teachers are less rule bound, comfortable making unique sense of their experiences, even if others do not agree with them. The conflicting opinions of others do not upset them. Their professional identities are not shaped by the opinions of others and they do not mind being set apart from the "tribe." As problem solvers, they will enter the debate but will often hold tightly to their views in unbending ways.

Still others are able to remain curious about what happens each day. They have an intuition about life's events and seem okay with suspending judgment by asking more questions. Two competing experiences are more interesting than stressful, and when decisions are made, they seem ready and open to consider the consequences, make midcourse corrections, and move on. Their professional identities are characterized by self-authorship, interdependence with others, and wisdom.

All of the above, then, will affect the "complicated conversations" within the professional learning community. All of the above will affect decisions about the most appropriate and growth-producing professional development needed for the professional development community; each will need differentiated content and experiences because of unique professional and development readiness.

The notion of reconceptualizing the received standards into more holistic transformative goals, for example, will evoke a variety of responses depending upon the readiness of each teacher. Those of us who seek to embrace curriculum wisdom problem solving for our designing/planning, teaching, evaluating, and organizing decisions need to be cognizant of the social, interpersonal, psychological, and developmental readiness of the members of the learning community. In our work with teachers, we have come to appreciate the complex and difficult psychological and political challenges of this work and yet embrace all of it as part of each person's 3S journey of understanding. Curriculum wisdom problem solving requires patience, yet the expectations are very high, requiring disciplined, practical, and sophisticated reasoning. The social, interpersonal, psychological, and developmental readiness of each member will in part determine his or her problem-solving paradigm. Additionally, developmental readiness will be a factor in the manner in which the teacher addresses the two fundamental challenges (reconceptualizing received standards and reflective inquiry capacity) and the four decision-making processes (designing/planning, teaching, evaluating, and organizing). Gaining insight into how each member makes meaning or sense of the world will help the TCL professional learning community understand how that meaning making will affect the curriculum wisdom problem solving and curriculum decision making. This readiness or meaning making dynamic is precisely what makes the deliberation so challenging and so important, and precisely why the negotiation strategies you learned about in chapter 4 are so essential.

WWYD (What Would You Do?)

How would you imagine yourself handling those questions at the faculty meeting? Would you have had the courage to ask the original question posed by the teacher–leader? If so, how might you have responded to the silence or comments that some teachers were thinking? These are the questions we must process if we are to find ways to have this professional learning community support curriculum-based teaching judgments at the personal, interpersonal, and societal levels. We need to ask each individual what she or he might need from others to do this work; that need may be different depending upon the problem-solving paradigm. If the teacher is already committed to the constructivist best practice (CBP) paradigm, she or he may occupy a different role in the learning community and may use the professional learning community to transition to the curriculum wisdom (CW) paradigm. If the teacher is already deeply committed to this kind of curriculum wisdom, his or her role in sustaining the work through mentoring or modeling might be appropriate. Regardless of developmental readiness the TCL professional learning community needs to support every teacher's efforts to enact the curriculum wisdom problem-solving cycle, replete with reconceptualized standards, systemic decision-making processes, acting and experiencing with currere narratives, and robust reflective inquiry. Exploring and developing a professional learning community suggests a commitment to breaking the cycle of *faddism*. Doing so proposes that educators distance themselves from workshops, and similar formats, which provide the *answers* to educational problems, to experience a more sophisticated professional inquiry journey that guides their personal and professional growth and development, strengthens their collegial relationships, and helps the growth and development of their students. Through this professional learning community, teachers are more likely to find practical ways to actively engage students in making sense of democratic ideals, than if done alone. We suggest using Barth's (2001) notion of critical friends as one way to begin.

Critical Friends

The cultivation of *critical friends* provides an important avenue for building a TCL professional learning community (Barth, 2001). Critical friends can be experienced in at least three ways: through students in your classroom; through a trusted colleague; or through a group of colleagues. Critical friends (Barth, 2001) are generally trusted colleagues with teaching and leadership ability who possess strong interpersonal skills; however, students are important participants in the professional learning community, as well. Whether your critical friends are students, an individual colleague, or a group of colleagues, we advocate using the currere narratives between and among all participants to facilitate the personalized journeys of understanding for all involved.

Regardless of the composition of the learning community, building trusting relationships is essential to cultivating and sustaining the curriculum judgments we advocate in this book. A critical friend is someone who, for example, asks provocative questions about your designing and planning decisions, provides data to be examined through another lens as you determine the criteria for judging the quality of your students' 3S journeys of understanding, and offers critique of your work as a friend. Critical friends take the time to fully understand the context of the work presented and the outcomes that you or the group are working toward. A critical friend may have been the one to respond to the comments some of the teachers were thinking.

Most importantly, the friend is the advocate for the success of that work. Costa and Kallick (1993) suggest that critical friends will work collaboratively to:

- be clear about the nature of the relationship, and not use it for evaluation or judgment;
- listen well: clarifying ideas, encouraging specificity, and taking time to fully understand what is being presented;
- offer value judgments only upon request from the learner;

- respond to the learner's work with integrity; and

- be an advocate for the success of the work. (p. 50)

Critical friends, as partners advocating curriculum wisdom problem solving, want to be able to freely express their thoughts, ideas, concerns, suggestions, apprehensions, and the like without judgment. A nonthreatening setting is a key component to developing comfort and trust within the community. Critical friends within a professional learning community dedicated to transformative curriculum leadership are committed to self-study and believe improving their practice cannot be accomplished without reflective inquiry. Critical friends move beyond congenial interactions (congratulating one another and offering pats on the back) to collegiality and deep deliberations (providing challenge and inquiry into issues that surfaced as they study their teaching practices). Critical friends fully embrace the journey, yours, their own, and others, and trust in the process, recognizing the inherent unpredictability of situations. They admit the possibility of error, understand that each moment is different from the one preceding it, and are attentive to the present circumstances, aware of the consequences of actions (Henderson & Kesson, 2004). Critical friends are alert to the implications of these consequences for our democratic way of life. If critical friends were in the room at that faculty in the previous vignette, we believe that the dialogue would have been fruitful and supportive and, most importantly, facilitated the teachers' 3S of understanding and therefore the students' 3S journey of understanding.

More Questions

Members of a TCL professional learning community are educators who know that in order to arouse the search for freedom in their students, they must be in search of their own (Greene, 1988). They are prepared to be aware of and confront the implicit injustices potentially lurking in the hidden and null curricula and may ask each other the same questions they ask their students:

1. Have we employed knowledge effectively in diverse, authentic, and realistically messy contexts?

2. Have we revealed personalized, thoughtful, and coherent grasp of subjects demonstrating the ability to think for ourselves?

3. Are we wide awake, willing to welcome new insights and refining core beliefs through conversations with diverse others?

4. Have we demonstrated the ability to effectively and sensitively interpret texts and the ability to read between the lines?

5. Have we extended or applied what is known in novel ways to become more cognitively, emotionally, physically, aesthetically, and spiritually attuned to ourselves and others?

These specific questions must be woven into ongoing 3S designing, planning, teaching, evaluating, and organizing decisions. Professional learning communities dedicated to curriculum wisdom problem solving proceed holistically and humbly, not literally and ideologically.

Students as Critical Friends in TCL Professional Learning Communities

If we are attempting to help students grow into people who can think for themselves, who can engage in life imaginatively and fully as life-long learners, and who are able to embrace democracy as a vibrant way of living, then providing opportunities for students to speak truth to power is essential. Viewed as dynamic makers of meaning, students are a storehouse of information, providing feedback for improving our wisdom problem solving and elevating our curriculum judgments. Students sharing their currere narratives in a safe and open environment are taking an important step on their 3S journey of understanding, and they are contributing to an important aspect of your 3S journey of understanding. To embrace a love of curriculum wisdom is to embark on a journey of discovery, and who better to help you discover the quality of your decisions than your students?

As transformative curriculum leaders, we believe that students need to make sense of events and must be treated as if they have minds of their own. By treating students as critical friends, not only will you be encouraging students to use their mental capacities to build more sophisticated understandings, but you will also be provided real and insightful feedback on the quality of your designing, planning, teaching, evaluating, and organizing decisions from the people most intimately involved.

Colleagues as Critical Friends in TCL Professional Learning Communities

About four years ago, we worked with a small school district in southeast Ohio in its quest to cultivate curriculum wisdom. In this section, we would like to share our experiences and reveal what we learned while working with the professional learning communities that grew out of this effort. Throughout this experience, those involved functioned as critical friends and advocates for the work.

The culture within the district and each school fostered a respect for teachers' knowledge and expertise, and it supported the transformative curriculum leadership movement. The challenge was to invite educators to research and explore "best practices" in teaching and learning and, in turn, examine their collective impact related to reconceptualized standards, systemic curriculum-decision making, acting and experiencing through currere narratives, and reflective inquiry on their 3S education efforts. Members of the professional learning community agreed to "step outside the box" (or least attempt to) and become open to learning about a lifelong professional inquiry journey as well as inviting their students to do the same. Professional readings, follow-up support, practice, feedback, reflection, and evaluation of teaching and learning practices were critical components of the work enacted by the learning community. These enactments promoted teaching and learning practices that were conducive to a transformative approach to education.

When members of this school community, including parents, board members, other staff members, and community members at large considered the vision and the changes they needed to make, they began to experience what Lord (1994) calls "productive disequilibrium." Transformative curriculum leadership represented major shifts in both perspective and practice, and some struggled with the changes. Further discord was prompted by the readings and the discussions around the readings as members struggled to make connections to their own practices.

As a result, a discussion within the professional learning community brought to light the following questions: How do we address our current standardized management teaching responsibilities while working on becoming transformative curriculum leaders (reflective ethical inquiry)? Can we measure learning success in a way that promotes the equitable treatment of students (reflective critical inquiry)? Can we consider diverse perspectives on what we are trying to accomplish (reflective multiperspective inquiry)? How do we provide ongoing communication with colleagues and community members who disagree with our positions (reflective political inquiry)? How will our work change power relations in the school/district (reflective political inquiry)? How does our work deepen our feel for democratic morality in education (reflective poetic inquiry)? How will a portfolio process impact working and community relations in the district (reflective political inquiry)?

This dissonance helped move the learning community in a positive direction, and the ongoing deliberative exchanges were supported through professional development activities in three ways involving colleagues as critical friends: (1) disciplined study about a variety of timely and relevant topics in small and large groups before, during, and after school; (2) participation in a higher education/K–12 school partnerships by having professors join the learning community, immersing themselves in study, with opportunities to secure university workshop credit for the members; and (3) finding time for sharing currere narratives, formally and informally, as data for designing, planning, teaching, evaluating, and organizing decisions. Acknowledging that educators develop at different rates and have different talents and interests, it was essential to provide professional development opportunities that gave high priority to collegial conversations, provided collaborative learning, and invited reflection (Darling-Hammond & McLaughlin, 1995; Zepeda, 1999). Holonomy—the delicate balance between autonomy and interdependence—was a factor as the members of the TCL professional learning community worked to build their reflective inquiry capacities. As a result of this kind of professional development, the following are a few examples of the professional leadership projects that were developed in the district.

Professional Leadership Projects (PLPs)

Members of the learning community created Professional Leadership Projects (PLPs) (see Figure 8.1 for an example of project requirements along with a framework). Specifically, the PLPs addressed the individual professional development goals listed on each member's Individual Professional Development Plan (IPDP), which outlined goals in relationship to the district's Continuous Improvement Plan, specific building goals, as well as the teacher's areas of improvement. Overarching questions for their PLP were carefully written after reflecting on their goals and how those goals aligned with the district initiatives. Working individually, with a partner, or in small groups, members crafted their PLPs.

The following are examples of PLP topics explored by members of the learning community, along with related questions, which offered *multiple corridors for participation* (Grossman, 2001):

Figure 8.1 Professional Leadership Project: *Collaborative Project Guidelines*

Requirements

1. A collaborative project group must be composed of three or more educators.
2. Complete and submit to the Local Professional Development Committee (LPDC) <u>one</u> project proposal and include all members of the group.
3. The project must connect to the district and building Continuous Improvement Plans (CIPs) and Individual Professional Development Plans (IPDPs) of the members of the group.
4. A letter of support from the building principal or program director must be included with the initial proposal and must include the names of the group members.
5. A work session log with meeting dates, times, and a detailed description of the activities and objectives of the work session must be included.
6. <u>One</u> copy of all materials (e.g., activities, artifacts, student assessments, etc.) must be submitted with the final project
7. Create <u>one</u> list of all group members involved in the collaborative project and include it with the final project.
8. A collaborative project may be completed for 15 hours or for 30 hours.

Framework

1. Identify the topic or need.
2. Consider and respond to the following questions:
   - What do the "experts" say about the topic or need?
   - What materials and resources are available to address the topic or need?
   - What materials and resources do I need to address the topic or need?
   - Identify the connections to the district and building CIPs and IPDPs.
3. Identify and review the student data to identify and to support the investigation of the topic or need.
4. Describe the action plan. Consider and respond to the following:
   - Describe the specific action(s) the group will take.
   - What will be the role and responsibility of each collaborative member?
   - Provide a rationale for the action(s) including the intended effects.
   - Who will be involved and/or affected by the actions?
   - What is the timeline for the completion and implementation of the project?
5. How will you document the process? (e.g., journals, logs, student/teacher work samples, video recordings, etc.)
6. What materials will be created? (e.g. lesson plans, assessments, activities, etc.)
7. Reflection—How do you see this project benefiting students and teachers?
8. After implementation of this project, how do you plan to share it with colleagues?
9. What are the next steps for this project or a portion of this project?

Source: Developed August 2001 by the director of Instruction and Professional Development and the Local Professional Development Committee in a small public school in the Midwest.

Creating Departments and Common Planning Time

- How can we coordinate and encourage nondepartmentalized staff members to work collegially as they research, develop, and plan options for the implementation of new departments, such as fine arts, careers, and special education?

- How can we explore and create ways to improve grade-level collaboration among regular education teachers and special education teachers (e.g., cognitive delay (CD), specific learning disability (SLD), gifted and talented, and intervention) at the elementary level?

Classroom/Team Practices

- How can we help the students in computer graphics class to work as a team to conduct research in connection with a constructive, real-world situation; to apply their knowledge and technological skills; and present their findings in a multimedia presentation that showcases the skills and abilities of each team member?

- How can we help second-grade students improve their reading skills so they will become lifelong readers?

- How can we help high school French students practice inquiry, engage in analytical thinking, and participate in reflective practices?

- How can our team of fifth-grade teachers collaborate with first-grade teachers from an urban charter school on a service-learning project that promotes literacy?

Special Education

- What is the most efficient and effective manner in which to address the following topics and enhance the delivery of services to students with exceptionalities?

  — Increased collaboration and reflective opportunities with the special education faculty

  — Increased dissemination of information to regular and special education faculty and to parents

  — Development of guidelines for administration of the gifted program

  — Coordination of program administration between gifted and special education faculty

  — Development of a lending resource materials library

  — Development of modified curricular objectives

- How can we provide students with special needs an outlet within the school that allows them to feel a part of the school community?

- How can we involve and facilitate eighth-grade students with special needs in the design of their career in and of life "transition plans" in preparation for high school?

Leadership

- How can we learn, apply, and reflect on the six core values we have defined as a school (honesty, students first, team-centered approach, loyalty, professionalism, and respect) and use them to guide our plans, decisions, and actions?

- How can I assist the faculty in enhancing team collegiality, increasing interdisciplinary integration among our content-area teachers and expressive arts teachers, and improving parent communication?

- How can I assist the teacher leaders in their role as "change agent" in continuous school improvement?

Impact on the District

- What is the role of the professional portfolio in teacher growth and development and review/evaluation?

- How can we use technology to improve communication, accountability, and information distribution/collection/analysis methods for students, faculty, and community?

We learned many important lessons about cultivating curriculum wisdom problem solving while working in the district and believe our work made a small, yet significant contribution to this body of knowledge. The professional development that spawned the projects we mentioned earlier included opportunities to engage in complex, critical questioning and thinking, exploration and engagement in discourse concerning current educational issues, and involvement in systematic school improvement processes (e.g., peer coaching, mentoring, professional portfolios, and action research).

Currere Interlude

I wish I could report fabulous experiences in my district with the wisdom problem-solving cycle illustrating many examples of reconceptualizing the received standards, building reflective inquiry capacities, and currere narratives providing rich descriptions of students' 3S journeys of understanding within a robust and intellectually stimulating professional learning community. I wish I could illustrate a professional development agenda that might give you more precise guidance about how to make this happen. I wish I could move you with news of a visionary platform for designing and planning curriculum experiences for students that cultivated and facilitated their journey of understanding, with teachers, other educators, and all stakeholders dialoging and deliberating about expressive outcomes, criteria for judging those performances of understanding, and generative learning experiences. But alas, I cannot.

And as we draw close to the end of this book, I will try to explain why. Remember: Transformative Curriculum Leadership is a journey, not a destination. Yes, we may all strive to meet the high professional standard outlined in this book, but we also need to find strength in the myriad small ways that parts of this vision may be going on in your school or district right now, today. We estimate that anywhere from 10 percent to 20 percent of teachers are not only ready for this wisdom challenge, but also may already be functioning in this way. They will not call what they do a curriculum wisdom problem-solving cycle and they may not know that they have reconceptualized the received standards into holistic understanding goals, but they are doing this nonetheless. Most often, teachers operating out of the wisdom orientation are popular among students. Students feel their love and acceptance but recognize that they have never worked so hard and more willingly in their lives. One of our teachers has been named by students the "best Black, White teacher" they know. When asked why, the students and parents report that she connects with students as a people, communicates an attitude of love and respect, knows her subject matter inside and out, and has extremely high expectations. This teacher, whether she knows it or not, is likely operating out of at least three working assumptions, which may be part of her beliefs about teaching and learning.

Three Working Assumptions

Transformative Curriculum Leadership operates on at least three working assumptions (Henderson & Kesson, 2004): First, curriculum work is an exercise in "practical wisdom." This wisdom is the capacity to judge rightly in matters relating to life and conduct, choosing carefully the means to the end, and sound sense especially in practical affairs (*Oxford English Dictionary*). Second, curriculum wisdom assumes a *love of wisdom*; a humble openness to a life of inquiry through a disciplined quest to judge rightly for students in societies with democratic ideals. The third working assumption is that curriculum wisdom is focused on the "democratic good life . . ." the exercise of responsible freedom in daily affairs and the responsible curriculum judgments of the teacher, which facilitate responsible student judgments. While I cannot dazzle you with stories about the perfect wisdom problem solving, reconceptualized standards, and currere narratives, I can share some of the ways that my colleagues and I exercised practical wisdom, with a disciplined quest to judge rightly for students in societies with democratic ideals, seeking opportunities to cultivate responsible curriculum judgments centered on the facilitation of responsible student judgments. Was every one of our decisions based on these assumptions? No. Could we have made better decisions, with more wisdom and more discipline? Yes. Was every decision we made motivated out of a deep love for children and their well-being? Absolutely! One out of three is not bad. In baseball, a 33 percent batting average will get you in the Hall of Fame.

While I do not want to sound flip, I want to take some time in this currere narrative to tell you about my district and the ways I attempted to work within these three assumptions. Yes, I fail; I succeed; I give up; I persist; I am patient; I am frustrated, but I am *always* tuned in to these assumptions in my quest to improve the quality of my democratically inspired judgments for teachers and students. What has no name vanishes. Now this kind of curriculum work has a name and is manifest in my daily actions to my capacity, whatever that might be.

Recall that in my district, the professional judgment was made to emphasize subject matter knowledge in order to help students gain basic skills not only to pass the tests, but also to access the broader world. Over the past few years, students enrolling in our schools were several grade levels behind in their basic skills. Some had been enrolled in so many schools and districts that they had tremendous gaps in their knowledge. A newly enrolled third grader might be reading at a preprimer level. With the high-stakes test only six short months away, a triage was put in place to get her up to speed. While I shuddered at what seemed to be a "skill and drill" experience, I also knew that for this student, at this time, in this way, this was the most practically wise decision. Teachers stepped up and provided the expertise, love, and energy to bring the child up to speed.

I worried, however, that we did not have the agility to transition out of a skill-and-drill format to give this student many meaningful learning experiences as well. My heart went out to our teachers. Many of them operated out of the constructivist best practices paradigm, but with the emphasis on subject matter alone, they had to let go of some of the more meaningful curriculum experiences for students. This was professionally frustrating for them. Working in a standardized management environment also was frustrating. It bears repeating, however, that some of these projects did not address the content standards in a purposeful manner. Some of the projects lacked a curricular focus and while they were fun and even entertaining for students, our focus as educators must include subject matter content experienced in democratically inspired and meaningful ways.

The politics in my district were such that if I tried to place one more project in the classroom, teachers would resist . . . justifiably so, I might add. Because of the challenges we were facing, we all felt a sense of urgency to ensure that students knew the content. It was difficult for teachers to make adjustments in their planning when for years what they had been doing "worked well." I shied away from bringing teachers together to talk about reconceptualizing the received standards, or teaching for 3S understanding, because I knew they were burdened enough. In order to continue working incrementally within the curriculum wisdom paradigm, I offered teachers professional development opportunities using the Wiggins and McTighe (1998) backward design. This, I thought, would be my "wiggle room." Over a 2-year period, approximately 16 teachers and administrators attended their 2-day workshop and returned very inspired to do this kind of work. My hope was that if teachers could become inspired by working for deep subject matter understanding within the constructivist best practices paradigm, at some point they would be cued up for the transition to the curriculum wisdom paradigm. Teaching for deep subject matter understanding, with authentic performances of understanding, is challenging and time-consuming work. While Wiggins and McTighe offer teachers assistance on their Web site, authentic learning projects such as these became more and more difficult. I attempted to engage teachers in problem-solving dialogue to find a way to facilitate this work more effectively. After-school meetings were held, but coaching, family, and graduate-course responsibilities forced some teachers away. About the same time, the testing accountability pressures were increasing. In addition to having 75% of students pass the tests, now students with disabilities were added to the list and expected to pass the tests. What professional development time and money we had was now shifted to standards-based education activities.

Another Attempt to Find Wiggle Room

Part of my responsibilities in the district included teaching the secondary methods course to preservice teachers working on their masters in education at a local university. I used this as an opportunity to teach preservice teachers about constructivist best practices concepts, with the hope of transitioning them to the curriculum wisdom paradigm at some point. The units they developed were absolutely amazing and very 3S indeed. I hope that in some small way I may have introduced these teachers to a curriculum for "becoming," which included the subject matter content, in one awesome unit.

Imagining a Professional Development Agenda

I have often dreamed about ways to set up a professional development experience for this kind of work. In the current culture of many districts, professional development time and money are spent on scientifically based teaching, leaving little room for extending this to include some of the curriculum wisdom problem solving. Assuming for a moment, that the politics would allow it, however, I would start by sending an e-mail to all staff, asking them to attend a dialogue session with me and other colleagues to discuss ways we might provide students with more meaningful curriculum experiences. I would schedule the meeting at a convenient time and make sure I had plenty of snacks. If possible, I would seek a stipend for those teachers attending.

At the meeting, we would discuss some of the frustrations they might be feeling about the pressures of the accountability movement. Lest we celebrate the problem, we would move on and begin dreaming about another way we might "be" with our students. I would tell some currere narrative about my experiences with this work and invite others to share theirs. A recorder would capture the essence of each story in flip charts for all to ponder. After a period of time, and when I was certain that there were no more stories to tell, I would ask whether any teachers might want to further pursue this work. A sign-up sheet would be passed around to build a roster. Those names would become the TCL professional learning community of the district.

I would seek graduate credit for our work and begin by asking teachers to read about democracy in education. Ample opportunities for sharing currere narrative would be essential. We would tackle, in the safety of our learning community, reconceptualizing the content standards, finding out how they may have done this already. We would work on building our reflective inquiry capacity by continuing our study of curriculum theory, philosophy, and just what it means to cultivate responsible curriculum judgments centered in the facilitation of responsible student judgments. More currere narratives would be shared to learn more about the possibilities for expressive outcomes and a student's 3S journey of understanding. Careful work would be done to develop rubrics, which would be used as criteria for judging the quality of the 3S journey. We would take time to pay attention to the needs of our professional learning community by determining how we will make decisions, how we will divide the work, how we will communicate with one another by respecting the developmental readiness of each member of the group. We would recognize that every community experiences conflict and would develop strategies and capacity for negotiation and resolution. As with most everything else in this book, we cannot give you precise protocols for enacting this work. Depending on the setting and the people involved, your process will be uniquely your own.

At some point, the learning community will need to engage with parents and other stakeholders. True, robust TCL professional learning communities must flourish if we are to advance transformative curriculum leadership. No less important, however, is the stakeholder learning community. As you will see in the next section of this chapter, the professional advocacy role and agenda of the stakeholder learning community must be robust for this kind of educational reform.

BUILDING STAKEHOLDER LEARNING COMMUNITIES

In this section we will explore what it means to build the second of the two local learning communities: a stakeholder learning community. While the role and therefore the agenda of each learning community may be different, the common purpose in this context is to encourage and support wise curriculum decision making in societies with democratic ideals. Stakeholder learning communities are composed of parents, community members, and others. Building stakeholder learning communities for the advancement of curriculum wisdom requires educating the general public on a number of levels, which will be discussed here. Educating a stakeholder learning community poses additional challenges as compared to professional learning communities for some obvious and perhaps not so obvious reasons.

Our experience has been that many educators working within the professional learning community may be challenged to fully understand this systemic problem-solving cycle and the sophisticated curriculum decision making that comprises this work. This book has been written for the express purpose of providing practitioners with practical advice and guidance to cultivate this work in their settings. If educators, who are in the schools working with students every day, are challenged by this theory, the challenge increases as we attempt to provide parents, community members, and others with appropriate conceptual and practical information to engender their support and advocacy. Building stakeholder learning communities requires communicating with and educating the general public about:

- The value of students' performances and demonstrations of 3S understanding

- Promoting and inspiring professional advocacy, evidenced by their trust in educators' curriculum judgments by establishing a supportive network with a particular democratically wise educational platform

- Negotiating wiggle room for curriculum wisdom decision making with reference to the SM paradigm and the CBP paradigm

Communicating for 3S education is not your typical home/school communication. Within the SM paradigm, teachers and administrators are taught to be good communicators. We are taught that we must avoid educational jargon when reporting information about a textbook selection, a particular educational program, or subject methodology. We are reminded that our language must be clear, precise, and straightforward when dealing with parents and community members. If parents or community members are confused by our communication, it is generally perceived to be the responsibility of the educator. The message must be coherent and reflect the vision of the school or district.

Communicating with stakeholders within the CW paradigm includes all of the reporting necessary within the SM paradigm and should include the value of students' performances and demonstrations of 3S understanding. A wide range of curriculum stakeholders need to know what it means to educate for deep subject matter understanding and democratic self and social learning. The better able we are to describe examples of what this kind of education looks like, and its value to the student, the school, and the society, the better the stakeholders will understand. The better they understand, the more likely they are to assist in establishing supportive networks for this work.

VALUING 3S PERFORMANCES OF UNDERSTANDING

Imagine for a moment the deep gratitude a parent or guardian might have if their child were involved in a curriculum project that helped the community. Further, if their child's role demonstrated his personal insights and deep subject matter understanding, the parent or guardian would naturally want more of the same kind of experiences for the child. Imagine the appreciation a parent or guardian might have if their child saw herself as an active, informed lifelong learner, capable of using subject matter understanding in ways that contribute to the elimination of suffering and injustice. Parents and guardians and indeed all community stakeholders would likely become natural advocates for this kind of work.

When curriculum projects are deeply satisfying and result in a meaningful difference for others, this kind of work would soon become a new standard of "accountability," now called "responsibility." We believe that if parents and other stakeholders understood 3S education, they would opt for it. They would, we believe, be thrilled that we are preparing their child for a life of personal and social responsibility, as well as critical and creative thinking.

EDUCATING FOR PROFESSIONAL ADVOCACY

Communicating 3S education also includes promoting and inspiring a kind of professional advocacy. Once we have shared information and projects about 3S education and its value for improving the quality of student's educational experiences and lives, we need to establish stakeholders as advocates and supporters of the robust teacher professionalism that comes with this interpretation. This professional advocacy is evidenced by stakeholders' trust in educators' curriculum judgments and by establishing a supportive network with a particular democratically wise educational platform. In order for 3S education to have sustainability, we need to educate our public in a way that not only advances this professional advocacy, but also communicates to them their role as essential supporters of this professional advocacy.

As has been stated repeatedly throughout this text, the CW paradigm foregrounds teacher judgment. In the current environment, teacher judgment has been all but eliminated. Student achievement is measured on standardized tests, and curriculum is viewed more as tangible products, such as textbooks and worksheets, than as a process of "becoming." The message to stakeholders needs to promote the value of teacher judgment in matters of curriculum and teaching in much the same ways that they value the judgments of their medical doctor, for example. When you seek medical advice, you certainly want a health-care practitioner who has all the necessary physiological, biological, and anatomical content knowledge information. You want a person who knows his or her stuff. Most importantly, you want a practitioner who makes good judgments about your health care, based on your age, weight, ethnicity, and medical history. You would be indignant and even horrified if your particular circumstances were not considered in the diagnosis, prognosis, treatment, and prevention planning. Health-care practitioners who have a reputation for making good judgments about our specific needs are honored with national and international reputations as "being the best in the field." Educators need to ask why we accept anything less for our students. We all need to ask why there is a tradition of respecting medical doctors' clinical judgments, when there is not a tradition of respecting educators' curriculum judgments. Stakeholders need to ask why they would accept anything less for their children. As teachers and educators make curriculum decisions through a disciplined examination and articulation of the educational path for the "good life" for each child, stakeholders need to be an essential part of the community that emerges to support the work.

As you can readily see, this kind of public communication to educate stakeholders is different from reporting newsy information to parents about what is happening in school. The transformative curriculum leader recognizes that she or he needs to identify a public that is ready for this kind of education, work with them to expand their understanding of what it means to teach for 3S education, and establish the group as a political base for growing 3S education. This is not just any type of learning community building; it is a specific type of learning community building with people who not only understand this curriculum interpretation, but also form a professional identity around the work. If 3S education is to be sustained, stakeholders need to advocate for the robust professionalism associated with this work. The same kind of robust professionalism enjoyed by and expected by doctors and lawyers. We want to communicate with parents, community members, and all other stakeholders that it is in their natural interest to have democratically wise designing, teaching, evaluating, and organizing curriculum decision making. We need to communicate that these decisions will ultimately yield much better results for student learning that is dedicated to a life of continuous growth.

Some reading this may scoff or shy away, believing that giving voice to parents and community members is tricky and can lead to untenable political situations. In our view, reaching out to stakeholders about the kind of professional identity we are building does not mean that we are reaching out so that they will interfere, replacing one kind of top-down management with another. Certainly we need stakeholders to be partners in this work. We need their input and knowledge during the deliberations to make the most informed educational decisions for the students. In a similar manner, you should be a partner in your health-care decisions. You need to share your health background and information so that the most informed health-care decision may be made. At some point, however, through the deliberations and the negotiating, most of us embrace the input of the health-care practitioner and with our full knowledge a decision is made in our best health-care interest. We ask again, why should this be any different in the field of education?

EDUCATING FOR NEGOTIATING

In addition to communicating with and educating the public about 3S educating and advancing professional advocacy, we also need to educate for negotiating the wiggle room for curriculum wisdom decision making. Negotiating is an essential skill if we are to advance this challenging curriculum work, and we need stakeholders to assist. The daily organizational and structural changes necessary for 3S education in the school will require careful negotiating. Teachers unions, school board members, and the wide range of curriculum stakeholders will need to be involved. Walker (2003) outlines key negotiation strategies that curriculum stakeholders need to employ in order to meet the challenges of any curriculum improvement. These strategies will be critical for negotiating the time and resources for curriculum wisdom decision making with reference to the other two paradigms and were discussed at length in chapter 4. These strategies include:

1. Achieving working agreement

2. Making principled decisions

3. Working constructively with teachers

4. Seeking substantial, lasting improvement

5. Facing conflict constructively

Most likely, there will be times when it will be necessary to take two steps back to take five steps forward as you negotiate with the stakeholders learning community. At times it will be necessary to go along to get along. There is great value in reminding all stakeholders that this is a journey, not a destination, and that if we persist, change can occur. Remember, the dominant paradigm and the constructivist best practices paradigm are the current reality and the good negotiator remains hopeful and courageous while working with and through each to make a case for the wisdom paradigm. Henderson and Kesson (2001) remind us that "an important characteristic of public intellectuals, and in this case, our stakeholder learning community, is that they strive to illuminate the most pressing issues of our day in a way that renders these topics more transparent, more explicable and transformable." Your work now should include being able to describe what this kind of education looks and feels like. Begin by finding the words to illuminate the pressing issues, making the topic digestible and real to those involved. When you are able to describe the rich, meaningful, and deep experiences that students and teachers are having as a result of this "love of wisdom," you will more naturally find yourself negotiating from a position of strength because, as Eisner (1994) points out, *meaning* is a basic human need.

Currere Narrative

We think many parents and stakeholders would be ready for this kind of advocacy. Each month for almost 10 years, I hosted a Curriculum Advisory Council meeting. You were introduced to this council in chapter 6. It was a pleasure to work with people so passionate about the work of the committee. Each month parents, community members, teachers, administrators, and students would gather to talk about our curriculum projects in the district. While we did not formally discuss specific 3S projects, the quality of our relationships and the depth of our discussions convinced me of the potential to engage stakeholders through professional advocacy. Do I believe that we could have gone to even greater lengths to bring this work to the fruition? Yes. I remain hopeful about that possibility.

I predict that in the not too distant future, educators across America will push back, drawing the proverbial line in the sand about the over emphasis on test scores as the only measure of student achievement. While many educators are relieved by the fact that disciplinary subject area specialists in our country have outlined what a "literate" person should know and be able to do in math, science, language arts, and social studies; and while still more agree with Gardner (1999) when he states that educators can use subject matter objectives to show students how one thinks and acts in the manner of a scientist, a geometer, an artist, or an historian, for example, emphasizing not only content standards, but also process standards outlining ways of knowing and inquiry for the future; most if not all educators yearn to offer more for their students. I know many teachers and other educators who believe that curriculum improvement can be a means for a vision about a society in which citizens are open to dialogue over their core beliefs and they want their students to be a part of that vision. Many, many teachers want to be part of learning communities (professional and stakeholder) that encourage students to be able to choose *not* to be comfortable, nonquestioning true believers (Henderson & Hawthorne, 1995). They want their students to grow each day, ready to participate in a society in which citizens accept the give and take of differing points of view because they possess a balanced outlook on life with a full appreciation of subtleties, ironies, and ambiguities. They work each day, full of resolve to help their students develop the critical maturity to celebrate and cultivate such democratic principles as fairness, justice, moral sensibilities, and the fullest realization of human potentials.

I think Gardner (1999) is correct when he states, "There are many great teachers—but the lack of coordination among classes and the absence of accountability to those 'outside the door' is lamentable. The lack of coordination and accountability regularly results in cases where students who move from one school to another discover almost no overlap between the two institutions' offerings" (p. 117), but we have gone to the other extreme. I believe that we have handcuffed teachers with such imbalanced, semiprofessional expectations that we have eliminated teacher judgment. I know many teachers who are ready and able to engage in disciplined inquiry into the relationship between democracy and education, willing to take full responsibility for elevated curricular judgments. I know more still, who if given the opportunity to learn through complicated conversations in supportive learning communities, would mature into this professional identity. Meaning is a basic human need (Eisner, 1994). You may say I'm a dreamer, but I'm not the only one.

In the next chapter, we will discuss the possibilities for educators committed to curriculum wisdom problem solving to engage with the broader public sphere. Working with other transformative curriculum leaders on projects that extend beyond their local settings just might be an important way to influence the local stakeholder community. Chapter 9 explores this visionary topic.

REFERENCES

Barth, R. S. (2001). Teacher leader. *Phi Delta Kappan, 82*(6), 443–449.

Costa, A. L., & Kallick, B. (1993). Through the lens of a critical friend. *Educational Leadership, 51*(2), 49–51.

Darling-Hammond, L., & McLaughlin, M. W. (1995). Policies that support professional development in an era of reform. *Phi Delta Kappan, 76*(8), 597–604.

Dewey, J. (1966). *Democracy and education.* New York: Free Press. (Original work published 1916)

Eisner, E. (1994). *The educational imagination: On the design and evaluation of school programs* (3rd ed.). New York: Macmillan.

Furman, G. C. (1998). Postmodernism and "community" in schools: Unraveling the paradox. *Educational Administration Quarterly, 34*(3), 298–328.

Gardner, H. (1999). *The disciplined mind: Beyond facts and standardized tests, the K–12 education that every child deserves.* New York: Penguin Books.

Gergen, K. (1991). *The saturated self. Dilemmas of identity in contemporary life.* New York: Basic Books.

Greene, M. (1988). *The dialectic of freedom.* New York: Teachers College Press.

Grossman, P., Wineburg, S., & Woolworth, S. (2001). Toward a theory of teacher "community." *Teachers College Record, 103*(6), 942–1012.

Henderson, J. G., & Hawthorne, R. D. (1995). *Transformative curriculum leadership* (1st ed.). Upper Saddle River, NJ: Merrill/Prentice Hall.

Henderson, J. G., & Kesson, K. R. (2001). Curriculum work as public intellectual leadership. In K. Sloan and J. Sears (Eds.), *Democratic curriculum theory and practice: Retrieving public spaces* (pp. 1–23). Troy, NY: Educator's International Press.

Henderson, J. G., & Kesson, K. R. (2004). *Curriculum wisdom: Educational decisions in democratic societies.* Upper Saddle River, NJ: Merrill/Prentice Hall.

Josselson, R. (1995). Imagining the real: Empathy, narrative and the dialogic self. In R. Josselson & A. Lieblich (Eds.), *Interpreting experience: The narrative study of lives.* (Vol. 3, pp. 27–44). Thousand Oaks, CA: Sage.

Kegan, R. (1982). *The evolving self: Problem and process in human development.* Cambridge, MA: Harvard University Press.

Kegan, R. (1994). *In over our heads: The mental demands of modern life.* Cambridge, MA: Harvard University Press.

Lord, B. (1994). Teachers' professional development: Critical colleagueship and the role of professional communities. In N. Cobb (Ed.), *The future of education: Perspectives on national standards in America.* (pp. 175–204). New York: College Entrance Examination Board.

National Commission on Teaching and America's Future. (2003). *No dream denied: A pledge to America's children.* Washington, DC: Author.

Nias, J. (1995). *Teachers' moral purposes: Sources of vulnerability and strength.* The John Jacobs Foundation Conference on Teacher Burnout, Marbach Castle, Germany.

Walker, D. F. (2003). *Fundamentals of curriculum: Passion and professionalism* (2nd ed.). Mahwah, NJ: Lawrence Erlbaum Associates.

Wiggins, G., & McTighe, J. (1998). *Understanding by design.* Alexandria, VA: Association for Supervision and Curriculum Development.

Zepeda, S. J. (1999). *Staff development: Practices that promote leadership in learning communities.* Larchmont, NY: Eye on Education.

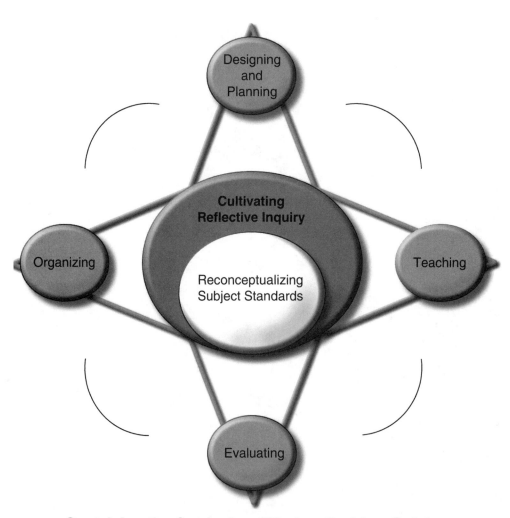

Sustaining the Curriculum Wisdom Problem Solving

CHAPTER 9

ENGAGING THE BROADER PUBLIC SPHERE

How can we motivate ourselves and our fellow citizens to risk our hopes as well as our time, effort, and resources in working to transform our democratically deficient societies? How can we sustain ourselves in struggle over the long time period it may take to achieve and to institutionalize deep democracy's habits of the heart and ways of community life, especially in the face of entrenched and powerful opposition? A prophetic pragmatism that struggles and builds toward the Beloved Community offers promising answers to these key questions of democratic character, and of the character of effective transformative movement toward deep democracy.

(Green, 1999, p. 135)

A REVIEW OF THIS TEXT

We have now reached the end of this book's professional journey. You have been introduced to a type of curriculum work that is transformative in two important senses. It challenges educators to elevate their professional judgments by practicing a sophisticated problem solving. There is a common sense understanding of curriculum problem solving in today's education field: set clear curricular goals, systematically decide how to achieve these goals, act on experience in making these decisions, and reflect on the results of your educational actions. This book invites educators and other curriculum stakeholders to deepen this commonsense understanding in specific ways as depicted in Figure 9.1. This image of the curriculum problem-solving cycle was introduced in chapter 3 in Figure 3.1. We now return to this image as a way to review the contents of this text.

Examine the recursive nature of the curriculum problem solving as presented in Figure 9.1. Educators are asked to articulate standards for a holistic 3S education. They are asked to consider the goals, performances, and criteria associated with teaching for a subject matter understanding that is embedded in democratic self and social understanding. This was the topic of chapter 2. Because this is such a challenging professional undertaking, most educators will need to cultivate their reflective inquiry capacities in order to clearly conceptualize and enact 3S educational standards. This was the topic of chapter 3. The systematic decision making associated with 3S education was addressed in chapters 4–7. As was mentioned in the essay that introduced this set of chapters, systematic 3S educational decisions require an "ecological" approach embedded in a strong sense of professional responsibility. This means that the fundamental processes of curriculum decision making—designing, planning, teaching, evaluating, and organizing—are not only treated as highly interdependent, but they are also handled "in house." They are not farmed out to outside curriculum stakeholders, including textbook publishers, state politicians, and hired test evaluators, who cannot credibly practice curriculum deliberation in an appropriate case-sensitive and democratic manner. The decision making advice in chapters 4–7 was, thus, offered in this spirit of professional empowerment. Finally, the

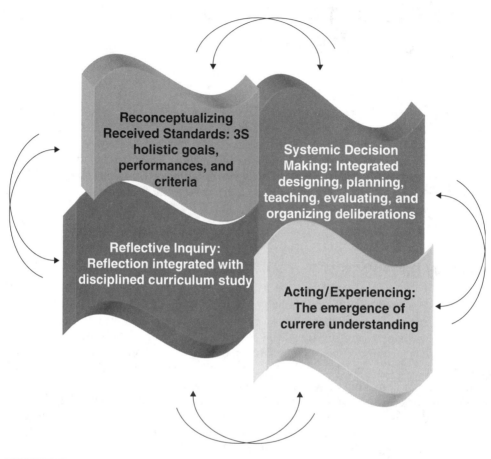

Figure 9.1 Curriculum Problem-Solving Cycle

enactment of the complete problem-solving cycle in Figure 9.1 will, for most educators, require professional and stakeholder learning community support. This was the topic of chapter 8.

We introduced our sense of acting/experiencing in chapter 1 in our discussion of the Latin noun *curriculum,* interpreted as the Latin verb *currere.* By taking this approach, we are acknowledging that teaching for students' 3S understanding requires a personal journey of self-understanding as a democratic educator. In succinct terms, 3S curriculum work necessitates 3S currere work. To enact a 3S educational course of action requires a certain running of the course. Rosie Gornik models this journey of democratic self-examination through her currere narratives and interludes in chapters 1–8; and in her currere farewell at the end of this chapter, she will provide advice on how you can compose your own currere narratives. Rosie describes her journey of self-understanding as a committed democratic educator and invites you to embark on your own personalized journey of self-understanding, through journaling or whatever other self-reflective method that works for you.

In chapter 3, we introduced the "reflective practice" embedded in the problem-solving cycle as a marriage of reflective practice and democratic curriculum inquiry. Our term for this marriage is *reflective inquiry*. We integrate reflection and inquiry because 3S democratic education requires such a close connection. Democratic curriculum inquiry is a key component of disciplined curriculum studies, which is a complex, interdisciplinary, and multidisciplinary field. We will shortly present a historical overview of this field. There are educators who separate curriculum studies from educational practice. We challenge this custom. We reject the separation of curriculum theory and curriculum practice and acknowledge that the standardized management and constructivist best practice paradigms contribute to this problem. Because the curriculum wisdom paradigm serves as this book's frame of reference, we want educators to base their actions on a disciplined inquiry into the relationship between democracy and education. We want educators to practice reflective inquiry as a central feature of their holistic problem solving; and as we noted in chapter 3, we use the term *inquiry* instead of *study* in recognition of the action-oriented nature of curriculum decision making.

Over time, the continuous recursive movement between conceptualizing 3S standards, engaging in systemic decision making, cultivating currere insight, and practicing reflective inquiry can result in *sophisticated curriculum problem solving.* This is the basic working assumption and the professional standard of this book, which we have attempted to model in every chapter. We hope that you can now comprehend, envision, and begin to experience our referent for elevated curriculum judgment.

This professional referent is transformative in a second important sense. As we pointed out in chapter 1, the work of transformative curriculum leadership generally requires deep-seated personal and interpersonal changes and is directed toward deep-seated societal changes. We have written the book with this multilevel interplay of transformations in mind, and we hope that you now have a good feel for what is entailed in curriculum work for "deep democracy" (Green, 1999). The overall goal of this book can be summarized succinctly: *the cultivation of deep democracy requires an education for deep subject matter, self, and social understanding.* Clearly, educators who choose to work in this transformative way must function as collaborative leaders who invite other curriculum stakeholders to join them in this historic adventure. In sum, transformative curriculum leadership is a highly personal, deliberative, reflective, inquiring, and collaborative undertaking.

AN AGENDA FOR BUILDING A COLLEGIAL IDENTITY

We now turn to the question of establishing a network of transformative curriculum leaders across diverse educational settings. Is such broadly based professional community building possible? Could a transformative curriculum leadership (TCL) collegial identity be established in regional, state, provincial, national, or even international contexts? As authors of this book, we have pondered such queries while writing this text. We don't know the viability of such a futuristic professional goal, but we do have hope. The remaining sections of this chapter have been created to introduce you to this line of visionary questioning. There is a general three-part agenda associated with building a TCL collegial network. Educators must understand the disciplined interpretation of curriculum-based teaching that underlies this book. They must embrace this understanding as central to their professional identity, and they must collegially act out of this understanding in multiple public forums. *In effect, they must find ways to engage the broader public sphere.*

We explore this agenda in two steps. We begin by presenting a historical narrative of curriculum studies in the North American context. We tell this story, which covers a period of 90 years, to deepen your understanding of the disciplined interpretation of curriculum-based teaching that informs this book. The TCL concept is based on the synthesis of a diverse set of influential curriculum theories, and we want you to acquire an appreciation of the complicated theoretical conversation underlying this book. Though learning about this conversation may make your head swim and may feel like an unnecessary sideshow, it may also motivate you to further explore the topic of democratic curriculum inquiry. We hope you will consider taking this step as an important part of your continuing education. If you do, you will definitely gain further insight into the disciplined interpretation of "curriculum-based teaching" that informs this book's problem-solving cycle, and you will acquire a deeper appreciation of the professional and public value of transformative curriculum leadership in societies with democratic ideals.

The question of engaging the broader public sphere as transformative curriculum leaders was raised in a 3-hour town meeting at the sixth annual Curriculum and Pedagogy Conference, which was held at Miami University in Oxford, Ohio, in October 2005. The question invoked a lively discussion, and we have invited two participants to contribute to this book. They are Kent den Heyer and Kathleen Kesson. Both Kent and Kathleen are teacher educators who already embrace the discipline of transformative curriculum leadership as central to their professional identity, and they both work collegially with a wide range of teachers and administrators in multiple school settings in Edmonton, Alberta, Canada and New York City. Their personal narratives illustrate two ways that transformative curriculum leaders can work as public intellectuals. Furthermore, as teacher educators, they interject two distinct academic voices into this practitioner-based book. This is an important consideration because the challenge of engaging the broader public sphere will require the combined collaborative efforts of school-based practitioners and college/university-based academics.

THE HISTORICAL NARRATIVE

Transformative curriculum leadership is based on a particular disciplined understanding of curriculum-based teaching, and we want to tell a story that provides historical insight into how we arrived at this understanding and why we feel this interpretation is so vitally important. The general field of curriculum studies, as it has emerged in the North American context over the past 90 years, possesses multidisciplinary, interdisciplinary, and transdisciplinary characteristics. *Multidisciplinarity* refers to the inclusion of multiple disciplines within a particular field of study. As Klein (1990) notes, it is an "additive, not integrative" characteristic of a field (p. 56). Klein goes on to state that "*interdisciplinarity* signifies the synthesis of two or more disciplines, establishing a new metalevel of discourse," while *transdisciplinary* approaches "are conceptual frameworks that transcend the narrow scope of disciplinary world views, metaphorically encompassing the several parts of material handled separately by specialized disciplines" (p. 66). As we tell our story, you will note that the disciplined interpretation of curriculum-based teaching that we are advancing in this book honors the curriculum and teaching field's multidisciplinary, interdisciplinary, and transdisciplinary characteristics. We feel that it is fortunate, and perhaps inevitable, given the complexity of education, that the curriculum and teaching field has developed in this way. It allows for a wide range of critical and creative theorizing.

Formally speaking, our disciplined understanding of curriculum-based teaching is poststructural, not structural, in its orientation. We don't think there is a precise structure—no protocol, procedure, rationale, taxonomy, or method—that educators can unvaryingly follow to ensure their success. We feel that those who promote a particular structuralist approach, particularly without acknowledging its limitations, are attempting to oversimplify a complex field of work. In effect, they are substituting a narrow technical rationality for a sophisticated educational artistry. Poststructuralism refers to the acknowledgment and celebration of the play of diverse perspectives in any human endeavor (Cherryholmes, 1988). Educators with a poststructuralist orientation would view a particular protocol, procedure, or method as simply one among many possible interpretations on how to proceed. For example, they would view a particular high-stakes standardized test as simply one interpretation of "quality" education. Our narrative is written with this poststructuralist sensibility. As we tell our story, you will notice that we continually recognize and honor the diverse play of interpretations that constitutes the contemporary curriculum and teaching field.

Our historical narrative revolves around two themes: *journey* and *judgment*. These themes can be abbreviated as JJ. Because transformative curriculum leadership can be abbreviated as TCL, we can summarize this book in an abbreviated sentence. *TCL is a collaborative effort to advance JJ in the context of a love of democratic wisdom.* We include a historical narrative in this book to explain this sentence. As we tell our story, we feel a sense of gratitude to the educational scholars, particularly the curriculum theorists, we will be highlighting. We could not have created our disciplined understanding of curriculum-based teaching without their contributions. We also want to acknowledge that we are keeping our story relatively brief, so please keep in mind that behind the few influential scholars we mention are many other important, supportive, and contributing voices in the curriculum and teaching field. In an important way, the individuals we mention are only representative of a much larger group of scholars. As our narrative unfolds, we will refer to other chapters in this book. We do this to clarify the complex gestalt of curriculum theorizing that informs transformative curriculum leadership. Though this is a practical book, it is based on years of theoretical work. Although we have kept our conceptual discussions to a minimum in this text, we want to acknowledge the thinking behind our problem solving advice.

Curriculum as Journey

Our story begins with Franklin Bobbitt in 1918. We introduced his contribution to the curriculum and teaching field in chapter 1. Bobbitt was a professor of educational administration at the University of Chicago and is generally considered to be one of the founders of the field of North American curriculum studies. Bobbitt helps us understand curriculum as a journey, as a long-term process with a certain degree of consistency. This interpretation of curriculum is not as commonsensical as it may seem. Many people, including many educators, think of curriculum as specific products: school district frameworks, scope and sequence charts, course syllabi, and textbooks. They rarely address curriculum at the experiential, process level; if they do, the decision-making process they have in mind is short-term: a lesson, unit, or course decision. Furthermore, they are not thinking about the importance of the principle of continuity with reference to their systemic decision making, and in 1938 Dewey composed an important and influential essay on this principle:

> The principle of the continuity of experience . . . may be called the experiential continuum. . . . The more definitely and sincerely it is held that education is a development within, by, and for experience, the more important it is that there shall be clear conceptions of what experience is. Unless experience is so conceived that the result is a plan for deciding upon subject-matter, upon methods of instruction and discipline, and upon material equipment and social organization of the school, it is wholly in the air. . . . Connectedness in growth must be. . . [the educator's] constant watchword. (Dewey, 1938/1998, pp. 17, 90)

Bobbitt valued the principle of continuity in education. He viewed curriculum as a long-term journey, and so do we. He proposed a systematic and comprehensive approach to curriculum work, and so do we. Our book is organized around reconceptualizing subject standards from a holistic and balanced 3S framework and then integrating this standard-setting into four decision making processes: designing/planning, teaching, evaluating, and organizing. We advance this comprehensive, ecological approach because we want students to have coherent educational experiences. However, as we also mentioned in chapter 1, Bobbitt envisioned a student's journey as a path containing about 700 standardized objectives, while we frame this journey in a different way. We will come back to this point in a moment, but first we want to introduce one of Bobbitt's doctoral students at the University of Chicago who went on to outshine his teacher. His name was Ralph Tyler.

Ralph Tyler was invited to join the University of Chicago faculty, and his teaching responsibilities included a course on curriculum called Education 360. In 1949, he published the teaching material in this course under the title *Basic Principles of Curriculum and Instruction.* This book, which refines Bobbitt's systematic approach to curriculum work (Kliebard, 1992), is presented as a problem-solving "rationale" that carefully integrates educational purposes, learning experiences, instructional organization, and learning evaluation. Tyler (1949) argued that curriculum workers should systematically ask themselves four questions:

1. What educational purposes should the school seek to attain?

2. How can learning experiences be selected which are likely to be useful in attaining these objectives?

3. How can learning experiences be organized for effective instruction?

4. How can the effectiveness of learning experiences be evaluated? (p. 1)

Tyler's highly influential rationale is based on an understanding of students' educational journey that is similar to Bobbitt's, one of his mentors, but with one important difference. Bobbitt identified specific objectives, while Tyler took a more deliberative approach. He wanted curriculum workers in a specific setting to decide on their own standardized goals, which he called behavioral objectives:

> Education is a process of changing the behavior patterns of people. This is using behavior in the broad sense to include thinking and feeling as well as overt action. When education is viewed in this way, it is clear that educational objectives then represent the kinds of changes in behavior that an educational institution seeks to bring about in its students. A study of the learners themselves would seek to identify needed changes in behavior patterns of the students which the educational institution should seek to produce. (pp. 5–6)

A Journey of Disciplined Understanding

We agree with Tyler that localized decision making is quite important, and the section III chapters are written from that perspective. However, notice how Tyler conceptualizes a specific curricular course of action. It is a journey through specific, locally determined behavioral objectives. This approach suggests that students' learning can be efficiently "produced" by an educational institution the way that cars and other standardized material products can be efficiently engineered and manufactured (Callahan, 1962; Kliebard, 1992). Perhaps Tyler didn't mean to suggest that curriculum work should promote standardized production (Hlebowitsh, 1993). If that's the case, then he should have been more explicit about this matter. We have. Beginning in chapter 1, we have carefully framed students' journeys' of understanding as characterized by a "productive idiosyncrasy" (Eisner, 2004). In fact, we highly recommend that you read Eisner's (1969) essay on the importance of individually expressive outcomes when facilitating students' educational journeys. This essay is generally considered to be one of the most influential publications in the history of American curriculum studies. We note in chapter 2 that students' expressive performances of understanding are a key component of transformative standards, and these standards serve as the paradigmatic focus—the "organizing problem"—for the section III decision making processes.

Our historical narrative now jumps to 1959. The launching of the Soviet satellite Sputnik in 1957, at the heart of the Cold War, created political shock waves in the United States. In that heightened social atmosphere, a curriculum conference was convened at the Woods Hole Center on Cape Cod. Academic specialists in psychology, mathematics, the sciences, history, and other disciplinary fields were invited to attend (Bruner, 1960). Only three of the invited attendees were educators, and none of these educators was a curriculum scholar (Marshall, Sears, & Schubert, 2000). Consider the implications of how this conference was organized. The meeting focused on teaching for disciplined understanding in certain high-profile subjects, particularly mathematics and the sciences. Academic disciplinarians were invited, but curriculum scholars were considered irrelevant. Why was this? Certainly curriculum specialists understood how to design and enact systematic educational journeys. The problem, perhaps, was their understanding of these journeys.

Given the influence of the Bobbitt-Tyler wing of the field (there were other curriculum scholars who will shortly make their appearance in our story), did curriculum specialists understand how to design and enact students' journeys of disciplinary understanding with reference to specific subject matter traditions? As we mentioned in chapter 1, just because students acquire specific standardized skills and knowledge (in Tyler's language, specific behavioral objectives) does not mean that they possess subject matter understanding. Just because students perform well on standardized subject matter tests does not mean they can explain, apply, or create with this knowledge. Understanding requires knowledge, but the two cannot be equated. The organizers of the Woods Hole Conference understood this important distinction; apparently, they were not impressed with the curriculum and teaching field's preoccupation with the standardized management of learning. The organizers looked elsewhere. They weren't looking for scholars who could clearly conceptualize behavioral objectives. They were looking for scholars who understood the cultivation of disciplined minds (Gardner, 2000). Their overall professional goal was to facilitate students' subject matter understanding.

The initial curriculum products associated with the Woods Hole Conference, such as the Biological Sciences Curriculum Study (BSCS) and Man: A Course of Study (MACOS), were quite limited and not particularly successful. In fact, MACOS was politically vilified in the United States Congress in the early 1970s. This would not surprise general curriculum scholars informed by the work of Bobbitt and Tyler because they understood the critical difference between curriculum as process and curriculum as product. Curriculum packages like BSCS and MACOS were bound to fail. They were products produced by academics who did not understand the general parameters of disciplined curriculum and teaching work. They may have understood the underlying disciplinary "structure" of their academic field (Ford & Pugno, 1964), but they did not understand that teaching for understanding requires comprehensive decision making. It requires skillfully deliberated and well-integrated designing, planning, teaching, evaluating, organizing, and communicating decisions. It requires the systematic work of section III in this book.

Our story now jumps to 1998. Through years of careful research on the nature of student understanding, which drew on the foundational work of Ernst von Glaserfeld, Jean Piaget, Lev Vygotsky, and many others (Fosnot, 1996a), educators came to appreciate the "constructivist" nature of student understanding. They grew in their recognition that students understand by actively constructing meaning. This growing awareness, which was fostered by the "cognitive psychology" revolution of the 1970s and 1980s, influenced policy work in all of the curriculum content fields. The National Council of Teachers of Mathematics (NCTM), the National Council of Teachers of English (NCTE), the International Reading Association (IRA), the National Council for the Social Studies (NCSS), the National Science Foundation (NSF), and many other professional subject matter associations published specific statements on "constructivist best practices." Steven Zemelman, Harvey Daniels, and Arthur Hyde provide a useful historical synthesis of some of this policy work. In *Best Practice: New Standards for Teaching and Learning in America's Schools* (1993), they offer curriculum and teaching advice on the following topics: reading, writing, mathematics, science, visual art, music, dance, and theater. Fosnot (1996b) also offers historical insight into constructivist best practices in the fields of science, mathematics, language arts, early childhood, and art education. For more current best practice information, consult the latest publications in the subject matter field that interests you.

One publication, in particular, stands out in this part of our historical narrative: Grant Wiggins and Jay McTighe's *Understanding by Design* (2005), which was first published in 1998. Much as Franklin Bobbitt's 1924 publication, *How to Make a Curriculum,* serves as an exemplar for standardized management curriculum decision making, Wiggins and McTighe's *Understanding by Design* serves as an exemplar for constructivist best practice curriculum decision making. We wish Wiggins and McTighe could have been present at the 1959 Woods Hole Conference to present their influential book. They could have assisted the academic experts in understanding how to design for students' disciplinary subject matter understanding. In effect, Wiggins and McTighe's text provides a bridge between the Tyler Rationale and teaching for disciplined subject understanding. They write:

> Ralph Tyler . . . underscored in his seminal book on design, *Basic Principles of Curriculum and Instruction* (1949), the need to think about curricular matters from the perspective of desired outcomes and the learner's needs. Indeed, more than anyone, Tyler laid out the basic principles of [the design process we advocate]. He proposed three criteria for effective organization—continuity, sequence, and integration—to show how the logic of curriculum should suit the learner's, not the experts', sense of order. . . . (Wiggins & McTighe, 1998/2005, p. 298)

As we acknowledge in chapter 5, the template that we introduce to guide design and planning decision making is informed by the template that Wiggins and McTighe created for their advice on designing, teaching, and evaluating decision making. We are certainly indebted to their important work, not only in chapter 5 but throughout this book.

The Limits of Subject Understanding

The curricular focus on teaching for subject understanding has an important limitation, which we introduced in chapter 1. Students who are on a path to deeply understand particular subject matter are not necessarily on a path to understand democratic goodness. "Smart" people are not necessarily "good" people. Gardner (2000) offers insight into this important curriculum consideration:

> Particularly at a time of rapid change, and at a time when the identity of "good guys" and "bad guys" is no longer so evident, many are searching for models of humaneness. This hunger has fueled recent efforts to craft a broader definition of intelligence. Traditionally, "intelligence" meant aptitude for school subjects and school skills. Those of us who seek a fuller view—who speak of personal intelligence, emotional intelligence, moral intelligence, wisdom—are all declaring that skill in the literacies and facility at a certain kind of problem-solving are not enough. We seek individuals who not only can analyze but also do the right thing; individuals who will be admirable not only as thinkers or creators but also as human beings. . . . We must accept the harsh reality that one can be intelligent without being moral; creative without being ethical; sensitive to emotions without using that sensitivity in the service of others. . . . Similarly one may appreciate what is ethical without showing any tendency to pursue the good in one's own life. (pp. 248–249)

As we have been quite clear throughout this book, our concern with the cultivation of democratic goodness has led us to frame the paradigmatic, organizing problem of curriculum work as teaching for a disciplinary subject matter understanding that is integrated with disciplined democratic self and social understanding. In chapter 1, we characterize this orientation as "holistic" in nature, referring to a balanced approach to students' subject matter, self, and social education. In chapter 2, we note that this holistic approach is informed and supported by many research studies that have clearly demonstrated the vital relationship between cognitive, social, and emotional learning (Elias, Zins, Graczyk, & Weissberg, 2003; Zins, Weissberg, Wang, & Walberg, 2004). Working out of this frame of reference, we introduce the concept of "holistic goals" in chapter 2 and then integrate this concept into our chapter 4 designing and planning template.

Holistic Journey of Understanding

There is a rich history behind our curriculum decision making orientation, and we want to briefly acknowledge this heritage. The holistic sense of journey underlying this book's wisdom orientation traces back to a wide range of influential philosophers, including Socrates in the West and Lao Tzu in the East (Henderson & Kesson, 2004). We cannot possibly acknowledge all of these individuals in our historical narrative, but we will highlight two philosophers that have clearly influenced this book's holistic orientation: John Dewey and Maxine Greene.

We begin with Dewey. In 1897, he wrote, "The teacher is engaged, not simply in the training of individuals, but in the formation of the proper social life" (Dewey, 1897/2004, p. 23). Dewey's influence on the progressive educational movement in the United States was quite profound (Cremin, 1961), and in 1938 he published *Experience and Education,* reminding all the progressive educators who were influenced by his writings that he was working out of a holistic orientation that balanced subject matter and self and social learning. He was concerned that some of these progressive educators were either too child-oriented while others were too society-oriented. He writes, "The educator is responsible for a knowledge of individuals and for a knowledge of subject-matter that will enable activities to be selected which lend themselves to social organization, an organization in which all individuals have an opportunity to contribute something" (Dewey, 1938/1998, p. 61). As the final words in the quotation indicate, Dewey is quite clear throughout his book that his balanced subject/self/social approach was directed toward providing students with active, participatory educational experiences that would cultivate democracy as a moral way of living. Dewey's concern with the integration of democracy and education is perhaps best articulated in his *Democracy and Education,* which was first published in 1916.

Many curriculum scholars in Dewey's generation shared his educational orientation.[1] They were equally concerned about the integration of democracy and education and, therefore, also promoted a more balanced approach to subject, self, and social learning. We will not include these scholars in our story, but we highly recommend a book that provides an insightful historical overview of this holistic frame of reference in curriculum

....
[1]John Dewey was born in 1859 and died in 1952.

problem solving: Daniel and Laurel Tanner's *Curriculum Development: Theory into Practice* (2007). The Tanners begin by noting that the holistic approach in the United States can be traced back to Thomas Jefferson's views on the importance of education in a freedom-loving society. They quote Jefferson: "If a nation expects to be ignorant and free in a state of civilization, it expects what never was and never will be" (Lee, 1961, pp. 18–19, cited in Tanner & Tanner, 2007, p.4). They then cite Lawrence Cremin's insight that "the entire course of American educational history is based on the gradual realization of the Jeffersonian ideal" (Cremin, 1965, p. 40, cited in Tanner & Tanner, 2007, p.4). After a thorough documentation of the views of hundreds of American educational leaders in the 19th and 20th centuries on the importance of a holistic approach to curriculum work, they conclude their book with this plea: "The problem of curriculum balance is a difficult and important one and is closely tied to the democratic ideal of all individuals having the fullest education possible" (Tanner & Tanner, 2007, p. 475).

An Emancipatory Point of View

The integration of democracy and education requires an emancipatory perspective on curriculum work. Our use of the "transformative" adjective to describe our curriculum leadership advice captures this perspective. As we note in chapters 1 and 2, the overall aim of a transforming democratic education is to free students from psychological and cultural constraints so that they can realize their "best selves" in personally and socially responsible ways (Noddings, 1984). This emancipatory point of view was called "social reconstructionism" in the early formative years of the curriculum and teaching field, and as cited in Stanley (1992), Hunt and Metcalf (1968) note that this curricular orientation was based on six fundamental assumptions:

> The concept of reconstructionism evolved from the basic notion that social change is inevitable: (1) The course of social change may result from undirected "drift" or it may be led in more-or-less directed fashion by some group or cooperating groups in the society. (2) It is better that social change be directed. (3) Since the future decrees some sort of collectivism—the choices being authoritarian . . . or democratic—some groups need to push for democratic collectivism. (4) There are many groups eager to direct social change, most of them in an authoritarian direction; and in the presence of a vacuum in leadership, they will do so. (5) The group most dedicated to democratic values, most knowledgeable about cultural trends, and in the most strategic position to direct social change, is school teachers. (6) School teachers, therefore, should be the architects of the new social order. (p. 278)

The pioneers of social reconstructionism in the curriculum field include Harold Rugg, George Counts, and Theodore Brameld (Stanley, 1992). These three curriculum scholars were peers of Franklin Bobbitt and Ralph Tyler, and we highly recommend that you take time to read their work. You will certainly deepen your own understanding of democratic education. Our narrative, however, will not dwell on the social reconstructionist literature; we instead jump to current curriculum studies.

As Stanley (1992) documents, social reconstructionism receded from view during World War II and the early years of the Cold War but resurfaced in the late 1960s as "critical pedagogy," and this change in language signified an important shift in the emancipatory perspective. There was a movement away from structured ideological positions—from "isms"—to more nuanced, poststructural perspectives. The reflective inquiry scaffolding in chapter 3 was designed to foster this sense of nuance. Stanley (1992) concludes his historical account of this shift in the North American emancipatory outlook as follows:

> This is a critical pedagogy of neither/nor, oriented by a poststructuralist rejection of false dichotomies, awareness of the unknowable, understanding the limits of rationality. . . . It is a pedagogy of hope in the face of the very formidable barriers to critical analysis. (p. 222)

All of Rosie Gornik's currere narratives in this book have been written to illustrate the subtle nuances of emancipatory work and the "formidable barriers" that critically informed democratic educators must daily face.

To teach for subject matter understanding that is integrated with democratic self and social understanding is to cultivate a Jeffersonian, freedom-loving way of living, and this view of how to educate for the "good" life is either unexamined, ignored, repressed, or suppressed in the standardized management and constructivist best practice decision-making orientations. If unexamined or ignored, the relationship between democracy and education is part of the "null" curriculum. If repressed or suppressed, the relationship is part of the "hidden" curriculum. We introduced the notion of the null and hidden curriculum in chapter 2 and then explored Maxine Greene's (1988) essay on the freedom from . . . freedom to "dialectic" as a way to more deeply understand what can be null or hidden in curriculum work. However, before providing a little more background on Greene's writings, it's important that we acknowledge Michael Apple's invaluable insights into the complex dynamics of the hidden curriculum. Apple (1993) summarizes his penetrating research as follows: "The program of criticism and renewal I avow interprets education relationally, as having intimate connections both to the structures of inequalities in this society and to attempts to overcome them" (p. 3). Apple's groundbreaking *Ideology and Curriculum* (1979) is a good starting point for his work on the hidden curriculum.

Greene's contributions to curriculum thinking and practice are immense and have been documented and enthusiastically celebrated in two edited books: William Ayers and Janet Miller's *A Light in Dark Times: Maxine Greene and the Unfinished Conversation* (1998) and William Pinar's *The Passionate Mind of Maxine Greene: "I Am Not Yet . . ."* (1998). Because we are keeping our story relatively brief, we will highlight only one brief chapter that Greene wrote in 1975 for an edited book, *Curriculum Theorizing: The Reconceptualists.* We choose this text for an important reason. Notice how the book's subtitle, which refers to reconceptualizing curriculum studies, suggests a relationship to our chapter 2 topic of reconceptualzing subject standards. As the editor of *Curriculum Theorizing: The Reconceptualists,* Pinar (1975) notes that the contributors, including Greene, who wrote on the topic of "curriculum and consciousness," are all attempting "to understand the nature of educational experience . . . [in light of] matters of temporality, transcendence, consciousness, and politics" (p. xi).

Pinar uses *reconceptualizing* for a particular rhetorical reason. He wants to communicate that the scholars in his edited book were reframing curriculum studies. They were establishing critical distance from such structuralist approaches as the Tyler Rationale and from empirical curriculum and teaching research that assumed that teachers' and students' behavior must be carefully defined and therefore controlled. In the place of this work, they advanced a diverse set of emancipatory, consciousness-raising projects. Greene (1975) illustrates this reframing in her chapter:

> It will be recognized that awareness begins perspectively, that our experience is always incomplete. . . . I have tried to show what this sort of interior journey can mean. Not only may it result in the effecting of new syntheses within experience; it may result in an awareness of the process of knowing, of believing, of perceiving. It may even result in an understanding of the ways in which meanings have been sedimented in an individual's own personal history. (p. 314)

Notice how Greene works with the journey metaphor, and notice how this quotation supports the curriculum-as-currere interpretation that we introduce in chapter 1 and integrate into all the chapters in this book.

Curriculum as Complicated Conversation

We'll have more to say on curriculum-as-currere in a moment, but first we want to explore the curriculum reconceptualzing theme in a little more depth. Pinar's use of this theme in *Curriculum Theorizing: The Reconceptualists* caught on and became an important but controversial point of reference in the curriculum field for a number of years. Because many curriculum scholars rejected the reconceptualist label as too confining, dehumanizing, or simplistic, the term eventually fell out of use. (In fact, Greene rejected being labeled as "reconceptualist.") In a 1988 publication, Pinar argued that the term *contemporary curriculum discourses* should be substituted for curriculum reconceptualization because "what started as an opposition to the mainstream and tradition of the field has become the field, although complicated, with several centers of focus" (Pinar, 1988, p. 7).

This idea of "complicated" curriculum discourses is further developed in William Pinar, William Reynolds, Patrick Slattery, and Peter Taubman's *Understanding Curriculum: An Introduction to the Study of Historical and Contemporary Curriculum Discourses* (1995). In this lengthy and influential book, curriculum is understood an "extraordinarily complicated conversation":

> It is what the older generation chooses to tell the younger generation. So understood, curriculum is intensely historical, political, racial, gendered, phenomenological, autobiographical, aesthetic, theological, and international. Curriculum becomes the site on which the generations struggle to define themselves and the world. (Pinar et al., 1995, pp. 847–848)

This multidisciplinary and interdisciplinary interpretation of curriculum studies informs our conception of reflective inquiry in chapter 3. We agree with Pinar and his three coauthors that understanding curriculum requires a "complicated conversation" involving multiple modes of address (Ellsworth, 1997), and we clearly make this point in chapter 1. We think, however, that curriculum work involves judgment and action as well as conversation. That's why our focus in chapter 3 is on cultivating a multidimensional reflective inquiry.

Interpreting Theory and Practice

The separation of theory and practice became a significant issue as the reconceptualization of the curriculum field gained momentum. The problematic nature of this split was explored in a special issue of the journal *Theory into Practice* titled "Grounding Contemporary Curriculum Thought." Jim Sears (1992), the guest editor of the issue, writes:

> None of the contributors [in this issue] questions that the "reconceptualists" have renewed the academic field of curriculum; the questions are what relevance is contemporary curriculum discourse to the curriculum director in Sioux Falls, what impact has it had on a state legislator in Albany, and what is its visibility to a parent of a "gifted & talented" child in Peoria. It is here that Jacoby [in *The Last Intellectuals*] draws a useful distinction between the academic whose first concern is furthering a university career through academic publishing, and the intellectual whose primary concern is affecting the public culture by writing in the educational domain. It is here that readers must render a judgment regarding the educational relevance, political impact, and public visibility of contemporary curriculum discourse. (p. 190)

We have written this book to be relevant and accessible to teachers, administrators, curriculum directors, state legislators, and all other curriculum stakeholders concerned about the democratic well-being of the United States and other self-identified democratic societies. We are working out of the multidisciplinary, interdisciplinary, and transdisciplinary spirit of contemporary curriculum discourse, and we hope that the transformative curriculum leadership we are advancing will have political impact over time. We realize that this will be a slow, evolutionary process because of the current dominance of the standardized management paradigm and the deep-seated personal, interpersonal, and societal transformations that we are advocating. However, we hope that many curriculum stakeholders, particularly teachers and administrators, will embrace the disciplined journey of understanding and the sophisticated problem solving that this book invites.

In the special *Theory into Practice* issue, Sears framed the theme of "grounding contemporary curriculum thought" in public intellectual terms. Beginning in the late 1990s, Sears began to work with about 30 other curriculum, teacher education, and leadership professors to create a professional association dedicated to this linkage between theory–practice integration and public intellectual commitment. This collaborative effort culminated with the organization of the Curriculum and Pedagogy Group, which organized an annual conference to refine and advance its professional mission and identity. The first annual Curriculum and Pedagogy (C&P) Conference was held outside of Austin, Texas, in October 2000. Patrick Slattery, another member of Sears's organizing team, wrote the foreword for the proceedings of the first C&P Conference. He reminisces:

> As I reflect back on the events of 2000 in preparation and implementation of the Curriculum and Pedagogy Conference, I am amazed at how quickly and efficiently a new community formed. More important, I am impressed with the sensitivity and dedication of all participants. Something significant is happening in C&P. Obviously, there is a tremendous need in the curriculum field for such a conference. It is exciting

to see some of the excellent presentations of the first conference now in press. Reflecting back on my experience as a field-based instructor in teacher education, I can see a parallel between my work with undergraduate students and the formation of C&P. In both cases, scholars, teachers, graduate students, artists, and researchers recognized a need to collaborate on a unified project of curriculum and pedagogy. Bifurcations of theory and practice, professors and PK–12 teachers, and curriculum and pedagogy are all dangerous constructions. We seek a more holistic approach. (Slattery, 2001, p. xiii)

Curriculum-Based Teaching

This book also rejects the bifurcation of theory and practice. In the terminology of this text, our decision-making advice and narratives are premised on the vital interrelationship between curriculum and teaching. We want you to say "curriculum and teaching" without taking a breath—without making any hard and fast distinctions. The French language is filled with elisions, which capture the soft boundaries, fluidity, and interplay of certain words, and we treat curriculum-and-teaching as an elided term. As you study our book, we hope you recognize that curriculum and teaching are deeply embedded in each other. Throughout this book, we have encouraged you to think in terms of curriculum-based teaching.

With reference to the C&P organization, its annual conferences, and its publications, including the *Journal of Curriculum and Pedagogy,* we use the term *teaching* instead of *pedagogy* for a reason. Because we are reaching out to a broad curriculum stakeholder audience, we feel "teaching" is a slightly more accessible word. The C&P organizers prefer to use "pedagogy," in part to refer to the emancipatory nature of critical pedagogy. Similarly, we recognize the emancipatory nature of democratic education but prefer to use "teaching" as one of our central terms.

Because we recognize that democratic education is deep-seated, transformative work, we feel that it is unfortunate when educators consciously, tacitly, or unconsciously ignore this important point. For us, the liberatory work embedded in democratic education is neither a "null" nor a "hidden" curriculum topic. The public rhetoric of the No Child Left Behind (NCLB) Act illustrates our point. This act is wrapped in a wonderful democratic sentiment, but what does the notion of "no child left behind" mean in practice? When educators work with this act, are they problem solving in an emancipatory spirit? Are they walking their talk? Or, do they say "no child left behind" but actually mean "no child left untested" and "no child left unsorted for class-based instruction"?

What if the constant barrage of high-stakes achievement testing, which is a current feature of the standardized management paradigm, actually leaves some students behind (Ohanian, 1999)? What if it is not fair to all students? What then? Does the NCLB Act allow for corrective actions for sensitive curriculum-based teaching judgments, or is there a separation of curriculum and teaching decision making? Does the act promote the bifurcation of curriculum and teaching? If so, who is making the curriculum decisions, and are these top-down decision makers turning teachers into unimaginative and inflexible test proctors? Where is the acknowledgement and affirmation of professional artistry?

Ohanian (1999) documents the injustices of the NCLB Act and similar standardized management initiatives. She describes top-down educational managers as "Standardistos" and provocatively challenges their curricular frame of reference:

> Although E. D. Hirsch [1987] is opposed to national or even state standards, believing that every school should make its own curriculum decisions, his endlessly proliferating lists of facts every school kid needs to know are at the heart of many Standardisto factoid-crammed documents. Give a Standardisto a pad of paper and a pencil and he goes nuts making lists of essential knowledge—without ever laying eyes on the children who must learn it. Intellectually, I get a good chuckle at the bizarre idea that I should teach the Edict of Nantes, non compos mentis, Planck's constant, the Slough of Despond, and scrotum to my students. But when we get down to the realities of classrooms, the realities of the individual children in our care, the antics of Standardistos are no longer funny: We need not wonder what alien power has taken over the collective cerebrums of Standardistos; what we need to do is fight back. (p. x)

Ohanian challenges educators to not confuse standardized knowledge achievement with subject matter understanding integrated with democratic understanding, and she pointedly documents the unfairness of current standardized management policies with its high-stakes testing mandates. We acknowledge Ohanian's critical insights and feel it is time for all curriculum stakeholders, particularly politicians, to stop mouthing democratic rhetoric and instead to start embodying a love of democratic wisdom.

Curriculum as Currere

There is an important reason why this fundamental change in curriculum orientation, which we have referred to as a paradigm shift throughout this book, is easier said than done. There is a reason why the love of democratic wisdom we are advancing may feel like an almost impossible dream. It is much easier to talk democracy than to integrate democratic insights into daily curriculum and teaching decision making. The necessary integration emerges out of a disciplined journey of understanding. Students' journey of understanding is inextricably linked to teachers' and other key curriculum stakeholders' journeys of understanding. The students' and the adults' journeys are two sides of the same coin; the adult, professional side of this coin is informed by Pinar's work on curriculum as currere.

In 1976, William Pinar and Madeleine Grumet argued for the importance of the autobiographical study of educational experience as a key feature of curriculum work in their book, *Toward a Poor Curriculum.* They used the term *currere* to describe this method of study. As we note in chapter 1, currere is the Latin infinitive for the Latin noun curriculum. *Currere* means "to run the course," while *curriculum* means "the course to be run." Currere refers to the experiencing of an educational course of action. Since 1976, Pinar has refined his method of currere in a number of publications. For an overview of this work, we recommend his 1994 collection of essays, *Autobiography, Politics and Sexuality: Essays in Curriculum Theory 1972–1992.* As we mention in chapter 1, all of Rosie Gornik's narratives, beginning in chapter 1 and ending in chapter 9, are informed by Pinar's work on clarifying a currere methodology. We will shortly present a currere narrative written by Kathleen Kesson, who provided leadership for the creation of Vermont's holistic educational standards. Our text's autobiographical narratives are particularly informed by Pinar's 2004 publication, *What Is Curriculum Theory?* We quote extensively from this book in chapter 1. In the introductory chapter of his book, Pinar (2004) explains that the purpose of practicing currere is to cultivate a deepening understanding of curriculum as complicated conversation. He writes:

> What is curriculum theory? The short answer is that curriculum theory is the interdisciplinary study of educational experience. . . . The method of currere—the infinitive form of curriculum—promises no quick fixes. On the contrary, this autobiographical method asks us to slow down, to remember even re-enter the past, and to meditatively imagine the future. Then, slowly and in one's own terms, one analyzes one's experience of the past and fantasies of the future in order to understand more fully, with more complexity and subtlety, one's submergence in the present. . . . The complicated conversation that is the curriculum requires interdisciplinary intellectuality, erudition, and self-reflexivity. This is not a recipe for high test scores, but a common faith in the possibility of self-realization and democratization, twin projects of social and subjective reconstruction. (Author's emphasis; pp. 2, 4, 8)

Pinar's final sentence captures the doubled nature of this book's journey of understanding. Through self-realization, educators clarify their moral responsibilities; and through self-understanding, educators gain insight into the facilitation of their students' journeys of understanding.

Curriculum as Deliberative Judgment

This challenge of facilitating students' understanding brings to the surface the second major theme of our historical narrative: the importance of informed curriculum judgment. This part of our story begins in 1969 with the publication of Joseph Schwab's first "practical" essay, "The Practical: A Language for Curriculum" (Schwab, 1969). Pinar, Reynolds, Slattery, and Taubman (1995) note this date in a dramatic way:

> The main [curriculum] concepts today are quite different from those which grew out of an era in which school buildings and populations were growing exponentially, and when keeping the curriculum ordered and organized were the main motives of professional activity. *That was a time of curriculum development.* Curriculum development: Born: 1918. Died: 1969. (p. 6; authors' emphasis)

The 1918 date refers to the publication of Franklin Bobbitt's *The Curriculum,* which we have already mentioned. Bobbitt's book is the first publication of a "synoptic" curriculum text in American education. As Pinar (2004) notes, a synoptic text is designed to "summarize curriculum scholarship and suggest its significance" (p. 7). We noted that Bobbitt organized his synoptic text around the advocacy of a particular protocol for standardized curriculum development. Many other educators followed in Bobbitt's footsteps, most notably Ralph Tyler with the publication of *Basic Principles of Curriculum and Instruction;* as we also mentioned, Tyler's "rationale" can be read as a refinement of Bobbitt's protocol (Kliebard, 1975/2004).

Eclectic and Practical Artistry

In this formative period of the North American curriculum field, there were scholars who challenged this management approach to the study and practice of curriculum. However, these more critically oriented scholars, including the social reconstructionists Harold Rugg, George Counts, and Theodore Brameld, worked within the confines of specific theoretical orientations. Joseph Schwab, who was a colleague of Ralph Tyler's at the University of Chicago, was disturbed by constrained nature of both procedural and critical theorizing. He felt that both approaches missed the mark. He felt that neither the proceduralists nor the critical theorists were working the way curriculum scholars should work. Neither properly understood the discipline of curriculum and teaching studies, so Schwab composed an essay, which he presented at an annual meeting of the American Educational Research Association and for which he received an unusual standing ovation. In this essay, he makes two basic points. The phenomena of "curriculum," referring to educational courses of action that facilitate human "growth," is so complex that it cannot be studied through any particular theoretical perspective—no matter how critically insightful. Curriculum scholars must be theoretically sophisticated; they must approach their discipline eclectically. Schwab (1969/2004) writes:

> All the social and behavioral sciences are marked by "schools," each distinguished by a different choice of principle of enquiry, each of which selects from the intimidating complexities of the subject matter the small fraction of the whole with which it can deal. The theories which arise from enquiries so directed are, then, radically incomplete. . . . It follows, then, that such theories are not, and will not be, adequate by themselves to tell us what to do with human beings or how to do it. What they variously suggest and the contrary guidances they afford to choice and action must be mediated and combined by eclectic arts. (p. 98)

Schwab's advocacy of the "arts of the eclectic" in curriculum work leads directly to his second point. He argues that this eclectic approach culminates in "arts of the practical," which are deliberative and cannot be reduced to precise protocols. In effect, Schwab argued that the field of curriculum is disciplined in two specific ways, and his organizing terms for these two key characteristics were arts of the eclectic and arts of the practical. The curriculum field is neither theoretical nor practical. It is both. Though Schwab extends his 1969 argument into three additional essays published between 1971 and 1983 (Schwab, 1971, 1973, 1983), his first essay is the groundbreaking one. We celebrate its publication, and we wish we had been at the annual AERA meeting when he presented his argument so that we could have joined in the standing ovation. We feel that his essay is, perhaps, the key moment in the disciplinary "birthing" of the curriculum field.

We now move to 1979, which is the publication of Elliot Eisner's *The Educational Imagination*. Eisner received his Ph.D. from the University of Chicago, and Joseph Schwab was one of his doctoral advisors. Working from Schwab's arts of the eclectic perspective, Eisner explores the arts of the practical in curriculum work through his organizing term of educational imagination. We have repeatedly cited Eisner's work in this book and note in chapter 1 that his understanding of the educational imagination is comprehensive and ecological. He explores the educational imagination with reference to curricular ways of knowing, program designing, teaching, evaluating, and researching (Eisner, 1994). In a recent edited book celebrating Eisner's highly productive career, the editors claim: "No one has been a greater champion of the broad utility of artistic and aesthetic paradigms for educational thought and practice than Elliot Eisner" (Uhrmacher & Matthews, 2005, p. xvii).

We now jump ahead to 1995. This is the date of the publication of William Pinar, William Reynolds, Patrick Slattery, and Peter Taubman's *Understanding Curriculum: An Introduction to the Study of Historical and Contemporary Curriculum Discourses,* a book we have already cited. This synoptic text provides the first comprehensive, in-depth examination of the arts of the eclectic in curriculum work. Their organizing term for the practice of the arts of the eclectic in curriculum work is complicated conversation. We have already quoted their curriculum-as-complicated-conversation definition, and we have noted that both our currere narratives and our chapter 3 reflective inquiry scaffolding are informed by this interpretation of curriculum. Patrick Slattery's (1995/2006) *Curriculum Development in the Postmodern Era* explores the implications of this orientation for the practice of curriculum development.

Let's now return to Schwab's practical essays, particularly his first 1969 publication. He argues that good curriculum judgments are based on case-by-case deliberations informed by arts of the eclectic and enacted through arts of the practical. With respect to Pinar's and Eisner's work, we could rephrase this as follows: Good curriculum judgments are disciplined by complicated conversation and educational imagination. This disciplined understanding of good curriculum decision making pervades this book. Schwab's linkage of the arts of the eclectic and the arts of the practical is an organizing principle of this text. Turning complicated curriculum conversations into sophisticated curriculum deliberations that are then enacted with imagination is how curriculum judgments become elevated.

Consider for a moment the overall design of our book. In chapter 2, we ask you to reconceptualize subject standards whereby you reframe the received standards from the dominant standardized management paradigm into transformative standards. You do this by conceptualizing the goals of 3S understanding, student performances of these understandings, and criteria for judging the quality of these performances. We recognize that this conceptual work is challenging; therefore, we provide guidance in chapter 3 on how to cultivate the necessary reflective inquiry capacities. In chapters 4–7, we offer advice on how your work on creating transformative standards can be integrated into designing/planning, teaching, evaluating, and organizing deliberations. As we discuss this comprehensive deliberative work, we encourage you to be as imaginative and creative as possible.

Journey and Judgment Are Embedded

Notice how the judgment theme in our story overlaps with our journey theme. The fact that curriculum-as-judgment and curriculum-as-journey are equally embedded in curriculum-as-complicated-conversation shouldn't be surprising. Transformative curriculum leadership is the collaborative effort to elevate judgments on the complicated problem of teaching for a holistic 3S understanding, while learning to address this complicated problem requires a particular professional journey of understanding. It involves curriculum-as-currere. In effect, judgment and journey are two sides of the same transformative curriculum leadership coin.

As we introduce in chapter 1 and constantly discuss throughout this book, the disciplined judgment/journey we are advancing is, in general, practiced in a context of paradigmatic tensions between the standardized management, constructivist best practice, and curriculum wisdom paradigms. This historical reality requires the exercise of professional judgment in three additional ways. Educators who work from a "love of democratic wisdom" orientation must find thoughtful, appropriate ways to *concur, comply,* and *invite.* In the context of case-by-case deliberations, wisdom-oriented professionals may actually concur with their colleagues who predominantly work out of one of the other two paradigms. These transformative educators may agree that teaching for a particular type of standardized achievement or for a particular type of subject disciplinary understanding is, in fact, the best way to proceed for a particular group of students in a specific time frame. This does not mean that these transformative educators have shifted away from their holistic frame of reference. They have simply made the judgment that, all things considered, a more constrained instruction is the best course of action for a particular educational situation.

Transformative educators may also decide to comply with the demands of those who strongly adhere to the standardized management or constructivist best practice paradigms. They may base their judgment on political inquiries as introduced in chapter 3 and acknowledged throughout this book. Though they may disagree with a particular curriculum decision, they may be legitimately concerned about not "burning bridges." By abiding by the constraints of a particular curriculum judgment, they may be in a better position to negotiate at a future date. Cuban (2003) discusses the "wisdom of practice" (p. 64) from this judgment perspective. With respect to the standardized management orientation, he writes: "But attention to raising test scores is not the same as restricting the school's agenda to those tests. And it is that wiggle room between selective attention to tests and a sole focus on scoring better that [permits diverse curriculum orientations]" (p. 35). Given current political realities, wisdom-oriented educators must, oftentimes, quietly and subtly seek out this wiggle room; undoubtedly, you have noticed that this pragmatic insight is a recurring theme throughout this book.

Finally, wisdom-oriented educators must make informed judgments on meaningful ways to invite their colleagues to undertake their own journeys of understanding. As we have made clear throughout this book, transformative curriculum leadership is a currere commitment. This is why chapters 2–8 are written from Rosie Gornik's first-person perspective. This book's decision-making advice is grounded in honest self-examination and soul-searching. There is no alternative. Given its democratic orientation, TCL is an inclusive collaborative process. Though TCL is not invitation only, it is only invitational. It is premised on a rigorous developmental commitment. Consider the book's three paradigmatic frames of reference. An educator working out of the curriculum wisdom orientation can understand the constructivist best practice and standardized management orientations because teaching for 3S understanding encompasses the latter two frames, but not vice versa (Henderson & Kesson, 2004). There is an expansive broadening of horizons embedded in this book's journey of understanding, and transformative educators must exercise judgment on how to invite others to expand their professional horizons in their own unique ways. Because Rosie Gornik's chapter 1 currere narrative is written as an invitation to the transformative work in this book, it illustrates how to practice this judgment. There is a subtle art to encouraging and confirming a deepening awareness, and we have written this book with this artistry in mind.

Curriculum as Hermeneutic Undertaking

The broadening of horizons is a central concern in the tradition of philosophical hermeneutics, particularly the work of Hans-Georg Gadamer (Gallagher, 1992). Philosophical hermeneutics, which has its formal beginnings in the 19th century (Grondin, 1995), addresses the art of cultivating a holistic understanding of some matter, such as a book, a concept, or a specific topic, through a flexible consideration of diverse interpretations on that matter. Philosophical hermeneutics requires a constant, back-and-forth movement between whole and part—between an emerging feel for the bigger picture and a nimble attention to various, and perhaps conflicting, perspectives. It possesses three key characteristics: holistic orientation, interpretive playfulness, and open-minded humility, and all three characteristics are clearly on display in this book. The book's holistic orientation—teaching for 3S understanding—is introduced in chapter 1 and clarified in chapter 2 as transformative standards. The interpretive playfulness that nurtures this holistic orientation is embedded in the reflective inquiry scaffolding in chapter 3 and in the deliberative decision making in chapters 4 through 7, while the informal and formal collegial support for this interpretive playfulness is introduced in chapter 4 and then carried forward in chapters 5–9. You may have noticed that the play of diverse perspectives is a central feature of our historical narrative. You are reading a story that draws on diverse curriculum theories for useful insights, not for definitive, all-inclusive statements. As we note at the beginning of this story, we have composed our historical narrative as poststructuralists, not as structuralists. We are practicing the eclectic artistry that Schwab advocates.

Finally, the open-minded humility that is a primary feature of a love of wisdom informs the entire book. Davidson (1998) provides insight into the vital relationship between humility and wisdom:

> Wisdom is knowing how little you know. Ignorance is the beginning of wisdom, Socrates cautioned us. Zen practitioners call it "beginner's mind," which is truly open and fresh, willing to remain innocent and receptive to life, not attached to our knowledge. It is the willingness to be empty, and thus open to learning and growing. This is the source of creativity and innovation, the key to continuous improvement. (pp. 36–37)

With reference to the tradition of philosophical hermeneutics, we could say that *Transformative Curriculum Leadership* is a book that promotes a democratic curriculum hermeneutics.

REACHING OUT TO THE BROADER PUBLIC SPHERE

We have now told a story that provides theoretical insight into transformative curriculum leadership. We hope our historical narrative assists your comprehension of the disciplined interpretation of curriculum-based teaching that underlies this book. We encourage you to further explore the curriculum literature that we have introduced. It will certainly deepen your understanding of this text and its position within the complex field of curriculum studies.

How can transformative curriculum leaders, who are committed to this disciplined interpretation of curriculum-based teaching, cultivate a broader public audience? How might they network with other like-minded educators and curriculum stakeholders beyond their immediate work environment? We now turn to these questions, which were discussed at the annual 2005 Curriculum and Pedagogy Conference in the context of a large town hall meeting. We present the narratives of two participants in this town hall meeting.

THE FIRST PERSONAL NARRATIVE

Kent den Heyer, a faculty member at the University of Alberta, is a Canadian educator. His narrative, which foregrounds the "historical agency" that is embedded in Transformative Curriculum Leadership, explores a number of ways that an emergent TCL network could effectively enter the public arena. There is a strong research emphasis in his narrative, and this is an important consideration since the public prestige of Transformative Curriculum Leadership could be quite dependent on the quality of the research supporting its advocacies. His narrative also models the broad holistic orientation of curriculum wisdom decision making.

Kent's Story

I begin my narrative by introducing the concept of historical agency. By "historical agency," I am referring to capacities expressed by groups in struggles over the conceptual resources that individuals use to interpret social and material life, such as ideals, images, and terms available to define and express identities, social goals, or visions of education (den Heyer, 2003a, 2003b). In contrast to more heroic notions of change agents propagated in textbooks, movies, and advertisements, historical agency speaks to the ways that we might envision ourselves as a collective yet distributed agent across a range of institutional locations and interests; diverse in what we think needs to be done to enhance education and social life but commonly committed to a "public education [that] is about educating the public" (Pinar, 2004, p. 232). What capacities might we express as an historical agent? Our capacities to offer diverse terms, images, information, and ideals that inform the public's imagination and deliberation about what education is, can, and ought to be. We might think of this role as advocating for support of a curriculum wisdom paradigm in the multiple "zones of influence" we occupy (den Heyer, 2003a).

In many ways, there already exists strong resonance within North America for the problem formulated in the curriculum wisdom paradigm, which seeks to advocate for "student performances of subject matter understanding embedded in democratic self understanding." As noted throughout this book, like the standardized management paradigm, curriculum wisdom is also concerned with student performances. However, compared to that paradigm, the wisdom paradigm is more scholarly. It calls for diverse performances of knowledge acquisition that provide multiple opportunities for teachers and the public to gain a clearer and deeper understanding of what students know and can do with knowledge.

Like the constructivist best practice paradigm, the acquisition of subject matter understanding is central to the wisdom paradigm. It improves on that formulation of the problem. It does so by asserting that such acquisition ought to enhance students' self and social understanding as democratic beings. Neither the standardized management nor best practices paradigm explicitly embodies this deep North American tradition for schools as sites where public democratic lives begin. In providing a place for the values of competing paradigms, educators operating out of a wisdom paradigm respect the diversity of values within contemporary society while explicitly connecting those values to its commitment and exploration of the democratic "good."

This book raises important questions on how to engage the public sphere. First, in what ways can we advocate for curriculum wisdom in the institutions where our desks sit right now? Second, given its already deep resonance within the political ideals found in North America, in what ways might we advance curriculum wisdom in the public imaginary to encourage political actions that support this paradigm? Third, what research can we collate to identify, justify, and advocate for public policies that support curriculum wisdom in public schools? These questions speak to several interrelated concerns central to the text's interpretation of curriculum-based teaching.

The first and second questions are concerned with the need to construct a disciplined professional identity. Such an identity is the necessary means to the end of bringing our expertise to the public deliberation of education. Extending this concern, the third question asks us to imagine in what ways we might impact the public imaginary in and through both conversations and policy. Let us address each question and the concerns to which they speak with specific examples. We start where our desks sit.

I have been an active member of the Curriculum and Pedagogy organization, which consists of university educators, public education teachers, and community leaders. This organization, which maintains an annual conference, journal, book series, and community outreach initiatives, seeks to explore and enact the inherent mutuality of education theory and practice. A key aspect of this work concerns encouraging the diverse ways we individually work, and, at the same time, cumulatively contribute to our historical agency, to engage the public in multiple sites. This work benefits from changes in what universities recognized as worthwhile scholarship. Such changes offer real opportunity to rethink the ways we, as diverse participants in education but united in support of a public education that is about educating the public, might more thoroughly engage in public intellectual work.

For example, Kent State University has adopted the "Boyer model" to support work not traditionally recognized as vital to the mission of the university. Boyer (1990) outlines five types of scholarship deserving of recognition in tenure and promotion decisions. His "scholarship of discovery" refers to research at a discipline's cutting edge. In the language of the research business, this scholarship is exemplified in the awarding of a Ph.D. for "a substantial original contribution to knowledge." Boyer's other categories—scholarships of integration, application, and teaching—attempt to broaden the types and locations of work recognized in the academe.

By way of fleshing out Boyer's hope for academe to recognize a more varied type of scholarship, one can envision under the category of scholarships of application, for example, university teacher-scholars creating and attending philosopher cafes, writing to newspapers, producing leaflets, addressing PTA and teachers' union meetings, and working more closely with teachers, students, principals, and superintendents. One can also envision greater engagement with government bureaucracies that set the conditions that shape what goes on in schools, questioning presuppositions and evidence used as bases for their decisions, and so on. In fact, we might imagine groups of scholars, teachers, parents, and students working together to study, work with, or interrogate local, state, and federal education bureaucracies as required. In doing so, in what ways would public discussions about education be enhanced?

Taking up such activities offers an opportunity to build on professorial capacities for public intellectual work. An equivalent question that scholars, teachers, and administrators might ask is "In what ways might schools as sites of intellectual life be enhanced if we invested in smaller class sizes, organized opportunities for teachers for extended study in their disciplines and develop leadership plans to encourage wisdom practices, and organized teaching schedules around grade-level teams?" The latter organization, for example, would give teachers the opportunity to meet weekly to discuss connections between their lessons, discuss student progress, and decide who might best engage a student whose behavior seems to have changed (which, we add, is a primary indicator of depression, drug abuse, and possible suicide)? Exploring the costs and opportunities of such arrangements requires that we identify critical friends such as superintendents, parents, and members of the media to advocate for public deliberation of such school practices. Paula, a teacher at a Philadelphia school, expresses well the frustration facing teachers who seek to work with students toward 3S understanding:

> It's not that the administration wouldn't say "we value democracy" or "we value students' critical thinking" or "we value students formulating their own thoughts on controversial issues." They're not opposed to that intellectually or pedagogically. They're only opposed to that when it's translated into actual classroom methodology, because it's contrary to the other things they're trying to achieve—which is the standardization of the curriculum. . . . (Shirley, 1993, p. 177)

Paula struggles to teach when only instruction is required. What other activities can we envision to support teachers like Paula?

The third question we proposed in this section—what research can we collate to identify, justify, and advocate for political action and public policies that support curriculum wisdom in public schools?—asks us to think about the public face of our work. It concerns impacting public conversation and policy. We have already mentioned several possibilities. We are fortunate to have other examples of how we might address this question.

The Public Knowledge Project (PKP) directed by John Willinsky at the University of British Columbia is dedicated to exploring the ways that "educational research can serve as a more useful and relevant source of professional development and political deliberation, both of which are no less critical to the future of our schools, I would hold, than improved test scores" (Willinsky, 2001, p. 6).[2] To do so requires "forging links

---

[2]The Public Knowledge Project's Website is available at www.pkp.ubc.ca.

between research and related classroom practices, teachers' experiences, curriculum resources, education policies, and public reports, in ways that would enable educators and people generally to make sense and make choices, to take in the broader picture and to focus on the learning experience" (Willinsky, 2001, p. 6). Following Willinsky, we argue that the success of this vital project requires thinking more experimentally about the ways we might engage and inform public deliberation about education.

In addition to offering the public a return on its investment in education scholarship in the form of accessible research, this outlet allows us to do some innovative engagement. For example, in the face of a public deinvestment in school arts, there exist many relevant studies using a host of methodologies linking the arts in schools to the positive development of students' intellectual, emotional, and social capacities. Members of the public, like educators, might find different reports cogent, some seeking statistical and or survey data while others are more inclined toward thick descriptions of programs and effects. What search terms might link, for example, ethnographic and statistical studies for public consumption? Organizing research to inform public concern—for example, whether we fund the arts in schools—can also be supported through public presentations by art and language arts teachers (among others) whose work with students would be enhanced with opportunities for a variety of creative studies in schools. Here we can see research and researchers and teaching and teachers coming together to inform parents, administrators, and politicians on crucial questions of how best to enhance the creative potential of young people. We also have other examples of attempts to connect a variety of influences that impact on the abilities of students to actualize their potential.

Recently, the Canadian government announced that it would spend 85 million Canadian dollars to set up 17 organizations across the country to inform Canadians about the link between health and learning. Like the PKP, this initiative seeks to collate and present research-based evidence for questions about health and learning for public deliberation. On a much smaller scale but in a similar vein, work is under way to integrate a broad range of social influences into the problematic of schools through a set of rubrics members of the public can use to judge the performance of their community and government leaders in support of a wisdom orientation in schools (den Heyer & Pifel, 2005). Specifically, this work seeks to identify the performance of social actors whose decisions impact students and teachers. It combines multiple types of research in various education fields to develop research-based indicators for what various public stakeholders such as parents, communities, political leaders, professors, teachers, administrators, and professional health and education organizations can and ought to do to support student achievement. Embedded in the rubrics are policies that, if enacted, research proves will be effective social supports for student successes.

For example, den Heyer and Pifel (2005) examined research (i.e., Kohler & Rigby's [2003] study) investigating the effects of health care on child development. From this research, it was determined that, in order to give children the best chance for educational growth and success, a community must provide accessible health care to those who need it. To measure the community's ability to provide this crucial service, one indicator (among others) was developed for the Community Indicator Rubric. It is depicted in Table 9.1.

A score of 4 would be obtained by a community that had high levels of care for children that was easily accessible both logistically and financially for parents. A community at

Table 9.1 COMMUNITY INDICATOR RUBRIC (INDICATOR ONE)				
Indicator	**4**	**3**	**2**	**1**
Accessibility to quality health care	Health care accessible to all who are in need with high levels of service	Health care limited by either inadequate accessibility or inadequate levels of service	Care available but limited by financial ability rather than need	Health care restricted to those who can afford it

Source: Based on "Indicators of Children's Development: Considerations When Constructing a Set of National Child Health Indicators for the European Union" by L. Kohler and M. Rigby, 2003, *Child: Care, Health & Development,* *29*(6), pp. 551–558.

this level would also be in a position to provide high levels of service for all in need. Communities would score a 3 by demonstrating one of the above qualities in a high degree, but limiting the other. Care that is allocated to those with the financial means first and given to a lesser degree to those who need it but can not afford it earns a community a score of 2. Finally, a health-care system that is reserved solely on the basis of high financial means would earn a community a 1.

In order to afford the resources needed to provide adequate health care to all in need, a community will need politicians who advocate for the reallocation of resources to make this happen, as well as show a willingness to work with experts in the field as to the most effective way to do this. This is represented in the Politician Indicator Rubric and presented in Table 9.2.

Table 9.2 RUBRIC FOR POLITICIANS (INDICATOR ONE)				
Indicator	**4**	**3**	**2**	**1**
Supports legislation that seeks to increase access to public health care for children.	Demonstrates knowledge of issues and research and introduces legislation that seeks to provide health care for all children.	Demonstrates some knowledge of issues and supports legislation that seeks to provide health care for all children.	Demonstrates little knowledge of issues and does little to change current funding formulas.	Opposes change to legislation and policy that perpetuates current trends in health care, which is limited to those who can afford it.
	Works closely with health care and social experts to determine best practices and policies.	Acknowledges expertise of education, health care, and social experts in formulating policy.		

The thrust of these research-based rubrics is to support teachers in the tremendously complex learning challenges and decisions they face daily. As one example, this type of research from university based educators can help initiate coalitions of interested scholars, teachers, students, parents, politicians, and community leaders in support of more wise social and political policies that support 3S understanding.

THE SECOND PERSONAL NARRATIVE

Kathleen Kesson, a faculty member at Long Island University in Brooklyn, New York, was asked to reflect on her collaborative work on the state of Vermont's Framework of Standards and Learning Opportunities. Her narrative provides a more in-depth account of one specific way that transformative curriculum leaders could engage the broader public sphere. They could work to reframe their government's subject matter standards in more holistic 3S terms. If they did not have the governmental access that was enjoyed by Vermont educators, they could, at the very least, reconceptualize the governmental standards, based on the guidance in chapter 2, and then present the results of their collaborative work in various public venues. Because Kathleen's story has a strong currere emphasis, her narrative adds another autobiographical voice to this book.

Kathleen's Story

In my late teens, I discovered existentialist literature. Simone de Beauvoir, Jean Paul Sartre, Camus, Heidegger, Hesse, and others of this ilk all changed my life and probably projected me inexorably into the 1960s counterculture. It is probably no surprise, then, that when I became an educator I was infused with the ideals of freedom and personal "authenticity." In the 1970s, following an early career in the theater, I got involved with the University Without Walls's system of experimental higher education and a consortium of "alternative" K–12 schools, including "free schools" (Miller, 2002) that were collectively involved in the exploration of forms of teaching and learning that were linked to democratic social change. The social context for this work was tumultuous: the issues of the day included the Black civil rights movement, the Vietnam War, women's liberation, gay liberation, and the proliferation of ethnic studies. Along with many other radical educators of my generation, I rejected the notion that education was primarily about gaining the knowledge and skills to join and perpetuate the "establishment," which we viewed as hopelessly corrupted by materialistic, racist, and militaristic values. Rather, I believed, education was (potentially) a revolutionary act, and should be oriented toward the various projects of social transformation—toward a society that was more just, more creative, more free, more sustainable, more peaceful, more egalitarian, and, to be honest, more fun! In short, we envisioned a society that would embody the aims of the countercultural revolution(s) of the 1960s and '70s, and we felt that learning could be harnessed to the enactment of this collective vision.

I spent a great deal of time in rural Oklahoma, working collaboratively with Native American individuals and groups to set up educational programs. Influenced by Eliot Wigginton's Foxfire project, our educational experiments were many and varied, and included projects such as setting up food cooperatives, where people pooled their incomes to purchase organic foods at low cost, learning to grow and distribute organic food, studying Native American history from Native Americans, protesting inequitable labor practices at a work site where many of us were earning a meager living, protesting the building of a local nuclear power plant, setting up community-based educational and artistic projects, and producing an underground newspaper filled with impassioned articles about these various projects. At the core of all of our work was the notion that knowledge should emerge from experience, that experiences could be directed toward social change, and that collective self-critique and reflection were an important aspect of this dynamic. We read some of Paulo Freire's writing and a bit of John Dewey, but were much more concerned with practice than theory. We were youthful idealists and felt quite sure that the world in which we would raise our own families (for those of us who would have families) would be radically transformed (along the lines of our own visions, of course) from the one that we grew up in and had rejected.

In the ensuing years, I held a variety of teaching jobs, raised my four sons (including home schooling them for a number of years), and finally, attended graduate school to study curriculum and instruction at the masters and the doctoral level. Throughout this period, my radical ideas about education were tempered by many things: more experience teaching children, being a parent, gaining a deeper and more inclusive understanding of the democratic process through extensive political work (I was active in the environmental, antinuclear, and peace movements), and importantly, my immersion in the scholarly curriculum field. I was fortunate (I say fortunate because it was entirely due to dumb luck, rather than any informed choices by myself) to land in a doctoral program in which my advisors were well versed both in critical theory and in the Reconceptualist thinking that was becoming preeminent in the field of curriculum.

In 1992, I moved to Vermont to take a position on the education faculty of Goddard College, an experimental school designed on the ideas of John Dewey. A newly minted education professor, I was excited about the opportunity to be a teacher educator at this historic school and hoped that it would be a place in which my progressive values might find a home. I was intrigued with what I had heard about Vermont and its approach to education. I knew that it was a leader in the "portfolio assessment" movement, and that it was home to a number of institutions of progressive higher education, including Vermont College, Bennington College, and Marlboro College, in addition to Goddard, and that these educational institutions had been influential in the development of Vermont as a politically progressive state. It seemed like a promising "laboratory" for progressive education ideas and practices.

Vermont is a small state, populated more heavily with cows and trees than people. Vermonters are known for thinking of themselves as fiercely independent (its one congressman, Bernie Sanders, reelected seven times, is the longest serving Independent in the history of the House of Representatives). The state embodies both traditional and progressive values. Its economy is still largely agricultural, and town meetings are still held annually in most towns and villages. Yet it is perhaps the most radical state in the Union, both historically and in the present day. It was the first state to outlaw slavery in its constitution in 1777, and it was a leading abolitionist voice by the 1830s. During the presidency of Ronald Reagan in the 1980s, more than 180 Vermont towns demanded a nuclear freeze in defiance of his policies. Vermont has no death penalty and virtually no gun control laws, but it is one of the least violent states. It has a strong environmental ethic—no billboards are allowed along its scenic roadways, and stringent environmental regulations govern development. Recently, it was the first state to legally acknowledge civil unions between gay and lesbian couples. Dating from around 1815, Vermont has a thriving secessionist movement, and even today, several hundred Vermonters belong to a democratic, grassroots solidarity movement committed to the return of Vermont to its original status as an independent republic. Democratic ideals, even notions of "radical" or "direct" democracy, are alive and well in Vermont.

In the early 1990s, people in the state of Vermont embarked upon an effort to construct a new state curriculum framework that might reflect their unique values. True to the historic town meeting ethos, at least 40 focus groups, consisting of more than 4,000 citizens, convened to discuss the question "What should students know and be able to do in the 21st century?" The result was *The Common Core of Learning,* a sparse document that specified "vital results" in four categories: communication, reasoning and problem solving, personal development, and social responsibility. These vital results were to be linked to integrated curriculum in three fields of knowledge: the arts, language, and literature; history and social sciences; and science, mathematics, and technology. The important point to note here is that the genesis of this process was rooted in a 3S position—that personal development and social responsibility were primary vital learning results, and that subject matter needed to be integrated with these vital results. I believe that the inclusion of social responsibility in such a prominent place in a state curriculum policy document is unusual. Many states include "civic and social responsibility" as a standard, but Vermont may be alone in its recognition that it needs to be woven into integrated subject matter throughout the curriculum.

Soon after I assumed my new position at Goddard College, I was a member of the state Science, Mathematics and Technology Commission, which was generously funded by the National Science Foundation, as well as a member of the Steering Committee for the statewide process of developing a curriculum framework based on this commission's work. I was intrigued with Vermont's unique approach to public education; with its strong tradition of local governance, there was no statewide textbook adoption process and no state-mandated standardized testing. Teachers and local schools appeared to have a great deal of autonomy and control over curricular and pedagogical decisions. I was interested in helping to preserve this, and I leapt at the opportunity to see what impact, if any, a progressive-minded curriculum theorist might have on the construction of a state policy document.

I spent a lot of time over the ensuing years engaged in deliberations with a wide variety of people: teachers, university subject matter specialists; teacher educators and university curriculum specialists, school administrators, parent and community members, and Business Roundtable members. The three curriculum commissions (arts, language, and literature; history and social sciences; and science, mathematics, and technology) were charged with reviewing the national standards set by professional organizations and deciding which ones we wanted to retain and/or reshape for our own purposes. This proved to be a daunting task, as anyone who has been involved with this type of work can attest. We pored through huge stacks of documents, deliberating and debating questions such as: What knowledge is of most worth? Who should determine what should be learned? How should subject matter be integrated? What are optimum subject matter pedagogies? What sorts of evidence might demonstrate learning? These questions address the perennial curriculum questions.

I contributed position papers on integrated curriculum and on the epistemology of science wherein I tried to set forth sophisticated ideas from the curriculum field in accessible, "public" language. One example of this was in the latter paper, where I argued for science teaching that recognized the cultural and political dimensions of science, as well as the contingency and historicity of knowledge claims. Guided by those of us in the curriculum studies field, lengthy discussions about the nature and relative merits of multidisciplinary, interdisciplinary, and transdisciplinary curriculum took place. We succeeded to the end in maintaining the "integrated" nature of the Vermont Framework, but throughout there was continued difficulty on the part of many participants envisioning learning standards that did not fit with more conventional behavioral objectives. From my perspective, the document that was ultimately approved by the State Board of Education in 1996 provided vital support for teachers of a strong 3S orientation; it enabled curriculum development built around the interconnections between strong, integrated subject matter, personal development, and civic/social responsibility. Teachers with a love of "democratic wisdom" could find inspiration and justification in the document for a variety of progressive curriculum innovations, and local districts and schools maintained a high level of autonomy over curriculum decisions. Teachers were further supported by much good work that was done to identify "constructivist best practices" within a progressive education framework. These were developed by the Learning Opportunities Committee and included such practices as authentic and varied assessment practices, cooperative group learning, student-designed projects around real-world questions, and other humanistic practices that valued the all-around growth and development (physical, social, emotional, cognitive, artistic) of students.

By 1996, we had a framework that was extraordinarily progressive (integrated, inquiry-based curriculum, attention to diversity and problems of bias and discrimination, mandates that students take part in community activities and participate in democratic processes, requirements that students be immersed in the arts, etc.). By 1997, the state had adopted a more equitable funding formula, and it looked as if issues of equity in educational opportunities would finally be addressed in a significant way. As well, educators in Vermont had been involved in a multiyear project to develop portfolios demonstrating competency in math and writing. It looked as if Vermont would soon be a progressive educators' dream—a state framework that supported genuine democratic education, equalized school funding, and an assessment system that was student friendly, authentic, varied, and designed for the improvement of instruction. But alas, the standardized management paradigm is powerfully entrenched in the public imagination, and following the adoption of the framework, there were pressures that threatened to dissolve some of the progressive advances.

The Vermont Framework suffered criticisms from near and far, including from university-based subject matter specialists and the Business Roundtable that it was "vague," lacking in specific objectives, and therefore of no real use to teachers, and so forth. Partly in response to these criticisms, new committees and commissions were set up to define grade-by-grade learning standards, bringing increased specificity to standard grade-level expectations. There are now documents that articulate grade-level standards in a number of subject areas. While undoubtedly many teachers appreciate such explicit guidance concerning what, how, and when to teach specific concepts, with such a move there is always a trade-off. Teachers have fewer opportunities to engage in reflective practice and exercise their professional judgment; hence such prescriptions contribute to the deskilling of teachers. Of course, a major reason for increasing specificity about what should be taught and when is the pressure for standardized accountability, which requires the alignment of curriculum, instruction, and assessment. The term *alignment* always brings to my mind a well-oiled machine with all the gears synchronized, mechanically going about its work, and indeed this metaphor is an iconic one for the standardized management paradigm. Predictably, under such increased pressures for increased, standardized forms of accountability, many of Vermont's progressive initiatives, including the use of portfolios, are on the wane.

The movement for increasing specificity of grade-level expectations (Ralph Tyler's behavioral objectives in new clothes) has had an impact on Vermont's university-based teacher preparation programs, requiring prospective teachers to demonstrate laundry lists of measurable competencies related to these grade-level expectations that are assessed using scoring rubrics. Though this approach might seem to indicate increased rigor and accountability, ultimately, increasing the focus on discrete skills (behavioral objectives) in either K–12 or university education makes it less possible to engage in more holistic, intellectually rigorous, personally meaningful forms of learning. This is the heart of the difference between the standardized management paradigm and the curriculum wisdom paradigm. At Goddard, and at other progressive colleges that prepare teachers in Vermont, the increasing and oppressive specificity of "outcomes" in teacher preparation programs had a stifling effect on the level and quality of the work that students produced. It is, I believe, a recipe for mediocrity in the teaching profession.

Conflict and disagreement is often at the center of public policy work. One interesting point of conflict in this policy process concerned efforts to include references to "ethical decision making" in the curriculum framework. There was no attempt to define a *particular* ethical perspective, only a suggestion that learning how to think about the ethics of social and cultural practices (such as genetic engineering, nuclear power, etc.) was a crucial component of learning to be a democratic citizen. I felt very strongly about this, as I believed that if students were educated to "think ethically" it would encourage them to become active democratic citizens who might embody the public interest when it came to social, environmental, and political decision making. However, our efforts met with resistance when drafts of the document that included the word "ethics" went to the State Board, demonstrating to me the timidity of policy makers when it came to issues that might provoke controversy or conflict. There were a number of battles over this principle, and ultimately, the State Board prevailed. The framework includes *no* reference to ethics or ethical decision making, although teachers in many schools certainly do include this as part of their teaching practice. Fortunately, in Vermont, they still have the room to shape their classroom pedagogies, to some extent.

On the bright side (from my perspective, at least!), the Framework did exhibit some tendencies toward being a living document, amenable to democratic input and adjustment. In June 2000, the Vermont State Board approved two new standards that emphasize sustainability of Vermont's environment and communities. Given my long commitment to environmental preservation, this issue was dear to my heart, and so I served on the grassroots committee that lobbied for these changes. The group was a consortium of government and nongovernment organizations and individuals interested in preserving Vermont's unique natural and cultural heritage. Again here, citizens gathered in community forums across the state to contribute diverse perspectives on the skills and knowledge Vermonters saw as essential to creating a sustainable future. More than 350 people participated in the forums. Following extensive drafts and revisions, the following two standards were accepted by the State Board and added to the Framework in March 2000:

> 3.9 Sustainability: Students make decisions that demonstrate understanding of natural and human communities, the ecological, economic, political, or social systems within them, and awareness of how their personal and collective actions affect the sustainability of these interrelated systems. 4.6 Understanding Place: Students demonstrate understanding of the relationship between their local environment and community heritage and how each shapes their lives.

As far as I know, Vermont is the only state that has made a strong commitment to the environmental education of its citizens, with such an emphasis on local culture, heritage, and "sense of place."

In this narrative, I have tried to portray a genuine grassroots effort to come up with a progressive curriculum framework that resonated with many Vermont citizens' deeply held democratic values. I have noted some of the controversy and conflict that accompanied this process. The "arts of the eclectic" were certainly present as we engaged in multiple forms of reflective inquiry: craft reflection (especially when we deliberated over and crafted the "learning opportunity standards" component of the framework) integrated with disciplinary, poetic, critical, multiperspective, ethical, and political inquiries. Participants grounded in curriculum studies were often the people pushing the edges of these reflective inquiry processes. The process proceeded with maximum democratic participation, although in the end, the "powers that be" prevailed in crucial decisions, as in the choice of the State Board to eliminate reference to ethics from the document. Sadly, the advent of high-stakes testing in the state demonstrates the power of the standardized management paradigm, even in a progressive social context with a history of democratic deliberation and decision making. The outcome of this story about trying to infuse a policy-making process with a curriculum wisdom perspective is mixed, but perhaps we can take heart from the Vermont story. Just this past February, Congressman Bernie Sanders hosted a critical panel on federal education policy. In his introduction to the discussion, he said:

> Many educators are concerned that the No Child Left Behind approach, as it is now being implemented, undermines the creative elements of education and encourages "teaching for tests" and rote learning—not necessarily the qualities we want to emphasize in a democratic society. (http://www.bernie.house.gov/statements)

How unusual to hear words from a public official that actually link issues of pedagogy to issues of democracy. As they say in Vermont, "Go, Bernie!"

Recently, I left the peaceful hills of the Green Mountain State to take a position in an urban teacher preparation program in the heart of Brooklyn. It is exciting to apply "democratic curriculum wisdom" to a whole new set of educational challenges. It has been 35 years since I first began my "currere journey" in the experimental world of alternative education during a turbulent time in American history. Of that time, I have spent the past 18 years educating teachers, carrying out educational research, producing policy papers and academic writing, and most importantly, engaging in the study of curriculum. Although my progressive values remain intact, I have perhaps become more of a pragmatist, in that while I no longer anticipate the radical social transformations that I once naively hoped for, I remain hopeful that we can progress toward a more just, creative, caring, peaceful society. Often I am discouraged by what seems backward movement to me: the high-stakes testing movement, the appalling lack of resources in many schools, the standardization of the curriculum, the deskilling of teachers, and so forth. I am discouraged by the "culture wars" and the efforts by powerful people in our society to turn back the clock on women's rights, gay rights, and civil rights. I fear for the future of our environment and worry about the world that we are leaving our children and grandchildren. I am profoundly disturbed by the militarism and imperialist tendencies of our nation. But I do believe, more strongly than ever, that education is pivotal to progressive social change.

My values have remained more or less consistent since my early years in the field. I still reject the notion that education is primarily about gaining the knowledge and skills to join and perpetuate the "establishment," or in more current parlance, the global corporate economy. I have not given up my hope that schools can, in the words of Counts (1932): "dare to build a new social order through educational activity." However, I am much less ideological than when I first embarked on this work. I have tried to be mindful of the criticisms of those who think differently and hold different values than I. One of my good friends and colleagues, Robert Nash, of the University of Vermont, promotes the idea of a "moral conversation" in which one looks for "the truth in what we oppose and the error in what we espouse" (2001, p. 178). To this end, I compel myself to read the work of conservative scholars such as Diane Ravitch (2000), who disparage just about everything that progressive educators stand for and with whom I often find myself at odds in the education/culture wars. Though not willing to surrender certain bedrock values, I try to open myself to their "truth" in the interest of becoming "more wise" in my educational judgments (see Henderson & Kesson, 2004). For example, Ravitch's claim that progressive educators have neglected subject matter in the interests of self and social change does have a certain truth-value, and my philosophy of education as embodied in the 3S perspective that has been articulated in this book reflects this understanding. Perhaps we need to do more to reach across our ideological barriers to carry on the "moral conversation" with those with whom we disagree.

It is difficult to be optimistic in the current educational climate. But we progressive educators need to find ways to keep our batteries charged, to continue to build our "disciplinary community," and to participate, as public intellectuals, in the ethical, political, and complicated policy conversations that might advance the project of democratic wisdom and a genuine pedagogy of emancipation. This, at least, is what I think and feel at this particular point in my "currere journey."

CONCLUSION

We conclude this book by returning to our welcoming comments near the end of chapter 1. We have written this book to encourage you to become a committed democratic educator who understands the nuances of educational growth in societies with democratic values. We believe that there is a reason why John Dewey calls education "the supreme art" (Dewey 1897/2004, p. 23). How does a society become a "deep democracy" (Green, 1999) without the daily efforts of dedicated educators? Who are these individuals? They are professionals, hopefully like yourself, who embrace this book's curriculum wisdom frame of reference, who welcome to the journey of self-understanding that accompanies a love of curriculum wisdom, and who courageously undertake the visionary work of transformative curriculum leadership. We applaud such educators and recognize that their victories belong to us all.

Rosie's Farewell Currere and Advice

Writing this book has been an incredible experience. Since we began the process in earnest about two years ago, I have experienced many of life's changes. My mother passed away, my daughter married, and my two other children graduated from college and moved away to start their own purposeful lives. I also changed jobs, having been promoted to assistant superintendent in a different public school district.

I have grown and changed in so many ways as a person, and in my understanding of just what it means to be a transformative curriculum leader. I can wholeheartedly state as never before that "I never knew what I thought until I read what I wrote." The learning never ceases because the study never ceases. Most importantly, I sincerely hope that you, the reader of this book, have learned more about your*self* as a person and as a transformative curriculum leader. As Fletcher (1993) so eloquently states, "A writer becomes vulnerable by revealing part of her inner life. This is the fine print in the reader–writer agreement: When we read, we expect to learn about the writer and, through the writer, about ourselves" (p. 25). I hope I have upheld my end of the agreement. This is the power of the currere narrative.

As we conclude this book, Jim and I felt strongly that I should leave you with more information and guidance about preparing and sharing your own currere narratives. Currere narratives are the energy source and the raw material that transformative curriculum leaders use to facilitate personal journeys of understanding. These journeys are a critical feature of curriculum wisdom problem solving. Currere narratives are more than simple storytelling. Currere narratives do more than just report a sequence of events with a tidy beginning, middle, and end. Pinar (2004) defines *currere* as a strategy "to study the relations between academic knowledge and life history in the interest of self-understanding and social reconstruction; to understand the contribution academic studies makes to one's understanding of his or her life" (pp. 35–36).

The focus of currere narratives is on the integral relationship between individual educational lives and their society's politics and culture. As you may have noticed as you read my currere narratives, I attempted to situate the personal details of my professional life in political and sociocultural contexts. I often revealed the subtext of each by highlighting, for example, inherent power relations, potential prejudices, or messy issues that had no resolution within my control.

Pinar (2004) provides specific guidance about the method of currere and outlines four "moments" in the method of currere: "The regressive, the progressive, the analytical, and the synthetical" (pp. 36–37). These moments highlight the importance of time awareness and critical interpretation in composing autobiographical narratives. In the regressive moment, "one returns to the past, to capture it as it was, and as it hovers over the present" (Pinar, 1994, p. 21). I modeled this regression in my currere narratives when I discussed, for example, all the forces in the environment that shaped me and in particular, those that impacted my emotional development. Pinar (1994) recommends bringing the past to the present by recording it in some manner. Because journaling has always been a part of my daily life, I had a vast amount of personal "past" material upon which to draw. Throughout my narratives, you will notice how I have consciously related the manner in which my past is still influencing my present.

In the second "progressive" moment, one looks to the future. Once again, throughout my currere narratives I dreamed and imagined what life in schools could be. In the currere narrative about the death of a student, I ask a series of questions in painstaking detail about what could have been, imagining a brighter future for all of us in schools. My currere narratives have helped me to wake up from the mind-numbing comfort of life's taken-for-granted realities so that I can become better able to direct and author my own life. Pinar (1994) reminds us that the "future is present in the same sense that the past is present" (p. 24). I wrote my currere narratives with this visionary perspective always in mind.

In the "analytic" moment, both the past and the present are critically examined for their personal impact; while in the "synthetical" moment, one integrates past reflections, future aspirations, and critical analysis into a plan for action. For example, in my currere narrative in the first chapter, after critically examining the series of events that resulted in the physical punishment of one of my students, after reflecting on painful past events in my family history, and after contemplating my future goals as a new teacher, I made significant changes in my practice. I made sure that corporal punishment would never again enter into my professional life.

In order to facilitate your currere narratives, I have compiled a few points to ponder that might assist you in understanding the currere methodology and its four autobiographical moments.

Points to Ponder

- Carefully compose your own currere narratives and respectfully encourage other curriculum stakeholders to do the same. This work facilitates personal journeys of understanding and these journeys are a critical feature of curriculum wisdom problem solving.

- Adopt an attitude of curiosity as a way to manage the discomfort of the unfamiliar.

- Avoid simple and tidy account of events, which Spence (1986) calls "narrative smoothing." Acknowledge all of the inconsistencies, tangents, dead ends, false starts, paradoxes, and so on. Such "bumps in the road" are part of a personal journey of understanding. Your currere narratives should include much more than a seamless recounting of events that flow from beginning to middle to end.

- Keep in mind that your currere narratives are highly contextual. You should be capturing very specific instances of personal growth, change, and action. Without the critical analysis and synthesis that calls you to transformative action, you are engaging in the composition of a personal story, not a currere narrative.

- Be aware of becoming too self-involved. The overall focus of this autobiographical work is not on personal therapy. You are facilitating your journey of understanding so that you can better serve and support your students' journeys of understanding.

- Keep in mind that currere narratives promise no quick fixes. This autobiographical work calls us to slow down, to reenter the past, to imagine the future, and to act with love and wisdom as our students embark upon their journeys of democratic growth.

I have a deep and abiding hope that the concepts and advice presented in this book will help you better serve children and other curriculum stakeholders. Hopefully, you now have a better understanding of the educational road to a democratic "good" life. By facilitating your journey of understanding, you are in a better position to encourage and support the journey of others, particularly students. By working in this way, you are contributing to the democratic future of our world.

Readers desiring to embrace this book's curriculum wisdom frame of reference— those who look forward to the journey of self-understanding that accompanies a love of curriculum wisdom—are invited to share their currere narratives for advancing this work on a weblog at this address: http://curriculumleadership.edublogs.org.

REFERENCES

Apple, M. W. (1979). *Ideology and curriculum.* Boston: Routledge.

Apple, M. W. (1993). *Official knowledge: Democratic education in a conservative age.* New York: Routledge.

Ayers, W. C., & Miller, J. L. (Eds.). (1998). *A light in dark times: Maxine Greene and the unfinished conversation.* New York: Teachers College Press.

Bobbitt, F. (1918). *The curriculum.* New York: Houghton Mifflin.

Bobbitt, F. (1924). *How to make a curriculum.* Boston: Houghton Mifflin.

Boyer, E. L. (1990). *Scholarship reconsidered: Priorities of the professoriate.* Princeton, NJ: Carnegie Foundation for the Advancement of Teaching.

Bruner, J. (1960). *The process of education.* New York: Vantage.

Callahan, R. (1962). *Education and the cult of efficiency.* Chicago: University of Chicago Press.

Cherryholmes, C. H. (1988). *Power and criticism: Poststructural investigations in education.* New York: Teachers College Press.

Counts, G. S. (1932). *Dare the school build a new social order?* New York: John Day.

Cremin, L. A. (1961). *The transformation of the school.* New York: Knopf.

Cremin, L. A. (1965). *The genius of American education.* New York: Vintage.

Cuban, L. (2003). *Why is it so hard to get good schools?* New York: Teachers College Press.

Davidson, L. (1998). *Wisdom at work: The awakening of consciousness in the workplace.* Burdett, NY: Larson Publications.

den Heyer, K., & Pifel, A. (2005). Extending the responsibilities for schools beyond the school door. Paper presented at the sixth Annual Curriculum and Pedagogy Conference, Miami University, Oxford, Ohio.

den Heyer, K. (2003a). Between every "now" and "then": A role for the study of historical agency in history and citizenship education. *Theory and Research in Social Education 31*(4): 411–434.

den Heyer, K. (2003b). The historical agency of Ted T. Aoki in scholarly fugues, communities and change. *Educational Insights, 8*(2). Available at www.ccfi.educ.ubc.ca/publication/insights/v08n02/aoki/denheyer.html

Dewey, J. (1966). *Democracy and education.* New York: The Free Press. (Original work published 1916)

Dewey, J. (1998). *Experience and education.* West Lafayette, IN: Kappa Delta Pi. (Original work published 1938)

Dewey, J. (2004). My pedagogic creed. In D. J. Flinders and S. J. Thornton (Eds.), *The curriculum studies reader* (2nd ed., pp. 17–23). New York: RoutledgeFalmer. (Original work published 1897)

Eisner, E. W. (1994). *The educational imagination: On the design and evaluation of school programs* (3rd ed.). New York: Macmillan. (Original work published 1979)

Eisner, E. W. (1969). Instructional and expressive objectives: Their formulation and use in curriculum. In W. J. Popham (Ed.), *AERA monograph on curriculum evaluation: Instructional objectives* (pp. 1–18). Chicago: Rand McNally.

Eisner, E. W. (2004). Artistry and pedagogy in curriculum. *Journal of Curriculum and Pedagogy, 1*(2), 13–14.

Elias, M. J., Zins, J. E., Graczyk, P. A., & Weissberg, R. P. (2003). Implementation, sustainability, and scaling up of social–emotional and academic innovations in public schools. *School Psychology Review, 32*(3), 303–319.

Ellsworth, E. (1997). *Teaching positions: Difference, pedagogy, and the power of address.* New York: Teachers College Press.

Fletcher, R. (1993). *What a writer needs.* Portsmouth, NH: Heinemann.

Ford, G. W., & Pugno, L. (Eds.). (1964). *The structure of knowledge and the curriculum.* Chicago: Rand McNally.

Fosnot, C. T. (1996a). Constructivism: A psychological theory of learning. In C. T. Fosnot (Ed.), *Constructivism: Theory, perspectives, and practice* (pp. 8–33). New York: Teachers College Press.

Fosnot, C. T. (Ed.). (1996b). *Constructivism: Theory, perspectives, and practice.* New York: Teachers College Press.

Gallagher, S. (1992). *Hermeneutics and education.* Albany: State University of New York Press.

Gardner, H. (2000). *The disciplined mind: Beyond facts and standardized tests, the K–12 education that every child deserves.* New York: Penguin Books.

Green, J. M. (1999). *Deep democracy: Community, diversity, and transformation.* Lanham, MD: Rowman & Littlefield.

Greene, M. (1975). Curriculum and consciousness. In W. F. Pinar (Ed.), *Curriculum theorizing: The reconceptualists* (pp. 299–317). Berkeley, CA: McCutchan.

Greene, M. (1988). *The dialectic of freedom.* New York: Teachers College Press.

Grondin, J. (1995). *Sources of hermeneutics.* Albany: State University of New York Press.

Henderson, J. G., & Kesson, K. R. (2004). *Curriculum wisdom: Educational decisions in democratic societies.* Upper Saddle River, NJ: Merrill/Prentice Hall.

Hirsch, E. D. (1987). *Cultural literacy.* Boston: Houghton Mifflin.

Hlebowitsh, P. (1993). *Radical curriculum theory reconsidered: A historical approach.* New York: Teachers College Press.

Hunt, M. P., & Metcalf. (1968). *Teaching high school social studies* (2nd ed.). New York: Harper & Row.

Jacoby, R. (1987). *The last intellectuals: American culture in the age of academe.* New York: Basic Books.

Klein, J. T. (1990). *Interdisciplinarity: History, theory, & practice.* Detroit: Wayne State University Press.

Kliebard, H. K. (1992). *Forging the American curriculum: Essays in curriculum history and theory.* New York: Routledge.

Kliebard, H. K. (2004). The rise of scientific curriculum-making and its aftermath. In D. J. Flinders and S. J. Thornton (Eds.), *The curriculum studies reader* (2nd ed., pp. 37–46). New York: RoutledgeFalmer. (Original work published 1975)

Kohler, L., & Rigby, M., (2003). Indicators of children's development: Considerations when constructing a set of national child health indicators for the European Union. *Child: Care, Health & Development 29*(6): 551–558.

Lee, G. C. (Ed.). (1961). *Crusade against ignorance: Thomas Jefferson on education.* New York: Teachers College Press.

Marshall, J. D., Sears, J. T., & Schubert, W. H. (2000). *Turning points in curriculum: A contemporary American memoir.* Upper Saddle River, NJ: Merrill/Prentice Hall.

Miller, R. (2002). *Free schools, free people: Education and democracy after the 1960's.* New York: State University of New York Press.

Nash, R. J. (2001). *Religious pluralism in the academy: Opening the dialogue.* New York: Peter Lang.

Noddings, N. (1984). *Caring: A feminine approach to ethics and moral education.* Berkeley: University of California Press.

Ohanian, S. (1999). *One size fits few.* Portsmouth, NH: Heinemann.

Pinar, W. F. (1994). *Autobiography, politics and sexuality: Essays in curriculum theory 1972–1992.* New York: Peter Lang.

Pinar, W. F. (2004). *What is curriculum theory?* Mahwah, NJ: Erlbaum Associates.

Pinar, W. F. (Ed.). (1975). *Curriculum theorizing: The reconceptualists.* Berkeley: McCutchan.

Pinar, W. F. (Ed.). (1988). *Contemporary curriculum discourses.* Scottsdale, AZ: Gorsuch Scarisbrick.

Pinar, W. F. (Ed.). (1998). *The passionate mind of Maxine Greene: "I am . . . not yet."* London: Falmer Press.

Pinar, W. F., & Grumet, M. R. (1976). *Toward a poor curriculum.* Dubuque, IA: Kendall-Hunt.

Pinar, W. F., Reynolds, W. M., Slattery, P., & Taubman, P. M. (1995). *Understanding curriculum: An introduction to the study of historical and contemporary curriculum discourses.* New York: Peter Lang.

Ravitch, D. (2000). *Left back: A century of failed school reforms.* New York: Simon & Schuster.

Schwab, J. J. (1969). The practical: A language for curriculum. *School Review 78*(1), 1–23.

Schwab, J. J. (1971). The practical: Arts of the eclectic. *School Review, 79,* 493–542.

Schwab, J. J. (1973). The practical 3: Translation into curriculum. *School Review, 81,* 501–522.

Schwab, J. J. (1983). The practical 4: Something for curriculum professors to do. *Curriculum Inquiry, 13,* 239–266.

Schwab, J. J. (2004). The practical: A language for curriculum. In D. J. Flinders & S. J. Thornton (Eds.), *The curriculum studies reader* (2nd ed., pp. 103–117). New York: RoutledgeFalmer. (Original work published 1969)

Sears, J. T. (1992). This issue. *Theory into Practice, 31*(3), 190.

Shirley, D. (1993). Promising practices in the social studies. In S. Berman & P. La Farge (Eds.), *Promising practices in teaching social responsibility* (pp. 163–181). Albany: State University of New York Press.

Slattery, P. (2001). Foreword. In K. Sloan & J. T. Sears (Eds.), *Democratic curriculum theory & practice: Retrieving public spaces* (pp. xi–xiv). Troy, NY: Educator's International Press.

Slattery, P. (2006). *Curriculum development in the postmodern era* (2nd ed.). New York: Routledge. (Original work published 1995)

Spence, D. P. (1986). Narrative smoothing and clinical wisdom. In T. R. Sarbin (Ed.), *Narrative psychology: The storied nature of human conduct* (pp. 211–232). New York: Praeger.

Stanley, W. B. (1992). *Curriculum for utopia: Social reconstructionism and critical pedagogy in the postmodern era.* Albany: State University of New York Press.

Tanner, D., & Tanner, L. (2007). *Curriculum development: Theory into practice* (4th ed.). Upper Saddle River, NJ: Merrill/Prentice Hall.

Tyler, R. W. (1949). *Basic principles of curriculum and instruction.* Chicago: University of Chicago Press.

Uhrmacher, B., & Matthews, J. (Eds.). (2005). *Intricate palette: Working the ideas of Elliot Eisner.* Upper Saddle River, NJ: Merrill/Prentice Hall.

Wiggins, G., & McTighe, J. (2005). *Understanding by Design* (2nd ed.). Alexandria, VA: Association for Supervision and Curriculum Development.

Willinsky, J. (2001). The strategic education research program and the public value of research. *Educational Researcher, 30*(1): 5–14.

Zemelman, S., Daniels, H., & Hyde, A. (1993). *Best practice: New standards for teaching and learning in America's schools.* Portsmouth, NH: Heinemann.

Zins, J. E., Weissberg, R. P., Wangf, M. C., & Walberg, H. J. (Eds.). (2004). *Building academic success on social and emotional learning: What does the research say?* New York: Teachers College Press.

INDEX